Perspectives on a Changing China

About the Book

Perspectives on a Changing China:
Essays in Honor of Professor C. Martin Wilbur on the Occasion of His Retirement
edited by Joshua A. Fogel and William T. Rowe

This collection of essays represents current research in modern (post-1800) Chinese history. All contributors are former students of Professor C. Martin Wilbur, one of the great names in the China field over the past forty years, who recently retired from a long tenure as modern Chinese historian at Columbia University.

While diverse in their subject matter, the essays reflect the historiographic concerns of a group of scholars whose views were formed at least partly in response to the view of modern China presented by Professor Wilbur and others of his academic generation. In a sense, the essays constitute the late fruits of pioneering efforts. Appropriately, an important theme addressed by several of the authors is how modern China is and has been perceived. Most of the essays embody, at least in part, a revision of previously held views.

Joshua A. Fogel and William T. Rowe are both Ph.D. candidates at Columbia University.

Published in cooperation with the
East Asian Institute, Columbia University

Perspectives on a Changing China

Essays in Honor of
Professor C. Martin Wilbur
on the Occasion of His Retirement

edited by Joshua A. Fogel
and William T. Rowe

Westview Press • Boulder, Colorado

Dawson • Folkestone, England

This volume is included in Westview's Special Studies on China and East Asia.

All rights reserved. No part of this publication may be reproduced or transmitted in any form or by any means, electronic or mechanical, including photocopy, recording, or any information storage and retrieval system, without permission in writing from the publisher.

Copyright © 1979 by Westview Press, Inc.

Published in 1979 in the United States of America by
  Westview Press, Inc.
  5500 Central Avenue
  Boulder, Colorado 80301
  Frederick A. Praeger, Publisher

Published in 1979 in Great Britain by
  Wm. Dawson and Sons, Ltd.
  Cannon House
  Folkestone
  Kent CT19 5EE

Library of Congress No.: 79-626
ISBN (U.S.): 0-89158-091-3
ISBN (U.K.): 0-7129-0879-X

Printed and bound in the United States of America

Contents

Acknowledgments

This book would not have been possible without the constant efforts of Anita M. O'Brien. The editors also wish to thank Dr. Dorothy Borg, Professors Thomas Bernstein, Wm. Theodore de Bary, James W. Morley, Andrew J. Nathan, and Herschel Webb of Columbia University, Gilbert Chan of Miami University of Ohio, Samuel Chu of Ohio State University, Hsueh Chun-tu of the University of Maryland, Ho Ping-ti of the University of Chicago, Allen Whiting of the University of Michigan, and Mr. John S. Service for their assistance in this project.

This volume was financed by the East Asian Institute of Columbia University, and by the personal contributions of the following friends, colleagues, and students of C. Martin Wilbur:

M. Searle Bates
Edwin G. Beal, Jr.
Deborah E. Bell
Professor and Mrs. Thomas P. Bernstein
Hugh Borton
Pauline Ho Bynum
F. Gilbert Chan
Dr. and Mrs. Thomas S. N. Chen
Sister Madeleine Chi
Samuel C. Chu
Mr. and Mrs. O. Edmund Clubb
Gwendolyn F. Dahlquist
Cora Du Bois
R. Randle Edwards
Professor and Mrs. Ainslee T. Embree
Professor and Mrs. Morton H. Fried

Mr. and Mrs. Bernard L. Gladieux

Professor and Mrs. L. C. Goodrich

Sidney L. Greenblatt

Thomas L. Kennedy

V. K. Wellington Koo

Jane Price Laudon

Professor and Mrs. Charlton M. Lewis

Bernadette Y. N. Li

Anne J. Lindbeck

Professor and Mrs. Allen B. Linden

Professor and Mrs. Pichon P. Y. Loh

Kuang-huan Lu

Professor and Mrs. John Meskill

Professor and Mrs. James I. Nakamura

Andrew J. Nathan

Susan W. O'Sullivan

Mr. and Mrs. Russell W. Schoch

Dr. and Mrs. Georges E. Seligmann

Mr. and Mrs. Ichiro Shirato

Professor and Mrs. Paul K. T. Sih

Odoric Wou

Silas H. L. Wu

Professor and Mrs. Ka-che Yip

W.T.R.
J.A.F.

An Appreciation

James P. Harrison

Students in the classes of C. Martin Wilbur never doubted the fascination of Chinese history or their professor's vast knowledge of this engrossing subject. As my experience in his Master's-level seminar in the spring of 1960 well demonstrated, however, they did not always share their professor's mastery of its complications. After some minutes of a rather incoherent presentation I made on the extraordinarily contradictory interpretations of the "truth of the Li Li-san Line" of 1930 in the history of the Chinese Communist movement, I recall well Professor Wilbur's terse comment, "Mr. Harrison has shown well an important lesson of Chinese history—its complexity." He could of course have added "confusion," but I appreciated the lesson, which he so aptly restated in his presidential address to the Association for Asian Studies on March 28, 1972:

> It is our job to try to understand Asian societies as they actually were in the past and as they really are today; to see them in great depth, in their multi-faceted variety; to view them with sympathy but with historical perspective and detachment.

Such sensitivity to complexities and historiographical problems, together with its necessary complement of brilliant research to unravel key problems of Chinese history, most distinguish the achievements of C. Martin Wilbur. He has helped to clarify key problems from many centuries of Chinese history for readers, students, and friends; for specialists, he has elucidated with particular skill first a crucial aspect of the social history of the Han dynasty, and later, in a series of writings, the remarkable conjunction of events that occurred in the 1920s (during this period, as the son of YMCA workers, he had been himself a student in Shanghai).

Surely it is testimony to an outstanding talent to be able to write the definitive studies of problems separated by the 2,000 years between the

Han dynasty and the 1920s. The former work, published as *Slavery in China during the Former Han Dynasty, 206 B.C.–A.D. 25* (New York, 1943), grew out of his 1941 doctoral dissertation at Columbia University, the institution where he also earned his Master's degree in 1933 with an essay on "Village Government in China." He did the research for the classic volume on the Han while assistant curator and then curator of Chinese archaeology and ethnology at the Field Museum of Natural History in Chicago from 1937 to 1943. A "Contribution to a Bibliography on Chinese Metallic Mirrors" (*China Journal* 20, April 1934) and the "History of the Crossbow" (*Smithsonian Report* for 1936) offered further testimony to his mastery of ancient Chinese matters.

Yet it was the colossal events of modern China that captured the attention of Professor Wilbur's later scholarship. Wartime service with the Office of Strategic Services and service with the Department of State from 1945 to 1947 helped to shift his interests, as, one suspects, did the intimate friendships with Chinese that have run throughout his life. The shift coincided with his assuming the responsibility for modern Chinese history in 1947 at Columbia University, the institution to which he devoted his subsequent career. Naturally, succeeding years demanded elaborate course preparations, and in addition Professor Wilbur gave unstintingly conscientious guidance to a growing number of students. The continuously stimulating nature of his courses and his admirable attention to the problems and progress of his students won the respect of all.

With equally characteristic thoroughness, Professor Wilbur mastered the available bibliography on modern China, in 1950 publishing *Chinese Sources on the History of the Chinese Communist Movement: An Annotated Bibliography of Materials in the East Asian Library, Columbia University*, and in 1953 editing Ichirō Shirato's *Japanese Sources on the History of the Chinese Communist Movement: An Annotated Bibliography of Materials in the East Asiatic Library, Columbia University, and the Division of Orientalia, Library of Congress*.

His first major publication on modern China, accomplished with Julie Lien-ying How, aimed to unravel some key problems in modern Chinese history. This was the indispensable *Documents on Communism, Nationalism and Soviet Advisors in China, 1918-1927: Papers Seized in the 1927 Peking Raid* (New York, 1956; republished 1972). There followed important studies on aspects of the early history of the Chinese Communist movement. These included a painstaking study of the founding of the Chinese Communist Party in Shanghai in July 1921, given in his introduction to Ch'en Kung-po's *The Communist Movement in China* (New York, 1960). This fascinating book had originally been a Master's essay at Columbia University in 1924, written by one of the twelve participants in the Party's First National Congress. The by now well known Wilbur style of meticulous scholarship was next applied to the "first Long March" of what became the Chinese Red Army, the flight of troops under Chu Teh, Chou En-lai, and others from Nanchang after the uprising of August 1, 1927 ("The Ashes of Defeat," *The China Quarterly* 18, April-June 1964). There followed "The Influence of the Past: How the Early Years Helped to Shape the Future of the Chinese Communist Party," in *Party Leadership and Revolutionary Power in China* (John Lewis, ed., Cambridge, Mass., 1970).

While producing some of the most careful and informative work on the history of Chinese Communism, Professor Wilbur continued to pursue studies of the Nationalists and warlords in the 1920s. In *China in Crisis: China's Heritage and the Communist Political System* (Ping-ti Ho and Tang Tsou, eds., Chicago, 1968) his "Military Separatism and the Process of Reunification under the Nationalist Regime, 1922-1937" was published. This essay provided the clearest succinct account to date of the intricacies and significance of the myriad military forces that bestrode China in the 1920s, and of the Northern Expedition of 1926-1928 during which Chiang Kai-shek's Nationalist armies achieved dominance. The importance of Professor Wilbur's work on the history of the 1920s is evident in the recently published *China in the 1920s: Nationalism and Revolution* (F. Gilbert Chan and Thomas H. Etzold, eds., New York, 1976). He wrote the foreword to the book, which is dedicated to him and includes essays by some of his former students. Professor Wilbur's most recent major work is *Sun Yat-sen: Frustrated Patriot* (New York, 1976). In it, he explores with finesse the late career of the "father" of Nationalist China, giving a clear summary of the earlier years of Sun Yat-sen and a thorough and convincing account of the formation of the alliance with Russia and of the first United Front between the Nationalists and the Chinese Communists. His continuing work in progress promises equally outstanding future contributions to our understanding of this extraordinarily complex period.

C. Martin Wilbur left far more monuments than his impressive publications during nearly thirty years as professor at Columbia University prior to retirement in 1976. His numerous students, including myself, will always be thankful for his teaching of

conscientious scholarship and humility in the face of the complexities of history, nowhere more necessary than in the study of the
world's oldest and largest continuous civilization. Professor Wilbur's
character, shaped in great part by the legacies of that great civilization, as well as by his family, schools (including Oberlin College,
B.A., 1931), professors, and friends, provided perhaps the greatest
lesson of all. He is a model gentleman appropriate to a tradition that
places such great stress on integrity. Special note must be given to
the support he has received in all respects from his wife of forty-five
years, Kay.

In addition to the accomplishments noted above, C. Martin Wilbur
was a founding member of the East Asian Institute, established under
George Sansom in 1947, and succeeded Hugh Borton as its director
from 1957 to 1964. With Franklin L. Ho he was a cofounder in 1958 of
the Chinese Oral History Project, which has created an important
addition to the remembrances of historical figures.[1]

Outside the Columbia community, the esteem in which Professor
Wilbur is held led to his election to the presidency of the Association
for Asian Studies in 1971-1972. His presidential address to that group
on March 28, 1972 (*Journal of Asian Studies*, August 1972), fittingly
described the "need for mutual understanding between China and
non-China," and for the "skeptical eye. This is what we need in the
study of China, past and present." For Professor Wilbur's skeptical
and brilliant scholarship, for his humanity, gentility, and persever-
ance in studying China with "sympathy, historical perspective, and
detachment," as he put it, we are all thankful.

Introduction

Joshua A. Fogel
and William T. Rowe

One of the most striking aspects of recent American revisionism in modern China studies has been what Samuel Huntington has called, in a more general context, "the change to change." On the surface, this includes a terminological shift from such value-laden words as "modernization" and "development" to the more neutral concept of "historical change." More basically, it implies a recognition that if the useful notion of modernization, in its most elemental form as the acceptance of human progress, may still be validly applied to societies other than our own, it may no longer be treated as synonymous with "Westernization." Thus historians of late dynastic China have been newly conscious of the dynamism inherent in that "changeless" society, and those of the twentieth century have increasingly focused on the adaptation of the inherited social and political culture with a new view to its positive as well as negative legacy.

The present volume incorporates eleven essays that portray various manifestations of this process of change in China since the founding of its last imperial dynasty in 1644. At the same time, it contains examinations of some perspectives taken on China at different points during this same period, in an attempt to highlight the very real role played by point of view in molding our understanding of the processes of Chinese history. One such examination, that of a predictive viewpoint, opens the volume. In this paper Olga Lang offers us a rare glimpse at the expectations held for China in nineteenth-century Russia, the Western nation in longest and most intimate contact with the Central Kingdom. By exploring the contexts and contents of two visions of China's future, created several decades apart by two widely popular authors, Ms. Lang is able to depict Russia's shifting conceptions of and attitudes toward China throughout the century, as well as that nation's own self-perceptions as it passed through an historical phase in certain ways comparable to that of its southern neighbor. The essay is particularly interesting for the attention it draws to the continuing interrelationship of historical scholarship, journalism, and myth.

Five essays then focus on specific institutional forms in Chinese history. In the first of these, Robert Lee offers a survey of Chinese attempts at institution-building in the exceedingly complex cultural milieu of the southwestern borderlands throughout the Ch'ing period. Mr. Lee shows that this effort reached its peak of intensity on the very eve of the 1911 Revolution, thereby strikingly reminding us that processes of "rationalization" and "development" have been enforced upon perceived inferiors by powerful civilizations outside of the West as well. The next two papers deal with Ch'ing formal administrative structures, yet both study these at points of intersection with evolved patterns of nonadministrative social organization (the family system and the local community, respectively). While neither Odoric Wou nor William Rowe takes a chronological approach, both clearly imply an active process of indigenous change: a process alternatively of deterioration from ideal forms in the later reigns of the dynasty, or of constructive and adaptive evolution, according to one's perspective. The final two essays of this section discuss more usual candidates for the label "modernization" in their analyses of Western-inspired programs of conscious innovation. Thomas Kennedy presents an early example from the military and economic sphere, and John DeFrancis evaluates recent and continuing efforts at reform of perhaps the most basic of Chinese cultural institutions, the written language.

Of course, one of the most important institutional tools in the hands of those who wish to direct the historical course of a society is its educational establishment. Despite the fact that C. Martin Wilbur himself has never chosen to address this connection in his published researches, it has formed one of the chief themes of his teaching of Chinese history. Three of his former students here demonstrate the influence of this emphasis. Treating three roughly successive periods of Republican China, Anita O'Brien, Ka-che Yip, and Jane Price all probe the implications of political events on the content and quality of education, and in turn the heightened importance of educational institutions within a rapidly shifting environment in shaping the attitudes of future generations of political actors. The progression in this sequence seems to reveal a movement from vocational to liberal and back to vocational emphases—in the final case the vocation being revolutionary change itself.

Students of Professor Wilbur have frequently considered the

hallmark of his approach to the study of history to be an impartial and critical (Mr. Harrison prefers the term "skeptical") attitude toward received wisdom in the field, treating the work of earlier scholars of all ideological persuasions with respect, but also with a keen eye for the intrusion of personal or political predilections. This approach of the teacher has quite naturally inspired many of his students to direct their inquiries toward the problem of writing history itself. In this volume, Ms. Lang's essay takes a step toward revealing the attitudinal framework behind a portion of early European sinology. The two essays that conclude the book focus more specifically on the historian's craft, analyzing through particular examples the outlooks underlying attempts by two groups of twentieth-century Chinese historians to reexamine their own past. In Joshua Fogel's article a comparative view of Japanese historiography of China is also offered. While both Mr. Fogel and Li Yu-ning arrive at conclusions that are their own, rather than necessarily those of their former teacher, they each reveal clearly the legacy of Professor Wilbur's passionately objective approach.

Professor C. Martin Wilbur seems today to belong to a remarkably distinguished generation of American China scholars—a generation that inherited a tradition of useful but often strongly subjective, intuitive, politically self-serving, or simply anecdotal writing on modern China, and through its own application of devoted scholarship and the techniques of the social scientist forged a view of China that made complex and subtle historical sense. Revisionism indeed is at work in this volume, but it is hardly a fundamental reaction against an earlier generation's work. Each of the contributors has undergone the stimulating experience of developing a research design under the guidance of Professor Wilbur and thus can attest to his striking academic flexibility. A proposed approach differing fundamentally from his own was never taken as a challenge to his academic correctness, but was rather welcomed as a fresh opportunity for both teacher and student to critically reevaluate current thinking on an historical subject. The quality of Professor Wilbur's own research speaks for itself. We hope that the diversity and critical spirit apparent in the essays in this volume are fitting tribute to his career as an educator.

Part 1

Prospect

Two Visions of the Future: Russia and China as Pictured in Two Nineteenth-century Russian Tales

Olga Lang

Russia and China are close neighbors, and Russia was the first Western country with which China concluded a treaty. Nevertheless, in the field of sinology Russians began to be heard only in the first quarter of the nineteenth century with the publication of Yegor F. Timkovskii's *Travels to China Over Mongolia*.[1] In the years that followed, the works of the "father of Russian sinology," Father Iakinf (Bichurin), made a substantial contribution to Western knowledge of China, and some were translated into several European languages.

In this essay I want to tell of two Russian stories less known outside their native land. Both presented a vision of life in the future, and both predicted that Russia and China were to become the most powerful countries in the world. This was a rather audacious prediction, both in the 1830s and 1840s when V. F. Odoevskii published parts of his *The Year 4338: Letters from St. Petersburg*, and in the late 1870s or early 1880s when G. P. Danilevskii wrote his "Life One Hundred Years After."[2] Both these writers, now almost forgotten, were very popular in their time. Odoevskii's story, in which Russia is presented as the leading country in the world and China as its junior partner, can truly be called a "utopia." In it the author presented a vision of future life in Russia as improved in accordance with his ideals. Danilevskii's sketch does not belong to this category, since a situation in which Russia, while better off than the rest of the world, still plays a secondary role and depends on the mercy of the Chinese emperor was not the ideal of a Russian patriot. This work should rather be called a satire; its main intention was to portray the decay of Western materialism, in sympathy with the views of Russian Slavophiles who asserted that the West was rotten and thus going to its doom.

Odoevskii and His Work

Utopian visions are rare in Russian literature. In the eighteenth and early nineteenth centuries, when this genre became rather popular in the West, there had only been six in Russia before the first part of Odoevskii's *The Year 4338* was published in 1835.[3] Odoevskii was also the first Russian fiction writer who paid serious attention to China. In *The Year 4338*, while the main role is played by Russia, it is a Russia viewed through Chinese eyes—eyes that are able to understand and admire this ideal country.

Prince Vladimir Fedorovich Odoevskii (1804-1869) was a significant figure in Russian cultural life from the 1820s through the 1860s.[4] His famous literary salon in St. Petersburg was visited by nearly all important representatives of the Russian intelligentsia of the time and was mentioned in all the memoirs of the period. He was highly respected as a philosopher and a musicologist, as a political writer, and especially as a writer of fiction.[5] His outstanding abilities and diligence allowed him to combine his studies and writings with a government service in which he achieved high position.

One of the most remarkable features of this talented man was his capacity for development. Throughout his life he was never satisfied, but constantly looked for new ways to discover the truth. He took philosophy as the principal guide for his moral and intellectual life. In the 1820s he organized a circle of young philosophers (*liubomudry*, literally, "lovers of wisdom") at the University of Moscow and was an ardent follower of Friedrich Wilhelm Schelling (1775-1854), along with Hegel the dominant German philosopher of the time, and of the now forgotten but then influential natural philosopher, Lorenz Oken (1779-1851). In the 1830s, while continuing to respect Schelling, Odoevskii succumbed to the mystical-philosophical trend of the times in trying to reconcile philosophy and religion.

Schelling's and Oken's idea of the necessity of uniting all branches of knowledge and arts into one philosophical system reconciled with religious feeling is largely responsible for what contemporaries termed Odoevskii's "encyclopedism," his desire to be familiar with all the most important branches of natural science. In the 1850s and 1860s he developed into a scholarly realist, but this takes us long beyond the time of *The Year 4338*'s publication.

As a fiction writer, Odoevskii evolved from the fantastic romanticism of the 1820s and 1830s, when he was influenced by the German writer and musician E.T.A. Hoffmann (1776-1822), to the realism of his last stories. His best works are the philosophical stories that reflect the intellectual life of the school of thought to which he belonged.

His political and social outlook also underwent changes. In his youth he was alien to all the progressive movements of the time, yet in the late 1840s he began to be interested in social problems and took a leading part in an organization known as "The Society for Visiting the Poor," later suppressed by the government. In the 1850s and 1860s he became an enthusiastic supporter of the emancipation of the serfs and of the liberal reforms of that time.

Odoevskii was a great admirer of the Russian people and firmly believed in their superior qualities. He saw the Western world perishing. His ideas are best expressed in his *Russian Nights (Russkie Nochi)*, a philosophical dialogue published in 1841 and considered his masterpiece.[6] The well-known critic and literary historian Nestor Kotliarevskii wrote that, "together with the philosophical letters of Chaadev and the articles of I. Kireevskii, *Russian Nights* was the first fruit of the ripening philosophical thought of Russia. Its seed was imported but it grew in Russian soil and fed not only scholars but everyone who cherished man as a thinking and feeling being."[7]

Odoevskii said in *Russian Nights*:

> [In the West] the sciences, instead of striving for the unity that could give them back their strength, are broken to pieces like flying dust. . . . The meaning of art is destroyed; the poet has lost his power, he has lost his faith in himself. . . . People do not trust him. . . . Religious feeling in the West is perishing. Its temples are now a political arena, its religious feeling merely a conventional display of petty parties. In a word: the West is going to its doom. . . .
>
> But Providence is preserving a people destined to show again the way abandoned by humanity, and destined to take first place among the peoples of the world. One new innocent people is worthy of this great exploit. Only through them or with their help is possible the birth of the new light which will embrace all spheres of intellect and social life.[8]

He was referring, of course, to the Russian people. "We have to save not only the body of Europe but also its soul."[9]

"The nineteenth century belongs to Russia!" With this ringing exclamation Odoevskii closes his *Russian Nights*.[10] And elsewhere: "There will be a Russian conquest of Europe, but it will be a spiritual one."[11] These ideas brought Odoevskii close to the Slavophile movement, one of the most important intellectual and political trends in Russia in the decades from the 1820s through the 1860s.[12]

But he never subscribed completely to Slavophile teachings and later expressed many ideas that the Russian Westernizers could share.

The Year 4338, however, was written when Odoevskii's faith in the superiority of the Russian people was unshaken. In this work he foresees a world dominated politically and spiritually by Russia, with China as its junior partner. Why China? I suggest the following explanation. Odoevskii's insatiable inquiring nature induced him to take a close look at China, the country for which, along with the Near East, Russian educated society developed increasing interest in the 1840s. Perhaps Odoevskii's personal acquaintance with Father Iakinf, this "last European sinophile," played a certain role in arousing his sympathy for China. But Father Iakinf was not the only source of Odoevskii's knowledge of China. He also read the books of nineteenth-century European sinologists and travelers, Timkovskii's writings, and those of Russian correspondents in China, who unlike their seventeenth- and eighteenth-century predecessors wrote more skeptically of that society. One therefore finds many negative remarks scattered among the references to China in Odoevskii's published works and unpublished notes.

In *Russian Nights*, Odoevskii saw China as the country of empty formalism. He used China as a case in point to express his opposition to eighteenth-century French philosophy, to prove his assertion that not every thought could be revealed by words, that words change their meaning with time, and that forms can continue to exist when the essence of the thought originally behind them is gone.[13] He began with Confucius and his philosophical definitions:

> Such is the word "morality." This word once [for Confucius] had a higher meaning. But what have the descendants of Confucius done with it? The word remains but now it does not mean for them anything else than an outward form of politeness, and behind it are deceit, insidiousness, all kinds of depravity, [while the real meaning] has become extraneous. China is in itself an interesting country and is an important example for the formalists. It is not without cause that the eighteenth century philosophers were enraptured by it: it fitted perfectly their destructive teaching. Everything they said is illustrated there. There is a form for everything: a form for education, for military art, even a formula for gunpowder and guns and cannon, but the essence is rotten, and rotten to such an extent that this state with its three hundred million inhabitants would collapse after the slightest European attack.[14]

Why then did Odoevskii choose China as Russia's junior ally in ruling his world of the forty-fourth century? Russia needed an ally, and perhaps Odoevskii imagined that this country with its citizens educated for docility would be willing to learn from Russia and accept its guidance, just as Russia in the eighteenth and nineteenth centuries had taken Western Europe as its own model.[15]

The Story of *The Year 4338*

Odoevskii's utopian vision was written in 1835-1838, about the same time as his *Russian Nights*, and projected into the remote future the idea expressed in his famous philosophical dialogue: "The nineteenth century belongs to Russia!" The author hoped that in the forty-fourth century the entire world would in fact belong to Russia and China.

His notes, preserved in the Public Library of Leningrad, and assiduously studied by P. N. Sakulin at the beginning of this century and by Orest Tsechnovitzer in the 1920s,[16] reveal that Odoevskii intended to write an historical trilogy. The first part would depict the period of Peter the Great (early eighteenth century); the second would be "our time," i.e., the 1830s; the third, Russia 2,500 years later.[17] "Future historians," wrote Odoevskii in his notes, "will use this periodization of history: from the world's beginnings until the birth of Christ; the middle ages, from the birth of Christ until the division of the world between China and Russia; and the period from the time of this division until their own time."[18]

Other countries, very powerful in the 1830s, would subsequently either disappear completely or be in full decay. *The Year 4338* described a rather funny-sounding learned discussion in which forty-fourth-century Russian scholars were convinced that the names for Germany in the nineteenth-century Russian, French, Italian, and German languages refer to four different peoples.[19] The English had come to such a state that they had had to sell their islands to Russia.[20] The French were not even mentioned. The main reason for this decay was seen by Odoevskii and his Slavophile friends in the crass materialism of the West.[21] Odoevskii evidently was not sure what would become of the United States. In one passage of the novel he had a Chinese say that the Americans became savages,[22] but in later notes he described an American poet traveling in Russia, and his occupation alone showed that America was in certain respects organized in the Russian fashion.[23]

The trilogy was never completed, but Odoevskii was occupied for many years with the third part of it, conceived as an independent novel. Even this novel was never finished, only two sections being published in the author's lifetime (in 1835 and 1840), but the numerous notes of later years found by Sakulin and Tschnovitzer reveal many of Odoevskii's further ideas on this topic.[24] Relying on the work of these two scholars I have also used these notes.

In the preface to *The Year 4338: Letters from St. Petersburg*, Odoevskii tells the origin of the story in the following way. He was in St. Petersburg, making public some letters that had been given to him by a very remarkable person. For many years this man had occupied himself in the study of mesmerism and had achieved such perfection in this art that he could put himself into a somnambulistic state and select a subject of concentration for his "magnetic" vision. While in this state he was able to write down all that his vision showed him. After awakening he forgot everything and read with great interest what he had written. He had been greatly impressed by the calculations of astronomers that in 4339, i.e., 2,500 years after his time, the comet Viela would unavoidably collide with our planet and he wanted to see what the world a year before this terrible event would be like. Thus he concentrated on this. After awakening, he found before him sheets of paper filled with writings from which he learned that in his somnambulistic state he had been a Chinese youth of the forty-fourth century, a student of the Main School in Peking bearing the unlikely name for a Chinese of Hippolyte Tsungiev. He had been traveling in Russia and had recorded his impressions in a continuing correspondence with a friend in Peking (who bore the more Chinese-sounding name Ling-king).[25]

The letters are full of expressions of the highest respect and admiration for Russia. Russia and China are closely allied, but there is no doubt as to who is the "elder brother" in this relationship, and the Chinese take their subordinate station very humbly and willingly. When arriving in the Russian capital Hippolyte writes to his friend, "Finally I am in the center of the Russian hemisphere and of the enlightened world!"[26]

> How much knowledge, how much thoughtfulness one sees in this people! One sees in them astonishing erudition and still more astonishing inventiveness. . . . I think with shame of the situation in our country, but of course we are a young people and here in Russia the enlightenment has thousands of years of history behind it; this alone should soothe our pride. . . . Looking at all that surrounds me, dear friend, I ask myself what would have happened to us if 500 years ago had not been born the Great Hun-King who finally awakened China from its centuries-long sleep, or more appropriately, its deadly

stagnation; if he had not annihilated the traces of our ancient childish sciences and replaced our fetishism with the true faith; had he not introduced us into the family of educated people. We might, in all seriousness, be now similar to the Americans who have become savages, who have no other way of making money than to sell their cities at public auctions, and then come to our country to rob us, so that they are the only people in the whole world against whom we need maintain an army.[27]

This situation described by Hippolyte reminds one somewhat of the Chinese press writings of a century later, in 1949-1960, praising elder brother Russia and regarding the United States as the chief enemy.

The Russians had introduced aviation to China but, as Hippolyte reveals, "only Russian victories over us had taught us this art." Thus Odoevskii presumed that Russian dominance over China, and probably also over other parts of the world, had not been achieved in a peaceful way but through military means. "All this took place because of our obdurate stagnation, in which our poets still now find something poetic," continued the Chinese traveler.

> Of course, now we run to the opposite extreme, to the thoughtless imitation of everything foreign. Everything in our country is done in the Russian way: our dress, our customs, our literature. The only thing we lack is the quick Russian wit, but in time we will acquire that also. Yes, my friend, we are lagging behind our famous neighbor. Let us hurry and learn while we are young and still have time.[28]

Here Odoevskii alludes to his own country in the 1840s, when the imitation of everything Western European became the butt of attacks by many writers and especially by the Slavophiles. He also acknowledges that the Russia of his time is still in many respects behind its European neighbors, but hopes that it will "overtake and surpass" them (to use the phrase very common in Soviet Russia of the 1930s). Simultaneously he also makes an accurate prediction for China, foreseeing its "catching up" development in Western technology.

But let us return to Hippolyte. The reason for his visit to Russia was the comet Viela, whose imminent collision with the earth had been foreseen by Russian scholars. An International Union had been formed to share the expense necessary to prevent the catastrophe, and Hippolyte's uncle had been sent by the Chinese emperor to St. Petersburg to introduce China into the union, and to get information about what had been done for the prevention of this calamity. Our hero had accompanied his uncle who, following the old Chinese custom, took along a relative as his secretary.[29]

Hippolyte occupied his time with sightseeing, and a Russian scholar named Khartin accompanied him, helping him to understand the structure of the Russian government and to see the great moral and material achievements of Russia. All of these aroused his great admiration. The most important of the inventions was one to improve the Russian climate. In the equatorial regions there had been created a huge storage system for heat, and a system of tubes directed this hot air to the colder northern climate.[30] Important also was the development of aviation. At a time when the idea of galvanization (the production of electricity by chemical action) had become very popular, the author foresaw aircraft as balloons moved by galvanic power.[31] The Chinese still did not know how to use them, and in fact were forbidden by their government to do so. "Our government was right," wrote Hippolyte, "considering the state of our education it is too early for us to think of that. Many accidents killing thousands of people prove the wisdom of the Chinese government's order." But the Russians just smiled when he spoke of this fear. They believed in science and the strength of their nature, so that for them to fly was just the same as for the Chinese to use railways.[32] Both Russians and Chinese thought it inconceivable that steam had once been used as a means of transportation.[33]

In the story and in later notes Odoevskii predicts numerous other scientific advances, such as travel to the moon, the invention of artificial fabrics, electronic communications, photo-duplication, and the hybridization of fruit. He describes also a tremendous urbanization process, such that by the forty-fourth century Moscow and St. Petersburg had merged into a single city.

The visitor and his guide discuss the disappearance of ancient books and manuscripts. "In this respect," says Hippolyte, "you are happier than we. Your climate has helped you to save at least some fragments of old writings, and you have been able to transfer them onto glass. In our country, however, what did not decay by itself was destroyed by insects, so that there are no historical documents for China."[34] No wonder that Hippolyte and his contemporaries felt that their true history had begun only five hundred years earlier, in the year 3800 when the Great Hun-king brought China into the civilized world. Yet even in Russia of the forty-fourth century there was little understanding of their historical tradition. Odoevskii did not foresee the deliberate destruction or falsification of historical documents by the later totalitarian political regimes in his country.

The most important feature of the new Russian society as seen by its Chinese admirer was its intellectual and moral progress. The main philosophical problem occupying Odoevskii at the time when *The Year 4338* was written, the unification of the sciences, had been solved. The sovereign of the country, who was one of the greatest poets of the time, had the happy idea of uniting the various specialties in the following way. To a person honored with the greatest rank, that of "philosopher" or "poet," were attached a number of historians, physicists, linguists, and other scholars, who were obliged to follow his instructions in preparing for him the material he needed. Each historian in turn had under his command several chronologists, philologists, antiquarians, and geographers; a scientist was similarly assisted by chemists, mineralogists, and so on.[35] "This distribution of occupations," said Mr. Khartin, "is profitable for all the participants. Knowledge that one lacks is provided by another. Some researches are carried out simultaneously from various sides. The mechanical work does not distract the poet from his inspiration and the philosopher from his meditation." Hippolyte thanked Mr. Khartin for his kindness and "sighed inwardly, wondering when the time would come when such organization of scholarly pursuits would be possible for China."[36]

This same aim was served by the Scholarly Congresses which assembled weekly in the Cabinet of Rarities, a tremendous zoological and botanical garden the size of a complete city. "Scholars, poets, musicians, artists, physicists, historians, all come here almost daily. They nobly share with one another their thoughts, their experiments (even the unsuccessful ones), their projects in initial stages, and hold nothing back, avoiding both false modesty and boastfulness."[37]

The emperor had organized the government of the country by entrusting various fields to his ministers. All high officials were trained in the School for Statesmen, which selected the best students from schools throughout the country. After having passed a very strict examination they were admitted to meetings of the State Council, and after several years had gained enough experience to be appointed to the highest government posts. Consequently, very young people were often among the highest statesmen. Only the freshness and activity of young men could withstand the pressures of their difficult duties.[38]

The post of head of the government, or minister of conciliation, was the most difficult. Under him were justices of the peace, selected from among the richest and most respected citizens. Their duty was to remain in contact with all the houses of the region entrusted to them and to prevent family disagreements, especially lawsuits.[39] The minister of conciliation was responsible also for the coordination of actions of all government offices and officials. "His duty was to observe all literary and scholarly discussions and to see that they continue only as long as they were useful for the perfection of scholarship, and never allow them to assume a personal character." (This looks very much like a form of censorship.) It was known that the lives of statesmen were usually short; their excessively difficult work killed them. Not only were they responsible for the peace and order of the state, but they were constantly preoccupied with their own moral improvement.[40]

Personal moral improvement was a concern not only of high officials but of some other inhabitants of forty-fourth-century Russia as well. During the special two months of rest, one at the beginning and one in the middle of the year, all government offices were closed. The citizens used this time for self-improvement, or if they preferred could devote themselves to their family affairs, and it was customary to refrain from visiting each other during these times. The Chinese visitor liked this plan very much.[41]

Having been invited to a party by the prime minister, Hippolyte was very excited about the opportunity to see the life of Russian high society. He was very favorably impressed by the style of the reception, which had none of the ceremonial politeness from which the Chinese still could not free themselves. The simplicity with which one was treated was combined with sincere cordiality. The guests were completely free; they could talk if they so chose, but could also keep silent. There was no idle talk, but the conversation once started was continued eagerly. Hippolyte was astonished to note that the guests spoke about the fatal comet much less than he expected, but when someone introduced the topic, the problem was discussed in a very learned way. Some people spoke about the great victories of the human mind over the powers of nature, and their belief in the human mind was so great that they spoke of the predicted calamity with an ironic smile.

The guests were offered wonderful fruits unknown to the foreign visitor; one picked them directly from the trees growing in the garden where the reception took place. Next to the trees stood urns with golden faucets. These contained not wine, as Hippolyte had thought, but an aromatic mixture of exciting gases tasting like wine and producing immediately in one who drank them the feeling of joy and liveliness. These gases were completely harmless and recommended by the physicians. They completely replaced wine in high society; wine was drunk only by simple artisans.[42]

The guests were entertained by means of a fashionable discovery called "animal magnetism." It was activated by one guest standing at a magnetic bath and the others holding cords which stretched from the bath. Some guests fell into a healthy, strengthening "magnetic sleep"; others lapsed into a somnambulistic trance. Hippolyte was not affected and could observe what happened. One somnambulist after another began to tell about his or her secret thoughts and feelings. Some of these thoughts were rather trivial, some less so. The result of these seances was that hypocrisy and falsehood were eliminated.[43] Those people who avoided participation in "group magnetism" were disliked and were suspected of harboring hostile thoughts and perverse inclinations.[44]

Some Thoughts on Odoevskii's Story

Such was the Russian utopia as conceived by one of the most outstanding representatives of the Russian nonradical intelligentsia of the mid-nineteenth century. It demonstrated the author's great love of his homeland and belief in its great mission. The work is especially interesting because in it, for the first time, China was conceived of as the future friend of Russia, willing to accept enlightenment from it and to share its power. For several years, it looked as if this prediction was going to be fulfilled.

In the preface to his story Odoevskii quotes the opinion of a friend through whose hands he received Hippolyte's letters:

> When thinking of the story told by this Chinese gentleman in connection with the situation in which we live now, one cannot say that he had made many mistakes. In the first place, human beings will always remain human beings as it was at the beginning of the world. The same passions, the same motives will remain. On the other hand the forms of their thoughts and feelings, and especially of their material life will change.[45]

Odoevskii's tale is thus suitably replete with evidence of technological change. The author notes that some of Hippolyte's observations seem to be logical developments of the technological trends of his own time. And indeed, as noted above, many of Odoevskii's predictions concerning technical progress came true.

There is much less evidence of social change. This work clearly shows its author to have been an aristocrat, imbued with the prejudices of his class. Politically and socially his ideal Russia of the forty-fourth century is not very different from the Russia of his own time. It is an absolute monarchy, although an enlightened one. High officials had to be men of outstanding moral quality, devoted to their work and striving like the whole society for their personal self-improvement. Yet forty-fourth-century Russia, like the one in which Odoevskii lived, was based on social inequality. The country was ruled by an intellectual elite; some of them worked very hard but were well compensated for their labors. There were very rich people, and also those who could allow themselves a life of leisure, only pretending to work when others did.[46] The rich had servants, perhaps even serfs; Odoevskii never mentioned that serfdom had been abolished. Censorship in a modified form was preserved. Even the idea of women's equality did not exist in this ideal society. All changes evidently benefitted only the upper class. Even the refined methods of intoxication were reserved for them, as was the obligation for good health care, and apparently also the elimination of hypocrisy by means of "animal magnetism." While Odoevskii does not speak at length about the social and political life of China, a few remarks in Hippolyte's letters reveal that it too has an emperor and an upper class.[47] This almost complete avoidance of the idea of social change is especially striking because at about the same time that *The Year 4338* was being written, the Frenchman Etienne Cabet wrote his famous utopia, *Voyage en Icarie* (Travels to Icaria), in which he described a society based entirely on the ideas of equality and social justice.

Regarding the unchanged human nature of which Odoevskii's friend spoke, in both Russia and China of the twentieth century efforts were exerted to prove him wrong. In my opinion these efforts could hardly be called successful. I remember Russia before 1917 and have visited the Soviet Union many times after 1960 and have closely followed its literature, and I would say positively that the "new Soviet man" of whom its leaders and some writers speak is a myth. In the sixty years since the October 1917 revolution the Russian national character has not changed. After 1949, Mao Tse-tung (the Hun-king of the twentieth century) made a daring attempt to change human nature and to speedily transform his countrymen into selfless idealists. At this writing it looks as if this attempt is also failing.

Danilevskii and His Times

Our second vision of the future predicts a greater role in the world for China and a secondary role for Russia in 1968, approximately a hundred years after its writing. It is called by its author a "fantastic story," but it is based in part on the views of several Russian sinologists of the period and perhaps was intended as a warning—both to the West and to Russia.

The author of the story "Life One Hundred Years After,"[48] Grigorii Petrovich Danilevskii (1829-1890), was a thinker of considerably less stature than Odoevskii and could not match his educational level. But he was a good storyteller and very popular in his time. He made translations, wrote poems (rather poor ones), short stories, novels, literary essays, economic surveys, and travelogues. His greatest achievements were his novels, especially those describing episodes of eighteenth-century Russian history. Some of his novels have not lost their interest even for the contemporary reader.

Danilevskii[49] was educated in institutions considered among the best of the 1830s and 1840s. He was first enrolled in the Noblemen's Institute at the University of Moscow and subsequently entered the Law School of the University of St. Petersburg. His studies were interrupted in 1849 when he was arrested under the assumption that he belonged to the socialist circle headed by M. V. Petrashevskii. The assumption was soon proven wrong—Danilevskii was never a radical, neither in his youth nor later. Nevertheless he spent two months in the Peter and Paul Fortress in St. Petersburg. In spite of this interruption he graduated from the university in 1850 and immediately entered government service as an official of the Department of Education, assigned to the desk handling Jewish affairs. Work in this area gave him a strong anti-Semitic attitude very clearly felt in his "Life One Hundred Years After" and other works.

When Danilevskii studied and began his government service, the "Jewish problem" was important in Russia.[50] The acquisition of the greater part of Poland after the Third Partition (1795), the annexation of Bessarabia (1812), and the Congress of Vienna (1815) added to Russia a Jewish population amounting to about 2 million in 1848. At the beginning, owing to the liberal spirit of the first part of the reign of Alexander I (1805-1809), the Jews were treated relatively mildly and had full liberty in trade and commerce. At the end of Alexander I's reign repressive measures began. Under Nicholas I (1825-1855) the government decided to pursue a policy of assimilation, and the most effective measure was considered to be the enlistment of young Jews from twelve to twenty-four years of age into the army. Here they were to stay for twenty-five years, as all soldiers did, and be educated with the eventual aim of baptism. These measures met with vigorous resistance by the Jews. Many recruited children (and there were among them many younger than twelve) died after their induction, and many Jewish soldiers preferred suicide to baptism. It was one of the most tragic episodes in the sad history of the Jewish people. In 1835 Jews were forbidden to settle outside of a certain "pale of settlement." Later, in 1840-1848, the government changed its tactics and decided to achieve assimilation by the introduction of state-run Russian language schools and restriction of the autonomy of Jewish communities. All of this was accompanied by numerous other oppressive measures and was coupled with the arousing of anti-Semitic feelings among the population, for example by the accusation that Jews were using the blood of Christians in their rituals.

A man of Danilevskii's conservative views was easily influenced by the anti-Semitic mood prevalent in his office.[51] His career was proceeding successfully and because of his outstanding abilities his official duties left him time for writing and for visiting the literary salons of St. Petersburg where he established contacts with the leading writers and Slavophile intellectuals of that time.

His writings were met with great approval by the reading public, so that in 1857 he left his office deciding to devote himself to a literary career, though during the next twelve years he continued to be active in public affairs. In the 1860s and again in the 1870s he traveled abroad, visiting France, Germany, England, the Slavic countries, and Turkey. Upon his return to St. Petersburg in 1868 he was appointed first assistant editor and, in 1882, chief editor of the new government daily, *Pravitel'stvennyi Vestnik* (Government messenger). Also in 1882, he became a member of the Chief Administration of Press Affairs.

His successful career as a government official was accompanied by the growth of his popularity as a writer, both in Russia and abroad. Starting in 1874 his novels and short stories were translated into French, German, Polish, Czech, Serbian, and Hungarian. In 1880 he published his best work, the historical novel *Mirovich*, which met with great approval by the Russian and foreign public. Danilevskii wrote in the "Golden Age of Russian Prose" in the second half of the nineteenth century, when he had to compete with such giants as Tolstoy, Dostoevskii, Goncharov, Turgenev, and the young Chekhov, and still he found many readers. In his own lifetime seven printings of his collected works were published, and he received high remuneration for his writings.

During the winter of 1878-1879 there occurred cases of plague in the Volga region, which led to panic in St. Petersburg. The plague was the main topic of conversation among the educated society of St. Petersburg, and so in one group meeting at the house of an old inhabitant of the city it was decided best to divert the conversation to other subjects. Following the example of Boccaccio, who wrote his *Decameron* during the plague in Florence in the fourteenth century, each of the members of the group was required to tell a fantastic story. Danilevskii was entrusted with keeping minutes of these gatherings, and later after careful rewriting he published them as his own works, under the title *Sviatochnye vechera* (Christmas evenings). Among them was the story that interests us, "Life One Hundred Years After."

The story reflects Danilevskii's anti-Semitic feelings, which were revived in the 1860s as the profits of some Jewish businessmen from Russia's growing industrialization led to a new wave of this feeling throughout Great Russia. The Jews, however, play a minor role in his story; more important politically is the role of China. And here again, as in the case of Odoevskii, we must ask why the writer, an outsider to sinology, became interested in China and represented it as so powerful in his future vision.

Danilevskii lived at a time when interest in China was growing both in Western Europe and in Russia. In the 1840s to 1880s, one could hardly find a Russian periodical not giving space to an article or at least a short note concerning the Middle Kingdom. In the 1830s the teaching of Chinese as well as Manchu and Tibetan began in Russian universities. The two wars with China, that of 1839-1842 and especially that of 1856-1860, increased this interest. In the latter war Russia took an active part. The Aigun Treaty (1858), the Tientsin Treaty (1858), and the Peking Convention (1860) confirmed Russian occupation of the Amur region and gave it all the advantages in China won by Russia's Western allies, England and France. Occupation of the Amur region was overwhelmingly approved by Russian public opinion, from the extreme right to the extreme left. It was considered not as seizure of Chinese territory but as a return to Russia of those territories occupied by the Russian Cossacks in the seventeenth century and acquired by China when, during the negotiations at Nerchinsk, the Chinese had displayed an army ten times the size of the Russian, forcing the Russian representative Golovin to accede to Chinese demands and sign the Treaty of Nerchinsk (1689). In the comments of the Russian press in the 1850s and 1860s it was stressed that these territories were not inhabited by Chinese, and not even by Manchus, but by various native tribes. The fact that these areas had been first occupied by Russians seemed to carry with it the right to consider the Amur region as part of Russia.

Danilevskii had certainly read articles about China in Russian and foreign journals and had seen how the attitude toward China was gradually changing. For a while the authority of the last Russian sinophile (and one of the last in Europe), Father Iakinf, was still influential. His books, *Kitai: ego zhiteli, nravy, obychai, i pros-veshchenie* (China: Its inhabitants, mores, customs, and education, 1840) and *Kitai v grazhdanskom i nravstvennom sostoianii* (China: Civil and moral, 1848), containing a great wealth of information, were widely read and discussed. Father Iakinf attempted to be objective by mentioning briefly some darker sides of Chinese life and national character but concluded that on balance "the good predominates over the bad."[52]

Yet in spite of the high respect in which Iakinf was held, his readers gradually ceased to accept this judgment. The detractors of China helped to spread notions that built up a stereotyped view of that country, which was reflected in the common speech of the day; for example, "a Chinese wall"—to symbolize exclusiveness; "Chinese ceremonies"—empty formalism; "Chinese writing"—something incomprehensible (equivalent, perhaps, to the English expression, "It's Greek to me"); and "Chinaism" (*Kitaism*)—an expression meaning narrow-mindedness, conservatism, and again empty formalism. Some observers often mentioned "Chinese laziness," and others "Chinese cowardice." The low comedy by N. A. Polevoi, *The Chinese War of Theodosia Sidorovna* (1842),[53] told how a single Russian woman armed only with an ovenfork and a poker defeated 60,000 Chinese cowards, fools, and clowns; it won great success with Russian theater-goers during its run at one of the best theaters in St. Petersburg.

The books of Father Iakinf also found reviewers who drew conclusions from the information supplied that were opposite to those of their author. I might mention two of these, written by critics having a great influence on Russian public opinion: the first was by the conservative Osip Senkovski (1800-1858), a brilliant linguist and professor of oriental languages at the University of St. Petersburg and editor of the popular periodical *Biblioteka dlia chtenia* (Library for reading);[54] the second was by the outstanding radical and Westernizer Vissarion Belinskii (1811-1848). These opinions can best be summarized by a few lines from Belinskii's review of *China: Civil and moral*: "The facts speak for themselves. . . . After having read the book by the venerable Father Iakinf, no one would become a sinophile. Precisely the opposite."[55]

In the meantime Russian sinology was developing. Members of the

Russian Ecclesiastical Mission and the scholars attached to it produced after 1820 a wealth of information about China past and present.[56] As Russian knowledge of China became more sophisticated, more realistic pictures of that country began to appear in the Russian press.

One could not say that Russians began to feel more sympathy for China, but perhaps the favorable depiction of the Chinese by the author of *Oblomov* and one of Russia's greatest nineteenth-century writers, Ivan A. Goncharov (1812-1891), had some effect. Goncharov was impressed with the activity and industriousness of the Chinese he saw in Singapore, Hong Kong, Canton, and Shanghai, and in his widely read travelogue, *The Frigate Pallas*, he stated that "this people is destined to play a great role in [world] trade, and possibly not only in trade."[57]

Other prominent Russians shared Goncharov's opinion about China's future. The later notes of Odoevskii, who in the 1830s and 1840s had depicted the Chinese as humble admirers of Russia, reveal that he saw the possibility that one day the tables might be turned. He further asserted that Father Iakinf himself shared this opinion.[58] Throughout Russian journals of the 1850s through 1880s one finds similar expressions of concern that China might become dangerous.

Like many intellectuals of his generation, Danilevskii was probably most influenced in his view of China by the articles of V. P. Vasiliev (1818-1900), a professor at the University of St. Petersburg and a member of the Academy of Sciences. Vasiliev was the most outstanding Russian sinologist of the second half of the nineteenth century, spent about ten years in China, and was the founder of the school that stressed a strictly scholarly approach to Chinese problems. He published a great deal on China and on Sino-Russian relations and discussed his ideas frequently with Russian intellectuals outside the China field. "For several decades . . . Vasiliev was for the Russian reading public at large almost the only recognized authority on China."[59]

Let us examine some passages from Vasiliev's article "Kitaiskii progres" (Progress in China), an article in which he recognized the great military potential of China. Vasiliev here expresses his great respect for Chinese scholarship and argues that China's present troubles stem primarily from the fact that as yet it does not want to acknowledge new European techniques and inventions.

> The spiritual culture [of China] is on a very high level. Humanitarianism, law, order, spiritual power, and honesty are the most

essential problems dealt with in Chinese theoretical works. . . .

They say Chinese are cowards, but how could it be otherwise when being armed only with bows and arrows one meets an enemy armed with long-range guns. . . .

Europeans compelled China to open her doors and all her seaports to their trade, and they penetrated even to Hankow, at the center of China. But since then the Chinese have succeeded in getting into their hands the trade in European commodities; even in the European business offices Chinese are employed as shop assistants. Chinese are not novices in trade and exchange. . . .

One can positively say that China has every possibility of achieving the highest point of intellectual, industrial, and also political progress. Her principle of the highest respect for science, and the striving of her whole people to study with unusual intensity . . . show that she could become the most educated nation in the world, and that she could produce scientists who would not only develop science together with the rest of the world, but would not stop at this level. Chinese historical scholarship, although far from satisfactory, had accustomed the Chinese to critical thinking, and to the profound and careful treatment of a subject. The thousand-year existence of that nation, organizing its whole life by its own efforts . . . promises that the new discoveries of other peoples in material subjects will find in the Chinese zealous developers and innovators. . . . There is no handicraft, no trade, no business in which one should fear that the Chinese will lag behind. And as everything will be produced carefully and inexpensively, the world might be flooded with Chinese products. It might proceed so far that the Chinese will lay hold of all trade and crafts of the entire world. . . .

Hand in hand with that, and even earlier, the political power of China could grow to an incredible extent. . . .

One should not forget that no other country has such an excellent possibility to create the strongest army in the world. . . .

Seizing the richest islands in the world, those of the Eastern ocean, China would simultaneously threaten Russia, America, and Western Europe. If the Chinese have strength they will have enough heartlessness to kill all recalcitrants, even the whole world. The whole world would be inhabited by Chinese alone—to that extent, our fantasies about the future, which we now call impossible, could come true.[60]

"Life One Hundred Years After"

In Danilevskii's vision of the future some of these ideas of Vasiliev find literary expression, but the author presents the fate of Russia as less hard than that of other countries in a world dominated by China.

The story is told by a young Russian named Poroshin and is set in Paris, considered by Russian intellectuals to be the highest center of Western civilization.

Poroshin had graduated from the University of Moscow, but he was not the sort of radical Russian student so prevalent in the 1860s. He was chiefly preoccupied with deistic philosophy and read with great interest items in the newspapers about supernatural phenomena, somnambulism, and mediums, but did not believe in their practical application, especially because their practitioners were usually quacks. When he arrived in Paris in 1868, he eagerly visited the seances and mesmerism displays that were abundant in the French capital at that time and was disappointed to discover that the "professors" conducting them were likewise charlatans. At length, however, he met an Armenian gentleman whose powers seemed genuine.

After some hesitation, Poroshin struck a bargain with the Armenian. At the sacrifice of seven years of his natural life and upon payment of a considerable sum of money, he would obtain the fulfillment of his wish to spend seven days in the world as it would be one hundred years from then. In addition to seven pills, one each for the seven days, he was presented with a strange oriental-looking suit and, to cover his expenses, several gold pieces bearing on one side the engraving "République Française—Liberté, Egalité, Fraternité" and on the other side some curious oriental characters. He swallowed the pills and fell asleep.

When Poroshin awoke he looked out of the window and saw that Paris was the same and yet not the same. The streets were full of people, as if a great feast was being celebrated. Tremendous ten-story buildings were draped with flags and big pictures. On the streets he saw three-storied omnibuses, palanquins, and wide *droshkies*[61] of several seats, covered with beautiful oriental-looking umbrellas. All the passengers were reading newspapers. This startled Poroshin, who did not expect to encounter such general literacy, even in France. Then he saw something that astonished him even more: behind the Place de Trône, where he was living, was a city well patrolled by armed soldiers in strange uniforms. Over the tower closest to him was a streaming red banner with a yellow dragon in the center. "What deviltry!" thought Poroshin. "How does a dragon come to Paris?"[62]

Poroshin went out into the street to investigate further. Well acquainted with Paris customs, he decided to go to a nearby cafe and read a newspaper. But the newspaper only confused him still further. He read there of the trains to England through the channel tunnel and of the African Middle Sea, created out of the Sahara by draining water from the Mediterranean. Something still more startling confronted him in the proclamation of a recent legislative act: "By the grace of God and the will of the sublime ruling Chinese people, we, the ministers of His Illuminous Majesty the Emperor of China and Europe, after thorough discussions in the parliaments of Europe, decree . . .".

After a moment or so of shocked disbelief, Poroshin sought clarification in a *Calendar*, a reference book useful for such problems.[63] From it he learned the following:

> In the middle of the nineteenth century the number of Chinese reached about 300 million, and already at that time political and social scientists had begun to become alarmed at the tremendously rapid population increase. At the end of the nineteenth century, about 500 millions, that is, half of mankind, were Chinese. During the first quarter of the twentieth century, the population of China grew to 700 million.

The inhabitants of the Middle Kingdom thereupon launched a major reform (thousands of years earlier than Odoevskii had predicted). They imitated all the practical technology of Europe, and especially the products of European genius in military science. They thus created a tremendous land force of 5 million soldiers and a giant steam-powered navy with a hundred ironclad warships[64] and twice as many gigantic, high-speed steam cruisers.

Having covered their entire country with a network of railroads, reaching into Western Siberia and Afghanistan, they first absorbed the "effeminate" Japan and then conquered and colonized the United States, aided by a second destructive conflict between the northern and southern states of that nation. Then, after transplanting to America a portion of their surplus population, they turned their attention to Europe. They sent their navy to the Atlantic, and in a tremendous sea battle destroyed the combined naval forces of the major European powers, the decisive factor in this engagement being the Chinese mastery of submarine warfare. In 1930, Europe was conquered by China.

Just as previously France, England, Italy, and Germany had annexed the second-class powers of Europe—Spain, Austria, Sweden, and Denmark—these nations were in turn swallowed up and abolished by the Chinese. They became Chinese colonies and were organized into a federation called (as a gesture of comfort to the native scholars and political theorists) "The United States of Europe." This federation was subordinate to the Chinese emperor, who from that time on was known also as "Emperor of Europe," as once the queen of England had borne the title "Empress of India."[65]

Trembling, Poroshin searched this *Calendar* for information on the fate of Russia and found to his relief that it alone had survived this general collapse and remained independent, because:

> during China's attack on Europe, [Russia] maintained a friendly neutrality, as a revenge on England for Palmerston and his successors, on France for the Napoleons, on Austria for her constant treachery and betrayals, and on Germany for Bismarck who "was pressing the Slavs to the wall."[66]

"Well," thought Poroshin happily when he read this historical account, "everyone got what they deserved!"[67]

With Chinese approval and support, Russia had been able to set up two dependent states of its own. First, it had been at last able to oust the Turks from the European continent and had organized in the Balkans a separate Slav-Greek-Danubian empire. Then, using the new railroads from the Urals to Khiva and from the new Chinese advanced post to Afghanistan, it had defeated the British at Peshawar, thrown them out of India, and established a new Russian state with its capital at Calcutta.[68] Thus his mother country, in Danilevskii's vision, had become the junior partner of China in world domination but was less dependent on its patron than China had been in Odoevskii's future world.

The Chinese had bestowed many favors on conquered Europe but had also exerted their own power and influence. They imposed a high annual tribute of 1 billion francs on the European continent, along with the obligation to use only Chinese raw materials in European factories. They abolished all national armies and navies and replaced them with a "Chinese gendarmerie" and provincial garrisons. In accordance with the old American system, each of the United States of Europe was allowed to function in its own particular way but had no right to possess any kind of arms. Even knives and forks had been eliminated and replaced by chopsticks.

Chinese cultural influence was noticeable. On the streets one saw men and women dressed in a mixture of Chinese and Western styles. The food in restaurants was partly Chinese, but since Chinese food was very appetizing the Frenchmen evidently did not mind. Everyone, also in Chinese fashion, smoked cigarettes containing opium.

In political matters the Chinese had been very tolerant. Germany was pleased that it could keep its "aristocratic *landtag*," Italy its popedom, and England its House of Lords and primogeniture. France had become a modified republic, whose presidents ruled in dynastic fashion. After the "dynasty of Gambettas"[69] ended, the state had been ruled largely by the Jewish house of Rothschild. In 1968 the ruler was Rothschild XII.[70] Jewish admirals commanded the French navy, and Jewish field marshals guarded French borders. All this was in the name of the Chinese Emperor Tsa-ou-tse, whose recent triumphant tour of Paris had occasioned the flags and festivities Poroshin had noticed. The French lived in peace and harmony with their Chinese conquerors. Formerly in that country, republic had alternated with empire—now the French had both, to their general satisfaction.

By the year 1968 great technical progress had been achieved. Each city had a central accumulator of electrical energy that supplied the streets, public buildings, and private homes with light and heating. A central administration provided water through a system of special tubes and faucets. One had only to turn a faucet and there would be warm or cold water, the temperature varying according to one's wishes. Cobblestone streets had been replaced by asphalt, and transportation was completely mechanized. Horses had disappeared—even the contestants in the horse races were artificial beasts moved by compressed air.

Poroshin noticed all this but had reservations, which he discussed with various French acquaintances. Above all, the Frenchmen irritated him by their acceptance of Chinese domination without a shade of protest. "What kind of republic do you have when you are conquered by the Chinese Emperor and in his decrees he calls you his slaves?" he asked.

"Oh, the Chinese are our best friends!"

"What kind of friends are they when . . . you pay them such terrible tribute, and their flags hang over the walls of this once glorious city?"

The Frenchmen then explained the advantages they now had. "We have been freed from the domination of lawyers," they exclaimed jubilantly, and informed him of their greatly simplified administration of justice. The public prosecutors would bring all defendants or suspects into a room filled with a newly invented gas called "spirito-chloroform." After one whiff they would lose their willpower and simply dictate to the stenographers all that they had done and what was in their innermost thoughts. After that, all police investigations, cross-examinations, denunciations, and inquests became unnecessary. Poroshin evidently was unable to respond to this.[71]

He next reproached the French for having "a dynasty of Jewish Rothschilds" ruling them. There had been enough anti-Semitic feeling in France when the author Danilevskii traveled there in the 1860s and 1870s, and the Frenchmen of that time (like the Russians in the circles he lived in) were of the opinion that the Jews were becoming too powerful financially. Now, in his imagined France of a hundred years later, the people told him that they did not mind this because Jewish power had advantages for everyone. Poroshin was informed that in the early twentieth century the Jews had concentrated in their hands all the gold and silver in the world. The Rothschilds had become presidents by using their power on the stock exchange, where they could influence the only classes having the right to vote. Under their presidency France had become a financial paradise. The state budget was completely balanced. Promissory notes on the gold and silver the Jews owned became paper money, which the population found far more convenient to use than metal coins.[72]

"Then have you accepted the Jewish religion?" asked Poroshin.

"To tell the truth we have no religion at all," answered his acquaintance (named Bonaparte) with a smile. "The Chinese are very liberal in this respect, and they concede us full freedom. Now instead of sermons we read editorials in our Sunday papers." In general, Mr. Bonaparte thought the Chinese "the most outstanding people in the world."[73]

Poroshin remained horrified by the decline in French mores and culture. He was disgusted by the Parisian women, who at home and on the stage were scantily attired; their costume consisted of a small girdle, costume jewelry, bracelets, and rings. Polygamy had become widespread. The favorite amusements in France had become fights of beasts, and of beasts and human savages. On the seventh and last day of his stay, Poroshin gave vent to his feelings in a conversation with a member of the French Academy. He reproached the Frenchman for the looseness of French sexual mores.

"We have no prejudices," came the reply. "We admire nature and reality."

"Your science and crafts go no higher than the earth! You have traded the rays of the sun for fertilizers, and the song of a free, poetic nightingale for the bellowing of a heifer being prepared for slaughter. . . . Your art and poetry have completely decayed. Your painting has been replaced by Chinese art, and by dry, lifeless photography. . . . And your music! It is Wagnerism carried to ludicrous extremes . . . and melody has disappeared without a trace. What happened to your drama, to your high comedy? You have stupid but realistic vaudevilles instead. You have exchanged Voltaire and Rousseau . . . for the dullards Liebich and Virchov."[74] Poroshin went on telling of the French negation of their culture.

"But we are true to nature," answered the academician, lighting an opium cigarette.

Concluding Remarks

Odoevskii and Danilevskii wrote about the future with different purposes in mind. Odoevskii wanted to show Russia in the remote future as having developed its great potential and, after many years of moral and intellectual progress, as having become the center of world enlightenment and the most powerful nation on earth. As a typical nineteenth-century intellectual, he believed in progress and was convinced that the technical advancement he foresaw would be followed by moral improvement. If his hopes have not been fulfilled now, about a hundred years after his death, it is yet possible that by the forty-fourth century he described, humanity may have changed in ways that will prove this optimist right.

Danilevskii's "fantastic story" was meant as a warning to the materialistic West and perhaps also to those Russians who admired it. He did not depict any significant social change; to a conservative like Danilevskii, the idea of such change did not occur. The technical progress he saw in his imaginary France of a hundred years after the time he wrote was followed not by moral improvement but by moral degradation.

For all their differences, though, the two writers have one important thing in common: they both predicted a great future for China. It is not astonishing that these two Russian patriots saw Russia as a powerful country in the future. Russia in the nineteenth century was already a great power. But for China the time when they wrote their stories—the 1840s and the 1870s—was the period of its greatest humiliation. Even to present it as a respectful but also respected junior partner in Russia's world domination, as Odoevskii did, was a daring prediction for that time. Danilevskii went even farther and predicted China as the conqueror of the entire world.

One could hardly reproach either of the two writers for not seeing the great role the United States would play in the future. Who had foreseen that before the end of World War I? More surprising is the prediction by both of the decline of the British empire, the most powerful country in the world in the middle of the nineteenth century. We do not yet see the sale of the British Isles at auction, as Odoevskii foresaw, but jokes of that kind were already made in 1976 by an American journalist who certainly had never read Odoevskii's story.[75]

It is particularly interesting that both authors saw Russia and China as becoming close allies in the future. In the 1950s it looked as if their predictions were becoming partially fulfilled. While Russia's role in the world was constantly growing, and China was becoming increasingly strong both militarily and politically, the two nations were presenting to the outside world a picture of close friendship. But unexpectedly, this friendship proved to be of short duration. Who in 1949 could imagine that the Chinese Communists, who won power in their country after having learned so much from their Russian comrades and being helped by them at the critical time, would prove so unlike the humble younger brother that Odoevskii had imagined and instead become bitter enemies of the heir of old Russia, the Soviet Union? This hostility became apparent in the 1960s, and who now knows how long it will last?

Part 2

Chinese Institutions and Institutional Change

Frontier Politics in the Southwestern Sino-Tibetan Borderlands During the Ch'ing Dynasty

Robert H. G. Lee

Historically, the Sino-Tibetan frontier in southwestern China has been relatively stable. This stability could be attributed to the absorption of the energy and attention of the Chinese nation in the opening and colonization of the Yunnan-Kweichow plateau, which possessed greater political and economic value than the Tibetan borderlands. Also, since the decline of the T'u-fan power in the eighth century, there had not been any important foreign threat from that direction. Thus for centuries the frontier passed virtually unnoticed through the pages of history until the rise of Mongol power and the Tibetan Buddhist church resurrected it from obscurity. The Mongols, traversing the region on their way to the conquest of Yunnan, imposed once more a single sovereign power over its many territorial lords, and the Buddhist religion provided the single cultural influence that could bind its isolated communities together.

After the Mongols left, the Ming Chinese stepped conveniently into the political foothold that the Mongols had secured for them. But the attention of the Ming government was focused upon the more congenial environment of the southern borders rather than upon the austere uplands to the west. It was not until the Ch'ing dynasty that the Sino-Tibetan frontier became the scene of active political expansion. The reason for this expansion was to be found in the political significance of the Buddhist church in Lhasa in relation to the prolonged struggle between the Manchus and the Jungars for supremacy in inner Asia. The attempt to integrate firmly the Sino-Tibetan frontier with China proper came, however, only at the end of the dynasty when the Ch'ing government was under increasing pressure from British India, which was plotting the separation of Tibet from Chinese control.

Geographically, the southwestern Sino-Tibetan frontier during the Ch'ing dynasty was composed of the following regions: northwest Szechuan, the Ta-liang Shan range in Szechuan, and northwest Yunnan. It covered roughly the territories located from longitudes 93°E to 103°E and from latitudes 27°N to 33°N. Here the Tibetan and Chinese cultures coexisted in uneasy equilibrium while both sought to extend their influence over the tribal peoples living in the area. Politically and ethnically the frontier presented the imperial government with an extremely complex situation.

The Sung-p'an Grassland

For the sake of convenience, the southwestern Sino-Tibetan frontier may be subdivided into three sectors: the northern or Sung-p'an sector, the central or Kham sector, and the southern or Yunnan sector. The Sung-p'an sector is the homeland of the Si-fan, the Giarong, the Ch'iang, the Polotse, and the Hei-sui Man-tzu.

The Si-fan

Si-fan is the name applied to the nomadic Tibetans who occupied the large expanse of grassland situated at the headwaters of the Yellow River, the Min River, and the Chin-ch'uan River (the present Ahpa Tibetan Autonomous Chou). The region is crisscrossed by many streams and dotted with swamps. The average elevation is over 10,000 feet and the climate is severe, with winter temperatures often falling to –20° F. In the Ch'ing period there were two large centers of settlement in the region: Sung-p'an in the east and A-pa in the west. Like most of the Tibetan nomads, the Si-fan, whose herds consisted mainly of sheep and yaks, lived in yak hair tents in the grassland during the summer and moved into shelters built of wood and earth in the ravines during the winter. There were also mixed pastoral and agricultural Si-fan who lived in permanent villages and cultivated the fertile soils found in the Min River and Chin-ch'uan valleys around Sung-p'an and A-pa. Due to the primitiveness of their agriculture methods, the yield of their crops such as barley, wheat, peas, and turnips was only from one-third to one-sixth of the number of seeds sown.[1] These products of the soil were exchanged for the meat and butter of the nomads. Generally speaking, animal breeding was the major economic pursuit of the Si-fan. In religion, the Si-fan were followers of the Gelugpa school of Tibetan Buddhism, and their monasteries were either located in the villages or followed the encampments of the migratory nomads. Because of the remoteness of Lhasa, the Si-fan monasteries had been dominated by the Labrang Monastery, a powerful center of Vajrayāna Buddhism in Kansu.

Politically, the Si-fan were supposedly under the jurisdiction of seventy-two *t'u-ssu*, or native chiefs, appointed by the imperial government, but the constant shifting of population and allegiance typical among nomads had rendered such an arrangement meaningless.[2] Actually, the imperial government paid scant attention to the Tibetan nomads living in the immense but sparsely populated region between Chinghai, Szechuan, and Kham. Tribal feuds were settled by force, and the victors, more often than not, received the tacit recognition of the imperial authority. Among the nomads, grazing rights in the tribal territory were vested in the tribe as a whole. In the mixed pastoral-agricultural region the territorial chief had sole control over the arable lands, and his position was hereditary. Since the power and prestige of the chief were dependent upon the number of his followers, the defection of his subjects to another chief was a frequent cause of tribal war.[3] With the exception of Sung-p'an, a garrison town, the Si-fan were usually left alone by the provincial government of Szechuan. The remoteness of the Si-fan homeland from any center of Chinese population was their best guarantee against interference in their internal affairs by Chinese officials.

The Polotse and the Hei-sui Man-tzu

As the Sung-p'an plateau falls to the edge of the Szechuan basin, its surface is deeply cut by numerous streams and altered by frequent earthquakes. Most of the cultivated lands are located in the drainage areas of the Cha-ku River and the Hei-sui River on slopes ranging from 5,000 to 9,000 feet in elevation. The growing season is about six months. Rainfall is variable. Below 6,000 feet is the arid zone where the monsoons are blocked off by the high mountain walls. Between 6,000 and 8,000 feet is the semiarid zone where agriculture is possible without irrigation. Between 8,000 and 9,000 feet is the forest zone. Above the forest is the grassland. The slope land is subject to severe erosion while the bottom land is often washed away by torrents. The soil in the grassland is better developed, but the temperature there limits its use.[4]

The youthful, V-shaped valleys, while providing only a poorly endowed home for their inhabitants, also safeguarded them from unwelcome outside interference. As a result the various tribes living there had preserved many peculiarities of speech and custom. Buddhism had penetrated the region but had not driven out completely the indigenous animistic faiths. Topography, a warlike disposition, and a remarkable skill in building fortified stone towers aided the native communities in resisting the imposition of effective Chinese rule.

The Hei-sui is one of the two major tributaries of the Min River. More than fifty small valleys are strung along its two hundred mile course. Each valley represents a natural site for one or more settlements containing from one hundred to two hundred families.[5] Among the settlers were the Polotse, who occupied some of the valleys in the middle course of the river. Tradition relates that they were the descendants of the Norsu contingents who were brought there from Szechuan and Yunnan to fight against the Ch'iang tribes during the Ming dynasty.[6] Very little is known about them except their reputation for robbing passing caravans. The rest of the population consisted of the Hei-sui Man-tzu, who were really a mixture of Si-fan, Giarong, and Ch'iang. The Polotse and the Hei-sui Man-tzu were traditional rivals. They both spoke a language that was unintelligible to the surrounding tribes and might have come from a single racial stock.[7] They carried on a constant feud with their neighbors and were known as habitual thieves. The underlying cause of their truculent behavior was probably the unproductiveness of their soil. The land was overpopulated in terms of its fertility, and many inhabitants migrated annually into the surrounding country to work as masons, well-diggers, hired hands, and yak drivers.[8] In religion they were followers of the Nyingmapa school of Tibetan Buddhism.[9]

During the Ch'ing dynasty, the Hei-sui region was under the nominal jurisdiction of the Somo *t'u-ssu* of the Chin-ch'uan region but political power seems to have been exercised mainly by local headmen. The yamen of the headman was a combination of official residence, courthouse, prison, hotel, and trading post. It was a four-storied, Tibetan-style stone building, one story higher than the common dwellings. The ground floor served as stable, food storehouse, and prison. The second floor was reserved for the stewards, traders, bondsmen, and litigants. The headman lived on the third floor with his family, relatives, and guests. The courtroom was any place the headman happened to be found. The chapel was on the fourth floor where visiting lamas usually stayed.[10]

The office of headman was hereditary and could be transmitted through either men or women. The headman practiced group endogamy. Since both polygamy and leviration were permitted, a shrewd headman could build up considerable political influence by marrying the widows of deceased colleagues, and by inheriting the wives of his deceased brothers who were also headmen. He could also marry his sons into headman families who lacked male issue. The wives of a polygamous headman generally resided in different localities and ruled in his absence.[11] An influential headman usually ruled over a number of settlements. Under him were petty headmen and village elders. The extensive landholdings of the headman were cultivated by tenants or bondsmen.[12] All of those who lived in the area under the authority of the headman were his subjects. Bondsmen were lawbreakers who had been sentenced to servitude or refugees who sought the protection of the yamen. Corvée labor was also performed by commoners whenever required by the headman.[13]

The Ch'iang and Giarong

Between the confluence of the Hei-sui and the Min rivers in the north and Wen-ch'uan in the south and between Mao-hsien in the east and Li-fan in the west lived the remnants of a once powerful people, the Ch'iang. In ancient times they had ranged extensively throughout the highlands of northwest China. During the Ch'ing dynasty they were found in their valley homes of stone and clay located on slopes between 4,000 and 8,000 feet. Their villages were guarded by stone towers, some of which rose to more than one hundred feet. Maize was their staple crop, followed by beans, buckwheat, and millet. Domestic animals included sheep, cattle, and hybrid yaks. Hunting and gathering medicinal herbs provided additional means of subsistence.[14]

The Ch'iang did not have any written language. They worshipped a sky god and a pantheon of nature deities, as well as Chinese gods. Although they were conquered by the Giarong during the reign of Ch'ien-lung (1736-1795), they had never been converted to Buddhism. Their life centered around their religious ceremonies, which were conducted by the *pi* who combined the functions of a shaman, magician, and priest in one person.[15]

The Ch'iang community was ruled by a headman, appointed by the provincial government, whose role seemed to be primarily the settlement of disputes. The Ch'iang, more than any of their neighbors, had been susceptible to Chinese influence. Many of them could no longer speak the Ch'iang language or understand the native tradition.[16]

The Giarong lived in the drainage area of the Great Chin-ch'uan and Little Chin-ch'uan rivers at the upper course of the Ta-tu River. The language that they spoke differed considerably from the Tibetan dialects. There were also differences between the two peoples in physical appearance, food habits, and other cultural traits.[17] Historically, the Giarong came to this region as conquerors from the west. Many Ch'iang settlements, for instance, were ruled by Giarong chiefs. The Giarong generally considered the area west of Ma-t'ang (i.e., the upper Great Chin-ch'uan region) as Giarong proper, and the area south of Ma-t'ang as a zone of conflict where a mixture of peoples prevailed.[18] After the suppression of the Giarong or Chin-ch'uan rebellion in 1776, the imperial government set up five military colonies in the rebel territory. These colonies were administered by Chinese officials, but the native population was still largely in the care of their own chiefs and headmen.

Giarong society was composed of a hierarchy of social classes: a small hereditary group of petty *t'u-ssu* (*darro*, or native chiefs) and headmen (*tschungro*) ruled over the commoners and slaves. The commoners included the *tschralba* and the *tokdamba*, as well as monks and artisans who had been recruited from the younger sons of the *tschralba* or *tokdamba*. The land was regarded as the property of the chiefs from whom each *tschralba* had received an individual piece as a hereditary investiture in exchange for service as a warrior. The *tschralba* were not required to pay taxes but were expected to serve the chief as retainer for twenty to thirty days annually and to furnish their own horses and weapons in war. *Tokdamba*, who were often the younger sons of *tschralba*, were farmers who had to pay rent to the chief. Slaves worked in the fields or tended the cattle of the chief without recompense except for food and drink. They could buy their own and their families' freedom with money. A freed slave could get a piece of land from his chief and become a *tokdamba*. None of the land held by the commoners could be sold or divided.[19]

Landholding among the Giarong was inextricably tied up with their family system. Each individual was identified by the name of the estate upon which he lived. Occupation of the estate involved the assumption of all the privileges and obligations associated with it. The estate could be inherited only by a single (usually eldest) son or daughter. Thus the younger sons either joined a monastery, acquired a new estate by clearing new lands, became artisans, or married into another family whose daughter had inherited an estate. The name of the estate never changed, although the family line might have been thinly diluted by a succession of adopted sons-in-law. A new family establishing itself on the estate whose previous occupants had died out often retained the name of the estate and assumed all its obligations.[20] The Giarong did not have any clan organization or even family surnames.

The Kham Plateau

The central or Kham sector has a total area of about 175,000 square miles, of which the Kham or Tibetan area has about 154,400 square miles, the Ya-an area, which is almost purely Chinese, has about 3,900 square miles, and the Chien-ch'ang (also known as Hsi-ch'ang) area of mixed Tibetan, Moso, Lisu, Miao, Chinese, and Yi settlements has about 16,700 square miles. Ya-an, at an elevation of 2,118 feet, is situated at the westernmost edge of the Chengtu plain. It is a tea-growing district and a center for Tibetan trade. The area is drained by the Ch'ing-i and Ta-tu rivers, both tributaries of the Min River, and is surrounded by the foothills of the Tibetan plateau, some of which are more than 10,000 feet high. The Chien-ch'ang region is often called the Ning District because it formerly belonged to the jurisdiction of the Ning-yuan Prefecture. It is a valley formed by the An-ning River, which flows north to south between the plateau and the Ta-liang ranges. The river joins with the Ya-lung near the Yunnan border as it empties into the Chin-sha, the upper course of the Yangtze. Because the valley constitutes one of the direct routes from Szechuan to Yunnan, it is also called the Chien-ch'ang "corridor." Kham comprises the basins of the Ya-lu-tsang-po (Brahmaputra), Nu (Salween), Lan-tsang (Mekong), Chin-sha, and Ya-lung rivers. The land, deeply furrowed by the canyons of these rivers and their effluents, slopes from the highlands in the northwest toward Szechuan in the southeast. It is a country of great contrasts. The average elevation is 13,000 feet, ranging from 8,000 feet at the valley bottoms to peaks of more than 16,000 feet. The temperature varies according to the altitude and changes abruptly from day to night. Rainfall is concentrated in the summer and fall months and varies according to latitude and altitude. The cultivated areas in Kham are concentrated at Danba (Tan-pa) in the Ta-tu basin, at Kanze (Kan-tzu) and Nyarong (Chan-tui, Hsin-lung) in the Ya-lung basin, at Ting-hsiang (Hsiang-ch'eng) and Tu-ch'eng in the Chin-sha basin, and at the Ba-t'ang plain.[21] It is a sparsely populated region even today.

The Khambas

Like all other areas where Tibetan culture predominated, the Khambas lived in a society dominated by Buddhism and segmented into rigid social classes. Politically the country was divided into numerous entities organized into either tribes or principalities and governed either by hereditary territorial chiefs or by the church hierarchy. The authority of the Peking or Lhasa government, transmitted through the secular or ecclesiastical rulers, was only indirectly felt by the majority of the people. The population in the valley settlement engaged in farming or in a mixed farming and herding economy, while the tribes in the northern grasslands were mostly nomadic rulers.

The ruling class in Kham consisted of a hereditary nobility and a hierarchy of church officials. The governing chiefs were called *t'u-ssu* in Chinese. They ruled over domains that varied greatly in size and influence. A *t'u-ssu* was created when a native chief received from the imperial government an official title confirming his authority within his own domain. At the beginning of the Ch'ing dynasty there were more than 380 *t'u-ssu* in Kham; by the end of the dynasty only about 180 remained.[22] The *t'u-ssu* were differentiated into a hierarchy of ranks that approximated the political influence of the holders. The Tibetan names for them were *gyalbo* (king), *deba*, and *bonbo*.[23] The territorial chiefs were assisted by officials drawn from noble families who held office by a rotation system. Village headmen were chosen either by the territorial chief or by the villagers themselves.[24]

The head of the Tibetan Buddhist monastery was the *k'an-po* or abbot. Among the Gelugpa monks, who were celibates, the *k'an-po* was elected by the brotherhood or appointed from Lhasa for a term of three or five years. Among the Nyingmapa monks, who could marry and have children, his position was hereditary. The *k'an-po* had full authority over the administration of monastic affairs. A *k'an-po* who was also a *tul-ku*, or reincarnation, ranked higher than one who was not. Under the *k'an-po* were the following monk officials: the *um-dse*, who lectured on the scriptures and led the monks in recitations; the *ge-ko*, who maintained discipline among the monks and participated in the internal and external administration of the monastery, including such activities as setting the time for planting and harvesting, and regulating market prices; the *e'ag-dso*, who administered the routine affairs of the monastery; the *tsi-dpon*, who was the accountant; and the *ner-pa*, who was in charge of commercial undertakings. The ordinary Gelugpa monks who had gone to Lhasa for a year or two of study were called *da-pa*. The student monk was called *btsan-ch'un*. Only a monk who had passed a public examination in one of the Lhasa monasteries was eligible to be elected abbot of a Gelugpa monastery. A monastery usually had one or more residing reincarnations who generally possessed great prestige and wealth. Aside from being supported by the income of the monastery, the individual monks also owned private property and were permitted to engage in trading and moneylending.[25]

The monastery usually possessed extensive landholdings and capital funds. As a landowner it exercised jurisdiction over the peasants who worked on the land. As a wealthy corporation it engaged in trade and moneylending. It was the only cultural center for the majority of the inhabitants where the Tibetan language was taught, the traditional arts practiced, and the theatrical entertainments performed. Always influential in localities where the territorial chiefs exercised undisputed power, the monasteries became the virtual rulers in localities where the authority of the territorial chiefs was weak. In places like Chamdo (Ch'ang-tu) and Draya (Ch'a-ya), they had direct control over the population.[26] The relationship between the church hierarchy and the nobility was very close. The great majority of monks in the lower ranks corresponded to the peasantry from which they came and with which their family and economic ties were not completely cut, while the church hierarchs holding large landed estates roughly compared with the lay nobility from which most of them originated.[27]

The economic basis of political power was the ownership of land. In Kham, as throughout Tibet, all the land was considered to belong to the ruler, who had the right to repossess it at will. The territorial chiefs and the noble families granted their subjects land allotments that could be inherited but not sold. Holders of the land allotments (*tse-ba*) were required to pay land rents as well as requisitions in kind and in labor. These requisitions, called *ula*, included products such as fuel, fodder, animals, and food, and services such as farming, herding, and transportation.[28] The *la-da* were peasants who received a small land allotment in return for work on the lands of the monastery. In general they were slightly better off than the *tse-ba* because they were protected by the monastery from unjust exactions by the chiefs.[29]

Khambas living as pure nomads on the northern grasslands were banded together into tribes of several hundred families who owned their pastures collectively. The tribe was subdivided into clans. Often the pastures were owned by the territorial chiefs, noble families, and monasteries who leased the land and herds to the herders, who paid a stipulated amount of animal products and a number of young animals annually to the owners. There were also herders who owned their own pastures and who agreed to take care of their neighbors' animals for an agreed share of the young animals and products. Unlike the nomad tribes, these landless and landholding herders did not combine into large groups, even though their way of living was similar to that of the pure nomads. Finally, a village might also have public grazing grounds where the valley-dwelling peasants could supplement their income by herding.[30]

The Khamba village was an armed settlement. Practically every family possessed some sort of weapons, which were used not solely for defensive purposes. Looting expeditions and intervillage feuds were often organized by the whole village and led by the herdsman or a lama, the loot being divided among the surviving participants. The families of those who died in battle were not compensated, but the village had the obligation to seek revenge for them. Blood feuds often became a vicious cycle that could only be broken by the paying of blood money accompanied by the taking of an oath.[31] The nomads, who lived a precarious life depending upon the health of their herds, often had no alternative other than to take by force from others what disease and drought had taken from them. The rugged environment of Kham had produced a race of men who fought hard to survive and whose only real solace was the Buddhist conception of possible rebirth into a better life.

The Forest Tribes and the Yi

Along the southern border of Kham, the Ya-lu-tsang-po River bores its way through the Himalayan rampart to emerge as the Brahmaputra in the Assam hills. Here, in an area about one hundred miles wide and two hundred miles long, the valleys and slopes of Kongbo, Pome, and Pemako are covered with lush vegetation, the gift of moisture-laden monsoon winds that have blown in through the mountain gap.[32] In this area there lived little-known peoples whom the Tibetans called Monbas and Lopas. Although both subscribed to Buddhism, there were many indications that they indulged in phallic worship. The Monbas and Lopas of Pemako paid allegiance to the territorial chief of Pome.[33] The people of Pome, although speaking a more or less intelligible Tibetan dialect, were not considered true Tibetans. There was a legend that a detachment of Chinese soldiers, on their way from Szechuan to Nepal during the Gurkha War (1791-1792), detoured into Pome and found the place so attractive that they married the local women and stayed there for good.[34] These dwellers of the Tibetan monsoon forest were keen hunters. Barred from the south by the Assam jungle and bypassed by the main Szechuan-Lhasa routes, this region had been ignored by most of the world.

More is known of the Yi (Norsu, Lolo), whose homeland is the Ta-liang Shan range extending roughly from latitude 27°N to 29°N between Szechuan and Kham proper, occupying an area about five hundred miles long and one hundred miles wide. Sinicized Yi were found in many parts of Yunnan and Kweichow, but those in the Ta-liang Shan region had clung stubbornly to their own culture. Living at an elevation between 4,500 and 7,500 feet, they subsisted upon a mixed pastoral and agricultural economy. A warlike people, they had long maintained an autonomous existence at the Sino-Tibetan frontier.

Yi society was built upon the labor of a subject population. The ruling nobility, called the Black Bones, possessed all lands and political power. Courageous in battle, they were quick to take offense at any slight or injury to their pride or possessions. Disdaining menial labor, they confined themselves mostly to the arts of fighting and governing. Their hieroglyphic script, divorced from practical use, had become merely esoteric symbols preserved only in the scriptures of a priestly class drawn from the commoners.[35] Their supernatural world was populated by a host of gods and spirits who controlled the natural elements and inflicted illness and misfortune upon the population.[36] Economically, they were primitive farmers who sometimes resorted to slash-and-burn agriculture, which caused the deforestation of large tracts of land. As animal breeders, they produced excellent horses, in addition to herds of sheep and goats.[37]

The clan was the basic social unit of Yi society. The nobility practiced class endogamy but clan exogamy. Members of the clan usually resided within the territory protected by their clan power. The clan chief held his position for life and acted for the entire clan in war and peace.[38] During the Ch'ing dynasty, a number of hereditary *t'u-ssu* were created who were made responsible for the behavior of the Yi people within their jurisdiction. However, unless they were men of proven ability, they were unable to exert much influence beyond their immediate followers.[39]

Warfare among the Yi resulted mostly from clan feuds. The issue of war or peace was decided in clan meetings. Commoners and slaves fought alongside the nobility in battle. The defeated clan either migrated to a distant locality or put itself under the protection of a friendly clan. If a member of the nobility was killed or committed suicide after having been captured by the enemy, the feud between the warring clans would continue for generations. Otherwise, peace could be restored through the mediation of an influential person with ties to both camps.[40]

The subject people, both commoners and slaves, were called White Bones; they were captives or descendants of captives of the nobility. Most of them were of Chinese origin, while others were of Si-fan and Moso origin. Commoners were generally descendants of slaves who had gained their freedom through faithful service to their masters or by the paying of ransom. They had become thoroughly assimilated into the Yi culture and constituted the great majority of the population. There had never been a recorded case of rebellion of the White Bones against the Black Bones, for the ambition of the commoners was not to take the place of the nobility but to become wealthy under the protection of their overlords. They took as much pride in the ancestral glories and military prowess of their masters as did the masters themselves.[41] Slaves, however, had a harder life. They could be sold, exchanged, or given away. A new slave was always tortured and ill-treated until his spirit was broken. An escaped slave had to be returned to his owner by whoever found him.[42]

Secured in the fastness of a rugged mountain chain, living a Spartan life of simple foods and pleasures, and glorying in the possession of a fighting tradition, the Yi had defied many attempts of the imperial government to subdue them. The fortified Chinese villages that surrounded the base of their mountain homeland testified to how their raiding expeditions had terrified the peasant colonies.

The Yunnan Frontier

The Yunnan sector of the Sino-Tibetan frontier included roughly the administrative areas of Li-chiang, Yung-ning, Wei-hsi, Chung-tien, and A-tun-tse (Te-ch'in). Geographically, it is a part of the Tibetan plateau located roughly between the latitudes 27°N and 29°N and dominated by the tremendous mountain chains running from north to south which separate, almost within echoing distance of one another, the tumbling waters of the Nu, Lan-tsang, and Chin-sha rivers. It is the meeting ground of the Ku-tsung, Si-fan, Moso, Yi, Min-chia, Miao, Lisu, and Lu-hsi peoples. The dominant group, however, is the Moso or Na-hsi. The penetration of Chinese influence into this region occurred at a much later date than it did in other parts of the Sino-Tibetan borderlands.

The Moso

During the latter part of the sixteenth century, the Moso people, under the leadership of their chief Mu Tseng, extended their power from their capital at Li-chiang west to the Nu valley, north to the vicinity of Pa-t'ang and Li-t'ang in Kham, and east to the Ya-lung valley. Moso colonies were planted among the native population who came under the rule of Moso officials. The Moso kingdom, however, maintained its allegiance to the Ming court. Its noble families took up the study of Chinese literature and sent their sons to participate in the state examinations. In the seventeenth century, the Khosote

Mongols of Chinghai under Gushi Khan embarked upon the conquest of the entire Tibetan plateau, and the Moso dependencies fell under their political sway. As a result, the fortune of the Moso kingdom was already declining when the Manchus conquered Yunnan. They were the first among the non-Chinese peoples in Yunnan to adopt the Manchu hairstyle, a token of complete loyalty. During the Wu San-kuei Rebellion the Moso chief, Mu I, died in prison for refusing to collaborate with the rebels. After the suppression of the rebellion, the house of Mu was unable to recover its former vigor. Although it was permitted to retain the hereditary *t'u-ssu* rank, the administration of its shrunken domain, beginning in 1723, was exercised by Chinese officials.[43] The impact of direct Chinese political control during the Ch'ing dynasty accelerated the process of acculturation, which made the Moso, relatively speaking, the most sinicized of all the Sino-Tibetan frontier peoples.

The basic political organization of the Moso was the village. Each village was governed by a set of prohibitions promulgated and administered by village elders. The village often owned public lands and forests, the proceeds of which went to the maintenance of village schools, assistance to the poor, and similar public undertakings. These activities were administered by an elected officer. The Moso had a very strong cooperative spirit. Villagers worked together on each other's fields during planting and harvesting time. In the mountain villages, sheep-herding played an important economic role.[44]

Moso clan organization was weak. Clan members got together only for the sacrifice to Heaven. The clan leader was an intelligent person of advanced age who arbitrated disputes among clan members and presided over the division of family inheritance. Some clans owned property, the income from which was used to defray the expenses of clan sacrifices, which were held twice a year.[45]

The indigenous Moso religious cult figure, the *dtomba*, was a person who presided over funerals and weddings, exorcised demons, treated illnesses, and performed magical feats. The Moso script would have been lost if it had not been preserved in the scriptures of the *dtombas*. For this reason, the *dtombas* were the transmitters of the indigenous literary tradition, keeping alive the ancient tales, history, songs, and geographical knowledge as incorporated in the scriptures. Despite his importance in the life of the Moso people, the *dtomba* was not a full-time practitioner; his main economic support came from farming or handicraft work. Actually the Moso were eclectics believing in a mixture of animism, ancestor worship, and Buddhism.[46]

Other Tribes

The Lu-hsi, a kindred people of the Moso who lived in the Yung-ning District north of Li-chiang, had the distinction of having the only completely matrilineal society in the Sino-Tibetan frontier.[47] The Ku-tsung and the Yunnan Si-fan were Tibetan tribes living in the border districts of Wei-hsi, Chung-tien, and A-tun-tze. The Lisu were a primitive tribal people living in the high mountains and depending upon hunting, collecting, and crude agriculture for subsistence. The Yi were immigrants from the Ta-liang Shan region. They were feared and disliked by their neighbors. Everywhere they went, they set fire to the virgin forests in order to obtain land for cultivation. The Min-chia and Miao were immigrants from south Yunnan whose numbers were quite small.

Common Characteristics of the Southwestern Sino-Tibetan Border Regions

This brief survey of the southwestern Sino-Tibetan border cultures and geography suggests certain conclusions that may help clarify our understanding of the Ch'ing imperial frontier policy. First, the rugged topography and general inaccessibility of the region favored the establishment of multiple, small autonomous political entities. None of these autonomous domains, however, had the requisite economic and population resources to become the nucleus of a new, expanding power. The Giarong chiefs were able to annex some of their weaker neighbors and put up a stubborn resistance to the Ch'ing armies sent to punish them. However, expansion of the Giarong power was accomplished to a large degree through political and marital alliances among the territorial chiefs. Even at the height of their power, their territorial limits were relatively small.

Second, despite the geographic factors that separated them as political units, other influences had been at work to bind the border peoples together, the most important of these being Buddhism, which drew pilgrims from everywhere in the borderlands to Lhasa and other holy sites in Tibet and Kham, thus partially breaking down the physical and intellectual isolation of the local populations. In every local monastery there were monks who had spent some time studying in the great Tibetan religious centers. In a population immobilized by poverty and feudal ties to the land, they constituted an elite, cosmopolitan group who were able, through religious and political means, to impose certain uniform patterns of behavior on peoples distributed over a huge territory. Buddhism was a cultural bond that aided the border peoples in resisting the inroads of Chinese cultural influences.

A third cohesive factor was the similarity in social structure. Without exception the border societies were ruled by a hereditary aristocracy. Although an exceptional commoner might aspire to become a church hierarch, his lack of aristocratic background would definitely hinder his progress. Class endogamy was rigorously observed by the territorial chiefs and local nobility. Marriage alliances were made between the noble families of different autonomous units. An ambitious chief, through a combination of marital manipulations and political sagacity, could extend his influence beyond his own domain. Furthermore, the ruling class, cemented by blood ties and a similar social outlook, tended to act as a conservative force in extending and perpetuating the traditional social patterns and in resisting changes that might undermine its privileged position.

Fourth, the land tenure system in the borderlands differed radically from the traditional Chinese system of private ownership. With few exceptions, the ownership of land was vested in hands of the native ruler: unless protected by the military might of the imperial government, no Chinese colonists could acquire land for cultivation without his permission. Since land constituted the basic source of political power, the reluctance of the local ruler to open his territory to Chinese cultivators was understandable. Without the presence of Chinese colonists, the political hold on the territory by the imperial government was often more nominal than real.

Fifth, the greatest barrier to Chinese colonization was the nature of the land itself. It was too rugged for the customary mode of Chinese agriculture. Unless the Chinese acquired the technique of pastoral life, which they did not, the penetration of Chinese settlers into the highlands would place them in small isolated valleys surrounded by warlike nomads occupying the intervening grasslands. The possibility of advancing in a solid line of agricultural settlements into a nomad territory, as happened in the Inner Mongolian steppes, simply did not exist in the Sino-Tibetan borderlands.

Frontier Trade and Chinese Settlement

Throughout Chinese history, frontier trade had always had political overtones. The most important single article of trade in the Sino-Tibetan borderlands was tea, grown in large quantities in the rain-soaked Ya-chou District below the plateau. During the Sung and Ming dynasties, the system of bartering Chinese tea for nomad horses under government supervision was considered an important frontier security measure. It was thought that by controlling the frontier tea trade, the government would be able to assure a steady supply of war mounts as well as a means of controlling the tribesmen through the threat of suspension of the tea traffic. During the Ch'ing period, the extension of imperial power over large numbers of horse-producing regions made it unnecessary for the government to barter tea for horses. But the tea trade continued under government supervision for its tax revenues and for its role in frontier policy. Tea was exported from Szechuan and Yunnan to the frontier peoples through a licensing system in which the merchants were required to pay a fee for a fixed number of permits. Each permit entitled the holder to sell a fixed amount of tea. Since the number of permits was regulated by the government, the merchants who were granted the permits had a monopoly on the tea trade.[48] In addition to tea, Chinese trading firms exported silk, cotton, pottery, tobacco, and hardwares while importing wool, hides, animals, deer musk, and medicinal herbs.[49]

Whereas in Manchuria and Mongolia the Chinese merchants had virtually the entire field to themselves, the Sino-Tibetan border peoples, especially the Khamba, were inveterate and shrewd traders. All the territorial chiefs and the lamaseries took part in trading. They had the financial resources as well as the experience to compete against the Chinese, and consequently trading on the frontier was conducted on a give-and-take basis. The Chinese brought their goods to such distributive centers as Sung-p'an, Ta-chien-lu, and Li-chiang where they met Si-fan or Khamba caravans coming from beyond the border. When Chinese agents ventured into non-Chinese territories, they had to seek the cooperation of the local authorities for the disposition of their goods. In nomad country, this cooperation was essential, for otherwise they stood to lose not only their caravans but also their lives. Since the traders were never accompanied by their wives, many of them married local women while they were living in tribal communities. The children of such unions inevitably lost their Chinese heritage unless they were brought back to China proper.[50]

By the end of the Ming dynasty, the population of Szechuan had been seriously reduced by decades of civil war. The Ch'ing authorities aided the resettlement of the province by promising land to immigrants, and more than 1.7 million settlers were recorded in the period from 1667 to 1707. There is little likelihood that this migratory wave extended to the Tibetan borderlands. On the contrary, the rise of *t'u-ssu* power after the fall of the Ming and during the Wu San-kuei feudatory seemed to indicate an expansion of tribal power into territories vacated by the Chinese. Chinese colonization of the southwest was infeasible until the power of the *t'u-ssu* had been curbed. This was accomplished by the removal of some of the most powerful *t'u-ssu* at the Kweichow-Szechuan-Yunnan frontier in 1726 under the active policy of O-er-t'ai, governor-general of Yunnan and Kweichow. In 1730, the *t'u-ssu* of T'ien-chuan and Ch'ing-hsi of Ya-chou Prefecture were eliminated.[51] This opened the way for Chinese settlement of the Ya-tu valley. In 1733, military and civilian colonies were established in the Chien-ch'ang corridor.[52] A traveller to Sung-p'an reported in 1744 that only the road along the Min River and the town itself belonged to the Chinese; the rest was tribal territory.[53] Planned colonization did not begin in Kham until 1906.[54] Thus the initial efforts to colonize the different sectors of the Sino-Tibetan frontier occurred many years after the Manchu conquest of Szechuan in 1663. Significantly, these frontier lands were opened to Chinese settlers only in the wake of military campaigns.

Nor did the settlers enjoy uninterrupted periods of peace and security. Between the narrow valley bottoms and the intermountain plains where the Chinese settled were the tribal peoples who occupied the intervening mountain ranges. The constricted and isolated Chinese settlements were fair prey to tribal raiders whenever the authority of the imperial government showed signs of weakness. Unfortunately for the settlers, beginning with the White Lotus Rebellion (1796-1802) in Szechuan, southwest China witnessed a succession of civil conflicts that seriously affected the ability of the government to provide adequate protection for its Chinese subjects in the frontier region. These were the Yunnan Muslim uprising of 1845-1873, the Taiping Rebellion of 1850-1864, and the Kansu Muslim uprising of 1863-1873, all of which had repercussions in the frontier region. It was clear that colonization was possible only with the costly maintenance of strong garrison points. The government was willing to do this only when it was convinced that national policy required the planting of Chinese colonies in the chosen areas. The Min valley, which was the military route to Kansu, the Ya-chou valley to the Kham highland and Lhasa, and the Chien-ch'ang corridor to Yunnan were strategically important and had to be kept open. The Wei-hsi, Chung-tien, and A-tun-tze route to Kham was unimportant militarily, and no government colonization effort was made in that sector.

Frontier Politics: The Rise of Manchu Power, 1642-1700

During the latter part of the Ming dynasty, two frontier powers rose beyond the borders of China, each seeking political supremacy in East Asia. These were the Manchus and the Jungar Mongols. Until the final defeat of the Jungars in 1757, the struggle between these two peoples profoundly affected the history of the entire inner Asian frontier of China. Because the Mongol tribes were followers of the Tibetan Buddhist church, Tibet became an important political prize for the contending powers. Consequently, events in the Sino-Tibetan borderlands had to be considered in conjunction with conflicts that occurred on China's northwestern frontier and in Lhasa. In this regard, Chinghai was of special strategic importance. A part of the Tibetan plateau, it was bordered on the northwest by the Jungar empire in Chinese Turkestan (Sinkiang), on the southwest by Tibet, on the northeast by Kansu, and on the southeast by Kham and Szechuan. One of the two principal routes from China to Lhasa traversed its whole length from Sining to Nagchu (Heiho). In hostile lands, Chinghai could menace the security of both northwest and southwest China, as well as sever the communication between China and Lhasa.

In the seventeenth century the Jungars, one of the four western Mongol tribes called the Eleuths (Oirats), rose in power under their great leader, Galdan. To escape their domination, the Khosote Eleuth, led by Gushi Khan (d. 1654), migrated from Urumchi to Chinghai. By 1633 he had firmly established himself as the lord of all the Chinghai Mongols. Taking the fertile pastures around Chinghai Lake (Lake Kokonor), the Mongols pushed the Chinghai Tibetans (Amdo-pas) into the high mountain ranges. In 1636 Gushi Khan extended his conquest into Kham where he ruled the Khambas directly through the establishment of Mongol fiefs and garrison stations and indirectly through Khamba monasteries and chiefs.[55]

In 1641 the Fifth Dalai Lama requested Gushi Khan's military aid in eliminating the power of Tsang-pa Khan, the secular Tibetan ruler, and in 1642 Tsang-pa Khan was killed by the Mongols. Gushi Khan, however, did not come to Tibet on an altruistic mission. His eldest son, Ochir Khan, was made king of Tibet and the second son, Dayan Batur Taichi, was made second in command. Politically, Tibet had become a dependency of the Khosote Mongols.[56]

Earlier, in 1639, the Manchu ruler Abahai, following the suggestion of the Khalka Mongols of Outer Mongolia, had invited the Fifth Dalai Lama for a meeting at his capital, Shengching

(Mukden). In 1642, representatives of Gushi Khan, the Dalai Lama, the Panchen Lama, and Ochir Khan arrived at Shengching with greetings and presents. The next year a Manchu envoy journeyed to Lhasa. These visits established the first political ties between the Manchus and the Buddhist church in Lhasa. In 1652 the Fifth Dalai Lama traveled to Peking where the Shuh-chih emperor received him with lavish attention. In 1653 Gushi Khan sent a tributary mission to the Ch'ing court and received a royal investiture of his khanate.[57] By these diplomatic moves, the Ch'ing empire had acquired two important allies in the struggle against the Jungars.

The excellent Manchu-Tibetan relations protected the western flank of the Ch'ing armies as they fought the Ming Chinese in southwest China. In 1662 the Manchu conquest of Ming China was completed, and Wu San-kuei was given a hereditary fief comprising the provinces of Yunnan and Kweichow by the Ch'ing court for his role in the campaign. Almost at once, Wu embarked upon a program of winning the friendship of the Dalai Lama and of consolidating his control over the tribal chiefs of the southwest. Over the trade route between Kham and Yunnan, which was reopened in 1659 at the request of the Dalai Lama, came Tibetan horses for Wu's cavalry in exchange for Yunnan tea. Wu brought pressure upon Mu I, the Moso chief of Li-chiang, to supply him with 1,000 Moso soldiers; Mu I's refusal aroused Wu's enmity. In 1668, Wu ceded to the Dalai Lama part of the Mu family domain. Again in 1673, when Wu unfurled the banner of rebellion, he ceded another slice of the Moso territory to the Dalai Lama.[58] When the Ch'ing court ordered the Khosote Mongols to dispatch troops to Szechuan via Sung-p'an to block Wu's advance toward Shensi, the Dalai Lama demurred and, in a letter, advised the K'ang-hsi emperor to make peace by dividing the empire with the insurgents.[59] Thus, although the Manchu policy of friendship with the Dalai Lama was unable to prevent the latter from attempting to fish in troubled waters, it succeeded in preventing the rebels from getting any military assistance from the Khosote Mongols through the Dalai Lama. This incident probably impressed the Ch'ing court with the latent danger of the church in Lhasa being under the control of a hostile power.

Frontier Politics: The Period of Expansion, 1701-1795

The eighteenth century was a period of expansion of Ch'ing power into the Sino-Tibetan borderlands. Some idea of this expansion may be gotten by comparing the number of *t'u-ssu* investitures in the seventeenth and the eighteenth centuries. The investitures were made by the Ch'ing court as a reward for those hereditary tribal chiefs who submitted voluntarily to the authorities of the imperial government, and for those tribal officers who won distinction in their service to the imperial armies. In Szechuan, thirty-eight *t'u-ssu* were awarded in the seventeenth century, one hundred and fourteen in the eighteenth century, and one in the nineteenth century. Most of those founded in the seventeenth century were located along the Min valley and in Ya-chou Prefecture. In Yunnan, seventy were established in the seventeenth century, forty-three in the eighteenth century, and six in the nineteenth century.[60] More tribal chiefs submitted to the Ch'ing authorities in Yunnan than in Szechuan during the seventeenth century because tribal peoples were distributed throughout Yunnan Province, whereas in Szechuan they were located mostly along border areas. As the Ch'ing armies entered Yunnan in pursuit of the Ming remnants, the tribal peoples along the route of march switched their allegiance from the Ming to the Ch'ing. On the other hand, during the seventeenth century, the power of the Ch'ing empire in the Sino-Tibetan frontier generally did not extend beyond that of the Ming period.

Beginning in the eighteenth century, a series of military campaigns was undertaken that carried the authority of the Ch'ing court far into the Tibetan plateau. In 1698 and 1703 the garrison commander of Sung-p'an brought the Si-fan tribes in the area under his control. In 1720, in response to complaints that the Golok tribes (nomadic Tibetans living in the Chinghai highland near the borders of Szechuan and Kham) were raiding the people, a punitive expedition under the command of the renowned Yo Chung-ch'i was sent across the grassland from Sung-p'an to A-pa. In this campaign many Golok strongholds were destroyed and a number of tribal chiefs were executed. Yo Chung-ch'i put the pacified region under the authority of the Giarong chiefs of Chaku valley and set up a string of garrison points and post stations along the strategic route to northern Kham. During the Chinghai campaign against the Khosote Mongols in 1723-1724 the Szechuan troops from Sung-p'an subjugated a great number of hostile tribes along the Szechuan-Shensi and Szechuan-Kansu borders as well as remnants of the Golok tribes in A-pa. In 1727, Yo Chung-ch'i again had to discipline the Goloks for robbery and put them under the direct supervision of the Sung-p'an garrison command.[61]

In the Kham region at the end of the Ming dynasty the power of the Khosote Mongols extended to the district of Ya-chou in Szechuan. In

1662, the native chiefs east of the Ta-tu River in Ya-chou switched their allegiance to the Ch'ing court. In 1700, the Khambas invaded the *t'u-ssu* territory, which the Ch'ing government had created, giving the imperial troops an opportunity to extend their power beyond the Ta-tu River to the banks of the Ya-lung River. In 1701 the entire area was put under the jurisdiction of a newly established Ming-cheng *t'u-ssu* (Changla), and a Chinese garrison was sent to Ta-chien-lu, the gateway on the road to Lhasa from Szechuan.[62]

Meanwhile the Fifth Dalai Lama had died in 1682, leaving the affairs of state in the hands of his prime minister, Sangge, who, resentful of the Khosote Mongols, befriended the Jungars. On the other hand, the Khosote Mongols, under the leadership of Dashi Batur Khan, the tenth son of Gushi Khan, had formally placed themselves under the protection of the Manchu emperor in 1698. In 1700, Lobtsan Khan, a great grandson of Gushi Khan, inherited the position of king of Tibet. Sangge, who attempted to poison the young khan, was killed by the latter in 1705. The Ch'ing court readily confirmed Lobtsan Khan's title.[63]

Among the Jungars, a new leader, Tsewang Araptan, had emerged. Taking advantage of the discontent of Tibetans who chafed under Lobtsan Khan's interference with religious affairs, Tsewang Araptan's Jungar army invaded Tibet in 1717 and put the khan to death, ending the political ascendancy of the Khosote Mongols in that country. A Chinese relief column was annihilated by the Jungars in 1718. The K'ang-hsi emperor was determined to regain Tibet in spite of the combined opposition of his councillors and the Chinghai Mongols. The former stressed the difficulty and uncertainty of the venture while the latter disliked the prospect of having to provide men and animals for the campaign. The emperor, however, thought differently. No doubt his pride was hurt by the destruction of the relief column, which could have a detrimental effect upon his hold over other Mongols, but there were other considerations as well. Tibet, he maintained, was a shield for Chinghai, Szechuan, and Yunnan. If it were occupied by the Jungars, none of these regions would ever enjoy peace again. In 1720, two armies, one crossing Chinghai from Sining and the other crossing Kham from Szechuan, met in Lhasa. The Jungars were completely routed.[64]

Since the southern army of the Tibetan expedition had to pass through Kham, which was not yet under Ch'ing control, Yo Chung-ch'i was dispatched there to secure the line of communication. Starting from Ta-chien-lu in 1719, Yo swept westward toward Lhasa. On the way he killed the Khamba chief of Li-tang and accepted the surrender of the chiefs of Ba-tang, Chaya, Chamdo, Tsawarong, and Lhorong Dzong. After the Jungars had been defeated, Yo went to southern Kham and secured the allegiance of the local chiefs of Gonbo.[65] To facilitate the movement of troops, he set up eighty-seven garrison depots along the route of march from Ta-chien-lu to Lari. This was the beginning of the occupation of southern Kham by the Ch'ing government.[66] Northern Kham remained under the control of the Chinghai Mongols. Two former officers of Lobtsan Khan, K'an-c'en-nas and P'o-lha-has, were appointed by the emperor to administer U (central Tibet where Lhasa is located) and Tsang (western Tibet) respectively. In 1723 the imperial troops were withdrawn from Lhasa, but the garrison forces remained in Kham.[67]

The Khosote Mongols of Chinghai were disappointed that Tibet had not been restored to their control. Taking advantage of the death of the K'ang-hsi emperor in 1722, their leader Lobdan Dandzin convened the Khosote tribes in 1723 and demanded that all Mongols renounce their allegiance to Peking. With the support of the grand lama of the Kumbum Monastery in Chinghai and the promised aid of the Jungars, Lobdan Dandzin proclaimed himself the "Great Khan." The Khosotes, however, were not firmly united; two chiefs defected to the Ch'ing side as soon as hostilities began. The Jungars could not come to their aid because their route to Chinghai was blocked by imperial troops. In 1724 the Ch'ing forces under the command of Nien Keng-yao and his able lieutenant, Yo Chung-ch'i, routed the rebels in fifteen days. Lobdan Dandzin managed to escape to the Jungars. During the short campaign a great number of Khosote Mongols were killed and many monasteries destroyed. The Chinghai Mongols never recovered from this catastrophe.[68] In Yunnan the native chiefs of Chung-tien, who had professed loyalty to Lobdan Dandzin, now asked to be put under Yunnan administration.[69]

After peace had returned, Nien Keng-yao, in a memorial to the throne, submitted a number of proposals for the administration of the Sino-Tibetan frontier, which became the basis of imperial policy. Nien suggested that the Tibetan tribes of the Sung-p'an, Kham, and Chung-tien regions, who had been under the control of the Mongols, should be put under the jurisdiction of their native chiefs and subject to the supervision of nearby Chinese civilian or military officials. Their tributes to the imperial government should be less than what they had sent to their Mongol overlords. They should be permitted to retain their traditional pastures. Kham should be divided between Szechuan and Yunnan. The "saddle tax," which the trading caravans of the Dalai Lama had been exacting from the monasteries of

Chamdo, Chaya, Ba-tang, and Li-tang, should be eliminated. In return, the tariff paid by the trading caravans at Ta-chien-lu to Chinese authorities should also be discontinued. All the Khamba tribes east of Lhoring Dzong, except Chamdo and Chaya, which were under the control of Living Buddhas (*tul-ku*), should be grouped under their own chiefs appointed by the court. Military garrisons should be established at all strategic points in Kham, and in the Sung-p'an grassland. A civilian post should be established in Li-tang in charge of finance and taxation.[70]

The implementation of the above policy was entrusted to Yo Chung-ch'i, who suggested additionally that the Chung-tien and Wei-hsi districts be returned to Yunnan, that the lands west of the Nu River be given to the Dalai Lama, and that the lands east of the river be put under the administration of Szechuan.[71] In 1725 the Ch'ing court eventually decided to put A-tun-tze, Chung-tien, and Wei-hsi under Yunnan administration; the Szechuan-Tibetan boundary was set at Ning-ching Shan, a mountain range located between the Lan-tsang and Chin-sha rivers, and a boundary stone was erected there in 1726.[72] In 1732 the representatives of Tibet, Szechuan, and Kansu met and divided the territories of the nomad tribes in northern Kham between Chinghai and Tibet. Forty tribes, later known as the twenty-five tribes of Yu-shu or Jyelkundo, were put under the control of the imperial commissioner for Sining (Sining *amban*), and thirty-nine tribes, also known as the Jyade tribes, were put under the control of the imperial commissioner for Tibet (Tibet *amban*).[73]

The elimination of Mongol power from the Sino-Tibetan borderlands did not mean the assurance of political tranquility on the frontier. Yi raids against Chinese settlements in the Chien-ch'ang corridor prompted a series of campaigns by Szechuan troops, which ended in the establishment of three Chinese military garrisons and the appointment of a subprefect for the administration of Lu-ning, the first direct Chinese presence in that rugged corner in southeastern Kham.[74] But the most serious problem was the containment of the Giarong tribes. In 1746, Solobun, the Giarong *t'u-ssu* of Rardan (Ta-Chin-ch'uan) attacked his neighbor in Tsanla (Hsiao-Chin-ch'uan). Although forced to give up his gains by the Szechuan authorities, he raided his neighbors again in 1747 and repelled provincial troops sent against him. This brought the first imperial campaign against the Giarong, which lasted until 1749. At its end, except for the restitution of the lands taken from his neighbors, the Giarong chief emerged from the war without serious impairment of his prestige or territory.[75]

The failure of the court to eradicate Solobun's power and the exposure of the weakness of the Ch'ing army in mountain warfare encouraged the Chaku *t'u-ssu*, Ts'ang-wang, in his 1752 bid for territorial expansion at the expense of his northern neighbors, the *t'u-ssu* of Somo and Cho-ke-chi. Ts'ang-wang was captured and killed in the winter of 1752. It was decided then that the position of *t'u-ssu* should be eliminated, and that the tribal territory of Chaku valley should be divided into five districts, each governed by a tribal leader who was appointed to a hereditary rank.[76] The rapid resolution of the Chaku incident was due to the fact that many Chaku inhabitants were not Giarong but Ch'iang subjects of Giarong conquerors. The fighting quality of the Giarong was again in evidence during the second Giarong campaign.

In 1758 Solobun's nephew, Langa, inherited the chieftainship and decided to emulate his uncle's military feats by subjugating the lands of the Gechitsa, Bati, and Bawant *t'u-ssu* in 1759. Thereupon, the neighboring *t'u-ssu* were mobilized by the court to attack Langa from the north and south, and they succeeded in freeing Gechitsa. The military power of Langa, however, remained intact. After Langa's death, his son, Sonan, renewed the aggression against his neighbor with the help of his brother-in-law, Tsengasang. The Ch'ien-lung emperor decided that a serious campaign was needed to punish the recalcitrant Giarong chiefs, and in 1773 an expedition was sent against them. The chiefs resisted for five years before succumbing to the imperial forces.[77]

In the aftermath of the war, five military colonels were established in the Giarong territories, which acted as garrison forces. Civilian colonies were created in lands that had been laid to waste. The remaining lands were settled by Giarong natives under the leadership of their headmen, who were subject to the supervision of the garrison commanders.[78] Although the victorious conclusion of the Giarong campaign was celebrated with much pomp and self-glorification by the court, it was a costly war that the emperor would have avoided if possible. The Chin-ch'uan territory was unimportant both militarily and politically. The colonization of the conquered territory was an afterthought, not the rationale for the initiation of the hostilities. The point stressed by court and provincial authorities alike was that no single tribal chief should be permitted to become unduly strong through the annexation of the territories of his fellow chiefs, since the safety of the borderlands depended upon the fragmentation of tribal power.

The occupation of Chin-ch'uan completed the consolidation of Ch'ing power over the Sino-Tibetan frontier in southwest China.

From the Sung-p'an grassland in the north to the Nu River in the south, the authority of the imperial government was recognized by all the tribal peoples. The power of the Khosote Mongols in Chinghai had been broken and the prestige of the Tibetan Buddhist church had been used to serve the imperial cause. The road to Lhasa had been secured. With the destruction of Jungar power in 1757 and the conquest of the Tarim Basin in 1759, any lingering menace to the Sino-Tibetan frontier from the northwest had been eliminated. Instead of being an external frontier demarcating China from a Mongol-dominated central Asia, it had become an internal frontier separating Chinese culture from tribal cultures.

In the closing years of the eighteenth century, the political hold of the imperial government over the Sino-Tibetan borderlands was further strengthened by the reorganization of the Tibetan administration following the Gurkha War of 1791-1792. In the wake of military victory, the Ch'ien-lung emperor ordered a sweeping reform of the Tibetan political structure. The imperial commissioners were raised to a rank equal to the Dalai Lama and Panchen Lama in official protocol. Their approval was required for all important official appointments and for the passage of the government budget. Candidates for the incarnations of all grand lamas, including the Dalai and Panchen lamas, were henceforth to be chosen in their presence by the drawing of names placed in a golden urn. The imperial commissioners were also entrusted with the military defense of Tibet. The restrictions thus imposed upon the autonomy of the Lhasa government meant that the Tibetan-administered part of the Kham territory had now come under the purview of the imperial commissioners in Tibet.

Frontier Politics: The Retreat of Imperial Power, 1796-1900

With the ascension of the Chia-ch'ing emperor in 1796, the period of territorial expansion came to an end. The nineteenth century witnessed the steady decline of the prestige and power of the Ch'ing empire. The new reign began with the rebellion of the White Lotus Sect, which devastated the frontier provinces of Szechuan, Shensi, and Kansu. Thereafter, a succession of internal revolts and foreign aggressions culminated in the Boxer Rebellion of 1900. These turbulent events adversely affected imperial control of the Sino-Tibetan borderlands. The provincial governments of Szechuan and Yunnan, weakened by years of civil warfare, were unable to deal effectively with frontier problems. At the same time, the extension of

British power from Burma and India to the Himalayan foothills stimulated British interest in the Sino-Tibetan borders and resurrected the fear of foreign invasion in the minds of responsible frontier officials.

The loosening of imperial control over frontier affairs was reflected in a resurgence of tribal power and a growing attitude of independence among the Tibetan authorities in Lhasa. This was evident in Kham. Of all the native Kham *t'u-ssu*, the inhabitants of Chan-tui (Nyarong) had been the most troublesome to the imperial government. Their territory was situated on the right bank of the Ya-lung River, next to the Hor territories, off the main road to Lhasa, and thus shielded from the eyes of Chinese officials. Since its incorporation into the Ch'ing empire in 1728, the provincial authorities had been compelled time and again to discipline their chiefs for raiding their neighbors. In 1814 an expeditionary force was dispatched against one of the five Chan-tui *t'u-ssu* for robbing the people of Hor Drango and unintentionally killing a Chinese officer. The culprit was killed and his domain divided among the remaining Chan-tui chiefs.[79] During the Hsien-feng reign (1851-1861) when the imperial government was beset by the Taiping Rebellion, a native chief, Gombu Nyamjyel, after forcefully uniting the entire Chan-tui region, conquered the lands of his smaller neighbors, invaded those belonging to the *t'u-ssu* of the Hor and Dege regions, and blocked the caravan route to Lhasa. In 1862 after a tea caravan was robbed en route to Lhasa, the Tibetan government petitioned the court for a combined Sino-Tibetan campaign against Gombu Nyamjyel. The petition was granted. At that time, however, a Taiping force under Shih Ta-k'ai had invaded Szechuan, and the provincial government was unable to spare its attention elsewhere. Finally, in 1865 the court agreed to a joint campaign just as the Tibetans were approaching Chan-tui with the aid of many Kham chiefs. Meanwhile Szechuan Governor-general Lo Ping-chang was engaged by the troops of Lan Ta-shun, another Taiping rebel. Fearful of the consequence of a Tibetan victory, he requested the Tibetans to stop their advance. When his request was rejected, Lo sent a detachment of his troops to participate in the fighting. The commander of the Szechuan force, instead of going forward, dallied in Ta-chien-lu until the Tibetans had killed Gombu Nyamjyel. The victorious Tibetans then demanded 160,000 taels of silver as the price for their withdrawal. Unwilling to meet such a demand, Lo suggested to the court that Chan-tui be given to the Tibetans.[80]

The weakness of the Ch'ing government was fully exposed by this incident. The succession of Tibetan governors of Chan-tui sought to expand their influence over their neighbors just as Gombu Nyamjyel had done. As a result, border disputes between Chan-tui and the *t'u-ssu* of Li-tang, Ming-chen, and Hor flared up repeatedly. The Chan-tui natives also became embittered over the arbitrary exactions of their Tibetan overlords, and in 1889 revolted against them. The governor-general of Szechuan, however, denied their petition for the restoration of Chinese control in order not to antagonize the Tibetans. Consequently, the Tibetans returned with more garrison troops.[81] In 1894 the Tibetan governor of Chan-tui intervened in a dispute between the neighboring chiefs of Hor Driwo and Hor Drango. This time, Szechuan Governor-general Lu Ch'uan-lin took the opportunity to chastise the Tibetans and reconquer Chan-tui. His proposal for putting Chan-tui and nearby Dege under direct Chinese administration was vetoed by the court due to the objections of the Manchu general of Chengtu and the imperial commissioner of Tibet.[82]

Chan-tui was only one trouble spot among many that the frontier officials had to deal with. There were many minor incidents involving the Goloks, the Yi, and the Khambas. With the end of the Taiping Rebellion, however, a new set of officials came to power in the empire. They were able to grasp the implications of the position of China as a member of the world community of nations and were concerned by the gathering shadow of foreign imperialism over their country. While the nation focused its attention upon the capital and the coastal provinces where men like Tseng Kuo-fan, Li Hung-chang, and Chang Chih-tung sought means of strengthening and modernizing the empire, frontier officials with less publicity were beginning to look at their problems in a different context. Their changing perspectives and attitudes paved the way for the drastic reorganization of the frontier administrative structure after the fiasco of the Boxer Rebellion. There was a sense of urgency in their discussions, for foreign explorers and political agents had begun to penetrate the inland provinces and the outlying dependencies in ever greater numbers with questionable motives.[83] The feeling of security bred by geographical isolation was gone forever.

Ting Pao-chen, the governor-general of Szechuan from 1876 to 1886, frequently expressed fear of British power in India and its persistent effort to open trade with Tibet. He asserted that the foreigners were adept in using the pretext of trade to further their territorial ambitions and that the ultimate goal of Britain was not Tibet but Szechuan.[84] During his administration Ting had to deal constantly with the internal feuds of the Khambas and their open defiance of imperial authority, such as obstructing the travels of Chinese officials and Western explorers. However, he resisted suggestions by impatient officials for the sinicization of the Tibetan people, the colonization of their lands, and the opening of mines and industries in their territories, stating that any effort to disturb the traditional culture of Tibet would only produce contrary results.[85]

By the time Lu Ch'uan-lin became governor-general of Szechuan, the situation in Tibet had deteriorated. The Thirteenth Dalai Lama was disappointed at the inability of the imperial government to protect Tibetan interests against British pressure and leaned toward the Russians for help. Lu insisted that Chan-tui should be taken away from the Tibetans because of its importance to the security of Szechuan. He professed fear that should Tibet be lost to either the British or the Russians they would assert their right to occupy Chan-tui, thus threatening the safety of Kham and southwest China. In replying to critics who warned that such a move would antagonize the Tibetans and lead to frontier troubles, Lu stated his belief that China would be able to overcome any hostile action taken by the Dalai Lama. The Anglo-Russian rivalry over Tibet, Lu asserted, originated from the Russian desire for the riches of India: Russia wanted Tibet only to get at India. The British knew this and would welcome Chinese efforts to strengthen Tibetan defense.[86] Lu, therefore, proposed the strengthening of Chinese control over Tibetan affairs, which had slipped dangerously; the reoccupation of Chan-tui, from his point of view, would be the first step toward such a goal.[87]

The imperial government not only rebuffed Lu on Chan-tui, but also his similar maneuver regarding Dege. The wife of the Dege *t'u-ssu*, who had illicit relations with the Tibetan governor of Chan-tui, imprisoned her husband and ruled the country with her younger son under the protection of her lover. After having defeated the Chan-tui force, Lu sent a detachment of his troops to Dege, released the imprisoned chief, and captured the wife and younger son. On the grounds that he was acceding to the old chief's request, Lu took over Dege and proposed to put it under direct provincial administration.[88] Again the court rejected Lu's proposal as liable to arouse the fear of the native chiefs and antagonize the Tibetans. But the return to the status quo did not win the respect and loyalty of the Tibetans and Khambas for the imperial government. Despite Chinese advice to accommodate the British, the intransigence of the Lhasa authorities on the question of trade finally led to the British invasion of Tibet. The unpredictable consequences of the British invasion and the slaying of an imperial commissioner in Kham finally forced the court to act. The disintegration of imperial control over the Sino-Tibetan borderlands had reached the point where China either had to forfeit its rights or reassert its sovereignty.

Frontier Politics: The Attempt at Political Integration, 1901-1911

The Boxer Rebellion represented the last stand of unenlightened conservatism in China. In 1901 the court, chastened by defeat, proclaimed a program of constitutional reforms that gave impetus to demands for a closer integration of China's outlying dependencies with the body politic. A precedent for such action had already been set in 1882 with the formation of Sinkiang Province in Chinese Turkestan. Contact with the West had aroused the traditional ethnocentric and antiforeign feelings of the Chinese people, which were given articulate expression in the nationalism of the educated class. Significantly, the nationalism of that period was colored by the fashionable Darwinian creed of "survival of the fittest." It was believed that the victims of Western imperialism were unable to survive because their national institutions had not evolved to the superior stage of development that those of the Western nations had attained. For this reason, in order to resist foreign aggression successfully, China would have to adopt the institutions that had made the West so strong. Within China, the border peoples were seen as lagging behind the Chinese in the evolutionary process; therefore, it was incumbent upon the imperial government to accelerate the pace of institutional and cultural change among them so that they would be able to survive in the modern world.

Acting upon a vague and unsubstantiated rumor that Russia was about to establish a protectorate over Tibet, and brushing aside Chinese sovereignty over the land as a mere "fiction," the British invaded Lhasa in 1904. Forcing the Dalai Lama to flee the country, the invaders dictated peace terms to the Tibetans. The events in Lhasa created deep anxiety among Chinese officials concerned with the safety of the Sino-Tibetan frontier. Szechuan Governor-general Hsi-liang suggested than an imperial commissioner should be stationed at Chamdo to maintain stricter control over the turbulent Khamba tribes. The court agreed to the proposal and appointed Feng-ch'üan, a Szechuan circuit official, to the post. He was instructed to strengthen the defense capability of Tibet and Kham by paying special attention to the establishment of military colonies and the training of troops. In 1905 Feng-ch'üan was in Ba-tang en route to Chamdo. Annoyed by the independent attitude of the Ba-tang *t'u-ssu* and especially the monks of the Ba-tang Monastery, he proposed to the court that the number of monks of any sizeable monastery should thereafter be limited to three hundred persons and that ordination should be stopped for a period of twenty years. Monks who were less than thirteen years of age should be returned to secular life. As a means of breaking up the power of the big monasteries, excess monks should be ordered to return to their home localities where small monasteries could be established. Feng-ch'üan also advocated recovery of Chan-tui from Tibetan control. Seeing that the Ba-tang plain could support a larger population, he started a program of Chinese colonization without consulting the local authorities. These measures naturally aroused the antagonism of the Khambas. Led by the monks of the Ba-tang Monastery, they attacked Feng-ch'üan and his entourage of officials and guards. On April 5, 1905, Feng-ch'üan and most of his men were killed in ambush while being escorted back to Ta-chien-lu by Khamba soldiers.[89]

Feng-ch'üan's death following the British invasion of Tibet hastened the program of political reorganization in Kham. In the summer of 1905 a punitive expedition led by Ma Wei-ch'i and Chao Erh-feng captured and executed the senior and junior Ba-tang *t'u-ssu* and the abbot of the Ba-tang Monastery. Ma Wei-ch'i then returned to Szechuan while Chao continued military operations in the Li-tang region. Hsiang-ch'eng was taken after a long siege in the spring of 1906. The senior Li-tang *t'u-ssu* escaped to Tibet. As a reward for his success, Chao was appointed to the newly created post of imperial commissioner for the Szechuan-Yunnan frontier; the Li-tang *t'u-ssu* government was abolished.[90] In a memorial on frontier policy, Chao proposed the complete elimination of the *t'u-ssu*, the training of new troops, colonization of Ba-tang and Hsiang-ch'eng, the opening of mines, the improvement of communication and roads for the promotion of trade, and the establishment of schools. Meanwhile a revolt of the monks of Yen-ching was put down by garrison troops. In 1907 Chao was appointed acting governor-general of Szechuan in addition to his frontier duties. Chao immediately carried out a program of improvement in Kham by establishing inns along the main trade routes, sending out colonies, appointing school officials, hiring an American engineer and a Japanese agronomist to assist in the development of mining and agriculture, setting up a tannery in Ba-tang, building a steel bridge over the Ya-lung River at Ho-kou, sending delegates abroad to study textiles and milling machinery, and inviting doctors to set up medical facilities. Ba-tang, Li-tang, and Hsiang-ch'eng were reorganized into the Chinese magistracies of Pa-an, Li-hua, and Ting-hsiang. The Ministry of Finance in Peking supported his efforts with an appropriation of one million taels of silver.[91]

In March 1908 Chao was appointed imperial commissioner of Tibet in addition to his post as frontier commissioner, while his brother Chao Erh-hsun succeeded him as governor-general of Szechuan to facilitate the implementation of Chao's frontier policies. Prior to his departure for Tibet, Chao and his brother obtained court approval for changing Ta-chien-lu's name to K'ang-ting and raising it to the status of a prefecture. In the autumn of 1908 Chao advanced toward Dege, which was torn by a fratricidal war between the *t'u-ssu* Dorje Senge and his brother, the usurper Nagwang Champe Rincha. Senge appealed to Chao for assistance. After forcing the usurper to flee, Chao reported to the court that Senge had voluntarily surrendered his domain to the government. He also expelled the Tibetan abbot in control of Ch'un-k'o and Kao-jih, two small enclaves within the Dege domain.[92] While these events were taking place in 1909, Chao resigned from his Lhasa appointment, possibly due to the opposition of the Tibetans as well as to the jealousy of Lien-yü, the incumbent imperial commissioner in Tibet.[93]

In November 1909, after a long exile in Outer Mongolia and China, the Dalai Lama returned to Lhasa and determined to resume control of Tibetan affairs. Lien-yü was equally determined to strengthen Chinese control over Tibet. The immediate point of contention between the two was the court's action in sending 2,000 Szechuanese troops under the command of Chung-ying to garrison Tibet and to back up whatever political changes the government might desire to implement later. When the troops arrived at Chamdo in the summer of 1909 their direct route to Lhasa was blocked by the Tibetans. Upon receiving a request for help from Lien-yü, Chao proceeded to Chamdo, where he sent Chung-ying with an escort through the friendly nomad territory of Jyade (the thirty-nine tribes) to Chiang-ta (Giamda). While at Chamdo, Chao accepted the profession of loyalty from the Jyade tribes and the peoples of Po-mi (Pome) and Pa-shu (Bashu). His troops also defeated the Tibetans who had resisted Chung-ying's advance, and occupied Liu-wu-chi (Riwoche), Shuo-pan-to (Shuopando), Lo-lung-tsung (Lhorong Dzong), and Pien-pa (Bemba). Taking advantage of the favorable situation Chao also wrested control of Chiang-chia (Markam), Kung-chüeh (Gonjo),

Sang-ang (Tsawarong), and Tsa-yu (Zayul) from the Tibetans in
1910. Since all these territories, including Chamdo, were located west
of the Sino-Tibetan boundary of 1727 and had been under Tibetan
authority, Chao memorialized the court that they should be put under
Chinese jurisdiction and that the boundary line should be moved
westward to the neighborhood of Chiang-ta. This proposal was
approved by the court over the opposition of Lien-yü, who advocated
their return to Lhasa.[94]

Later in the year, Chao subjugated the inhabitants of San-yai
(Sangen), whose frequent raids against their neighbors had provoked
a Tibetan expedition in 1908. On April 21, 1911, Chao was appointed
acting governor-general of Szechuan. The post of imperial commissioner for Szechuan and Yunnan frontier affairs, upon the
recommendation of Chao, was entrusted to Fu Sung-mu. Chao and
Fu were instructed by Peking to effect the complete elimination of the
t'u-ssu system in Kham. On his way back to Chengtu, Chao,
accompanied by Fu, removed the *t'u-ssu* of the Hor territory, expelled
the Tibetan governor of Chan-tui, and established Chinese administration in the territory of the Ming-cheng (Chala) *t'u-ssu*. On August
2, 1911, he finally arrived at Chengtu to take over his duties as
governor-general. In the following month, his advocacy of railroad
nationalization brought about the outbreak of popular riots in
Szechuan. On December 22, at the age of sixty-four, Chao Erh-feng
was killed by revolutionaries.[95]

Meanwhile events in Lhasa entered a critical stage. The Dalai
Lama had fled to Darjeeling on February 24, 1910, upon the approach
of Chung-ying's troops. On February 25, an imperial decree stripped
him of his title and directed that a new reincarnation be found to take
his place. Rivalry between Chao and Lien-yü over control of Kham
territory then took an active turn. In the winter of 1910, Lien-yü sent a
detachment of troops under Chung-ying to occupy Po-mi, which had
earlier professed support for Chao. Apparently the people of Po-mi
had no intention of surrendering to Chung-ying and put up such
strong resistance that Lien-yü had to ask Chao for assistance. In the
summer of 1911 Po-mi was finally conquered with the assistance of
troops from Ba-tang. Lien-yü and Fu Sung-mu, the new frontier
commissioner, each wanted to keep Po-mi under his own jurisdiction.[96] Before the question could be resolved by the court,
revolution in China broke out and the Tibetans eventually regained
control of the district.

While the Po-mi campaign was in progress, Fu Sung-mu
proceeded to depose the remaining Kham *t'u-ssu* who had not yet
surrendered their seals of office to the imperial government. In

August 1911, Fu memorialized the throne for the establishment of the province of Hsi-k'ang. Before his proposal could be acted upon, the whole edifice so laboriously built up by Chao Erh-feng disintegrated with the collapse of the Ch'ing dynasty and the evaporation of Chinese control in Tibet. The forebodings of Chinese frontier officials were realized as the Dalai Lama returned from India with the backing of British power. Thereafter, the British became a party, directly or indirectly, in every dispute involving China and Tibet. The Tibetans recovered most of their territories lost in Chao's campaigns, and in 1933 the Sino-Tibetan boundary was finally stabilized along the Chin-sha River some distance east of the 1727 line.

During this period the Sung-p'an and Yunnan sectors of the frontier had remained quiescent. The Yi, however, were as obstreperous as ever. They had apparently recovered completely from a government expedition in 1868 in which thousands of slaves had been freed from their owners. In 1908 Chao Erh-hsun, governor-general of Szechuan, decided to pacify the entire Liang Shan region in conjunction with his brother's efforts in Kham, but the expedition was temporarily interrupted by the death of the emperor and the empress dowager. In the following year, two government forces operating in the northern half of the mountain range met and effected the surrender of more than 100,000 tribesmen; in 1910 the troops campaigned in the southern end of the Yi homeland. As a result of these measures, many Yi *t'u-ssu* were deposed. Subsequent events showed, however, that Yi power had not been broken, for new Yi leaders arose to take the place of those who had been removed.[97] In the warlord era after the Revolution of 1911, the Yi tribes were able to exchange opium for guns and ammunition from the provincial troops, thereby considerably strengthening their ability to defy the local authorities.

Conclusion

Historically, the expansion of the Ch'ing empire into the Sino-Tibetan borderlands came about through a combination of circumstances. First of all, as successor to the Ming, the empire simply inherited territories that had belonged to the previous dynasty. Then there were the political and military considerations arising from the confrontation with the Jungars, which led to the seeking of allies and buffer states in Chinghai and Tibet. Once political rights had been established, there was a reluctance to relinquish control even when the foreign threat had disappeared. The assumption of control involved a concomitant responsibility for the defense and maintenance of internal tranquility in the dependent territories. Thus, step by step, more political ties were created until the borderlands were firmly incorporated into the political structure of the empire.

The Sino-Tibetan borderlands were administered largely through the tested *t'u-ssu* system, an instrument of indirect rule whose prototype could be traced as far back as the Han dynasty and whose perfected form was first adopted in the Ming dynasty. It was particularly suited to the frontier where the rugged terrain favored a proliferation of small, independent tribes. The *t'u-ssu* system tended to perpetuate fragmentation of tribal power and prevent the growth of any strong frontier kingdom able to challenge the imperial authority. The abolition of the *t'u-ssu* in Kham was motivated by the threat of real or imagined foreign aggression but was ill-considered in view of the political and cultural development of the region. The substitution of direct for indirect rule involved the imposition of Chinese laws and moral codes upon a people whose social heritage was radically different from the agrarian Confucian society of China proper. Chao-Erh-feng's experiment in grafting Chinese political and social forms upon the traditional institutions of the Khambas, judging from the post-1911 developments in Kham, was largely a failure. The Chinese magistrates had little genuine authority over the population: the *t'u-ssu* either came back into power, or power shifted to the lesser leaders and village headmen.[98]

It was the arrival of the Communist revolution in Kham and the subsequent destruction of the political and economic power of the Khamba religious hierarchy and feudal landed aristocracy that finally brought about the firm integration of Kham into the Chinese body politic. This was accomplished only after the suppression of armed uprisings by the Khambas lasting from 1955 to 1959.[99] As of now, the administrative boundaries of the Sino-Tibetan borderlands closely resemble those of the Ch'ing period: the Sung-p'an grassland and Kham east of the Chin-sha River are under the jurisdiction of Szechuan Province with autonomous areas allocated to various ethnic minorities; western Kham or Chamdo is under the jurisdiction of the Autonomous Region of Tibet; and the Yunnan frontier is divided among various autonomous areas. Highways and airlines now serve many points in the borderlands. The sinification of the native peoples is proceeding at an accelerated pace, as their traditional cultures crumble under the weight of China's political and military power.

The Political Kin Unit and the Family Origin of Ch'ing Local Officials

Odoric Y. K. Wou

In the past two decades, sinologists have devoted a great deal of attention to the study of family origin and mobility of official gentry in China. They are concerned with these fundamental questions: From what social strata did the Chinese official gentry come? How much was their status independent of the social status of their forebears? How much mobility was there in China?

Their findings based on available quantitative data indicate that there was a high degree of academic mobility in China.[1] Merit and talent were indeed rewarded. Studies of career mobility show that family background had influence but that seniority was a more important determinant of official advancement.[2] On the whole, one gets the impression that Chinese society was relatively open and that family background had little influence on the degree of mobility.

One limitation of these studies is the methodology that the authors use to analyze the family origin of the subject. Family origin is usually investigated on the basis of the status and profession of the subject's forebears, namely his father, grandfather, and great-grandfather. Such methodology is influenced by Western studies on social mobility, which tend to correlate parental status with the subject's status and career.[3] To a certain extent, it is also limited by the nature of the quantifiable material. Examination lists only give the names and social status of subject's paternal father, grandfather, and great-grandfather. They do not provide information on other members of the family.

The methodology and nature of the material thus lead sinologists to ignore the fact that the Chinese family, and the official gentry family in particular, was an extended family or a lineage,[4] members of which shared common interests and were bound by a network of supportive ties to insure mutual assistance and protection. These reputable families were known as *kuan huan chih chia* in Chinese.

We have a vivid description of this kind of interlocking interests for four powerful clans (*ssu ta chia-tsu*)—the Chias, the Shihs, the Wangs, and the Hsuehs—in the famous early Ch'ing novel, *The Dream of the Red Chamber*.[5] Every official, the novel tells us, had an "official protective charm" (*hu kuan fu*). This charm consisted of a list of the official's relatives who held important positions elsewhere, or of a number of related families having important connections with government circles who would come to his rescue in case he ran into trouble. As the Chinese saying puts it, officials often protect each other (*kuan kuan hsiang hu*). Even the central government of the Ch'ing dynasty recognized that a political unit of related kinsmen was likely to place family interests ahead of government duties. Regulations under an elaborate system known as the "Law of Avoidance" were drawn up and frequently revised as a measure to check officials' power and to prevent them from forming a kinship coalition.

This essay focuses on such a "political kin unit" as a means of understanding the family origin of local officials in the late Ch'ing period. The questions it attempts to answer are: What is a political kin unit?[6] How large is it, and how much collective power is it able to wield? From what family background did the Chinese local official gentry come?

Sources

The data for this study are drawn from the *t'ung-kuan lu* (literally, "fellow official records") or directories of provincial officials. These directories, each consisting of four *ts'e*, were vitae sheets (*lü-li*) of incumbent provincial officials.[7] These career records, which were written by local officials about themselves, were forwarded to the Board of Civil Appointment for evaluation upon an official's entry into the government and during his triennial assessment. The records were later collected and published by the provincial government, obviously to leave behind a record for posterity.

These career records are extremely varied. Some are very brief, consisting of the official's name(s), titles, ranks, and position, his date of birth, place of origin, academic achievements, and a short history of his career. Others give an extensive history of his public career. They record the dates on which he was appointed, assumed office, and handed over business, places where he held government posts, dates when and places where he served as examiner, the manner in which he was recommended, special tasks he was commissioned to undertake, his rating in the triennial assessment, impeachments and punishments, and the dates and methods of purchase of degrees and offices.

The lengthy career records, in addition to the above information, report on the official's relatives. Information on kinsmen is included in two places: his forebears are entered at the top of the record, and members of his generation or younger generations are placed at the end.[8] For the male agnates, their name, relation to the subject, degrees, and official career, if they had any, are recorded. For female agnates, only the ones who were married prominently are given lengthy treatment. Otherwise, they are simply named or completely left out of the record. Sometimes juniors are not even named; only the number of that relation is given, as for example five daughters and two grandsons.

Meticulous care is given to the type of relation a kinsman had with the subject, and specific familial terminology is used. The generation (*pei-fen*) is indicated. For more remote forebears, the exact preceding generation is given, as, for example, "ancestor of sixth preceding generation" (*liu-shih tsu*). The degree of closeness on the horizontal axis is pointed out. The terms used are: of the same father (*pao*); descent from the same grandfather (*t'ang* or *t'ung t'ang*); descent from the same great-grandfather (*ts'ung t'ang*); and descent from the same great-great-grandfather (*tsai ts'ung t'ang*). For the spouses, the order of their marriage is shown: first marriage (*yüan-pei, chü,* and *ch'i*); second spouse (*chi chu* or *chi ch'i*); third spouse (*hsü chü*); and concubine (*ch'ieh*).

Affinal kin (relatives by marriage) are included under the females who either married into or out of the family. Relatives of the female who married into the family are indicated by their relationship to that female member.[9] Affinal kin of the female who married out of the family are shown by their relations to that female's husband.[10]

These directories include all officials from the provincial governor to the district magistrates.[11] A few even include minor officials below the district magistrate rank.[12] All directories include both substantive and expectant officials.

This study uses the following directories: Honan (1837), Shantung (1859), Anhwei (1871), Kiangsu (1880), Honan (1898), and Chihli or Chifu (1904).[13] It covers a period from 1837 to 1904 in an attempt to trace the change in the political kin unit from the time before the Opium War through the Taiping period to the end of the dynasty. It covers five eastern provinces. Directories on the south, west, and northwest are either unavailable or contain no information on kinsmen of the officials. There are two reasons for choosing two directories from Honan for analysis. First, directories from Honan are most informative and cover the longest span of time. Second, these two directories, separated by sixty-one years, can give us some insight into changes within the same province.

The Political Kin Unit

A man's occupational life is usually affected by the kind of family into which he is born, for he draws his financial resources and social support from his family. The educational climate at home furnishes him with a thought pattern, role model, and attitude essential for his educational and occupational attainments later in life.

The importance of family background to a man's career was even more pronounced in traditional China, where society was overwhelmingly family-oriented. Family considerations and mutual assistance among members were taken as facts of life. Moreover, since most elite families were extended families, the kin unit a male offspring could draw upon for socioeconomic support was larger than its Western counterpart. Of course, the size of a man's supportive base depended on what type of help he was seeking, and in turn upon which particular unit within the overall kinship structure he wished to draw.[14]

The largest Chinese kinship structure was the clan (*tsu*), members of which believed that they were descended unilineally from a common ancestor, actual or mythical.[15] The smallest unit was the primary family, the *chia*, comprising usually the ego, his spouse, their children, and sometimes the ego's parents. In between were two units of different sizes. A lineage was a structure in which common unilineal ancestry of the members was traceable genealogically. A branch (*fang*) was a subdivision of a lineage or sublineage.[16]

Kinsmen could also be divided functionally into various units, members of which had different degrees of functional corporateness. Ritually, a group of agnates and their spouses were described as within the relationship of five grades of mourning (*wu fu*), a circle of relatives drawn up in regard to a given ego. Members of the unit were bound by a structure of mourning obligations, and intermarriage was strictly prohibited within the boundaries.[17] Economically, kinfolk also formed a unit. The entire lineage or segment of a lineage might form an economic body based on joint ownership of land. Cultivated land was either rented to tenants with the proceeds used for collective purposes, or circulated among group members who were then charged for the expenses of these collective activities. To the government, such a unit became a body for corporate taxation.[18]

There was also a *political* kin unit, the one defined by the Law of Avoidance (*kuan-yuan-hui-pi*). The law delineated a group of related kin whom the government thought would be likely to coalesce to promote their family interests at the expense of the government. Members of this group who had attained political prominence were legally required to be separated physically as a means of guarding against favoritism and nepotism. Originating as an unwritten law in the Han dynasty, it had become an effective government device for checking local power and clusters of influence.[19] It had been written down in the T'ang dynasty and further elaborated in the Sung and Ming dynasties. By the Ch'ing dynasty, the Law of Avoidance had become a comprehensive set of codes incorporated in the *Collected Institutes of the Ch'ing Dynsty (Ta Ch'ing hui-tien)*, and was carefully defined in the *Statutory Amendments to the Collected Institutes (Ta Ch'ing hui-tien shih-li)*.[20]

Within this elaborate legal system, there were various categories of avoidance. First, officials were prohibited by law from taking positions in their own native province, the province of their temporary residence (*chi-chi*),[21] and the neighboring provinces within a distance of 500 *li*. Second, under the Law of Avoidance for tutor-disciple, an official was required to avoid serving in the same province as his tutors. But the most complicated part of the Law was the Avoidance of relatives (*ch'in-tsu hui-pi*). The law prescribed that kinsmen avoid becoming officials in the same province and required one of them, usually the junior or the one lower in rank, to serve in another province. The types of kinship involved in this system varied from the central government to the local government.

A metropolitan official (*nei-kuan*) should not serve in the same office as his grandfather, grandson, father, son, paternal uncle, nephew, brother; mother's father and brother, wife's father and brother, son-in-law, sister's son; father's sister's son, mother's sister's son, and those related to him by the marriage of his children.

Provincial officials (*wai-kuan*) were required to avoid the following relatives: relatives within five grades of mourning; father's sister's husband and son; mother's father and brother; mother's brother and sister's son; wife's grandfather, father, brother, and nephew; wife's sister's husband, son-in-law, and his son; sister's son; and granddaughter's husband.[22]

There are two broad categories of kinship incorporated in the political kin unit: consanguineal kin (*tsung-tsu ch'in-shu*) and

affinal kin (*yin-ch'in* or *wai-yin ch'in-shu*). The types of consanguineal kin included are identical with the ritual kin unit of the five
grades of mourning. The ritual kin unit spreads out vertically over
nine generations from great-great-grandfather down to great-great-
grandson (*chiu-tsu*), the exact circle of kin who may face capital
punishment in the event that ego commits a high crime such as
treason. Horizontally, it covers the stem and three collateral branches.
The affinal kin included in the political kin unit consist of relatives of
ego's mother, wife, daughter-in-law, daughter, granddaughter, aunt,
and sister.

The Law of Avoidance viewed members of this unit as close
relatives. The 1664 (third year of K'ang-hsi) regulation designated
specifically the following relations as "close blood kin" (*ti-chin*):
grandfather, grandson, father, son, paternal uncle, and brother. The
1729 (Yung-cheng, seventh year) code defined mother's father and
brother, wife's father and brother, son-in-law, and sister's son as
"extremely close relatives" (*chih-ch'in*). In 1821 the Tao-kuang code
added a number of relations to this category: daughter's son, sister's
husband, granddaughter's husband, those related by marriage of
one's children, father's sister's son, and mother's sister's son.[23]

The government was distrustful of patrilocal kinsmen, particularly those who were involved in criminal justice, taxation, scrutiny,
investigation, and the impeachment of officials. In explaining why
officials in these duties should strictly observe the Law of Avoidance,
the 1664 code stated:

> Clansmen (*tsu chung chih jen*), considered distant by mourning
> regulations, still harbor tremendous familial affection (*ch'ing-i*) for
> one another if they reside in the same locality. The one with the lower
> rank should practice avoidance. However, if they belong to distant
> branches of the same family and are dispersed in different prefectures
> and provinces, or if their native residence is not the same though they
> may have a common surname, they are obviously distant kinsmen and
> are not required to practice avoidance. On the other hand, those who
> are members of the same five grades of mourning, even though
> separated residentially, must observe the Law of Avoidance.[24]

Indeed, there existed a kind of corporateness among members of the
political kin group. For the agnates, they were participants of the
same five grades of mourning and often came together in ritual
observances. The law forced an official frequently to update his
knowledge of both the consanguineal kin and affinal kin in the
unit—their whereabouts, degrees, official posts, and official history.

This information was to be placed in the record and forwarded to the Board of Civil Appointment for inspection every time an official was appointed, promoted, or transferred to a new position. This gathering of information promoted an effective link among the members.

For the prominent members there was undoubtedly more interaction. At one time or another, prominent agnates must have served in the same family council. Though separated geographically by law, official kinsmen came together at times of weddings, funerals, and other festive occasions. In fact, official gentry in the Ch'ing period seldom hesitated to show off their family connections and collective power. As described in a Ch'ing novel, *The Scholars,* a scholar of the Lu family introduced his nephew to another scholar by saying, "This is our nephew. He is the grandson of our uncle who was Prefect of Nanchang." When the nephew later married, the story goes on to say, the Lu family had more than eighty lanterns inscribed with official titles. Combined with the lanterns of the bride's family, also headed by an official, these official lanterns filled three or four streets to overflowing.[25]

Members of the political kin unit often connived to support and protect each other in legal cases. For instance, Liu Tieh-yun, the famous author of the novel *The Travels of Lao Ts'an,* began his official career by offering his services to a friend of his father, Wu Ta-ch'eng, director-general of the Yellow River Conservancy. As a prefect in Shantung, Liu incurred the hatred of Yuan Shih-k'ai, who later charged him with the crime of misappropriating imperial property. Liu's brother-in-law, Ting Pao-ch'uan, governor of Shansi, protected him by enlisting the help of Prince Ch'ing in his defense. When Liu was finally exiled and died, his classmate, Mao Shih-chün, governor of Kansu, also related to him by the marriage of their children, arranged to have his casket brought back.[26]

Sometimes assistance among relatives went beyond the limit of the political kin unit. An excellent illustration is the relationship between the two well-known Ch'ing governors, Tso Tsung-t'ang and Hu Lin-i. Tso and Hu were related because Tso's son-in-law and Hu's wife were brother and sister, children of T'ao Chu, governor-general of Liangkiang (Kiangsu, Kiangsi, and Anhwei). As a result of this linkage, Hu Lin-i, who was then serving in the *mu-fu* of Liangkiang Governor-general and Imperial Commissioner Tseng Kuo-fan, recommended Tso to Chang Liang-chi, governor of Hunan and as such also a subordinate of Tseng. Tso afterward also joined Tseng's *mu-fu.* When Tso was later charged with corruption and unruliness, it was Hu who interceded and rescued him.[27]

This was the kind of kinship coalition and familial consideration that the Law of Avoidance aimed to prevent. The law cautioned officials that kinship often led a person to favor *(hsun-ssu)* and take care of *(chan-ku)* his relative. Even though it was not stipulated that remote affinal kin should avoid each other, it was stated that, if a superior should find them "harboring private interest," he was to report them immediately for impeachment. The law urged supervising officials to pay extreme attention to familial relationships and instructed them to be always ready to transfer one of the kinsmen to a neighboring province. It also told officials serving in the Department of Appointment to pay special attention to the dialect of the candidate who came for an interview in order to spot if he had misrepresented his native residence.

Officials should state, the law went on to say, all their property holdings in detail and specify all relations with their kinsmen. Should an official, before he took office, not know that his post was within the 500 *li* limit of his native residence, he must report it within three months after he had assumed office. By that time, he should have knowledge of the distance. Those who failed to observe the law would be demoted one class and transferred to a neighboring province.[28]

The Core of a Political Kin Unit and the Unit's Power

The Law of Avoidance only defined the boundaries of a political kin unit: it did not reveal the supportive kin network an official perceived to be his own. Since there might be as many as several hundred individuals included in the unit defined by law, intimate contact with every single member would be impossible. An official must have maintained various degrees of closeness with members of this huge group. Distant kinsmen who were not prominent apparently were on the periphery. Some forms of interaction and communication were kept up with them, but these were relatively weak, probably restricted to ritual contacts for consanguineal kin and formal contacts for affinals, unless they became prominent.

Those who were close kinsmen or prominent distant relatives of the official, however, had more frequent contacts, stronger attachment, and more communication. They clustered to form a *core* within the political kin unit. The size of this core varied from one official to another depending on how many prominent relatives he had. Obviously, the greater the number of prominent kin, the larger the core of his political kin unit. Moreover, the core was always open to change. Every time a kinsman attained prominence, he would be incorporated into the core and his ties of kinship strengthened. The actual size of the core within a given official's political kin unit and the amount of political power his kin unit possessed can be gauged from the number of his kinsmen and the degrees and offices they had attained, as listed by that official in his career record.

The largest core found in our material belonged to the kin unit of Ts'ao Ho-chi, an acting district magistrate of Wei-shih County in Honan in 1898.[29] His kindred had the longest history in officialdom. Ts'ao traced his own clan back to an ancestor who was a *chin-shih* in the Sung dynasty. His family at one time had migrated and resettled at Lu-chiang (Kiangsi?). Ts'ao put down in his record a long list of kinsmen from his great-great-great-great-great-great-grandfather down to his sons and nephews covering ten generations on the vertical axis and three collateral branches. His core comprised 208 persons: 160 agnates and 48 affinal kin from 36 families by marriage. The group produced 84 officials and 32 degree holders, a total of 116 prominent members.

Most of his relatives of the older generation were dead. We know, however, that his great-grandfather was still alive.[30] If we presume that all kinsmen older than his great-grandfather had already passed away, then Ts'ao had listed forty-six deceased kinsmen in the record. This is significant, for it shows that officials were still cashing in on the prestige of their dead kin and found it profitable to include them in their official history. The case of Ts'ao is a rather atypical one since few officials dated their history that far back; it therefore should not detain us here.

Two other cases are more illustrative of the collective power of these reputable families. Hsu Wei-cho, district director of studies in Chia-ting County, Kiangsu, in 1880[31] listed 57 agnates and 10 affinal kin, a total of 67, in his record. Table 3.1 gives the categories of kinship, the number of persons in each category, and the number of deceased in the core of Hsu's political kin unit.

Hsu reported 24 categories of kinship, 15 from his lineage and 9 from 6 other families by marriage. Twelve members were dead, 55 still living. Sixteen of the relatives, most of them deceased, came from older generations; 10 came from his own generation, and 41 from two younger generations. Hsu recorded 36 prominent members, 58 percent of the core. Of these there were only 19 degree holders, 17 of them officials. They had won a total of 32 degrees: 11 were purchased and 21 were earned through the civil service examination. Among the 17

TABLE 3.1
Categories of Kinship Recorded by Hsu Wei-cho

Categories of Kinship	Number	Number of Deceased
Agnates		
Great-grandfather (ts'eng tsu)	1	1
Great-grandmother (ts'eng tsu mu)	1	1
Grandfather (tsu)	1	1
Grandmother (tsu mu)	1	1
Father (fu)	1	
Mother (mu)	1	
Paternal uncles (pao po shu)	3	1
Brothers (pao hsiung ti)	5	
Elder sister (pao chih)	1	
Nephews (pao chih)	13	1
Nephews' sons (pao chih sun)	18	
Wives (ch'i)	2	
Sons (tzu)	4	
Daughter (nü)	1	
Grandsons (sun)	4	
Affinal Kin		
Great-grandmother's family (Chu)		
Father of great-grandmother	1	1
Grandmother's family (Li)		
Father of grandmother	1	1
Brother of grandmother	1	1
Mother's family (Chou)		
Mother's father	1	
Sister's family by marriage (Jen)		
Sister's husband	1	
First wife's family (Chu)		
Wife's grandfather	1	1
Wife's father	1	1
Second wife's family (Chou)		
Wife's father	1	1
Daughter's family by marriage (Chiang)		
Daughter's father-in-law	1	
Daughter's husband	1	
Total	67	12

officials, 12 received substantive posts, 5 expectant. Four served in the central government, 13 held positions in provinces. With the exception of one high official in Peking, they were low-ranking officials between the seventh and ninth ranks. Nine out of the 36 prominent kinsmen were deceased, and 27 were still living.

His kinsmen had served in eleven districts in five different provinces. Unfortunately, we have no information on dates of office and therefore we are unable to check if they were serving simultaneously in the same province. It is nevertheless interesting to note that his father, one of his brothers, and one nephew had been district magistrates in Shantung Province. Both his father and one of the brothers had served, presumably at different times, in the same Hsin-yang District in Shantung. A brother-in-law and a brother had been subdirectors of studies in two separate districts in Kiangsu Province in which he was then serving as a county director.

Another example is Yao Li-hsien, a district magistrate of Hsiang-ch'eng in Honan in 1898.[32] Yao gave a list of 169 kinsmen in his career record (see Figure 3.1), 131 agnates and 38 affinals covering 26 categories of kinship. Twenty-nine of them were dead and 140 were living. Yao's core included 71 prominent members, 35 from the agnates and 36 from the affinals, 47 of whom were still alive. When translated into degrees and official positions, this kinship group had produced only 10 degree holders—2 *chü-jen*, 5 *chien-sheng* (2 of them dead), 1 *fu-pang* (dead), and 1 *sheng-yüan*—and 61 officials. The offices they held are represented in Table 3.2.

The scope of political power in Yao's core was broad. His relatives had held offices in 62 districts in 14 different provinces. Six of them had worked in the central government. His kinsmen had been officials in 25 different districts in Honan, where he was then serving as district magistrate. They included a nephew of his grandmother, the father and uncle of his grandmother, two of his uncles, his father, two of his great-uncles, his cousin, his aunt's husband, his sister's husband, two fathers-in-law of his, his wife's brother, and his son-in-law. It is likely that none of them had violated the Law of Avoidance. Yet Yao's record shows that he had not only built up a tight network of supportive kinship ties within Honan but had linkages radiating from that province to different parts of the country.

His record also demonstrates the kind of marital alliance into which officials sometimes entered. First, two of his sisters married the same man in the Lü family, who was a district magistrate in Honan. Second, one of his sisters married Yuan Chao-li, a *chü-jen* and a secretary of the Grand Secretariat in Peking. This marital bond was reinforced in the next generation when Yao's own daughter married their son. Third, his mother and his first wife came from the same Ch'en family that boasted two local officials in Kwangtung, two expectant officials, and two degree holders. His first wife was in fact the niece of his own mother.

Family Origin of Local Officials

The information on their relatives that local officials placed in their career records provides us with an idea of the kind of family background from which they came. The following is a survey of 932

Figure 3.1
The Core of Yao Li-hsien's Political Kin Unit

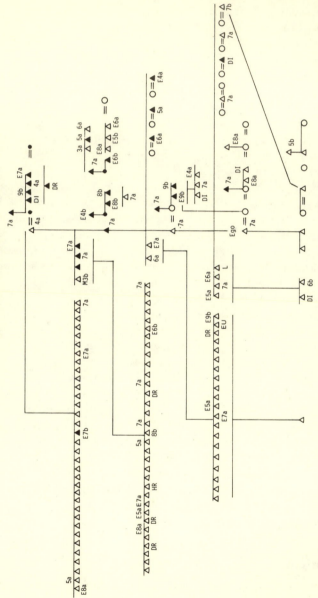

Official ranks in the Ch'ing period were divided into 9 categories, each in turn subdivided into 2 classes: *cheng* (indicated by *a*) and *tsung* (indicated by *b*). Numbers represent the highest prominence achieved by the particular individual. I consider here substantive posts higher than expectant posts, and expectant posts higher than examination degrees.

Black symbols indicate deceased kinsmen. E=Expectant; DI=Degree Irregular; DR=Degree Regular; M=Military; L=Literary Prominence; EU=Expectant Unclassed Rank; HR=Hereditary Rank.

TABLE 3.2
Offices Held by the Kinsmen of Yao Li-hsien

Substantive	No.	Expectant	No.
OFFICES HELD BY LIVING KINSMEN			
Judicial Commissioner (3a)	1	Intendent (4a)	2
Director of Banqueting Court		First Class Subprefect (5a)	3
(3b)	1	Chou Magistrate (5a)	1
First Class Subprefect (5a)	1	Second Class Subprefect (6a)	2
Magistrate of Independent		Secretary in Lieutenant	
Chou (5a)	1	Governor's Office (6a)	1
Chou Magistrate (5a)	2	District Magistrate (7a)	4
Second Class Subprefect (6a)	2	Salt Receiver (8a)	2
Second Class Compiler in		Prefectural Secretary (8a)	2
Hanlin Academy (7a)	4	Assistant District	
District Magistrate (7a)	6	Magistrate (8a)	1
Secretary of Grand Secre-			
tariat	1	9th Rank	1
Chou Subdirector of Studies		Unclassified Rank	1
(8b)	1		
OFFICES HELD BY KINSMEN BEFORE THEY DIED			
Major (3b)	1	Prefect (4b)	1
Intendent (4a)	2	Law Secretary in Lieu-	
Chou Magistrate (5a)	2	tenant Governor's Office	
District Magistrate (7a)	5	(6b)	1
Second Class Assistant		Second Class Subprefect	
Chou Magistrate (7b)	1	(6b)	1
Subdirector of Studies (8b)	1	District Magistrate (7a)	2
Subdistrict Magistrate (9b)	1	Chou Subdirector of	
Jail Warden (9b)	1	Studies (8b)	1
		Deputy Police Master and	
		Jail Warden (9b)	1
Total	34		27

Numbers in parentheses indicate rank of office.

officials who held substantive posts in the five provinces of Honan, Shantung, Anhwei, Kiangsu, and Chihli between 1837 and 1904. Altogether, these officials listed 16,180 kinsmen in their records (Table 3.3): 15,189 agnates and 991 affinal kin. The mean number of relatives per official, that is, the average size of the core of the political kin unit, for the entire period is 17. In none of our samples is this figure lower than 12 or higher than 35. Both these figures come from Honan Province and indicate that in the period between 1837 and 1898 the average size of the core of the political kin unit in that

TABLE 3.3
Number of Relatives Listed (i.e. Core of the Political Kin Unit)
by Province and Number

Province	Number of Officials	Number of Relatives Listed in the Core			
		Agnatic	Affinal	Total	Mean
Honan 1837	221	2,567	170	2,737	12
Shantung 1859	123	1,955	37	1,992	16
Anhwei 1871	90	1,460	97	1,557	17
Kiangsu 1880	195	3,325	202	3,527	18
Honan 1898	85	2,481	472	2,953	35
Chihli 1904	218	3,401	13	3,414	16
Total	932	15,189	991	16,180	17

province almost trebled. The 1898 figure for Honan (35) is outstandingly high, suggesting that there were clusters of powerful families in that province at the time.

If we take the core as a unit for analysis of the family origin of local officials, we find that (see Table 3.4) for the period under study 92 percent of local officials came from a family background with at least one prominent kinsman (that is to say, they were not from commoner families). In no province and year sampled was this figure lower than 85 percent. Again, Honan stands out as the province with the highest percentage of officials from prominent family backgrounds, 99 percent for both 1837 and 1898. Thus practically every official in that province had at least one prominent relative, and this had not

TABLE 3.4
Prominent Background of Local Officials

Province	Percentage of Officials from Prominent Family Background	Mean Number of Prominent Kin per Official
Honan 1837	99	6
Shantung 1859	85	5
Anhwei 1871	88	6
Kiangsu 1880	91	8
Honan 1898	99	16
Chihli 1904	87	5
Mean N=6,440	92	7

changed except in intensity in sixty years. The mean number of prominent kinsmen per official for the entire period was seven. With the exception of Honan in 1898, which registered a mean of sixteen, the mean for the other provinces varied between five and eight.

By prominence, we refer to two broad categories: academic prominence and official prominence. Academic prominence refers to those who held examination degree(s) only and had no official positions. This includes both those who obtained their degrees by the regular channel of civil service examination and those who followed the irregular avenue of purchase. Official prominence refers to all officeholders, with or without degree(s), who obtained either substantive or expectant positions. We exclude those relatives who possessed titles of honor conferred upon them by the government in return for services rendered by members of their family.[33] For the period between 1837 and 1904 (see Table 3.5), 68 percent of the prominent kin of the provincial officials were officially prominent and 32 percent academically prominent. The percentage of officially prominent kin increased during the Taiping period and at the end of the dynasty.

Our findings reveal two tendencies that, while incidental to our study of family origins, are of considerable interest in themselves. First, our figures show a high proportion of officially prominent kin without a degree. From 1837 to 1904 (Table 3.6), 60 percent of the official kinsmen entered the government with no degree. This high percentage may be due to the fact that the majority of the officially prominent kinsmen, as will be shown later, were holding low-ranking positions that did not require a degree. Secondly, among the degree holders (including all academically prominent kin and officially prominent kin who had degrees), 63 percent were regular

TABLE 3.5
Proportion of Prominent Kinsmen with Academic Prominence and Official Prominence

Province	Academic Prominence	Official Prominence
Honan 1837	39%	61%
Shantung 1859	29%	71%
Anhwei 1871	37%	63%
Kiangsu 1880	36%	64%
Honan 1898	25%	75%
Chihli 1904	26%	74%
1837-1904 N=2,056	32%	N-4,384 68%

TABLE 3.6
Degrees Received by Kinsmen

Province	Official Kinsmen Without a Degree	Degrees Received	
		Regular	Irregular
Honan 1837	52%	64%	36%
Shantung 1859	64%	59%	41%
Anhwei 1871	63%	58%	42%
Kiangsu 1880	58%	58%	42%
Honan 1898	61%	69%	31%
Chihli 1904	61%	65%	35%
Mean	60%	63%	37%

Total Number of Degrees Earned=3,846
Number of Kinsmen Without a Degree=2,594

and 37 percent irregular. The percentage of purchasers is low, considering the prevailing practice of buying a degree at the time.[34] But the percentage of purchasers was noticeably higher during the Taiping Rebellion and its aftermath, and declined after the Hundred Days' Reform of 1898. This stems from the fact that the purchase system became very unpopular at the time of the reform, a wave of protest against it having been launched by high officials and gentry such as Chang Chih-tung and Chang Chien. Moreover, the degrees must have lost much of their value by then; modern education was coming into being, and the examination system was abolished in 1906.[35]

Of the officially prominent kin, 78 percent served in the local government, 15 percent in the central government, and only 7 percent in the military (Table 3.7). Sixty-two percent received substantive

TABLE 3.7
Percentage of Officially Prominent Kin Serving in the Central Government, the Local Government, and the Military, by Rank (1837-1904)

Rank	Central Government	Local Government	Military	All Categories
High	30%	53%	17%	5%
Middle	17%	73%	10%	32%
Low	13%	82%	5%	63%
All Categories	15%	78%	7%	

TABLE 3.8
Proportion of Officially Prominent Kinsmen in Substantive and
Expectant Positions, by Rank (1837-1904)

Rank	Substantive	Expectant
High	80%	20%
Middle	66%	34%
Low	58%	42%
All Categories	62%	38%

posts and 38 percent were expectant officials (Table 3.8). When officially prominent kin are categorized into high (ranks 1 to 3), middle (ranks 4 to 6), and low (ranks 7 to unclassed),[36] we find an overwhelming majority (95 percent) holding middle- and low-ranking positions. This is obvious for two reasons. First, we are most likely to find relatives of local officials holding lower-ranking positions. Second, institutionally there were more middle- and low-ranking positions than high-ranking positions in the government.

However, career records of higher-ranking officials reveal (1) a greater percentage of officially prominent kinsmen serving in the central government or the military, (2) a higher rank occupied by these kinsmen, and (3) a greater percentage of these kinsmen occupying substantive posts. In fact, high-ranking officials (ranks 1 to 3) had a third more kinsmen with substantive posts, twice as many kinfolk in the central government, three times more relatives in the military, and almost four times as many kinsmen in high-ranking positions than did low-ranking officials. This confirms the common belief that power breeds power and that power tends to congregate at the higher level. But on the whole, most of the familial linkages of these local administrators consisted of middle and low officials in the provinces. Even the high provincial officials had only 30 percent of their officially prominent kin in the central government and 29 percent in high-ranking offices (Table 3.9).

Our data show (Table 3.10) that 32 percent of all local officials had prominent affinal kin. The total number of affinal kin recorded by the officials is 991 (refer to Table 3.3). This small percentage seems to support Robert Marsh's finding that distaff influence, that is the maternal branch of the family, played an insignificant role in official advancement.[37] The statistics reflect the nature of the Chinese society of the time, which was essentially male chauvinistic. A man would consider it a disgrace if he had to depend on affinal influence to move up the social ladder. In most cases, it was the female rather than the

TABLE 3.9
Percentage of Officially Prominent Kinsmen Holding High,
Middle, and Low Ranking Positions, by Rank (1859-1904)

	High	Middle	Low
High	29%	37%	34%
Middle	16%	47%	37%
Low	8%	39%	53%

These statistics are drawn only from Shantung 1859, Honan 1898,
and Chihli 1904.

TABLE 3.10
Proportion of Local Officials with Prominent Affinal Kin

	Honan 1837		Shantung 1859		Anhwei 1871		Kiangsu 1880		Honan 1898		Chihli 1904		%
RANK	O	PK	O	PK	O	PK	O	PK	O	PK	O	PK	
High	9	5			3	2	5	2	6	2	5	1	43%
Middle	70	29	35	4	30	7	25	14	29	19	78	5	29%
Low	142	68	88	9	57	13	165	81	50	30	135	3	32%
Percentage	46		11		24		50		60		44		

O=Number of officials   PK=Number of officials with
                                              prominent affinal kin

male who married upward. This does not mean that powerful
families of equal status would not intermarry to form a coalition. As
the example of Yao Li-hsien indicates, they even found it beneficial to
reinforce marital ties for generations. Our statistics show high
officials having a slightly higher percentage of prominent affinal kin
than middle- or low-ranking officials. We do not find a trend of
increase in this percentage toward the end of the dynasty, except in
Honan, which displayed a rise of about 15 percent in sixty years. We
do find, however, a tremendous variation among provinces, ranging
from 4 percent in Chihli to 60 percent in Honan.

Conclusion

This essay demonstrates that the study of family origin and
mobility of the Chinese official gentry should not be limited to an
analysis of the background of only the forebears of the subject, as has

heretofore been the case in Western studies of social mobility. Since Chinese gentry families were mostly extended families, the number of supportive kinship ties the Chinese official gentry could draw upon for success in their political lives was much greater than those of the elite in Western society. It is more meaningful therefore to use the political kin unit, as defined by the Law of Avoidance in the Ch'ing administrative codes, as an analytical framework.

As illustrated by officials in their career records, the collective political power possessed by these groups of kinsmen proves to be greater than that of the stem family above. The core of the political kin unit, where political power was concentrated, consisted of an average of seventeen members with an average of seven prominent individuals. More powerful cores could include up to several hundred members with more than one hundred prominent kin, all male and some deceased. Contrary to what has been shown by other authors, our data indicate that 92 percent of the local officials in the late Ch'ing period had at least one prominent relative. Only a minor fraction of local officials came from a commoner's background with no prominent supportive kin ties at all. Our findings also show that the majority of these prominent kin ties were located in the provinces. Most of the official kinsmen held substantive, middle-, or low-ranking posts. High-ranking officials, as we have commonly believed, proved to have a higher percentage of relatives occupying higher positions in the government. All these figures demonstrate that, after all, traditional Chinese society was not such an "open" society as it was sometimes believed.

4

Urban Control in Late Imperial China: The *Pao-chia* System in Hankow

William T. Rowe

The problem of local control beneath the lowest level of formal government has held an enduring fascination for students of China. Questions such as those of social organization, of structures of local power, of the flow of fiscal resources, and of social disorder and state responses to it, have all appeared to demand a prior understanding of subbureaucratic administration. And from the early empire to contemporary Maoist society, scholars have discovered seductively elegant systems, which reveal to further scrutiny only deeper and deeper complexity. Thus arises the continually felt need for reevaluation of our knowledge in this area.

The *pao-chia* system of the Ch'ing dynasty is one such local control system that has attracted frequent attention, an attention that in English language scholarship seems to have clustered into two major spurts. Analysts of Ch'ing political institutions, such as Hsiao Kung-ch'uan and Ch'ü T'ung-tsu, may be said to have comprised the first generation of scholarship in this field, and yet such is the elusiveness of *pao-chia* that even its classic treatment in Hsiao's *Rural China* has a revisionist ring, dedicated to the view that there was less to the system in practice than met the eye. This work, it will be recalled, argued that *pao-chia* had begun to attenuate rapidly almost upon its endorsement by the early Ch'ing emperors, and that by the 1860s it had "ceased to operate even in the imperial capital."[1]

But the system that *Rural China* thus buried has since been

The author wishes to thank professors Andrew Nathan of Columbia University and James Polachek of Princeton University, and Mr. Su Yun-feng of the Institute of Modern History, Academia Sinica, Taipei, for reading and commenting on earlier versions of this paper. This chapter is drawn from my dissertation in progress, which concerns various aspects of the society of late imperial Hankow. A portion of the dissertation research has been funded by a grant from the Social Science Research Council/American Council of Learned Societies.

resurrected in the works of recent scholars concerned with the analysis of specific local systems. While earlier antecedents might be cited, the chief influence on this revival of interest in *pao-chia* has probably been the recent work of Philip Kuhn on the origins of the local self-government movement in Republican China.[2] While there is still much disagreement within this school, the consensus appears to be that *somebody* in fact was doing the job for which *pao-chia* had been intended, and it would serve us well to discover who that somebody was. In this paper, based on evidence from the city of Hankow, I hope to define more clearly the surprisingly large role that the system and its heirs played in Chinese urban society of the nineteenth century.

Law and Order in the City

One November evening in 1878, a charcoal seller and a professional musician were drinking together in a Hankow wineshop. Having perhaps exceeded their capacities, they commenced a rendition of some bawdy tunes for the benefit of the assembled crowd. A local bullyboy named Chang, however, was not at all pleased by their singing and offered the suggestion that it was vile and blasphemous. In this sentiment he was vocally supported by his companion, a local fireworks dealer. The charcoal seller, himself described as "never a paragon of virtue," took up the challenge and a spirited argument ensued. The barkeep finally succeeded in reconciling his noisy customers, simultaneously ushering them all out of his shop, and the matter appeared settled.

The next morning, though, the charcoal seller appeared at the fireworks dealer's shop and offered to continue the debate as to his singing abilities. The latter, suspecting the presence of nearby accomplices, stood for the abuse until two local military students, fellow villagers of the dealer, happened by and once again showed the charcoal seller the door. This second repetition being too much, the fireworks dealer, Chang, and the two students the following day paid a call on the charcoal seller, dragged him down to a teahouse by the waterfront, and beat him to within an inch of his life.[3]

Crime and violence indeed lurked below the surface of nineteenth-century Hankow life. To many Western reporters the town was remarkable for the order and tranquillity exhibited by its densely crowded population, but Chinese observers knew that this tranquillity was illusory. Hu Lin-i echoed a popular official view in noting that the "Wu-han cities have always been a violent place."[4] The characteristic incident related above demonstrates a number of the reasons why: a large number of men without families in a more or less foreign locale who were engaged in occupations that were neither prestigious nor economically secure; a vast array of fairly disreputable sites suitable for confrontations; and ready-made factional lines along which to escalate hostilities. A basic cause of the problem may be identified as the great ethnic and occupational diversity of Hankow's population. Even the most ideal citizens among the city's sojourner merchants were prone to rowdiness, and as an 1850 commentator reported, their various *hui-kuan (landsmannschaft)* hosted scenes of unparalleled debauchery, inasmuch as "men on the road are more difficult to control than those at home."[5] The swarms of boatmen and porters likewise drawn by the trade, as well as the sizable lower-class population native to the city, found outlets for their energies and frustrations in the incredibly numerous teahouses, wineshops, and opium dens of the town. Formal or informal collective ties, either of trade or of local origin, provided additional lines of friction as well as psychological support for the would-be troublemaker.[6]

The disparate rough-and-ready elements of Hankow were not all attracted by legitimate professional callings such as those in the above story, nor was crime in the city always derived from such rambunctiousness or passionate displays. The widely heralded wealth of the town's great merchants made it an ideal target for parasitic criminal activity. The large beggar population and other marginal groups could slip in and out of theft as the economic situation demanded, but they had competition in this area from professionals acting either independently or as members of the city's well publicized robber gangs. More urbane thieves were known to assume the role of important traveling merchants, while lesser criminal types were content to maintain their anonymity among the great market's shifting population. Robbery was an enduring feature of Hankow life.

"Victimless crimes," such as gambling, prostitution, and the opium trade, also thrived in Hankow society. Here again, a bad economic turn frequently forced those households with tenuous economic positions to throw open their doors as gambling houses, or to rent out their wives and daughters, but probably the greater part of this activity locally was in the hands of large-scale professional organizations. Lin Tse-hsu described enormous opium warehouses that he raided in the 1830s[7] and stated that although his crusade had remarkable success, it was merely a temporary measure. By 1850, one once again had only to make the appropriate hand signal in any of the city's wineshops or teahouses for the drug to be produced for sale, and as late as 1911 one report listed 1,492 opium dens in Hankow.[8] Prostitution was a diverse enterprise, specialized so as to best serve each economic stratum of the population. As a center for the skin trade, of course, Hankow suffered the fate of any large port city, and we are told that otherwise pious leading local businessmen contributed to the problem by offering women and gambling on their commercial premises as a service to their valued transient suppliers and customers.[9] Prostitution activity was periodically stimulated by waves of homeless female refugees fleeing to Hankow from the flood-devastated Han River valley, who found a preexisting distribution network for their services in the city; an occasional reference can even be found to a professional female slave trade, importing women for illicit purposes from more distant famine-stricken areas.[10]

To the extent that all of this activity was syndicated, it seems logical to suspect a major role for the secret societies, which Esherick has pointed to as most heavily concentrated in Hankow and similar dominantly commercial cities.[11] In fact, secret societies thrived in Hankow; the British consul spoke, for example, of the "hundreds of secret societies existing in our midst."[12] Regarding their connection with organized crime, however, I must regrettably add my name to the list of those whose interest in secret society activity exceeds their powers of discovery.

The problem of crime was persistent, but it was the threat of general social upheaval—either spontaneous or organized—that weighed most heavily upon those charged with local control in Hankow. While their worst fears were seldom realized (until perhaps T'ang Ts'ai-ch'ang's famous uprising attempt of 1900), a variety of incidents occurred with sufficient frequency to ensure the vigilance of local officialdom. Some of these conflicts were simply responses to crises in the local economy. In 1801, for example, the rapid influx of refugees from the flood-devastated Han River valley led to a rapid inflation of rice prices and a subsequent grain riot—the classic pattern of similar disorders in both China and Europe.[13] Again, a specific economic grievance, but this time with a slightly higher level of consciousness and direction, led to the 1894 action of several thousand Hankow peddlers who clashed with police, set fire to a number of government yamens, and "attempted to foment a rebellion (*ta-pien*)."[14] However, both these sorts of incidents could be and were resolved fairly speedily by action to remove the source of the grievance.

More troubling was the continued rise of secret society agitation, particularly in the years after the Taiping Rebellion (1850-1864). In the rebellion itself, a sizable minority of the local population had for various reasons actively cast their lot with the insurgent cause.[15] In the reconstituted Hankow society of the years following the city's final recovery by imperial forces, organizations such as the Ko-lao Hui (Elder Brother Society) took root and directed a rather nonspecific antiadministration movement, which bore its first fruit in an aborted rising in the spring of 1883. This incident, which merits a fuller discussion apart from this essay, so alarmed local officialdom that it precipitated a wholesale overhaul and intensification of local security and control systems throughout the province of Hupeh. Hankow itself was once again confirmed in official eyes as a perennial tinderbox of violence and sedition.[16]

In response to these specifically urban problems of social disorder, the various levels of local administration governing Hankow had over the course of time evolved a number of government-run control devices. These included military patrols, gatekeepers, paid informants, neighborhood guardhouses, and, by the later years of the century, a system of local complaint bureaus. All of these instruments together, however, were not deemed sufficient to accomplish their task in the city. Their indispensable corollary was to be provided in several forms by the community. One aspect of this was the variety of law enforcement and conflict resolution facilities maintained by the many and powerful guilds and local-origin associations of the city, a topic that will not be treated here. The second form of community-sponsored assistance was to be via the *pao-chia* network.

Pao-chia as Regimentation

According to local sources, the *pao-chia* system was implemented in Hankow at the beginning of the Ch'ing dynasty, but the first serious attempt to institute a full-scale system of population control seems to date only from the early eighteenth century, in the wake of the K'ang-hsi emperor's detailed *pao-chia* instructions of 1708.[17] Thereafter, on this local level one can see at least *pro forma* revisions and reforms responding to the major periodic edicts on the subject promulgated by each of the Ch'ing rulers. The imperial government clearly demanded a continuing interest in *pao-chia* matters on the part of its provincial and local officials. In the Tao-kuang period (1821-1851), for example, the Hukuang governor-general and the Hupeh governor dutifully submitted annual palace memorials on the status of the system in this province, in which are revealed the major uses to which the government expected it might be put: combating opium smoking, salt smuggling, and the nagging problems of rebellion that plagued mountainous Hupeh Province. At the same time, these reports were so formulaic as to leave little doubt that genuine concern with the care and maintenance of *pao-chia* was to be vested at a more grass-roots level of administration.[18]

In Hanyang *hsien*, the county that governed Hankow, a fairly detailed *pao-chia* code remained on the books seemingly through the end of the dynasty. The oldest version of this code of which substantial portions survive is that of 1813. Yet while the code was drawn up on a county-wide basis, the details of its enforcement in Hankow were made the responsibility of the two submagistrates of that city. Locally, at least, it was recognized that the problems of enforcement, and of control generally, differed in Hankow from those elsewhere in the *hsien*.

The inconceivably ambitious goal of *pao-chia* in Hankow as throughout China was the complete regimentation of the population into decimal groups of households, which could then be arranged into a control hierarchy under successive levels of headmen. At each level of the hierarchy, the units were designed to incorporate within themselves the twin principles of collective and one-man responsibility for community behavior. In the largest of these units, the *pao* of approximately one thousand families, the one responsible individual was a headman known locally as *pao-cheng* or *ti-pao*. As of 1813, Hankow was allotted eighty-five of these functionaries.

Regimentation required first of all enrollment. While Hsiao Kung-ch'uan notes that as national policy this process was to include only adult males,[19] in Hankow the process seems to have been somewhat more ambitious. One local writer describes each of the local headmen theoretically "conducting a thorough house-by-house investigation of the number of persons male and female, and recording their native place and surname, witnessing evidence of their home district registration, and ferreting out those rebellious drifters who have no local ties."[20] Census reports for all of Hanyang *hsien* were issued on this basis in 1711, 1813, and 1888.

At this point a word must be added regarding home-district or native-place registration (*chi-li*, or simply *chi*), particularly inasmuch as I know of no work in English that treats this subject in any detail. This institution is frequently confused with *pao-chia* enrollment, no doubt largely because of the tendency to translate both concepts with the English word "registration." As the above quotation illustrates, in Hankow at least, the two institutions were entirely distinct, and in fact fully one-half of the individuals included in the 1813 *pao-chia* enrollment were registered natives of some place other than Hanyang *hsien*.[21] This number included, of course, the various travelers and seasonal merchants whom the city attracted, but also a substantial number of permanent residents of the place, many of whom had even been born there. These were people belonging to families that had migrated to Hankow for one reason or another but had never changed their registration, either because they did not meet the local prerequisites for doing so (such as ownership of real property), or because they dealt in a regional specialty product or service and might therefore be prohibited by their guild from doing so.[22] Registration was important. It affected upward mobility by enabling one to enter certain schools, by allowing one to receive a *hsien* stipend as a state-supported scholar, and by facilitating one's candidacy for the local civil service examinations. It was also important socially, for it strictly determined to what secondary organizations one might belong. I have found no evidence, however, that local registration in Hankow either inhibited geographic mobility or played any role whatsoever in the areas of local control or public security.

Pao-chia enrollment, on the other hand, was specifically designed to serve these purposes. Once the constituency of each decimal unit had been legally established, it was thought that keeping track of the registered natives and other permanent residents, at least, would be a relatively easy task. Then, as one Hankow writer optimistically put it:

> If it happens that a newly-arrived and unfamiliar individual comes to reside within the group, he will first be interrogated and then driven out by the *ti-pao*. If it turns out that someone has concealed him, that person will be dealt with according to uniform criminal procedures. This policy is a continuation of the old mutual assistance concept of eight families surrounding a well.[23]

However, even the most nostalgic of Hankow policymakers recognized that the situation as it existed was not to be resolved by any resurrection of the well-field system, if for no other reason than the high percentage within the city's population of both long-term and short-term sojourners, upon whose presence all but the most die-hard physiocrats acknowledged that the economic life of the city depended.

Aside from general population resistance, two constant nemeses could be found in Hankow to any such registration system: the traveling merchants of all economic levels who passed through the city, and the harbor dwellers of either temporary or permanent duration. Rather detailed regulations for the control of the former group were set out in the 1813 *pao-chia* code, some of the more interesting of which were the following:

> The various Buddhist temples (*an-miao*) and inns (*fan-hsien-tien*) of Hankow which take in lodgers must post placards with the names of these lodgers, and must keep sequential record books with the names of the lodgers, their native places, and their *pao-chia* affiliations. . . .
>
> Native residents of Hankow, and those outsider families who have established residence there, who open any sort of business establishment, be it a *hang*, a warehouse, a small shop, or a dealership, whether gentry or nongentry, must all investigate those merchants who come and go from their place of business. They are responsible for posting and keeping up to date a *pao-chia* placard, so that confusion and subversive elements may be avoided. . . .
>
> In the future, all will come under the auspices of *pao-chia*, and at their first arrival it will be determined whether or not they are troublemakers. Those great resident and traveling merchants who deal only with responsible *hangs* and warehouses in Hankow will inevitably recognize that they have no need to fear this enrollment. It is only those vagrants and rebellious elements from outside the *hsien* and province who either make their living through physical intimidation, or who pilfer like dogs and rats, who will find no place to stay other than at small out-of-the-way inns, or in those makeshift mat-sheds along the banks of the Han.[24]

Thus, if this did not put a stop to criminal activity, it was at least designed to ensure poor living conditions for the criminal.

The general prescription for dealing with both dangerously mobile groups—the traveling merchants and the boat people—put a heavy emphasis on collective responsibility for each group member's actions. Where regimentation based on place of residence, such as *pao-chia* strictly defined, was not practicable, other measures such as five-men or ten-men mutual security bonds were recommended for dealing with the merchants.[25] As for the harbor dwellers, while they were already theoretically incorporated into the Hankow *pao-chia* structure (a number of the city's *pao-cheng* were specifically designated as *shui-pao-cheng*, or "water headmen"), other regimentation systems were also periodically employed for this segment of the population. One such device, applied with fleeting success to the grain tribute boatmen, was to collect them into ten-boat mutual liability groups (confusingly also labelled *chia*). Unlike the simultaneously operative *pao-chia* units, however, these *chia* were not a function of location; they were as binding in Hankow harbor as when the boats were under way or moored elsewhere.[26]

The confusing multiplicity of these regimentation schemes for the more mobile elements of Hankow's population suggests strongly that none could have had a firm and long-lasting effect. In fact, as early as 1818, the compiler of the *hsien* gazetteer complained that "although Hankow is but a single *chen* [town], its merchant population all rent their living quarters and thus are one place in the morning and gone from there in the evening." Consequently, he went on, neither they nor the harbor dwellers may be enrolled with any expectation of success.[27] Sixty years later, a local reformist writer echoed the historian's lament:

> Lodgers who come to Hankow either dwell in rented houses or stay at wayside inns. Today they may dwell in Chü-jen ward but tomorrow move to Yu-i. The following day they may be found in Hsun-li or Ta-chih ward. Before the investigations of the *ti-pao* can catch up with them, they have already moved three or four times. No matter how diligently one attempts to investigate their whereabouts, how can one do it?[28]

I would contend that not only were transients never successfully integrated into the regimentation process in Hankow, but that even as regards long-term residents the process was either never effectively enforced in the city or had become at least by the very early nineteenth century little more than a cherished memory. For one thing, in no source I have encountered is mention made of the existence of any decimal population unit, or of the lower-level headmen (*p'ai-t'ou*, *chia-t'ou*) who were to have been the system's grass-roots support.[29] A brief analysis of Hankow population figures as reported through *pao-chia* enrollments provides us with a glimpse of the regimentation system in decay.

From the first, the system must have had great difficulty in keeping pace with the town's rapid population growth, which had continued unabated since its founding in the middle of the Ming dynasty. If we compare the figures from the 1711 and 1813 enrollments, we can see that while the population of the submagistracy encompassing Hsün-li and Ta-chih wards had risen from 51,649 to 52,282 (an increase of only about 1.2 percent), over the same period the population of the two remaining wards, Chü-jen and Yu-i, had leaped from 47,732 to 76,900 (an increase of 61.1 percent). Clearly, the latter two wards had been more recently settled, and over the course of the eighteenth century the center of gravity of Hankow had shifted in their direction. However, notwithstanding the fact that by 1813 the majority of Hankow's population was congregated in these two wards, they were allotted at that time only twenty-one *pao-chia* headmen (*pao-cheng*), giving them a population/headman ratio of about 3,652:1. By contrast, the population of Hsun-li and Ta-chih wards was represented by sixty-four *pao-cheng,* for a far smaller ratio of 816:1.[30] These figures leave little doubt that the distribution of *pao-cheng* promulgated in 1813, and the corresponding size of the *pao-chia* units they commanded, far from reflecting the contemporary situation was based on a population distribution pattern that was more than a century out of date. Consequently, by the beginning of the nineteenth century the reality of the *pao-chia* regimentation process in the daily life of a Hankow resident was already, at best, very much a function of where in the city that resident happened to dwell.

Furthermore, it is readily apparent that a great portion of Hankow's day-to-day residents escaped this enrollment altogether. Taking the population of the *chen* as a whole based on the 1711-1813-1888 *pao-chia* totals, we find a steady increase from 99,381 to 129,182 to 180,980, or a net growth over a 177-year period of 81.1 percent.[31] This seems not unreasonable in light of other descriptive sources, indicating that the effectiveness of at least the census-taking *pao-chia* machinery remained at a somewhat consistent level. In absolute terms, however, these figures remain far lower than those given by even the most cautious reporters. To cite but three examples: in 1745, the governor of Hupeh estimated the population of Hankow at 200,000.[32] In 1858, Laurence Oliphant, Lord Elgin's secretary and a normally acute observer, gave Hankow the lion's share of a total Wuhan population of 1 million, estimating that before the recent Taiping devastation the number would have been twice that.[33] Ten years later, a Western guidebook stated that Hankow's population was roughly 600,000.[34] Even allowing that the Western commentators may have included some elements of the city's transient population that the *pao-chia* investigators may not have concerned themselves with, the vastness of these discrepancies strongly implies a general weakness in the enrollment procedure itself. And the inability, readily acknowledged by local observers, of the *pao-chia* to provide even reasonably accurate census figures leaves little doubt of its failure in its infinitely more demanding task of enforcing the principle of collective responsibility among Hankow's huge and dynamic population.

If *pao-chia* as a regimentation device was grossly ineffective in the nineteenth century, it was never without its proponents. Even as they lamented its failure in practice, elements among the local gentry reiterated their belief in the system's principles—undoubtedly in part because it smacked of home rule. The anonymous reformist essay of 1876 (which we have already had several occasions to cite) is typical of this view.[35] The compiler of the T'ung-chih period *hsien* gazetteer, after reprinting the 1813 *pao-chia* code, similarly voiced his support: "When the people perform it dutifully, it is almost as beneficial as a program of collective education."[36]

Local official feeling on the matter was generally more cautious and varied with the prior experience of the individual. An aggressive administrator with a faith in *pao-chia* could, however, attempt to reinvigorate the system for a time. A prominent example was Lin Tse-hsu, whose phenomenally successful antiopium campaign in Hupeh seems to have included a major effort to revive *pao-chia* regimentation in the province, with a special emphasis on control of transients in Hankow and other major cities.[37] A second period of official interest in the more collective aspects of the system came in the late 1870s at the hands of a certain Hanyang magistrate, Ts'ai, who with his successors and colleagues launched a major law and order campaign in Hankow.[38] Ts'ai was concerned, apparently with excellent reason, at the recent upsurge of activity of local toughs in the city and the growing collaboration they seemed to be receiving from other segments of the population such as shady merchants and yamen clerks. The assault on this rise in crime featured an intensification of enrollment compulsions and a renewed demand for the posting of *pao-chia* placards (*shih-chia-p'ai*), as well as an increased role for the *pao-chia* headmen, to whom we shall momentarily turn.

Clearly, the *idea* of *pao-chia* remained alive in Hankow throughout the nineteenth century. Regarding the system's efficacy in enforcing membership in decimal groups, however, it is evident that what fleeting successes officials like Lin and Ts'ai might have achieved were highly unusual and moreover brought about only through great effort and coercive force. Enrollment drives were periodically carried out, and *shih-chia-p'ai* occasionally were seen in the town (although local correspondents often noted that even these were indifferently maintained), but the reality of the control network was not behind these displays. The consistently vital aspect of the *pao-chia* system in Hankow lay in its least collective component.

The Case of the Disembodied Headmen

I have elsewhere explored the usage *"ti-pao"* (translatable as "local guarantor") and argued that in Hankow and perhaps all of urban

China it was used interchangeably in the late Ch'ing with the title *pao-cheng* or *pao-chang*.[39] If etymology is a reliable tool of historical reconstruction in this case, a subtle but significant shift may be perceived behind the growing acceptability of the former term as a substitute for the latter two. While *pao-cheng* is a title specifically applicable to the head of an administratively designated *human* unit (the thousand-household *pao*), the term *ti-pao* and its variant *ti-fang* were clearly derived from a *territorial* unit over which this functionary exercised authority. This verbal transference may have implied a recognition that the headman's claim to legitimacy had become liberated from its dependence on a regimented unit of population, which was no longer presumed to exist. Other, nonlinguistic factors such as the headman's growing connection with the rounds of gatekeepers and watchmen, as well as his role in regard to real property rights, also indicate that at least by the post-Taiping period the Hankow *pao-cheng*'s jurisdiction was defined in territorial rather than in human terms.[40] Indeed, if one wishes to posit this realignment as taking place a century earlier, it helps explain the authorities' remarkable willingness to ignore the differential rates of population growth within the city, noted above, in their deployment of *pao-chia* headmen.

For practical purposes, in any case, the evidence is overwhelming that even while *pao-chia* as a vehicle of regimentation withered, the functionaries, whose utility had originally been conceived as that of shepherds to these groups, continued to thrive and to play an indispensable role in their society.

The most basic function of the local headman in Hankow was as an independent guardian of the neighborhood peace. A very large number of reports in the contemporary Chinese press testify to the fact that a good many *pao-cheng* of the city did execute these duties rather diligently. One headman, we discover, apprehended a dangerous madwoman prowling the neighborhood; another reported to the magistrate a crime of violence observed in an urban gravel pit; a third brought to justice the culprit of a nasty ethnic confrontation aboard boats in Hankow harbor.[41] It should be stressed that reports such as these are free from normative or exhortative content—they are simply sensational journalism in its most rambunctious form. As such, they provide eloquent attestation to the performance of peacekeeping functions by Hankow's *pao-cheng* well into the last quarter of the nineteenth century.

Local official sources reveal more clearly the broader range of the headman's duties in combating criminal activity. Many of these duties derived from the still-held expectation that he be familiar with all persons residing within his jurisdiction. He was, for example, routinely called in for consultation (*hsieh-t'ung*) by either a yamen runner or the local officials themselves to suggest suspects in a current case or to provide background on accused or accusers. He was also apparently a necessary party to the serving of subpoenae, inasmuch as an 1884 document notes that whenever the Hanyang magistrate wants to "summon or arrest" (*huan-huo*) an individual, he must first send a runner to enlist the cooperation of that person's *pao-cheng*.[42] Here the headman clearly served less as a government strongman than as an aid in identification of the party to be summoned and as a witness to the arrest; on occasion, however, he could also be employed in the more menial role of jailer, as when required to escort a prisoner wearing a cangue to be displayed before the scene of his crime.[43]

One of the headman's most basic police functions was, as we have seen, acting on his own authority and initiative in the reporting of crimes and in the apprehension of wrongdoers. To better achieve this purpose, the *pao-cheng* was expected to make regular personal rounds of his territory, supplementing the government troops that were also assigned to neighborhood patrols. In the post-Taiping years, as the problem of urban toughs (*p'i-kun*) became ever more severe in Hankow, official exhortations to intensify these patrols were correspondingly more frequent, culminating in the crackdown campaign spearheaded in the late 1870s by Magistrate Ts'ai.[44] From several of Ts'ai's proclamations during the winter of 1877-1878 we can reconstruct the neighborhood anticrime procedures of the time. Throughout the evening hours, a watchman under the direction of the local headman was assigned to patrol each street or block (*tuan*). The headman himself, in addition to making personal rounds at key periods, was to be on call to assist the watchman at any point. If a crime was detected in progress, a gong would be sounded and theoretically the entire neighborhhood would respond. Now, Ts'ai stipulated that each *tuan* further appoint one local "brave" to make additional evening patrols, again under the guidance of the headman.

The following year, Ts'ai's colleague, the subprefect of Hankow Chang Chin-chia, undertook even more strenuous efforts in this area. His proclamation of December 1878 reads in part:

> To all *pao-chia* personnel of Hankow: know that this office has issued funds for the repair of enclosing gates (*cha-lan*) of various streets of Hankow. The responsibility for this project has been assigned to the

two submagistrates of Jen-i and Li-chih, and construction has commenced in the tenth month. Henceforth, as a security measure, all *pao-chia* headmen, accompanied by a watchman, are to proceed from street to street strictly carrying out the daily opening and closing of the gates. Out-of-the-way streets, small lanes, and nonfrequented places are to be locked up at eleven P.M. every night. The major streets and marketplaces, where many people come and go, are to be locked at some time after midnight. . . . If the night patrols discover a gate which has been left open, the responsible *pao-chia* headman and watchman will be brought to trial and punished severely. There will be no leniency.[45]

Aside from the prevention and prosecution of street crime in their neighborhoods, Hankow *pao-cheng* were used with some success by the administration to combat more general patterns of antisocial behavior. The system, as we have noted, was expected to be of use in local antismuggling and antiopium campaigns, and, whereas the enforcement of collective responsibility principles had dubious success in this area, the headmen themselves occasionally proved to be of some usefulness for these purposes. For example, in 1830 an attempt was made with reportedly good results to have Hankow *pao-chia* leadership regularly board all boats entering the harbor with the goal of closing down the thriving black market in salt.[46] Of course a campaign of this scope relying essentially upon nongovernmental personnel could not have enjoyed a long life span. Other consistent official nemeses against which local headmen were coopted as policing agents included the circulation of counterfeit or otherwise nonapproved currency and the epidemic violation of zoning regulations (such as encroachment upon public property, and violations of the restriction of certain streets to certain kinds of porterage traffic).[47]

Obviously, however, the most nagging official fear that the headmen were designed to ameliorate was the rise of organized rebellion or other general social disorder. Occasionally, *pao-chia* personnel are credited with a role in maintaining the remarkable freedom from antiadministration unrest that the city enjoyed, and no doubt the network of spies that Lin Tse-hsu and others maintained to this end included many local headmen.[48] Yet the likelihood is that nongovernmental organizations such as the guilds and local origin associations of Hankow deserve more credit for maintaining this tranquillity, and in fact *pao-chia* functionaries often proved particularly inept in dealing with popular movements, as the following incident reveals.

Throughout the 1870s local officials had engaged in a tug-of-war with the celebrants of the fifth lunar month's "Dragon Festival," alternately forbidding the festival's observation and tolerating it, despite its tendency to touch off ethnically inspired incidents between the various provincial groups of Hankow. In 1878, instigators had roamed throughout the city whipping up such enthusiasm for the festival that the authorities at first thought it best to adopt an attitude of cautious acquiescence. By the time they had become truly alarmed and had issued a proclamation banning further activities, it was already too late and the notice had little or no effect. The celebration was to culminate in a competition among the dockworkers and boatmen of each pier of the city to produce and set to sail the most suitably resplendent dragon boat. When the scramble to procure building materials (by any means) had led to the predictable flurry of hostilities and lawsuits, blame was fastened by the officials for this widespread misconduct chiefly upon the cognizant *shui-pao-cheng*, who were threatened with the cangue.[49]

The reasons for the ineffectiveness of the *pao-cheng* in this case were, I think, three. First, the headmen probably felt no great threat from the activities that they were assigned to regulate in this instance and no doubt anticipated enjoying or even participating in the festivities themselves. Secondly, the system was here confronted directly with one of its two traditional nemeses in Hankow, the harbor-dwelling population over which its control was least effectively established. Third, and perhaps most telling in this case, the headmen were here forced into conflict with one of several types of groupings in the city, which, when they did not specifically reinforce their authority, provided an alternative leadership of much more compelling legitimacy than the *pao-cheng*. In this case, these were the leaders (*fu-t'ou*, or *pang-t'ou*) of the informal guilds or work-gangs that operated on a pier-by-pier and anchorage-by-anchorage basis in the city.

The preceding summary of the *pao-chia* headman's peacekeeping functions in Hankow may have created the impression that his role was in fact nothing more than that of the beat-pounding local constable, with whom he has often been compared. In actuality, although his gradual divorce from any enforceable system of community enrollment made his police duties stand out in starker aspect, the *pao-cheng*'s most fundamental role was in providing "security" in its more general sense: he was the "knower" of his neighborhood, and it was from this capacity that his powers in theory derived. Thus his duties within the judicial process itself went far beyond those of law enforcement. Tsung-li Yamen archives on local cases in Hankow reveal the great variety of areas in which the *pao-cheng* was called upon as an independent expert to give oral or written testimony on goings-on within his jurisdiction.[50] In criminal cases he was asked the whereabouts of a suspect or of stolen property. In civil matters even more intimate knowledge was expected: pedestrian traffic flow within his neighborhood, the details behind an alleged forfeiture of mercantile bond, the circulation and backing of notes issued by a local money shop (*ch'ien-chuang*).

In many respects, the *pao-cheng*'s role as "guarantor" remained a viable one throughout the late imperial period. He guaranteed, first of all, the identity of people, and for this purpose stood by as yamen clerks interrogated witnesses from within his ken. Meadows observed in the Canton of the 1840s that when one of a headman's constituents applied to the yamen in any matter, the *ti-pao* must "certify that the applicants are the people that they state themselves to be. For this purpose, a wooden seal or stamp is given to him, and no petitions or accusations are received at the yamen unless a *ti-pao*'s seal is affixed to them." In all probability similar procedures were followed in contemporary Hankow.[51]

Equally significant, and probably more important as a source of the *pao-cheng*'s power, was his role as the guarantor of *property*. It is unclear whether the headman himself was custodian for real property deeds (*ti-ch'i*) within his jurisdiction, but he was certainly the legally recognized local authority on matters of land title. The *pao-cheng* was routinely called upon as a neutral witness to recount the history of a property and to attest to its present ownership.[52] Beyond simple matters of title, this functionary as chief overseer of a given section of territory was responsible for surveying and recording boundaries of individual plots. In most cases, where boundary markers (*chieh-pei*) existed, this was simply a formality. When uncertainty or dispute arose, however, the headman's advice was binding in yamen cases.[53] It would appear to follow from these duties that the Hankow *pao-cheng* was a necessary party to all transactions involving land title. This impression is supported by at least one recorded case in which an educational fund of Hanyang *hsien* in purchasing a plot of Hankow land called in the cognizant headman to specify its proper measurements.[54]

Additionally, the *pao-cheng* was regularly called upon to serve as custodian (*k'an-shou*) of personal property temporarily in public hands. This might include found items, for which the headman also bore disposition responsibility,[55] as well as property impounded by the administration. In one 1875 case, for example, the Hankow *taotai* responded to complaints that a local merchant had defaulted on debts to his Western trading partners by seizing the merchant's household furniture and charging its care to the neighborhood headman.[56]

Pao-chia leadership in Hankow, incorporating as it did all of the above legal and quasi-legal powers, can be seen to have been a force of considerable consequence on the local scene. Beyond these functions, however, the *pao-cheng* quite possibly played one additional role that may have greatly altered the nature and scope of his power: that of tax-collection agent. We know that in rural China the local headmen often assumed this function, and one recent study has concluded that their role in the fiscal process increased significantly over the course of the nineteenth century.[57] In the city of Hankow, a 1747 source credits the headmen with an unspecified role in the collection of "commercial taxes" (*shang-shui*),[58] and yet, among the wealth of material on *pao-chia* operations and theory in that town in the nineteenth century, I have found no references to this particular function. I am led to suspect that the tax-collection role either had been legislated away from the headmen (perhaps in the reorganiza-tion of 1807) or had simply been usurped by other forces. These forces, of course, might have included yamen functionaries, guilds, or government-licensed brokers. Nevertheless, the fiscal powers of the *pao-cheng* continued, at the very least, in an indirect form. An example may be seen in the 1877 attempt of the provincial government to set up in Hankow a charitable agency (*hsi-tzu-chü*) modeled after one then existing in the neighboring provincial capital, Wuchang. Once the decision had been arrived at to endow this office chiefly by means of a special levy on shops in the neighborhood, it was this neighborhood's local headman who was entrusted with the task of determining which shops could afford to be assessed what amount.[59] This, indeed, is the stuff of which real power is made.

Who Was Served?

Our discussion thus far has centered on the various duties of *pao-chia* headmen in Hankow and on the quite considerable degree to which these duties were faithfully performed. Insofar as this was the case, the headmen clearly served as useful appendages of the administration in its attempt to penetrate below the lowest official level (in Hankow, the submagistrate) in regulating the urban population. There were, however, continual systemic dysfunctions that redirected the utility of the *pao-cheng* away from the administration and toward other forces on the social scene. To better understand these tensions we must consider several more questions: how were the headmen appointed, how were they paid, and, perhaps most important, who were these men? Like previous writers, I must confess to the lack of fully satisfactory data on these subjects, but certain answers do suggest themselves on the basis of local materials.

In Hankow as elsewhere the *pao-chia* leadership was supposed to be generated from within the local community. Most writers have assumed that this in effect meant selection by an entrenched local elite. Meadows, who observed firsthand Canton city in the 1840s, is worth citing in detail on this point:

> When the post of a *ti-pau* becomes vacant, either through death or super annuation, the householders of the quarter meet in a temple to select a person to fill the vacancy. Previously they generally post notices that a *ti-pau* is wanted for such and such a locality, and that candidates must offer themselves at the election, which is to take place on a certain specified day. . . . [In actuality, a few] influential individuals make the real decision.[60]

Meadows adds that once the choice is made, a petition is submitted to the magistrate with the name of the newly elected individual, who is then invariably approved. There is little reason to suspect that a similar pattern did not pertain in Hankow, or in most other large urban centers of the time. The chief difficulty is to identify who in fact these "influential individuals" were.

It is very tempting to view the contest for appointment of *pao-chia* headmen as one aspect of the larger struggle, waged on many fronts in late imperial China, between yamen functionaries and an older, nonofficial elite. Some writers, such as David Faure, see the *ti-pao* as increasingly captured by the yamen underlings. Faure produces evidence that by the late 1860s many Kiangsu headmen were in practice appointed by this group, tying this phenomenon in with the growing "bureaucratization" of Chinese society.[61] In Hankow, where the "elite" comprised an amalgam of merchant, merchant-gentry, and literati types, there is also some evidence for this view. We know that the yamen clerks formed a powerful interest group on the local scene, and from gentry grumblings in the post-Taiping period we learn that their influence did indeed extend into *pao-chia* matters. An anonymous Hankow essayist in 1876 argued forcefully that the city's central *pao-chia* administration should be removed from the submagistrate's offices, where it had fallen prey to the evil machinations of clerks and runners, and be vested in a newly organized, gentry-staffed *"pao-chia* bureau" (*pao-chia chü*).[62] This suggestion, evidence of a strong *feng-chien* (autonomy under local leadership) tradition at work in urban society, does not seem to have triggered an immediate official response, although such institutions later became commonplace in major Chinese cities. Nevertheless, viewing headmen in Hankow strictly in terms of a gentry/clerk dichotomy seems somewhat strained. Rather, their activities seem to indicate that they were clients of no single social group.

As unsalaried public functionaries, whose duties by the nineteenth century clearly approached full-time employment, the headmen were ideal, almost necessary, targets for corruption. Their legitimate income was derived from several fragmentary sources. First, they generally received a notary's fee for attaching their seal to documents for upward transmission, and probably also for witnessing property transactions. To this may have been added an approved percentage derived from their unclear role in the urban tax collection process. They were almost certainly remunerated further by donations from their neighborhood constituency.

As early as the beginnings of the Ch'ien-lung reign (1736-1795), however, the prefectural gazetteer lists a catalog of financial abuses indulged in by Hankow *pao-cheng*.[63] For example, "when rats and crows among the people present litigation against one another, tantamount to hanging or drowning themselves, the *pao-cheng* stand willing to present evidence for either side, like foxes picking the bones of the population." Among their other crimes are included "serving as lackeys for the local wealthy" (*mai-fu ch'ai-p'in*), "being derelict in the collection of commercial taxes" (*yin-ni shang-shui*), and "harboring traitorous elements" (*pao-ts'ang chien-chiu*)—all for a suitable price. Behind each of these four items, of course, we may perceive a separate interest group in Hankow, members of which were eager to purchase the headmen's favors: lower gentry professional "pettifoggers," the propertied rich, merchants, and professional thieves. The historian notes that while these abuses were rampant in Hankow they were as yet almost unknown in rural areas, and with remarkable insight he connects this phenomenon to the tremendous multiplication of the urban headman's administrative duties. From the headman's original function as little more than a neighborhood watchdog, his responsibilities have expanded gradually in a number of directions, and with the growing burdens of the job have come growing opportunities for corruption.

It seems clear that by the nineteenth century, urban society had become increasingly dependent upon the labors of the *pao-cheng,* to the point of indispensability. Having neither a proper official billet assigned to them, nor any longer a meaningful integration into a decimal group structure, these indispensable men had begun to emerge as an interest group in their own right. Several writers have commented upon the contradiction between the *pao-chia* headman's significant responsibilities and his generally low social status. Hsiao Kung-ch'uan emphasizes in addition the systemic flaw of legally prohibiting gentry members from holding a position that clearly demanded literacy as one of its many prerequisites.[64] In Hankow the solution arrived at seems to have been the rise of a professional class of headmen, an occupational group aided in their solidarity by the ease of communications and geographical proximity that the city provided. Evidence of this may again be found as early as the first decade of the Ch'ien-lung period. Although *pao-chia* leadership in Hankow as elsewhere was legally an annually rotating position, the same man in practice frequently served many one-year terms in succession—sometimes even assuming a new identity for this purpose, thus "eliminating all trace of their past evils with one stroke of the pen."[65]

In the post-Taiping years, a curious phenomenon supports this view of *pao-chia* headmanship as a career occupation, and its practitioners as a specific interest group. Of the nine Hankow headmen to whom I have found reference by name, all from this period, *four* were surnamed Su.[66] From all other evidence (newspapers, lists of examination candidates and donors to various projects, and so on) it appears that the Su surname was not especially prevalent in Hankow, in fact somewhat less common there than in China as a whole. This of course does not suggest that these men were other than local natives but does seem to add greater significance to their prominence within this very limited sample. Furthermore, we find that three of these Mr. Sus bore the given names Cheng-hsiang, Yung-shun, and Yung-hsiang, with the characters *"hsiang"* (favorable omen) and *"yung"* (perpetual) occuring twice. Evidently these men were members of the same lineage, possibly with the latter two brothers and the former (who is mentioned a decade before the others) their father or uncle. It then seems probable that these Sus, at least, were practicing their family trade of *pao-chia* headmanship in Hankow.[67]

If this is indeed the case, from the fact that the latter two gentlemen were serving simultaneously in different parts of the city, it would also seem that there was little necessary connection between the neighborhood of one's origin and one's *pao-chia* assignment. This helps to explain the insistence of our 1876 reformist writer that in the reorganized *pao-chia* system that he envisions for the city, the selection of headmen be restricted to "long-time residents of the area," preferably local gentry members.[68]

In spite of these factors, it would be simplistic to view *pao-chia* leadership in Hankow as no more than a class of local bullies or hired strongmen who preyed upon the more defenseless elements within the neighborhood population, in collusion with its more powerful forces. This is, it is true, the picture of local headmen in the empire as a whole held by many Chinese observers in the post-Taiping years. The journal *Shen Pao*, for example, ran a campaign against such abuses, which culminated in a front-page editorial in August 1879 that lamented the remarkable frequency with which complaints against oppression by *pao-chia* personnel had appeared in that newspaper's pages.[69] Curiously, though, none of the many nineteenth-century references to Hankow headmen in *Shen Pao*'s pages or elsewhere make note of oppression or corruption by headmen in that locality. The catalog of offenses in the 1747 gazetteer finds no echo later, and even the anonymous reformer of 1876 has nothing but good to say about the headmen's efforts in the face of insurmountable odds. I would not argue that impropriety had disappeared in that city but suggest that, in contrast to the perception of rampant corruption in the early Ch'ien-lung period, in later years this corruption was felt to be held within tolerable limits. *Pao-cheng* with their spectrum of functions were necessary to the city's smooth operation, and such abuses as payoffs and careerist behavior, far from destroying the headman system, were the very factors that allowed it to work.

In spite of the threats to public order catalogued earlier in this chapter, Hankow throughout the nineteenth century remained an internally rather stable society. At the same time that the city was open and the population free-flowing, the most striking thing about Hankow was that it *worked* as a social unit. Powerful nonadministrative forces such as guilds, local origin associations, and, in later years, Western diplomatic and commercial agents, felt a keen interest in this stability and kept potentially irresponsible and disruptively rapacious elements in check. The local neighborhoods, too, played a role in this self-nurturing and equilibrating process. If the neighborhood community allowed the headman certain liberties, these liberties were granted in return for his responsiveness to local needs. The law enforcement role that, as we have seen, the headmen rather dutifully performed, was clearly perceived as in the community interest. At least as often as the headman exercised these powers on his own initiative, his assistance was actively solicited by the victim of a crime or some other member of the neighborhood population. A typical case involved a restaurant proprietor who awoke one morning to find the corpse of a beggar curled up beside his exterior hearth, where the proprietor supposed he had died of exposure during the night, and thereupon summoned the local *pao-cheng*. This stalwart, unsatisfied with the· proprietor's theory, diligently pursued the possibility of foul play before reporting the matter to the administration.[70]

The headman was accessible and approached by neighborhood people of whatever social station and was genuinely seen as their immediate link to the administrative process. Perhaps more importantly, as the nineteenth century progressed, he increasingly served as intermediary between the populace and the various community service organizations outside the official sphere. One of the earliest of these was the Lifeboat Society founded in 1839. This worthy endeavor, though granted official sanction and protection, was essentially a gentry and merchant cooperative project that operated rescue craft in Hankow harbor during the city's frequent spells of heavy weather. According to the society's bylaws and the reports of early observers, when corpses were recovered, *pao-chia* headmen assumed the responsibility for identification, notification of next of kin, and disposition of personal effects.[71] More significant numerically on the Hankow scene were the gentry- or merchant-sponsored charity halls (*shan-t'ang*) of the city, which provided a variety of social welfare services and proliferated rapidly from the early Tao-kuang period until the end of the century. The *pao-cheng* assisted in delivery of these services, for example reporting cases of unidentified corpses or of deaths in indigent families. On the basis of such information one Hankow *shan-t'ang* alone distributed in the 1830s an average of 3,000 free coffins per year.[72]

One is left with the impression that Hankow *pao-chia* headmen, although very likely of extraneighborhood origin in many cases, remained very much agents of the neighborhood community. It is worth noting that none of the welfare functions just described were part of the headman's role as originally conceived but were an adaptation to the growing needs of late imperial urban society.[73] The headman's role grew to meet these needs. Moreover, one of his chief sources of income was donations and levies drawn from the merchants and residents of his area, a fact that linked the headman's interests at least in great measure with the financial well-being of his constituents. Over the course of time, the *pao-cheng*'s ties with neighborhood finance were further strengthened, as watchmen, local braves, and gatekeepers followed each other upon the urban neighborhood scene. All of these functionaries were, like the headman himself, reimbursed out of a fund administered by the latter.[74] Thus at least for security purposes the *pao-cheng* increasingly approximated the treasurer of what may be termed an informal "neighborhood association."

The genuine neighborhood leadership roles assumed by Hankow *pao-chia* headmen is most strikingly revealed by the circumstances surrounding the city's first major attempt at public street lighting in 1882. The effort originated with a proclamation from the local administration as part of a coordinated public security system for the high-crime months of the deep winter, but, significantly, was to be realized on a strictly neighborhood basis and at private neighborhood expense. The official proclamation called simply for traditional-style bamboo and paper lanterns to be hung at regular intervals with lamp oil supplied by local households according to a nightly rotating schedule. However, the several *pao-cheng* serving along the length of one of the city's modest thoroughfares felt that these flimsy lanterns would be unlikely to survive the severe Hankow winter and so, with approval of their constituency, initiated an alternative plan for the local collection of funds toward the purchase and installation of Western-style metal streetlamps. The experiment proved so successful that it was soon imitated by the more major streets of the city, and Hankow's first real public utility came into being. In this remarkable fashion the headmen, a traditional institution designed merely to effect imperial control, demonstrated their potential not only for local leadership but as agents of "modern" technological innovation.[75]

Conclusion

What survived through most of the nineteenth century of the *pao-chia* system in Hankow was thus both less and more than had been envisioned by its original architects. As a device for herding the population into neat decimal units, the system had proven itself not up to the demands of a cosmopolitan center of this kind. As a vehicle of administrative control, the institution of headmen was the only remainder of the ambitious scheme that the early Ch'ing emperors had drafted, but these headmen continued to play a vital role in the maintenance of public security and the enforcement of law. However, given the complexity of the urban social system and the multifaceted position of the headmen in that political and social system, they were not nor could they be agents of any particular group of actors on the scene. While the officials profited from their often commendable performance of duty, the headmen's powers could also be effectively exploited by local wealthy interests and by the ubiquitous yamen functionaries. More particularly, the *pao-cheng*, as professional subofficials whose activities were increasingly indispensable in an ever more intensely "urban" milieu, took their own interests as primary in balancing the demands of each group. And yet, whether by design or not, the chief beneficiary of the headman's various activities was often none other than his neighborhood constituency. Consequently, he remained a major contributing factor toward social stability and control.

Mausers and the Opium Trade: The Hupeh Arsenal, 1895-1911

Thomas L. Kennedy

At the close of the Sino-Japanese War, in late 1895, the Hanyang Arsenal mirrored the accomplishments and failures of China's Self-strengthening Movement. Although Hanyang was in many ways a remarkable example of rapid strategic industrialization, it was completed too late and had produced too little to aid the Chinese side during the war. The arsenal was part of a comprehensive program for strategic industrial development that Governor-general Chang Chih-tung of Hunan and Hupeh had conceived ten years earlier while serving in Kwangtung and had struggled unceasingly to achieve. Chang's plans called for modernization of the extractive and smelting industries, establishment of technical and scientific education, railroad building, weapons standardization, and strategic defensive planning. All were measures designed to free China's strategic industry from dependence on costly foreign materials, fuel, and technical manpower and to remedy other critical weaknesses that had developed during the 1860s and 1870s.

But a decade proved to be insufficient time for Chang to realize this ambitious scheme given the inertia of China's traditional society and economy and the difficulties imposed by the complex and pervasive network of foreign influences in the economy. As he and his purchasing agents in Germany hesitated over a change to machinery that could produce model 1888, 7.9 mm. Mauser magazine rifles, several precious years slipped by. When capital resources proved inadequate to move ahead simultaneously with construction of the arsenal and the associated Hanyang Ironworks, Chang gave priority to the ironworks, draining 1.5 million taels from the arsenal's appropriations to finance its establishment. Though a wise choice for long-range industrial development, these transfers drastically slowed construction of the arsenal. Only two of its projected five plants had been completed by the summer of 1894. One of these, the rifle plant,

which had been constructed with wood rather than sheet metal as
specified in the plans, was gutted by fire on the eve of the war. Rebuilt
under wartime pressure, it was completed in less than a year,
suggesting that it and the other plants at the arsenal as well could
have been completed more promptly and been producing for the
Chinese side during the war, had it not been for delays occasioned by
official indecision and shortages of capital. Bottlenecks in the
building supply industry slowed the overall pace of establishment
still further, and, at the last minute, shortages of trained management
and technical personnel delayed the beginning of production.
Chang's new technical and scientific training programs, financially
strapped and beset by a multitude of problems, had lagged behind the
required pace of development and were unable to supply the arsenal's
needs for skilled personnel.

Beyond the hesitancy of the leadership, the capital shortages, and
the inability of related sectors of the economy and society to respond
to the needs of strategic industrialization were more fundamental
problems that undermined Hanyang's strategic potential. Notable
among these was the lack of national leadership to coordinate and
direct the efforts of the arsenals in various provinces. The absence of
such direction from Peking led to outbreaks of self-defeating
interprovincial competition between Chang and his counterpart—
the munitions czar of North China, Governor-general Li Hung-
chang of Chihli—which slowed the work of establishment at
Hanyang. A more basic problem was the officially sanctioned
tradition of government monopoly in the ordnance industry. This
not only closed the door to the possibility of private capital, but it also
ruled out the "merchant-management and official supervision"
formula that had been employed to mobilize capital and talent and
spur modernization in the transport, mining, and textile industries.
As a consequence, the establishment costs of Hanyang had to be
wrung from already overtaxed provincial resources through financial
schemes devised by the fund-raising genius of Chang Chih-tung.
Funds came from Kwangtung where Chang had originally intended
to establish the arsenal, from the opium and salt revenues of Hupeh,
and from a variety of loans, contributions, and special appropriations.

The most pernicious influence during the establishment years at
Hanyang was the international environment. What Chang had in
mind was balanced strategic industrialization, but what the times
called for was rapid defense-oriented modernization. Intensifying
imperialist pressures, particularly from near neighbors Russia and

Japan, demanded immediate development of modern military power. For example, Russian pressures in the north led the Ch'ing government to forego progress in industrialization at Hanyang temporarily and shift appropriations for the ironworks to investment in strategic rail lines in Manchuria. The result was a shortage of capital for the ironworks, which prompted Chang to dip into arsenal appropriations, robbing Peter to pay Paul as it were, and slowing progress on the arsenal to a snail's pace.

For all these reasons, production did not begin until 1894, and then the arsenal turned out only several thousand rounds of 7.9 mm. Mauser ammunition daily. Production of rifles commenced a year later in the summer of 1895. The rebuilt plant was capable of producing only 50 percent of the 9,000 rifles per year that it had originally been designed to produce; in fact, it produced only a small fraction of that reduced capability. Meanwhile, production of two 3.7 cm. caliber quick-firing guns per month also began in the summer of 1895. These modest achievements cost dearly. And, since the arsenal's capital was being used for the ironworks, the arsenal accumulated a crushing burden of debts. In late 1895, Chang calculated the accounts payable to foreign firms for equipment and materials at more than 600,000 taels.

At the time Chang was serving as acting governor-general of the Liangkiang provinces (Kiangsu, Kiangsi, and Anhwei), an office to which he had been named during the war. From this post, he petitioned the throne for authority to use Liangkiang foreign loan funds and southern maritime defense funds to clear Hanyang's debts and finance a general expansion of production facilities at the arsenal. This would include the introduction of smokeless powder production (required for magazine rifle and quick-firing gun ammunition) and the production of larger caliber quick-firing guns. Chang argued that funds for modernization of strategic industry would be better invested at Hanyang than at either of the Liangkiang arsenals, Kiangnan and Nanking. Experience during the war had shown that the Kiangnan Arsenal in Shanghai was strategically vulnerable; the Nanking Arsenal, in a crowded urban setting, could not be expanded. Hanyang, on the other hand, had equipment for production of the most modern ordnance. It was at a secure inland site, centrally located on the principal arteries of water transport and, therefore, better suited than Kiangnan to supply a broad area. But postwar austerity prevailed. Chang was granted a loan of 600,000 taels from southern maritime defense foreign loan funds sufficient only for payment of existing debts at Hanyang and no more. The proposed expansion and modernization had to be postponed. The loan was never repaid.[1]

In 1896, after returning to his post in Hupeh, Chang separated the ironworks from the arsenal and placed it under the direction of a commercial corporation headed by the bureaucrat-entrepreneur Sheng Hsuan-huai—a move calculated to facilitate the provision of private capital to the ironworks and to free the arsenal from the burden of further support. The arsenal remained a provincial enterprise under Governor-general Chang's direction. It was subordinate to the Hupeh Provincial Iron Administration and Foreign Affairs Bureau (T'ieh-cheng yang-wu-chü) until September 1904 at which time Chang reorganized that bureau. This move, presumably prompted by the sweeping military reforms recommended by the Commission for Army Reorganization and approved by imperial edicts in September 1904, removed the arsenal from the bureau and subordinated it to the General Bureau for Military Industry in the province (Chu-sheng ping-kung tsung-chü). Reorganization did not bring any drastic changes in the direction of the arsenal's affairs; Chang Chih-tung remained firmly in control at least until he left the governor-generalship of Hunan and Hupeh in 1907. In 1908, the General Bureau for Military Industry in the province was consolidated with the provincial government (Shan-hou chü) and was redesignated the Military Industrial Office (Ping-kung-so). This office controlled the funds for the arsenal and associated plants until early 1910 when the Military Industrial Office was combined with the arsenal and funds for the arsenal were handled through the newly established Provincial Finance Office (Tu-chih kung-so). These changes from 1908 to 1910 probably represented attempts by the imperial government to extend its control over the arsenal, centralization being a well-known aim of the authorities in Peking during these years. They seem to have been unsuccessful, however. In early 1911, Minister of War Yin-chang cautiously attempted to assert imperial control over the director and personnel of the arsenal while reaffirming the governor-general's supervisory authority in all important matters and reassuring the staff that there would be no change in personnel, salaries, expenditures, or manufactures. From this it is clear that the primacy of provincial control under the governor-general of Hunan and Hupeh was not seriously contested until 1911 at the earliest.[2]

The arsenal expanded steadily during the decade following the war. The five main plants for the production of small arms, guns, small arms ammunition, gun ammunition, and gun carriages were operational by the end of 1895. Beginning in 1897, Chang undertook a major expansion of facilities aimed at developing self-sufficiency in the production of quick-firing guns, magazine rifles, and the ammunition that they employed. Pursuant to an edict encouraging the development of defense industries in provinces where basic raw materials such as coal and iron could be found, Chang placed an order with the German firm, Carlowitz and Company, for equipment to produce two to three tons per day of crucible steel required for quick-firing guns and fifty tons per year of smokeless powder required for quick-firing gun and magazine rifle ammunition. He petitioned the throne for an additional annual allocation of 400,000 taels from maritime customs proceeds to defray the costs of establishing the new production facilities, purchase of additional quick-firing gun machinery, and support of stepped-up levels of production after establishment. Though the income realized from this request fell far short of the estimated requirements, Chang moved ahead with the establishment of the smokeless powder and crucible steel plants at Ho-shan, a site six to seven *li* removed from the ordnance plant. The smokeless powder plant began test production in late 1901. Though beset by difficulties, it remained in operation through the end of the dynasty. The crucible steel works, however, was a casualty of the short-fall in annual income. The refinery, one of the two principal divisions with a daily output capacity of 1,600 to 1,700 pounds of steel, commenced trial production in mid-1904. But the shaping mill in which the steel was to be formed into bars was never completed. Consequently, the quality of the steel turned out was never put to the test. Early in 1905, the refinery also halted operations due to shortages in operating capital. Thereafter, the equipment depreciated rapidly. Idle machinery, some of which was never removed from the warehouse, was allowed to rust. The roof was not installed on the shaping mill and equipment there stood exposed to the weather. Though the steel works never entered into production, the facilities at Ho-shan were referred to as the Steel and Powder Works (Kang-yao-ch'ang).[3]

Meanwhile, by 1899 the arsenal had acquired equipment to produce 5.7 cm. caliber guns and had added a cartridge plant. The erection of new buildings also necessitated the establishment of brick and tile works at four nearby locations. During the next few years a machine shop, a molding shop, a boiler shop, a forge, a brass working shop, and a pattern shop were established. Pursuant to these changes, in 1904 provincial authorities petitioned the throne to have the official designation changed. The new name, the Hupeh Arsenal

(Hu-pei ping-kung-ch'ang), reflected the provincial status and the diverse activities conducted in the various shops more accurately than the previous terminology (Han-yang ch'iang pao-ch'ang), which denoted an ordnance plant in the city of Hanyang and nothing more.[4]

These were the major facilities comprising the Hupeh Arsenal at the close of the dynastic era in 1911. In 1910-1911, the arsenal, not including the Steel and Powder Works, occupied a site of 237 *mou* outside the city of Hanyang on the banks of the Han River. On the east, it adjoined the Hanyang Ironworks now under the management of the Han-yeh-p'ing Iron and Steel Smelting and Refining Company. The two plants shared the use of a small rail line, which extended from the Yangtze River pier of the ironworks north to the Han River pier of the arsenal, bisecting the arsenal grounds. To the west of the arsenal beyond the Lung-teng Dike was the Steel and Powder Works, which was also served by the rail line. The arsenal's various plants, shops, engineering offices, and drafting rooms were located in the southern portion of the grounds while the northern portion housed the administration, purchasing, and finance offices as well as living quarters for workers and officials, and barracks for the military.[5]

The establishment of new production facilities at the Hupeh Arsenal ceased in the middle of the first decade of the twentieth century at about the same time as a sharp decline occurred in annual income. Overall income, which comprised both annually allocated regular income and special appropriations, grew steadily through 1906, reaching more than 1.5 million taels annually and then falling off abruptly to about half of that figure. This growth was due to the unrelenting efforts of Governor-general Chang Chih-tung to strengthen the arsenal's financial base. In 1898 and 1899, he was successful in gaining imperial authority to tap the Hankow and Ichang customs proceeds for a total allocation of approximately 150,000 taels annually to support the new steel, smokeless powder, and heavy ordnance production facilities. In 1899 also, with imperial approval, Chang transferred the income from taxes on opium crossing the borders of Hupeh to support the arsenal. This fund grew in the next few years from 100,000 to more than 350,000 taels annually. Similarly, the Hupeh grain likin, which had been imperially approved for provincial use in 1891, was reallocated in 1899 to provide regular operating capital for the Steel and Powder Works. From 1903 to 1905, regular annual income averaged more than 1 million taels, of which almost one-half came from the proceeds of opium taxes.[6]

In the years after the Sino-Japanese War, unfixed income comprising loans, contributions, special appropriations, and the proceeds from the sale of munitions also provided an important part of total income varying from several hundred thousand taels to more than 800,000 taels annually. Initially, unfixed income came from loans, private contributions, and special allocations. Proceeds from the sale of munitions, first noted in 1899, had increased tenfold by 1902 to more than 400,000 taels, peaking the following year at more than 750,000 taels. This surge in the domestic market was presumably related to the embargo on import of munitions imposed by the powers in the Boxer Protocol of 1901, which remained in effect until August 1903. For the next three years, 1904-1906, income from sales averaged more than 350,000 taels annually. During these years income from opium taxes also soared, augmenting both regular and unfixed income. In 1904 Chang received imperial authorization to employ part of the proceeds of the Hunan-Hupeh consolidated opium tax revenues to support an expansion of facilities for small arms and ammunition production. During 1904 and 1905 more than 450,000 taels were allocated from Hunan opium taxes as regular incomes. In 1907 Chang retroactively allocated 300,000 taels from the consolidated opium tax proceeds to the arsenal's account as unfixed income for 1906, possibly to avoid having these funds fall under the control of the Head Office for the Collection of Excise on Native Opium, established at the end of 1906 as part of the imperial government's new comprehensive opium reform program.[7]

Not only did overall income increase markedly in the decade after the Sino-Japanese War, but the fraction derived from opium sale revenues grew from several hundred thousand to nearly half a million taels annually by 1906, comprising more than 28 percent of total income after the turn of the century. Following the establishment, in late 1906, of the Head Office for the Collection of Excise on Native Opium at Wuchang and a new provincial collection office in Hupeh, income from opium revenues disappeared from the arsenal's accounts entirely. Overall annual income plunged from 1,531,613 taels in 1906 to 805,201 taels in 1907, necessitating an abrupt curtailment of production. The results of this were immediately visible in the shrinkage of another important area of unfixed income: proceeds of munitions sales fell off from an annual average of more than 350,000 taels prior to 1907 to a figure of 100,000 to 200,000 from 1907 on. Despite the imperial government's efforts to rebuild the arsenal's financial base beginning with the allocation of 261,000 taels of imperially controlled opium revenues in 1908 and 1909 and increased allotments from the Hankow and Ichang customs revenues commencing in late 1908, overall income remained far below its 1906 level[8] (see Table 5.1).

The financial impact of opium tax reform on ordnance production was devastating. Quick-firing gun production, in which Hupeh had been the national leader, was wiped out entirely. Chang had originally entertained great plans to make quick-firing guns, but by mid-1895 he had purchased equipment through Ludwig Loewe and Company of Berlin adequate to produce each month only two 3.7 cm. caliber quick-firing guns on the pattern of the Gruson Werk of Magdeburg-Buchau. More machinery was on order to arrive in 1896; with this, the arsenal management expected to double 3.7 cm. quick-firing gun production and initiate production of 5.3 and 7.5 cm. caliber quick-firing guns. Production of the 3.7 cm. quick-firing gun reached a total of 222 during the next decade, but neither of the latter models was ever produced in significant quantities though machinery for production of 7.5 cm. caliber guns was eventually installed. Chang went on to formulate even more ambitious plans, however. Driven by the extension of imperialist pressures from the littoral to the hinterland in the years following the Sino-Japanese War, in early 1897 he resolved to develop the domestic capability to produce giant 12 cm. caliber quick-firing guns and ammunition for use in the Yangtze forts. But German firms such as Krupp were reluctant to share the technology employed in this ordnance. Despite the tireless efforts of the Chinese ambassador in Germany, Hsü Ching-ch'eng, Hupeh was able to obtain only limited amounts of production equipment through Ludwig Loewe, and never actually produced these guns. Instead, in the years from 1897 to 1899, the arsenal installed production equipment for the 5.7 cm. caliber quick-firing gun on the Gruson Werk pattern, and these became the mainstay of Hupeh's heavy ordnance. Output reached eight per month, employing imported steel. The bolt mechanism of the original German model was modified at Hupeh, and 479 pieces were completed. But production was suspended in 1906, following the Commission on Army Reorganization's recommendation to the throne that 7.5 cm. be adopted as the standard caliber for quick-firing artillery. This caliber was regarded internationally as the best for field artillery, combining destructive power and mobility. Though Hupeh was equipped to make these guns, it was financially strapped by the elimination of opium revenues from its income in 1906 and never commenced production. Instead it allocated its drastically reduced financial resources entirely to the production of small arms and

TABLE 5.1
Annual Income of the Hupeh Arsenal, 1895-1909
Unit: ch'ang-p'ing taels; 1 tael=approximately $0.69

Year	Total	Regular Income: Hupeh Customs, Salt and Opium Taxes	Unfixed Income: Special Appropriations, Loans, Arms Sales, etc.	Income from Opium Revenue	
				Income	% of Total
1895	577,663	373,780	203,883	199,147	34.5
1896	1,152,491	351,573	800,918	171,522	14.8
1897	646,548	436,624	209,924	233,093	34.5
1898	732,864	457,409	275,455	120,553	16.4
1899	915,664	707,538	208,126	316,049	34.5
1900	1,268,200	816,243	451,957	469,368	37.0
1901	1,175,282	851,160	324,122	1,383,384	32.6
1902	1,175,733	681,197	494,536	221,929	18.8
1903	1,932,513	1,139,101	793,412	521,799	27.0
1904	1,859,823	1,039,149	820,674	478,765	25.7
1905	1,547,735	934,744	612,991	465,602	30.0
1906	1,531,617	574,472	957,145	441,994	28.8
1907	805,201	399,913	405,288	--	--
1908	810,136	632,785	177,351	104,400	12.8
1909	1,139,254	815,969	323,285	156,600	13.7

Source: HPKC, "Shou-chih ke-k'uan ssu-chu ch'ing-tse : "shou-k'uan hsiang-hsia."

ammunition. The suspension of quick-firing gun production became permanent.[9]

Production in the related areas of gun ammunition and gun carriages was also halted in 1906. The Gun Ammunition Plant turned out projectiles, primers, and percussion caps. The rough forms of the projectiles were cast in the Projectile Casting Shop from first- and second-grade cast iron produced by the Hanyang Ironworks. About 70 percent of the 10,000 forms cast each month met the specifications of the Gun Ammunition Plant and were processed into projectiles. The remainder were discarded. Though shot and shell of a variety of calibers from 3.7 cm. to 8.7 cm. were cast, the chief products were 3.7 cm. shells, 10,000 of which could be completed each month, and 5.7 cm. shells, of which 7,000 could be produced monthly. Total output reached 200,000 of the former and 400,000 of the latter. Cartridge casings were made in a separate shop. Technological problems involved in the smelting and strength testing of brass in this shop severely restricted the arsenal's output of finished rounds. By 1906, when the Gun Ammunition Plant halted production, it was completing 7,000 5.7 cm. shells per month but the Cartridge Plant was turning out only 6,000 cartridge cases and only about 3,500 of these met required specifications. The result was to halve the effective monthly output of the Gun Ammunition Plant. Gun carriage production, which was entirely specialized on carriages for the 5.7 cm. quick-firing gun, had kept pace, reaching eight carriages per month when it also was halted.[10] Although the production of quick-firing guns, gun ammunition, and gun carriages at Hupeh had been hampered by technological difficulties and was dependent on imported steel, the monthly output was substantial. The financial collapse of 1906 brought an end to all this, reducing the arsenal to a rifle and cartridge plant.

Production of smokeless powder for rifle ammunition was maintained, but operations in the powder works, long plagued by technological and personnel problems, were cut back after the financial crisis of 1906. Trial production of smokeless powder had begun under the supervision of foreign technicians late in 1901 employing imported materials. In the years from 1902 until 1910 facilities for the production of nitric acid, sulphuric acid, alcohol, and ether were added. Output, which included smokeless powder for both rifle and gun ammunition, increased from 100 pounds per day to about 200 pounds before the financial contractions of 1906 forced elimination of powder for gun ammunition and cutbacks to 100 pounds per day of rifle powder. The quality of the powder produced was uneven, however, and problems with the production of some of the constituents forced prolonged reliance on imported materials. To produce sulphuric acid needed to make nitrocellulose, the chief constituent of smokeless powder, high-grade sulphur was purchased domestically and treated with nitric acid. A foreign specialist was hired to set up and supervise the production of acids in 1902, but the treatment plant was not completed and production did not begin until 1909. By this time, more than 100,000 taels in personnel expenses had been incurred with no tangible results. When sulphuric acid was finally produced, it was so impure and the acidity so low that it could not be used to make nitrocellulose and it was necessary to continue importing. Another trouble area was the production of acetin with which the nitrocellulose was treated to produce smokeless powder. Output was limited by lack of equipment. However, arsenal authorities spent scarce investment funds for new powder-cutting machinery, some of which did not function as well as the machinery already on hand, but failed to augment the equipment used to produce acetin. Consequently, the production capacity of this vital constituent of smokeless powder was only half of the amount required for daily output of 200 pounds of powder. The remainder had to be purchased from abroad.[11]

The explanation for these conditions seems to lie, to a large degree, in the ineptitude of technological personnel both Chinese and foreign. This was particularly ironic in view of Chang's determined efforts dating back to the mid-1880s to promote scientific and technical education. By the end of the dynasty, no less than sixty-nine different institutions for vocational education had been established in Hupeh. The Technological Academy (Kung-i hsüeh-t'ang), established in 1898, was expressly for the purpose of training engineers and technicians for the arsenal and other industrial enterprises in Hupeh. Tragically, this institution, constrained by the biases of traditional society, the disdain of the socially elite for manual work, and the limited vision of its first several directors, was unable quickly to train the technological personnel required for smokeless powder production.[12] Consequently the Hupeh Arsenal had to look to foreign technicians to direct this sophisticated area of operations. The first powder engineer engaged took leave and never returned to his post, after which the foreign specialist on acids took over his duties in addition to his regular tasks. This individual, a Swiss Ph.D. who knew little or nothing of powder making, drew a salary of £130 a month, an astronomical figure by Chinese standards of that day. Though neither powder nor acid production was satisfactory, inexplicably he was retained at least until 1910, when imperial inspectors reported his lack of qualifications and charged that over the years he had drawn an enormous salary without producing any concrete results.[13]

Another view of the technological conditions in the Smokeless Powder Plant was given by Mr. L. Dupre, a well-qualified British chemist, who was hired in 1904 to direct the production of smokeless powder. Dupre remained only until 1906 when, subsequent to a determination by the Commission on Army Reorganization that the quality of the smokeless powder produced at Hupeh was unsatisfactory, he was discharged. Dupre's memorandum submitted to the British consular authorities at the time of his dismissal, though obviously an attempt to excuse his own failure to produce good powder, shows the extremely difficult conditions with which foreign technicians had to cope. He pointed to the lack of essential equipment, the inadequacy of machinery used to clean nitrocellulose, and the unsatisfactory quality of the saltpeter used to produce nitric acid, among other serious problems. He also complained of the director's favoritism toward certain poorly qualified Chinese chemists and hinted that the director was in collusion with Carlowitz and Company, which had supplied most of the equipment, in order to keep from Governor-general Chang the true state of affairs.[14] It was probably after Dupre's departure that the Swiss took charge of smokeless powder production and conditions deteriorated still further.

Chang began a changeover to employment of Japanese rather than German technicians beginning in 1906. But in 1910 the unqualified Swiss Ph.D. was still ensconced at the head of the powder and acid plants, a translator was serving as overseer of the powder plant, and a coppersmith supervised sulphuric and nitric acid production.[15]

The Hanyang Mauser rifle and the ammunition that it employed became the sole products of the Hupeh Arsenal following the cutback of 1906. Production of the German 7.9 mm. Mauser "Infantry Rifle Model 1888" had begun at Hupeh late in 1895 in a plant purchased from the Ludwig Loewe Company, which had taken over the Mauser Works. The machinery had been badly damaged in a fire of the previous year, and initial production amounted to only several rifles per day. Gradually, as the plant was completely restored and the artisans gained experience, output increased to fifty completed pieces each day.[16] This weapon, popularly known as the model 1888 Mauser, was actually patterned on the Austrian Mannlicher rather than the Mauser. The important difference between the two was in the bolt action that delivered the cartridge into the chamber. The model 1888 could not be used as a single shot weapon unless the magazine was empty, and its magazine could be reloaded only by inserting a clip of five cartridges. The insertion of the clip in the magazine greatly increased the incidence of jamming. In the true Mauser action, individual cartridges could be loaded in the chamber while there were cartridges in the magazine, and a partially filled magazine could be filled with individual cartridges without introducing a clip, giving greater flexibility and reliability in battlefield employment. In 1895, Chang favored a change to produce the Spanish Model 1893 Mauser, a rifle of slightly smaller caliber, which could be reloaded with individual cartridges whenever the magazine was partly depleted. But these hopes seem to have faded in late 1895 with his failure to gain access to funds for a general expansion of the arsenal.[17]

Chang kept the Hanyang rifle under close comparative scrutiny. In early 1897, at the behest of the imperial government, tests were held involving it and the Kiangnan Arsenal's 8.8 mm. magazine rifle to determine whether or not one would be suitable for adoption as a standard small arm. In the judgment of the foreign technicians from the Hupeh Arsenal who supervised the testing, the Hanyang Mauser closely conformed to the German model 1888 prototype and it was superior to the Kiangnan weapon in ten critical respects. However, the really crucial tests, comparing it with other foreign arms, were not made. Moreover, the foreign technicians misrepresented the model 1888 as a first-rate modern weapon surpassing the new Belgian Mauser. Actually, the Belgian Mauser model 1889 was the first with an improved mechanism that allowed for loading either individual cartridges or five rounds stripped from a clip into the magazine, a clear advance over the model of 1888.[18]

Chang did make international comparisons in the following year, 1898, while studying the matter of standardization of calibers. He favored a smaller caliber rifle for lightness, ease of handling, and economy. The imperial government failed to adopt a national standard caliber, however, and Chang lacked the financial resources necessary to purchase the new machinery needed to convert Hupeh's production to a smaller caliber. In comparative range and accuracy tests held in 1900 involving German, Kiangnan, and Hupeh rifles, the German weapons outperformed the Hanyang Mauser by a narrow margin. However, the latter clearly surpassed the 8.8 mm. Kiangnan magazine rifle. An edict directed that since the 7.9 mm. Mauser was the better rifle it should be produced by all arsenals; Kiangnan began changing over its production through economy-minded modifications of existing equipment. By 1901, the model 1888, 7.9 Mauser rifle was in production at both of China's modern ordnance plants.[19]

Though lacking the improved loading mechanism of late model Mausers, the model 1888 did conform to prevailing international specifications for small arms at the turn of the century. It was a 7.9 mm. caliber, bolt action, multiple loading weapon weighing nine pounds three ounces, with a muzzle velocity of more than 2,000 feet per second. Produced from German steel, the important parts stood up remarkably well under sustained firing tests.[20]

Chang continued to favor a change in rifle model, however. He discussed the need for an expansion of production facilities at Hupeh with the empress dowager during the winter of 1903-1904. Later in 1904, he gained imperial approval for a plan to use the consolidated tax on local opium from Hunan and Hupeh to support this undertaking, including a changeover to production of smaller caliber rifles. This plan became bogged down during the next year, however. The income realized from the consolidated opium tax, though substantial, fell far short of the figure of 800,000 taels that Chang had estimated would be required, and other income did not materialize.

Furthermore, much of what was received was consumed by the increased costs of current production to meet supply requirements in North China created by the Russo-Japanese War. Finally, the determination of a new standard small arm was taken over by the Commission on Army Reorganization. By October 1906, that body had not reached a decision. In the meantime, the Kiangnan Arsenal had converted again, this time to production of the model 1905, 6.5 mm. caliber Mauser. The possibility of a corresponding changeover at Hupeh, long delayed by financial shortages and diversion of resources, was finally ruled out by the financial collapse of 1906. China's two leading arsenals were once more producing different caliber small arms.[21]

The financial collapse also forced production cutbacks from fifty to thirty per day of the 7.9 mm. Hanyang Mausers. Output, nevertheless, reached a total of 121,972 weapons (an annual average of almost 9,000 rifles) by the end of 1909. In 1910, following the international trend toward the production of shorter small arms, Hupeh began producing 7.9 mm. carbines. During the first half of 1910, 8,266 carbines were completed. At the same time, the arsenal improved the rear sight and added a protective wooden cover to its regular Mauser rifle. By mid-1910, 5,896 of these improved Mausers had been completed. These weapons, with eighty-seven precision-made parts, could be turned out at the rate of thirty per day at a cost of about twenty-one taels per rifle for labor and materials.[22]

As in other areas of production, small arms manufacture was beset with problems. Though there was a need for replacement and augmentation of rifle machinery, the plant was adequate for the production of model 1888 Mausers at the rate of fifty weapons per day. Far more urgent were the problems of supply, personnel, and administration. The steel employed in rifle barrels, for example, was purchased from Germany at a cost of 1.37 taels per barrel, not including shipping charges, despite the fact that steel of comparable quality was available from the Kiangnan Arsenal in Shanghai at the lower cost of 1.2 taels per barrel. Poorly qualified personnel and confused administration undermined production efficiency. The new director named in 1910 had an employment background in the purchase of nitrates and sulphates but no experience with either ordnance or machinery. Below the director was a staff of more than six hundred, fifteen to twenty of whom held some kind of supervisory or clerical responsibility, often ill-defined. Though the operations of the rifle factory were cut back drastically after 1906, the size of the work force was undiminished. Some workers were not physically present in the plant and about one-quarter were underemployed. The lack of clearly defined management responsibilities and close supervision of the work force no doubt adversely influenced production: 20 to 30 percent of materials used in barrel and stock production were wasted. Quality control was seriously deficient: inadequate inspection procedures resulted in irregularities in as many as 50 percent of the rifles turned out.[23]

By 1910 the total output of small arms ammunition at Hupeh had reached almost 64 million rounds. Monthly production peaked at 800,000 rounds. Even after 1906 when financial restrictions forced cutbacks in production, monthly production was set at 600,000 rounds. Moreover Hupeh, unlike Kiangnan, never became involved in the costly enterprise of producing cartridges of various calibers. Virtually all of its output was 7.9 mm. Mauser ammunition. However, technological problems resulted in waste of about 40 percent of the work and materials employed in the production process: it was necessary to produce 1 million rounds to meet the production quota of 600,000 perfect cartridges. The cost per cartridge was correspondingly higher. The waste was due in part to shortages or operating deficiencies of vital equipment such as that for processing brass for cartridges. Though the rollers on this machinery were seriously marred, they were in regular use. Another serious problem was in smelting brass. Both the ratio of constituents and the process employed departed from standard practice with the result that the surface of the finished brass was irregular and the quality uneven. Even in cartridges that were passed for distribution, firing tests showed that about 2 percent were defective due, for the most part, to the poor quality of the brass. The irregularities in smokeless powder employed in the cartridges also resulted in wide variances in ballistic performance.[24]

Technological pitfalls such as those encountered in the refining and processing of brass stemmed from the inadequacy of technical supervision. Until 1910 the Small Arms Ammunition Plant had no officially designated director. Supervision of the work force of 381 was in the hands of a foreman and six bosses. There were also three managers whose duties were primarily clerical and three secretaries. The Brass Smelting Shop and the Cartridge Plant, which were used jointly with the Gun Ammunition Plant until that closed in 1906, employed staffs of twenty-one and sixty-three personnel, respectively, also under the direction of foremen or bosses. Each of the three plants enjoyed autonomy under its foremen and would not brook inquiry from without. When a director of the Small Arms Ammunition Plant was finally designated in 1910, he proved to be a man totally unfamiliar with industrial production.[25]

Production at the Hupeh Arsenal was carried on despite overwhelming technological, personnel, supply, and financial problems that eroded its strategic industrial power. Nowhere were these problems more graphically illustrated than in the arsenal's record of expenditures. The purchase of materials for production consumed 41 percent of all funds expended from 1895 through 1909, personnel costs and administration another 28 percent, and 13 percent was disbursed to other organizations in the forms of loans and advances, most of which were not repaid. In short, the cost of production consumed two-thirds of the arsenal's expenditures and the extraordinary lending function that it performed immobilized almost one-half of the remaining third. A modest 18 percent was left for capital improvements[26] (see Table 5.2).

The cost of operating a modern defense industry in a social and economic setting where technological modernization was just gaining a foothold was necessarily high. Chinese metallurgical technology, for example, simply had not progressed by 1906 to the point where domestic refineries could produce ordnance steel for artillery. Nor could complex industrial processes such as those required for the production of smokeless powder be introduced without close supervision by highly paid foreign technicians. But these expense factors were aggravated unnecessarily by management policies. Purchasing of foreign matériel was at best haphazard and possibly corrupt.[27] The prolonged reliance on costly foreign imports in the production of smokeless powder no doubt contributed to the high overall level of expenditures for matériel. This situation resulted primarily from the gross incompetence of the Swiss technician and the Chinese management personnel in the Smokeless Powder Plant. The latter, lacking any understanding of smokeless powder production themselves, not only retained the Swiss but also followed his advice unquestioningly with respect to purchasing and other matters.[28]

From this it can be seen that the problem of high matériel costs was aggravated by ill-advised management decisions. Undisciplined management was also responsible for the burgeoning personnel and administrative costs. Remarkably, official salaries increased sharply after the cutbacks of 1906 so that the percentage of the annual budget spent on personnel and administration was somewhat higher than it had been previously. Why was this so? Several factors contributed to personnel and administrative costs. First, the continuing need for

TABLE 5.2
Annual Expenditure of the Hupeh Arsenal, 1895-1909
Unit: ch'ang-p'ing taels; 1 tael=approximately $0.69

Year	Total	% for materials	% for personnel and admini-stration	% for loans and disburse-ments	% for capital investment
1895	456,878	6	19	18	57
1896	1,135,583	6	10	41	43
1897	703,378	14	24	20	42
1898	717,823	28	32	7	33
1899	984,460	35	30	10	25
1900	1,331,252	70	25	1	4
1901	1,093,358	44	32	11	13
1902	1,165,183	41	32	10	17
1903	1,975,788	44	26	17	13
1904	1,709,204	49	26	11	14
1905	1,538,408	49	28	14	9
1906	1,491,420	64	30	3	3
1907	893,579	38	43	--	19
1908	862,089	33	36	10	21
1909	1,214,545	38	29	17	16

Source: HPKC, "Shou-chih ke-k'uan ssu-chu ch'ing-tse": chih-k'uan hsiang-hsia."

foreign technical supervision in both ordnance and powder production throughout this period elevated costs. The extent of dependence on foreign advice seems to have declined, however, to the point where only two foreigners were employed in 1910. Moreover, the cost of foreign technicians was not a huge item of expense, varying from 10,000 to about 50,000 taels annually. The tragedy was that so much was a total waste given the notorious incompetence of some foreigners. From a quantitative standpoint, the salaries of Chinese officials and artisans were of far greater importance. Over the years, the work force in the arsenal, excluding the Smokeless Powder Plant, increased from 590 to 1,431 artisans and laborers despite the production cutbacks of 1906. In addition to the work force, there were more than one hundred official managers and clerical staff and eighty-three security personnel. The Smokeless Powder Plant employed another 287 in the work force and more than forty official managers and clerical staff. In 1910, imperial inspectors judged the personnel system to be lacking in organization, principle, and clear definition of responsibilities—the greatest source of waste in the arsenal. They attributed the growth in numbers of official personnel as late as 1910 to Director Wang Shou-chang's appointment of personal friends to newly created posts. The warehouse was grossly overstaffed and there was widespread duplication of supervisory responsibilities.[29] The uncontrolled increase in numbers of personnel even after the financial contractions of 1906 sapped the arsenal's meager resources to pay the salaries and wages of underemployed workers and managers and multiplied the indirect costs of administration.

The failure to clarify financial responsibilities at the highest levels of provincial administration resulted in confusion in the handling of arsenal appropriations. This, in turn, ultimately led to a series of loans and transfers of funds from which Hupeh emerged, in 1910, the loser. Since the arsenal itself did not have the authority for financial management, when funds were forwarded, they were received by the supervisory agencies: by the General Bureau for Military Industry in the province until 1908 and thereafter by the Military Industrial Office. Since there were no constraints on the arsenal to plan expenditures within the limits of projected income of these supervisory agencies, it sometimes happened that expenditures exceeded income with the result that there would be a shortage of funds. When this occurred the governor-general would intervene and transfer funds from other provincial agencies to meet shortages created by overspending at the arsenal. Similarly, the absence of budgetary controls on other provincial organs led to overspending, which sometimes left them short of funds. When this was the case, as it often was, the governor-general would make transfers from the arsenal's accounts to balance the financial interests of the various provincial bodies. The net effect of these transfers, by the end of 1909, left the arsenal with accounts receivable of between 1.8 million and 1.9 million taels for loans and advances to various provincially sponsored commercial enterprises, government bureaus, schools, and other provinces. Not only had no payment been made on these accounts, but no arrangements for repayment had been settled.[30]

The high cost of production and the unrepaid loans made by the arsenal diminished the portion of financial resources available for capital improvements and made impossible the replacement of model 1888, 7.9 mm. rifle machinery with equipment to produce a more recent model. The financial contractions of 1906 following the centralization of control over opium tax revenues made the financial strictures limiting capital improvement even more severe. After that time the only important acquisitions of new equipment were for the powder plant, and there the technological problems involved in production were grave and new machinery alone could not provide a solution.[31]

The distribution of arms and ammunition from the Hupeh Arsenal reflects the complex balance of national and local priorities that motivated Chang Chih-tung and his successors in Hupeh during the last years of the dynasty. On the one hand, the record of shipments from the arsenal points to Chang's earnest efforts to support Chinese forces wherever they might be engaged against foreign foes. For example, in early 1899, the arsenal shipped small arms and ammunition to Chekiang to bolster provincial forces there against an anticipated invasion by Italian troops at San Men Bay. But the entire quantity requested could not be sent since, as Chang explained, arsenal reserves had been depleted by shipments to the capital. Supply of imperial forces guarding the capital was assigned a high order of priority. During the Boxer uprising in the summer of 1900, Hupeh was directed by edict to supply ammunition to the imperial troops, some of whom were fighting alongside of the Boxers. Unable to produce the smokeless powder needed for magazine rifle cartridges at Hupeh, Chang bought smokeless powder from Kiangnan and packed cartridges at Hupeh. On August 10, as the allied expeditionary force pressed on Peking, he formulated detailed plans to ship cartridges to the imperial forces concealed in shipments of tribute grain. Though Chang did not support the Boxers, he reasoned that China's position at the peace table would be stronger if Peking were not occupied by foreigners. But the transport time was nine days and foreign troops entered Peking on August 14 as Chinese resistance collapsed. Nevertheless, Hupeh continued to supply units in north China during the summer and fall of 1900. Despite Chang's strong opposition, China was forced to accept a two-year ban on imports of munitions and war matériel in the Boxer Protocol signed in September 1901.[32]

The impact of the Boxer Rebellion was evident in 1901 when shipments of arms and ammunition from the arsenal came to a virtual standstill during the foreign occupation of north China. Large-scale distribution commenced again after the departure of foreign troops began in late 1901 and peaked in late 1903 and 1904 when the arsenal worked around the clock to supply units in north China as Russo-Japanese tensions mounted and fighting finally broke out in Manchuria. Chang's fears notwithstanding, the ban on the import of war matériel probably had very little effect in limiting the production of the Hupeh Arsenal. Practically from the beginning, the signatory powers were known to have had second thoughts about the ban since it made it more difficult for Chinese authorities to maintain order and ran counter to the powers' own trade interests. Therefore, import of strategic materials probably continued despite the ban. The high level of matériel costs at Hupeh from 1900 on through the ban period would support this view.[33]

Though the Hupeh Arsenal at Chang Chih-tung's bidding struggled to meet the needs of other provinces and especially the imperial government for arms and ammunition, Chang and his successors also did much to husband logistical power in Hunan and Hupeh. Small arms are perhaps the best case in point. Of the 130,726 rifles produced through 1910, 50 percent was retained in Hunan or Hupeh. Most of these, 29 percent of the total, never left the arsenal. Similarly, 50 percent of all small arms ammunition was distributed to units in Hunan and Hupeh; 34 percent was retained at the arsenal. Fifty-five percent of the artillery pieces and 86 percent of the gun ammunition were also kept in Hupeh and Hunan, most at the arsenal.[34]

Ironically, this enormous hoard of munitions that Chang and his successors accumulated over the years was employed against the dynasty that he had worked so tirelessly to support. On the very first day of the uprising at Wuhan, October 10, 1911, the arsenal guards under the command of General Li Yuan-hung surrendered the arsenal to the revolutionaries after only token resistance. The prize was reported to be forty-eight guns in the five to seven cm. caliber range and an unspecified number of smaller caliber field artillery pieces, 20,000 modern rifles, and more than 3 million cartridges, as well as large quantities of powder. When the counterattacking imperial forces temporarily regained control of the arsenal on December 9, they found that the revolutionaries had stripped the arsenal of everything, even the important machinery, before fleeing.[35]

Conclusions

The Hupeh Arsenal was one of the key institutions upon which the fate of the Ch'ing dynasty hung, the largest producer of small arms in an embattled empire where imperialism had staked its claims and rebellion smoldered just below the surface of society. It was, at the same time, a bulwark against the tide of political change and a chrysalis in which the technology of twentieth-century militarism was evolving. Technological and industrial accomplishments at Hupeh were considerable. While gradually freeing itself from dependence on all but a few foreign technical advisers, it developed a huge and diversified productive capacity. But, in 1911, it was a rifle and cartridge plant, nothing more, producing at only a fraction of its potential. Between Chang Chih-tung's dream of self-sufficient modern strategic industrial power and the reality of the Hupeh Arsenal in 1911 lay a gulf of unfulfilled plans and unrealized ambitions. The causal factors that defeated plans and frustrated ambitions are part of what makes the arsenal important to an understanding of this period of Chinese history. They answer that question asked so often by historians of the late Ch'ing period, "What went wrong?"

What did go wrong? The Hupeh Arsenal's operational deficiencies and unrealized potential were partially due to the supervision and conduct of operations and partially a consequence of the society and the international environment in which the arsenal functioned. Certainly the most important factor that deterred Hupeh from realizing its great production potential was the financial collapse of 1906. Reliance on the proceeds of opium taxes for a large portion of income must be regarded as unsound financial planning. In a modernizing situation, sooner or later this source of revenue would have to be eliminated. Still, in the search for capital to finance strategic industrialization, Chang had few places to turn: levies on foreign trade, private contributions, and the traditional tax revenues of the provinces that he controlled. The ports of Hunan and Hupeh handled only a small fraction of the foreign trade that passed through the coastal provinces. But opium, imperialism's most potent contribution to nineteenth-century China, was an important item in the agriculture and trade of Hunan and Hupeh.[36] Chang could not afford to overlook the income from opium taxes in his search for capital.

Technological problems also seriously affected operations, causing a high degree of waste. The inability to overcome technological problems that hampered production was primarily the result of the lack of qualified personnel—Chinese and foreign. Technological education in China had simply not kept pace with the needs of institutions like the Hupeh Arsenal. Still Hupeh did not retain a large staff of foreign technicians as some Chinese arsenals had in the 1870s and 1880s. With a few exceptions, the foreigners seem to have introduced the technology for which they were hired and then to have left. But one of the exceptions proved disastrous. The incompetent and highly paid Swiss technician in the powder works not only impeded the self-sufficient production of high-quality smokeless powder, but his salary resulted in incalculable waste of the arsenal's operating capital. Chinese technical personnel operating with little or no foreign supervision also exhibited a low level of competency. Waste due to faulty procedures in production was great. This situation would presumably improve as time passed and the work force gained experience, provided that, in the meantime, unskilled workers had not ruined good equipment; but time was running out. The waste due to imperfect technology was still high in 1911.

Another factor that limited the production of the Hupeh Arsenal and its capacity to strengthen China's defenses was its dependence on foreign supply. The need for processed materials, such as acids and ordnance steel, exceeded the existing supply capability of the domestic economy and required costly imports. The prolonged failure to develop domestic sources for these items kept supply costs high. Equally important, it forced China's leading small arms plant to look to industrialized Western nations such as Germany, the very imperialists against whom China was arming, for the materials needed to maintain production.

Matériel costs along with personnel and administrative expenses comprised the arsenal's operating costs; together they consumed two-thirds of all expenditures. A small portion of personnel expense went for salaries for foreign technicians, most of which was wasted. Costs for Chinese personnel were multiplied needlessly by favoritism, featherbedding, and overstaffing. The high costs for domestic personnel and administration probably stemmed from the fact that this arsenal was organizationally a branch of the Hupeh provincial government. The personnel administrative practices were those of a traditional Chinese government agency rather than the cost-effective administration required of a high-overhead modern industry. What were permissible levels of personnel efficiency in the traditional bureaus simply could not be tolerated at Hupeh. But the need for a thoroughgoing reform in this area was perceived too late.

The arsenal's extraordinary function as a lending agency also stemmed from its position in the government hierarchy. It was, in a sense, a conduit through which Chang channeled imperially sanctioned allocations for the arsenal, in the form of loans, to lower priority provincial organs and enterprises. Almost half of the one-third of operating capital remaining after operating costs were deducted was consumed by these loans, most of which were unrepaid. The total remaining for investment in plant and equipment was spent mostly during the early years. Though the scarcity of funds for new equipment affected every sector of the arsenal's operations, it was most critical in small arms production. There, the failure to purchase new equipment for a smaller caliber rifle with a more modern action meant that the Hanyang Mauser, though a serviceable weapon, was already obsolescent by 1911.

The imperial government in 1910 took the first steps toward initiating reforms at Hupeh when it launched an inquiry that identified the arsenal's most serious deficiencies, but the hour was already too late. The combined pressures of imperialism and rebellion had set a timetable for modernization that China's lumbering economy and its tradition-bound leadership were unable to meet. But the history of the Hupeh Arsenal is more than a partial autopsy of the imperial Ch'ing cadaver. The dream that Chang had for this arsenal and its imperfect realization were also a part of the early development of twentieth-century China, a linkage between the declining tradition of the nineteenth century and the developing modernity and the new problems of the twentieth. Perhaps the most striking example of this linkage is Chang himself, a paragon of traditional Confucian political virtues, irreversibly and uncompromisingly committed to modern strategic industrialization and the educational and economic changes that it entailed.[37] Credit for the arsenal's production achievements must go in large measure to this Confucian statesman whose tireless efforts brought it into being, securing its operating capital and the imperial sanction for its operations. But the tendency of Chang and Hupeh's other supervisors to retain most of the munitions produced in the provinces under their own control, at a time when a national commitment and the national strength were becoming ever more important to China's survival, underscores the essentially provincial nature of the arsenal. In the decades that followed, this tendency to assemble and maintain logistical power at the local level was widespread among provincial leaders who did not share Chang's Confucian loyalty to the center. It became the hallmark of provincial militarism.

Mao Tse-tung and Writing Reform

John DeFrancis

Chinese writing reform has run a tortuous course during the past few decades of active concern about the matter. The same characterization can be made of Mao Tse-tung's involvement in the reform and his influence on the course of events.

The first indication of Mao's interest in writing reform dates from early 1940, during a particularly difficult period in the anti-Japanese struggle. In January of that year, in the course of his discussion *On New Democracy,* Mao devoted several pages to a characterization of Chinese culture in the society of the transitional "New Democracy" that he envisaged as emerging from the joint rule of several anti-imperialist classes. He described the New Democratic culture as national, scientific, and popular in character. The popular character of the new culture required that it serve the people so that it would be possible to lead them in the fight against the enemy. "In order to achieve this aim," he said, "the script must be reformed under certain conditions, and the language must be close to the masses. It should be realized that the masses are the infinitely rich source of revolutionary culture."[1]

These remarks, which have been quoted over and over again by those interested in reform of the writing system, are a mixture of precise terminology and vague specifications. Mao contrasts *wénzì* ("script," "writing") with *yányǔ* ("language," "speech").[2] The former must be reformed, the latter must be close to the people. It is not clear, however, just how the script was to be reformed, or just what Mao had in mind by the phrase *zài yídìng tíaojìàn xià* ("under

Editor's note: The author, a leading scholar of Chinese linguistics, prefers the use of the Pinyin romanization system for the discussion of language problems in the People's Republic of China, where this system is employed. Consequently, this article alone in the present volume utilizes this system. Well-known personal and place names remain in the Wade-Giles or Postal Atlas systems, as applicable.

what conditions"), since he never explicitly spelled out the conditions. It is, perhaps, a commentary on the nature of society in China, and on the obtuseness of people who later had opportunities to speak with Mao, that no one appears to have had the temerity or the imagination to ask him to elaborate on his remarks and to specify just what conditions he had in mind.

It may be that some light is thrown on these matters by developments in the area of writing reform that occurred later in 1940. At that time, following a decade in which the "latinized New Writing" (or "Sin Wenz," i.e., Chinese written in Latin letters) created for the Chinese language in the Soviet Union had gradually penetrated into various areas of China, a call was issued for the establishment of a "New Writing Society in the Shensi-Kansu-Ninghsia Border Region." The ninety-nine original sponsors of this call were later joined by fifty-three other persons. Most of the top Communist leaders, including Mao Tse-tung, were among the signatories. Mao Tse-tung was also a member of the small honorary presidium that came into being with the establishment on November 7, 1940, of the Shen-Kan-Ning Sin Wenz Border Region Society.

The statement calling for the establishment of this organization stressed the following points:

> The great New Culture Movement of May 4th . . . was limited to an extremely small group of progressives, while the masses remained centuries behind. The reason for this is China's political and cultural backwardness, but the difficulty of the ideographic script is also one of the most important factors. . . . A Great Wall has been erected between the masses and the new culture. . . . This has facilitated the imperialist invasion of the Chinese nation. . . . We do not at all propose to effect an immediate substitution of the ideographic script by the New Writing, nor to call a halt toward continued modification of the latter. . . . What we want to do now is to use Sin Wenz to teach illiterates, so that they will be able in a short time to use it to study politics and science and also the ideographs. But the New Writing must be studied until it can be read and written and only then will it be possible to go beyond it to the study of the ideographs.

Apart from the denunciation of Chinese characters as impediments to mass culture, a theme popular at the time, what is most noteworthy in the foregoing citation is the emphasis on achieving mastery of the "New Writing" before going on to learn characters, which were envisaged as remaining for some time while undergoing continued modification. This emphasis on the use of latinized writing as an entity in itself, that is, not merely as an adjunct of characters or as a tool for learning characters, was reinforced at the time by the announcement that the border region government had given legal standing to the New Writing by legislating for it equal validity with the traditional script in reports, petitions, accounts, correspondence, and other documents, and that henceforth the most important of the laws and public announcements of the government were to be published in both the New Writing and the old characters.[3] A few months later Mao Tse-tung personally endorsed the New Writing movement in the first printed edition of *Sin Wenz Bao* [New Writing Journal], which came out on May 15, 1941.[4]

Apart from signing statements endorsing the New Writing there is no evidence that Mao Tse-tung played an active role in activities related to the promotion of the new script. Nor is there any clear indication as to the extent to which he understood, much less supported, the full implications of these developments, which if actually pushed along the lines indicated would have had such portentious effects on the future of the Chinese writing system. It may be that Mao's actions represented merely the offhand acquiescence of an important figure whose support was solicited by individuals more actively involved in writing reform and more intent on carrying it through to a radical conclusion: that of soon, or at least in the not-too-distant future, replacing the ideographic script with a latinized or romanized writing. Or perhaps Mao supported only part of the reform, without clearly indicating where he stood on each of the main issues involved. Or again it may be that he subsequently abandoned his earlier support for a radical change and adopted a more moderate approach to the form and timing of changes in the script.

In any case, the emphasis on romanized writing was abandoned in the years immediately preceding and following the establishment of the Chinese People's Republic in 1949. This development was considerably influenced by some remarks made by Mao Tse-tung in 1950 and 1951.

Mao's views, which were expressed to various persons on different occasions, were first reported in speeches made on February 5, 1952, before the inaugural session of the Committee for Research on Chinese Writing Reform and were published the following July in the inaugural issue of the new journal *Wenzi Gaige* [Writing Reform]. Most important was the report made by Ma Hsu-lun, the minister of education and chairman of this newly established official committee, who stated:

Because writing reform is a major matter in the cultural development of our country, last year we asked Chairman Mao for instructions, and the Chairman did give us instructions, requesting that we investigate this matter. Three or four months ago, the Chairman also instructed us: the writing system must be reformed, it should take the phonetic direction common to the languages of the world; it should be national in form, the alphabet and system should be elaborated on the basis of the existing Chinese characters.[5]

The passage containing Mao's views, which is presented above with the same punctuation as in the original Chinese, actually consisted of four sentences that show an interesting progression from the quite general to the increasingly specific:

1. "The writing system must be reformed." This sentence is a paraphrase of the first comment on reforming the script made by Mao in *On New Democracy* and is equally general and vague. The phraseology could encompass anything from a slight modification in the form of Chinese characters to their complete abandonment in favor of some other system of writing.

2. "It should take the phonetic direction common to the languages of the world." This appears to rule out that Mao intended only a slight change in the traditional ideographic script. The use of the phrase *pīnyīn fāng-xiàng* ("phonetic direction") can only be interpreted as a call for the adoption of a writing system based on the phonetic principle underlying the written form of all the languages of the world except those that continue to employ Chinese characters, namely Chinese itself, Japanese, and Korean (in South Korea only, however).

3. "It should be national in form." More literally, this may be rendered as "The form should be a national one." This appears to be a call for creating a phonetic script that would be distinctively Chinese, just as the *kana* syllabaries, which are based on Chinese characters, are distinctively Japanese, and the Hangul phonemic script, which is not based on Chinese characters, is distinctively Korean.

4. "The alphabet and system should be elaborated on the basis of the existing Chinese characters." This apparently makes more specific the national form that the new writing should adopt. The *zìmŭ* ("alphabet") presumably cannot, like the Korean, be national in form but not based on Chinese characters. Instead, it would seem that something like the old Zhùyīn Zìmŭ ("Phonetic Alphabet"), which had been elaborated on the basis of the traditional Chinese characters, was closer to what Mao had in mind. Less clear, however, is his intent in including in what was to be elaborated on the basis of

the existing Chinese characters not only the *zìmŭ* ("alphabet") but also the *fāng'àn*. This term, which has been variously rendered as "scheme" or "plan," is perhaps here better interpreted as "system," since it apparently applies to the alphabet taken as a whole, that is, as a system of orthography.

Immediately after the passage cited above, Ma Hsu-lun went on with his report as follows:

> In accordance with the Chairman's instructions we have established this Committee in order to carry on research. Next, taking into consideration the difficulty of written Chinese, the Chairman instructed that it must be put in order and simplified, and he also instructed that the printed form should make use of *kăi shū* ["standard style"] and the handwritten form may make use of *căo shū* ["cursive style"]. In addition, because the pronunciation of Chinese characters is hard to remember, it is necessary to note the pronunciation. Right now the People's Liberation Army is expanding the use of the Phonetic Alphabet as a help in literacy study. If the Phonetic Alphabet is to function as the prevailing system for the notation of pronunciation, whether there are places where it can be improved also needs our discussion and investigation.
>
> Now that our Committee has been established, it is necessary to assume such a revolutionary political task. As to how to proceed, I invite everyone to discuss this.[6]

One of the persons who took up the discussion of writing reform was Wu Yü-chang, who had participated in the creation of latinized New Writing, was an ardent promoter of the system in the 1930s and 1940s, and held the position of vice-chairman of the Committee for Research on Chinese Writing Reform. At the inaugural meeting of this committee he said:

> In June of the year before last [i.e., in June 1950] Chairman Mao spoke with me. He advocated that the simplification of Chinese characters be promoted first, and that carrying out script reform should not be divorced from reality. I felt then that Chairman Mao's directive was quite correct. In accordance with Chairman Mao's instructions, the letters used in alphabetic writing should also adopt a national form. Now the Phonetic Alphabet has already shown its utility, and research can progress based on it. We must do away with the idea that it is necessary to use the Latin or Cyrillic alphabet. The letters we use should be relatively close to Chinese characters and capable of accurately representing the sound-elements of Chinese.[7]

Kuo Mo-jo, like Wu Yü-chang an early and ardent supporter of latinized writing, also presented Mao's views at the inaugural meeting. He said: "Chairman Mao has instructed that we should prepare to take the phonetic road, and that the alphabet should adopt a national form."[8]

In their reporting of Mao Tse-tung's views, all three speakers brought out two points: first, that the Chinese writing system should adopt the principle of phonetic representation, and second, that the alphabet chosen should be national in form. Wu Yü-chang added a third important point, namely that in the work of writing reform priority should be given to simplification of characters. While the first point was in accord with the hopes and expectations of those reformers, especially the exponents of latinized New Writing, who had confidently anticipated support of their aims from the new government, the last two of Mao's instructions were bombshells that completely disconcerted the reformers and sent them scurrying along completely new paths.

Particularly upsetting was Mao's directive that priority be given to simplification of characters. This meant that the previous stand adopted by supporters of phonetic writing, namely that the characters constituted a barrier to literacy for the mass of the people, had to be abandoned. In their earlier arguments against characters the reformers had stressed the difficulty of the traditional script for most people. Some implied, and others directly stated, that the characters were a tool in the hands of the ruling class.

The argument that the characters had a class nature received a devastating blow with the publication of Stalin's *Marxism and Linguistics,* a work that came out in Chinese only a month after its publication in Russian in June 1950. In this work Stalin refuted the thesis advanced by N. Y. Marr, long a dominant figure in Soviet lingusitics, that language is part of the superstructure erected on the basis of the economic structure of society at a given stage of development, and that linguistic change follows a change in the economic basis when a new class takes over. On the contrary, said Stalin, language serves society as a whole, is not part of the superstructure, and remains basically the same despite revolutionary changes in society.[9]

In his remarks at the inaugural meeting of the Committee for Research on Chinese Writing, Wu Yü-chang said that in a spirit of self-criticism he acknowledged his previous errors in thinking that writing was part of the superstructure, and that it had a class nature, errors he perceived as such only after reading Stalin's treatise.[10] In referring specifically to writing, it should be noted, Wu Yü-chang significantly extended Stalin's pronouncements about language into an area that strictly speaking was not within the sphere of Stalin's discussion. Linguists have long attempted, without much success, to get across the idea that language (speech) and writing (symbols on paper) are by no means identical and indeed may differ very widely, as is particularly true in the case of Chinese. It might have been fruitful for the reformers to explore whether Chinese writing, as distinct from Chinese speech, could indeed be characterized as having something of a class bias because it conformed to Stalin's criterion of "serving one class to the detriment of others." This argument was not advanced, however, and the reformers permitted themselves to be routed by the use of Stalin's pronouncement that language equally served all classes of society. With varying degrees of enthusiasm, the reformers expressed their support for giving priority to simplification of characters.

There was less unanimity regarding how to apply the interpretation of the phrase "national in form" to the phonetic script that was to be adopted. A strong impetus was given to the already existing Phonetic Alphabet because the symbols so obviously resembled Chinese characters. Both Ma Hsu-lun and Wu Yü-chang in their reports had indicated approval of the system in terms that left it unclear as to whether they were speaking only for themselves or were reflecting the views of Mao Tse-tung. In any event, much attention was devoted to the possibility of adopting the Phonetic Alphabet either in its original form or after some modification.

There were others, however, who developed new alphabets that could be considered national in form. Some were related to the traditional Chinese characters. Others were distinctively different and unrelated either to the characters or to Western alphabets. The Committee for Research on Chinese Writing Reform, which had among its responsibilities that of reviewing various proposed schemes of phonetic writing and developing a new one, elaborated a preliminary draft of a new Chinese phonetic alphabet and submitted it to Mao Tse-tung for his consideration in 1953. Ma Hsu-lun reported that Chairman Mao found the new scheme "still insufficiently simple and convenient" and returned it for "further study."[11]

The phonetic alphabet devised by the committee was not displayed to the public. Just what it looked like is therefore unknown. It was apparently related to the traditional Chinese characters, however, as appears from the following abstract of committee discussions that apparently represents a paraphrase of Mao's comments:

Chairman Mao is of the opinion that although the phonetic alphabet devised last year is simple in its method of phonetic spelling, its strokes are still too complex, some being more difficult to write than the Phonetic Alphabet [Zhùyīn Zìmǔ]. . . . A phonetic script does not need to be made in a complicated block form, such a shape being inconvenient for writing and especially for linking. It is precisely because the direction of strokes in Chinese characters is haphazard that there appeared the cursive writing that aimed at breaking the square form. A phonetic script should in any case be simple; it should make use of the existing simple strokes and cursive script of the Chinese characters; the force of the strokes should basically, to the fullest extent possible, tend in one direction ["lean to one side"], and should not be complicated. People's opinions on the project should be widely solicited; it must be made really simple and easy, and only then can it be carried out.[12]

In the same year in which Mao expressed the foregoing views, he is reported by Li Chin-hsi, a prominent reformer who had helped to create the Guoyeu Romatzyh ("National Language Romanization") in the 1920s, to have made some additional comments on phonetic writing. Li reported:

In 1953 Chairman Mao issued the following directive: the phonetic script should be compatible with Chinese characters. It cannot be supposed that on a certain day after being promulgated it will immediately be put into effect. It is necessary to prepare for it to be *used jointly* for a period of time. [Emphasis added by the person who quoted from the recorded statement.] . . .

In 1953, at the time when the Committee for Chinese Writing Reform met, in response to a request for instructions, Chairman Mao said: I approve changing over to the use of Double Spelling in order to replace Chinese characters. [Because of the fact that, in the various language families of the world that use a phonetic system, a "syllable" or a word generally consists of "phonemic" letters spelled in the flowing water form (i.e., linked sequentially), length is disregarded. China's Phonetic Alphabet was already limited to Triple Spelling for each syllable. At this committee meeting some people proposed: go a step further and change to the use of Double Spelling. Chairman Mao indicated "Approved."][13]

The references to "Triple Spelling" and "Double Spelling" have to do with only one of the many problems raised by Mao's intervention in the work of reforming the Chinese writing system. The abstract of the committee discussions notes that after Mao's views were reported, they received the unanimous approval of the members, who also felt that the course of action laid out for them was quite clear. In point of fact, as the subsequent discussions amply revealed, his directives were far from clear, and when they were clear, it was difficult to reach agreement on how to carry them out.

The triple versus double spelling problem, as elaborated by Li Chin-hsi, was one of the more bizarre manifestations of the tortuous efforts to carry out Mao's wishes. The problem had to do, among other things, with the question of how many phonetic symbols should be used to write a Chinese syllable. Phonemic scripts, such as the old latinized writing of the 1930s and 1940s, may require as many as six letters to represent four phonemes in a syllable (exclusive of tones), as in the syllable *zhuang*. The Phonetic Alphabet required a maximum of three symbols, as in ㄓㄨㄤ for *zhuang*. Li proposed reducing the number to two. He defended this on the grounds that it conformed to Mao's "national in form" criterion since it followed the precedent of the ancient Chinese *fǎnqiè* system, in which the pronunciation of one character is indicated by the use of two other characters, the initial of the first being combined with the final of the second.

This idea that Mao's request for phonetic symbols "national in form" might be satisfied by other considerations than the shape of the symbols themselves took a variety of forms, including the notion that any system, even one based on the Latin alphabet, was national in form by the simple fact that it represented the Chinese language. Such interpretations existed among reformers from the very beginning of Mao's pronouncements on the subject and grew in strength as it became increasingly clear that all his specifications, particularly the one that "the alphabet and system should be elaborated on the basis of the existing Chinese characters," could not be met. One of the chief problems, apparently, was that of linking the symbols in a continuous fashion, as is done in handwritten English, Russian, and other alphabetic systems. The failure to solve this problem on the basis of the Phonetic Alphabet and other schemes based on Chinese characters led increasingly to disillusionment about the possibility of ever achieving success along these lines. In March 1954, when the vice-chairman of the Committee for Research on Chinese Writing Reform summarized the program of his committee, he omitted any mention of the "national in form" idea.[14]

Two years later, in February 1956, the committee finally came up with a draft phonetic scheme based on the Latin alphabet. After extensive consideration a revised scheme was promulgated by the National People's Congress in February 1958. Officially known as

Hànyǔ Pīnyīn Fāng'àn ("Chinese Phonetic Scheme"), it is generally referred to simply as Pinyin.

The most authoritative statement on the changeover to the Latin alphabet was made by Premier Chou En-lai in a report delivered on January 10, 1958. Chou stated:

> As to adopting Latin letters for the Chinese Phonetic Scheme, might this be in contravention to the patriotic sentiments of our people? Why were we not able to create a set of our own letters or simply to continue using the Phonetic Alphabet? Beginning in 1952, the Committee on Chinese Writing Reform devoted almost three years to the task of creating our own alphabet (including revising the Phonetic Alphabet), but without being able to achieve satisfactory results, and only then was the decision finally reached to abandon it and to adopt the Latin alphabet.[15]

What was Mao's attitude toward this manifest failure to carry out his wish for a phonetic writing that was national in form? It does not appear that he ever made any public pronouncement on this matter. There does exist, however, a clandestine record of remarks made by him on this subject in the course of a speech delivered on January 24, 1956, before the Central Committee of the Chinese Communist Party on the problem of the intellectuals. It is a remarkable statement that is worth quoting in full:

> Comrade XXX's speech was well done. I approve of all his views regarding writing reform. Do you approve or not? There is no great problem as regards the masses. Literacy will be very easy. But there are some people who feel that while it is fine and dandy to use Roman letters for spelling sounds, it is a pity that Roman letters were not invented by the Chinese. If the Chinese invent something and foreigners adopt it, since this is "using China to change barbarians," there is no problem. But if foreigners invent something and the Chinese adopt it, since this is "using barbarians to change China," then there is a problem. Comrade XXX is correct in saying that foreign letters are better. The letters are few, and when written lean to one side. Chinese characters cannot compete with them. Some professors say: "Chinese characters are the best writing system in all the countries of the world." I think that is not necessarily so. Therefore we choose Roman letters. For example, Arabic letters [sic! should be numerals] were also invented by foreigners, but doesn't everyone use them now? Roman letters made their appearance in Rome, but aren't such countries as England, America, and Russia [sic!] all using them? I have not studied the history of writing. In the past they also all had

their own writing. It is said that our Chinese characters were created by Cang Jie, but I think that is not necessarily so. Socialism did not emerge from Russia, yet Russia also learned from it. We should take over everything good from abroad and transform them into our things in order in one or two decades to catch up with the advanced international level. It was precisely so in the Han and T'ang dynasties. During the T'ang dynasty there were seven kinds of musical performances and dances, of which six came from abroad. They were well known in the T'ang dynasty and after being performed for a long time were converted into something Chinese.[16]

These informal remarks indicate that Mao acquiesced in the failure to meet his demand for a script "elaborated on the basis of the existing Chinese characters." It is also worth noting that, in addition to expressing his own approval of a script based on Latin letters, Mao felt that "there is no great problem as regards the masses." One important source of opposition is suggested by Mao's critical reference to "some professors." That the chief source of opposition did indeed come from the intellectuals is confirmed by a comment made by Chou En-lai in the course of a talk with a former French Minister of Education in the early 1970s. Chou said:

In the 1950s, we tried to Romanize the writing. But all those who had received an education, and whose services we absolutely needed to expand education, were firmly attached to the ideograms. They were already so numerous, and we had already so many things to upset, that we have had to put off the reform until later.[17]

In short, it would seem that while the masses and some intellectuals, particularly the left-wing intellectuals who had expressed themselves in favor of latinized writing in the 1930s, 1940s, and early 1950s, could be counted upon to accept the reform, it could not be carried out because of the opposition of the main body of those who had already received an education.

In accepting a script based on Latin letters, Mao Tse-tung was returning to a position similar in some respects to that of the 1940s when he came out in support of the latinized New Writing. This reversal does not, however, appear to include support for the earlier position of reformers who had succeeded in obtaining for latinized writing a standing of equal validity with the traditional script. That is to say, in contrast to the earlier outpouring of all sorts of publications wholly in latinized writing, the new Pinyin system adopted in 1958 has been used chiefly for annotation of Chinese characters, occasionally in publications containing passages in characters and equivalent passages in Pinyin, but hardly ever (only in a handful of children's booklets, so far as I know) in publications completely devoid of characters.

Such a restricted use of Pinyin may have been influenced by Mao Tse-tung's directive reported by Wu Yü-chang to give priority to simplification of characters. Apart from requesting priority in this area of reform, Mao provided further guidance as to how such simplification should be carried out. His instructions were given in response to a proposal for the simplification of seven hundred characters.

Ma Hsu-lun reported that Mao had rejected the proposed simplifications at the same time as he rejected the proposed phonetic alphabet, remarking that both were "still insufficiently simple and convenient" and should be subjected to "further study."[18] Further details of Mao's strictures were provided in the abstract of the committee discussions in the following paraphrase of his remarks:

> The 700 simplified characters that have been proposed are still not simple enough. In creating simplified characters it is necessary to make greater use of the cursive form, to seek out rules of simplification, to create basic forms, and, conforming to these rules, to proceed with simplification. The number of Chinese characters must be greatly reduced. Simplification can only be considered such if there is simultaneous simplification in form and number.[19]

The work on simplification of characters, which actually began immediately after the establishment of the new government in 1949 and went through several stages of official and public discussion,[20] culminated in an official list of simplified characters that first came out in 1964 and was reissued with a few relatively minor modifications in 1974.[21] This latter edition contains 2,258 simplified characters that have replaced 2,295 original characters. As these figures show, the simplification involved in these lists was chiefly a matter of reduction in number of strokes, that is simplification in form, in the case especially of many recurring partials such as the radicals (e.g., 訁 was reduced to 讠).

The second aspect of simplification, namely reduction in number of characters, has been effected chiefly through the publication in 1955 of a list of some 1,050 variant characters that were to be eliminated.[22] The problem of determining just how much reduction has been made in number of characters is in fact more complicated than it seems on the surface. Part of the difficulty stems from the existence of variant forms and hence from the problem of obtaining a precise and unambiguous list of original characters that can be used as a starting point to determine how many have been eliminated. For example, if 為 and 爲 are counted as two characters, the adoption of the simplified form 为 can be conceived as having effected a reduction of one character, whereas if they are counted as one there is no reduction in number since there is simply a one-to-one replacement.

The elimination of variants, while certainly helpful, is not nearly so significant as the reduction in number of nonvariants. The distinction is an important one that is too often overlooked. In her careful study of the problem, Chang Su-chen has concluded that of the 10,000 characters in the Chinese Telegraphic Code, there has been a reduction of only about 7 percent: 4 percent representing mere variants and only 3 percent being nonvariants. The author pointedly concludes that Mao Tse-tung's request that the number of characters be greatly reduced does not seem to have borne much fruit.[23]

One of the reasons for the failure to progress far in the direction demanded by Mao Tse-tung is his own injunction that "in creating simplified characters it is necessary to make greater use of the cursive form."[24] However, although the use of this form can be maximally helpful in effecting a reduction in the number of strokes in a character, it is of no use in, and indeed is a brake on, reducing the number of characters.

The overall simplification of characters is based on the application of three principles—the phonetic, the semantic, and the graphic—with the use of cursive forms being one aspect of graphic simplification. Of the three principles, only the phonetic principle is of any real service in effecting a reduction in number of characters. This can be done in part by seeing to it that in a character made up of a radical plus a phonetic, the latter is regularized so that all characters with identical or similar pronunciation are formed with only one or at most a few different phonetic elements having this pronunciation, as in the example of the simple phonetic *yi* 乙 used in *yì* 亿 for 億 ("hundred million") and in *yì* 艺 for 藝 ("skill," "art"). It can be done even more effectively by completely replacing a complicated character by a full or partial homonym of similar or even unrelated meaning, as in the use of *dŏu* 斗 ("peck") for *dòu* 鬪 ("to fight"). In this case 斗 has acquired the new pronunciation *dòu* in addition to the old pronunciation *dŏu*.

Indeed, if the phonetic principle were used to the fullest, it would be possible to eliminate all but about 1,350 characters (one for each distinct syllable of sound, counting tones), or even 400 (one for each syllable regardless of tones—this latter, though hardly desirable, being merely the application to characters of the same misuse of Pinyin as occurs when it is written without tones, as happens very often in the People's Republic of China).

In a study made by Sally M. Ng, it was discovered that of the approximately 2,300 characters included in official lists of simplified characters, only some 10 or 11 percent have been simplified on the basis of the phonetic principle.[25] About 7 percent represent merely a reduction in number of strokes, and the remaining 3 or 4 percent represent a reduction in number of characters by the adoption of full or partial homonyms. It is thus apparent, as Ms. Ng justly concludes, that the phonetic principle has played a distinctively minor role in character simplification. It is also apparent that it has played an even less important role in the area where it could actually be most effective, that of reduction in number of characters.

While Mao Tse-tung's interventions in the areas of character simplification and phonetic writing have received a mixed reception and have had quite uneven results, there is one area where he appears to have had great success. This is the area, more properly belonging to language planning than to script reform, of promotion of a standard language.

During the earlier period when the old latinized writing was being actively promoted, the position adopted by its most active supporters was that the new script should be used to create separate dialect romanizations (e.g., for Cantonese, Hakka, and so on) for local use as well as to create one for the standard language for use on a national basis. This position was officially abandoned after 1949 in favor of one calling for the application of a phonetic script only to what has come to be called Pǔtōnghuà. Hence the Pinyin system is used only to write this "Common Speech."

While Mao Tse-tung is not reported as having made any pronouncement on this extremely sensitive issue of dialect versus standard romanization,[26] the supporters of the former position, who had felt that their approach would prevail after 1949, were set back by the official support given to Stalin's views as expressed in his remark concerning "the necessity of a *single* national language, as the highest form to which dialects, as lower forms, are subordinate."[27] Stalin's comments, which dealt chiefly with a situation in Russia that, from a linguistic point of view, differed significantly from that in China, were used in what was essentially a political attack on supporters of dialect romanization as subverters of national unity.[28]

Given this background, Mao Tse-tung's directive issued in 1958 that "all cadres should learn Pǔtōnghuà"[29] acquired a special significance. It has been frequently quoted in support of the nationwide effort to promote Common Speech and has lent weight to the emphasis on the ascendancy of this standard over the dialects.

In a situation in which dissent runs the risk of political reprisal, it is difficult to gauge the extent to which former supporters of dialect romanization have actually been won over to the official position that romanized writing should be applied only to Common Speech (apart from its use in non-Chinese languages, of course) and that education from the earliest grades on should be conducted in this standard language.[30] In any case, given the absence of expressed opposition, most observers have concluded that this approach has been accepted by the population at large, even by those in dialect areas.[31]

Promotion of Common Speech to the point where it is spoken by all Chinese, including those in dialect areas, is commonly advanced as a prerequisite for the ultimate transition to a romanized system of writing. This seems to be the chief condition that would accord with Mao's early pronouncement that "the script must be reformed under certain conditions." No date is given for the achievement of the requisite conditions.

Reformers interested in accelerating progress toward the destined goal frequently pepper their exhortations with quotations from Chairman Mao. If Mao is cited as an advocate of reform, his opponents are blamed for failure to proceed more rapidly. They are presented as inveterate opponents of reform in all three of its main aspects that have been supported by Mao Tse-tung, namely simplification of characters, adoption of a phonetic script, and promotion of Common Speech. The following is a typical example of changes that have been circulated widely since the resumption of extensive discussion of writing reform in 1973.

> Since Liberation, the Liu Shao-ch'i–Lin Piao gang of swindlers has opposed writing reform. They viciously attacked the simplification of characters by saying it "will turn out very badly in the future," slandered the adoption of Latin letters in the Chinese Pinyin scheme as "slave mentality," and prated that "It won't cause anyone's death if Common Speech is not promoted for a hundred years."[32]

No details are provided to back up these allegations. The discussion of the complex issues underlying all aspects of language reform rarely goes beyond the polemical level of quoting a few phrases from Mao in support of a particular stand and attributing to those currently in disfavor a few phrases in opposition to the currently accepted position. The manner in which the quotations are handled is itself frequently suspect. For example, in recent discussions of writing reform Mao Tse-tung is quoted ad infinitum as having said: "The writing system must be reformed. It should take the phonetic direction common to the languages of the world." The rest of this statement, that is the added restriction that the phonetic notation should be national in form and should be based on Chinese characters, has apparently not been cited since Pinyin was officially adopted at the beginning of 1958.[33]

If the selective and incomplete quoting of Mao Tse-tung's views makes it difficult to reconstruct the evolution of his thinking, his influence on writing reform is even more difficult to gauge. It is apparent that the actual course of events in this area has by no means coincided with what is known of his pronouncements and interventions in the area of writing reform. But it is also apparent that much has been going on in this area behind the scenes. The failure to publicize Mao's Party speech in support of Pinyin is one clear example of this. Indeed, it would seem that the major decisions regarding writing reform have been made essentially on the basis of discussions within the confines of the government and the Party and beyond the purview of the public at large.

One of the most striking examples of the fact that what is displayed to the public is only the tip of the iceberg is a curious episode that happened in 1975. On May 31 of that year Peking radio broadcast the following announcement:

> The State Council of the P.R.C. has authorized the NCNA to issue the following public notice: from September 1, 1975, the Chinese phonetic alphabet will be used as the single standard for the spelling in Roman script of all Chinese personal and geographical names. This will apply to all foreign-language documents, passports, certificates, and publications written or printed in Roman script in China. The Chinese phonetic alphabet will also be used for other Chinese phrases that need to be transliterated into Roman script. Foreign-language documents, passports, certificates, and publications written or printed in the old system of transliteration prior to September 1, 1975, may continue to be used after that date.[34]

September 1 came and went, but the projected change from a sort of debased Wade-Giles romanization to Pinyin did not take place. On September 6 the Reuters news agency, on the basis of pronounce-ments by "a Foreign Ministry spokesman," reported from Peking that "China has postponed the introduction of a new system of transliterating Chinese characters into the Western alphabet." Although no reason was given for the postponement of the change announced in May, the news dispatch further quoted Chinese officials as saying that "the announcement could have been a mistake, or premature."[35] It would appear from this curious phraseology that there was disagreement not only on whether or not to make the proposed change but even on what reason to advance for the repudiation of the earlier announcement.

One interpretation that has been advanced for this episode is that the dissemination of the May announcement not by the Writing Reform Committee but by Peking radio and the official news agency, organs controlled by Mao's wife and the group subsequently denounced as the "Gang of Four," suggests that this was not a decision reached by those duly constituted to deal with such matters but represented rather a maneuver aimed at bypassing regular channels by a group that could not otherwise achieve its aims in extending the use of Pinyin.[36] On the other hand, a German student, in a letter written early in 1977 from Shanghai, reports what was apparently the view then current in China that "the stagnation in the development of language reforms may also be the result of the 'bad influences' of the Four."[37]

The latter interpretation is consonant with the fact that during the Cultural Revolution elements generally regarded as akin to the "Gang of Four" were the most violent opponents of Pinyin, being responsible for such actions as removal of Pinyin from street signs and the mastheads of newspapers at that time.[38] Moreover, after the downfall of the "Gang of Four," hitherto unreported interventions by Mao in the area of writing reform were attributed to him in publications the control of which had presumably been taken from the "Gang." The *Guangming Daily* for December 31, 1976, specifically charged the "Gang of Four" with sabotaging Mao's directives on writing reform. It further reported that in 1960, Mao Tse-tung, on seeing an army recruit studying a *Chinese Pinyin Textbook*, smiled and said: "This Pinyin writing is very good. Study it diligently." The same publication reported on January 28, 1977, that Mao had personally opted for resumption of its semimonthly page on writing reform,[39] though, it should be noted, the contents of this page were largely limited to discussions of character simplification and dealt hardly at all with the issue of Pinyin.

These murky glimpses into behind-the-scenes conflict over issues involved in writing reform, a conflict so intense as to explain the slow progress attained to date, suggest that extreme caution should be used in evaluating developments in this area on the basis of what is obviously only fragmentary evidence. It is particularly apparent that the simplistic invoking of a few quotations from Chairman Mao does not do justice to the complexities of his role and its impact on the course of events. This especially must be borne in mind now that Mao's death has removed any possibility of clarification from him on his intention with respect to Chinese writing reform.

Part 3
Education and Political Change

7

Military Academies in China, 1885-1915

Anita M. O'Brien

Toward the end of the nineteenth century the Ch'ing dynasty faced many threats to its security but had no competent army with which to respond. Soldiers were held in poor esteem by the populace and there seemed scant hope of strengthening the national defense force. Officers were chosen by an antiquated examination system, modelled after the civil service examinations, which rewarded physical strength and nonmilitary talents. This system was not revamped significantly until two provincial officials—Li Hung-chang and Chang Chih-tung—became convinced that China's army could be improved only through the development of an educated corps of officers. Li's military academy, established in Tientsin in 1885, and Chang's academy, opened in Canton in 1887, were the first phase of a modern approach to military education in China, which would come to fruition in the first decade of the twentieth century and shape China's military leadership in decades thereafter.

Military Schools before 1901

Until 1901, candidates for posts in the Ch'ing armies had to pass physical tests in mounted and dismounted archery, swordsmanship, bow-pulling, and stone-lifting, as well as written tests of their ability to reproduce from memory one hundred or more words from a military classic. There was little precedent for government-sponsored schools not based on these traditional examinations. Thus, when Li proposed the establishment of a military academy in 1885, he was truly breaking new ground. A key element of Li's philosophy was to make the military career respectable. Therefore, he called for the establishment of a separate school based on Western techniques to train young men from "good families."[1] The Wu-pei hsüeh-t'ang, or "Old Prep" as Li's academy came to be called in the military world,

157

was the initial step in a long process.[2] The first class of over a hundred men enrolled for a two-year course in such subjects as astronomy, geography, science, draftsmanship, arithmetic, and military studies —mainly German-style drills, taught by German instructors through interpreters.[3] Target practice and maneuvers were held monthly at military posts in the vicinity of the school. In 1887, a five-year course was added and forty youths aged twelve to fifteen, having some previous education, were selected by examination for the program. The first three years of the course were devoted to general studies, with military subjects introduced in the fourth year.[4] These elements—an entrance examination, a specified age group, previous education, and a general curriculum followed by military courses—were incorporated later into the nationwide program of military education.

Equally concerned with strengthening China, Chang Chih-tung in the south was setting up military schools in conjunction with the Westernization of China's armaments. Stung by China's quick defeat in the war with France in 1885, Chang was determined to entice men from good families into a new officer corps for his provincial army, so he opened the Naval and Military Officers' School in Canton in 1887. To further his desire to raise the status of the military profession, Chang planned to give military training only to literate civilians. Like Li's academy, Chang's followed the German model, with courses in cavalry, infantry, artillery, and military engineering. Unlike Li's school, however, its curriculum included courses in German and English language, and the best graduates were to be sent abroad for further study in foreign military academies.[5] Both of these elements were adopted by later academies.

The school at Canton accepted 70 students in its first year and had increased its enrollment to 115 by 1889.[6] As with Li's academy in Tientsin, students at the Canton academy were encouraged to take military or civil examinations upon graduation.[7] The potential problem of placing graduates with technical skills in a traditional employment environment was solved by using academy graduates as instructors or minor officers in the battalions and schools of Li and Chang. So few were trained at the schools, however, that their contribution to China's modernization effort was insignificant.

Neither of these early academies lasted into the twentieth century, but by the time they closed others had opened.[8] Chang was transferred in 1894 from Canton to Nanking, where he opened a new school the following year. Five German instructors trained the 150 students at this school, which was financed by customs revenue.[9]

When Chang was again transferred to Wuchang he set up yet

another academy, the Hupeh Military Preparatory School, along similar lines. Although the student body consisted of only about 120 pupils, the staff was large: two Chinese superintendents and more than twenty supporting members, including Chinese and German instructors. Chang maintained direct control over the foreign staff. The school was financed by salt taxes and the surplus from the Wuchang mint. Four thousand men applied for entrance, even though Chang had limited applicants to "all expectant civil or military officials, men with civil or military degrees, students of the classics, and the sons of reputable gentry or official families from any province."[10]

By 1896, Li and Chang had been joined in their efforts by two other provincial officials concerned with educating a modern officer corps. In the north, Yuan Shih-k'ai had opened several battalion schools for training men in German language and in cavalry, infantry, artillery, and supply techniques[11] while Liu K'un-i, who had succeeded Chang in Nanking, had backed the military academy there. Liu continued to use German instructors in the Nanking school but reportedly was hostile to them.[12] He declined to renew the German contract when it expired in 1898, even though he retained a German lieutenant as chief instructor. A military observer noted that Liu was tempted to hire lower-paid Japanese instructors but decided against it, perhaps because of bad reports about a Japanese-style military school in Wuchang.[13]

The Japanese school was an experiment established by Chang Chih-tung in 1899 at the urging of the Japanese government. At first, the German officers at the school were afraid of being supplanted by the new Japanese instructors who, in the words of one observer, would "accept all the drudgery and are satisfied with small pay." The school soon failed, and it was thought that the experience would cause other governors to decide against military academies along Japanese lines.[14]

In fact, though, support for the Japanese model was to grow. In time, German instructors were largely replaced by Japanese and students going abroad for further training usually went to Japan. It is interesting to speculate as to why the Chinese turned away from Germany toward Japan when military academies were established in greater numbers.

The early vogue for the German model, of course, was based on Chinese admiration for German military power and efficiency. Germany's troops were an impressive sight when performing precision drills. Moreover, Germany did not appear to pose a threat to

China, a key factor for officials who found it difficult to trust a Western country that offered to share its military knowledge.[15] A further consideration was that a German presence in China could be used to offset British domination of such organs as the Maritime Customs Bureau, and thus the Chinese could play one country off against another. For their part, the Germans cultivated Chinese provincial leaders in order to provide a market for arms, mainly those manufactured by Krupp. Krupp actually offered subsidies to prospective German instructors of Chinese troops.[16] Obviously a German instructor, equipped with German weapons, was an excellent model. Krupp's 1895 contract to supply China with machinery is evidence that this strategy worked, if only temporarily.[17] These German advantages in helping China to develop its military education program disappeared when Germany seized Kiaochow Bay and acquired the Shantung Peninsula as a sphere of influence at the end of the decade; Germany having proved itself just as untrustworthy as the other Western powers, the Chinese turned to Japan.

There were a number of practical reasons why Japan gained the upper hand. For one thing, after Japan's strength was demonstrated by its stunning defeat of China in 1895, Chinese officials could feel confident that training by Japanese instructors would be worthwhile. Further, Japanese teachers could be paid less than European ones, no minor consideration for provincial officials who had to finance military academies from their own treasuries. In addition, at a time when advanced military training facilities were unavailable in China, using the Japanese model would permit Chinese military students to supplement their basic training in China with higher education in Japan, at far less cost than equivalent instruction in Germany or France. The shorter distance between Japan and China also made supervision of Chinese students there easier and less expensive than it would have been in Europe. Finally, the Japanese language was easier than German for a Chinese to learn. Thus, instruction in Japanese in the academies would be facilitated by the greater availability of interpreters and the larger number of students able to understand the language. In turn, a Japanese could learn Chinese more easily than could a European, so the number of Japanese who knew Chinese was larger.

As the number of military schools increased, the demand for qualified teachers rose. Although Germany's initial foothold in military training in China was taken over by Japan, by 1906 the Chinese no longer had to rely on foreign instructors of any nationality, for by that time enough Chinese instructors had been trained in China and Japan to do the job.

Organizational Developments, 1901-1915

The failure of the Boxer uprising in 1900 finally convinced the Ch'ing court that China's military establishment had to be remodelled. As in the past, Chang Chih-tung was a leader in the reform. Chang and Liu K'un-i submitted a memorial urging military education reform, in response to which the court agreed to abolish the military examinations. In August 1901 existing degree holders were ordered to be available for retraining at new military schools to be established throughout the country.[18] The following month those provincial officials experienced in the organization of military academies—Li, Liu, Chang, and Yuan—were commanded to pass on their knowledge to governors and governors-general of other provinces. They were exhorted to

> lose no time in establishing similar academies and schools, and . . . to use every effort in bringing up armies of the Empire to a state of super-excellence, so that the country may depend upon them for the defense of hearths and homes as if surrounded by a strong wall.[19]

The court had at last come down clearly in favor of training capable officers. Its willingness to abandon old-fashioned military testing methods, as well as the lack of controversy over their abolition, testify to the bankruptcy of the old system.

But there was still no centralized plan for a uniform type of military school. Decisions were left up to each province, with far from satsifactory results. The Ch'ing court was required to issue yet another decree in March 1902, criticizing provincial officials for delays in reporting on their new academies, and stating that no further delays would be tolerated.[20]

Not unexpectedly, such officials as Liu, Yuan, and Chang were among the first to respond to the new decrees. Two weeks after the first decree the *North-China Herald* reported:

> Viceroy Liu K'un-i has instructed his military secretary to . . . inform all officers in Nanking that from henceforth none shall be allowed to ride about in sedan chairs, that they will not be required to don their official . . . robes when in the presence of high, superior officials, and that as soon as the new military classes for study to be inaugurated in each

battalion have been established, all officers, under colonel and
lieutenant colonel, will be required to attend them and improve their
minds in modern military science, etc. Those declining to attend said
classes will be permitted to resign their posts, which will be filled by
those willing to learn.[21]

Besides sending fifty-five of his training school graduates to Japan for
further education, Yuan established the Army Preparatory School at
Paoting in 1902, selecting literate soldiers for the eight-month course.
Within a year, six different training schools had been set up at
Paoting. Chang Chih-tung also continued to be active, establishing a
middle school at Wuchang, which was attended by 240 "literate and
healthy" students, ages fourteen to twenty-three. Military academies
were also quickly founded in Kiangsi, Kweichow, and Szechuan.[22]

In February 1903, it was reported that the possibility of establishing
regional military colleges was being discussed. Under this plan,
eventually implemented in 1908, schools would be built in Tientsin,
Wuchang, and Chengtu to provide higher military education for
surrounding provinces.[23]

In December 1903, the Commission for Army Reorganization was
inaugurated to supervise and inspect troop training. Under the
direction of Prince Ch'ing, Yuan Shih-k'ai, and T'ieh-liang, the
commission was divided into three sections: administration, command, and education.[24] The impetus to establish a nationwide
military plan may have come from court recognition of variations in
provincial response to the edicts; or perhaps the success of certain
academies was too threatening to be allowed to continue out of the
court's control. In any case, the result was a recommendation in
September 1904 that training be standardized through a hierarchy of
schools. Army primary schools would take graduates of civilian
primary schools for a three-year general education course that would
be supplemented by basic military training. Four middle schools, to
be located in Chihli, Hupeh, Kiangsu, and Shensi, would offer a two-
year course and four months of practical training in the ranks. Also
planned was an officer's course of one and one-half years, plus six
additional months with the army. Two years at a staff college would
end the military education for the best young officers.[25] The
commission plan had elements of both centralization and decentralization: initial education would be under the auspices of the
provinces in order to assure them of a minimally educated lower
officer corps, but those students continuing on to higher schools
would fall under the influence of central authority. The two highest

schools would provide a national orientation. This ambitious plan was taken over by officials of the Republic after the collapse of the Ch'ing dynasty. At last a truly national system of military education was taking shape in China.

By the end of 1904 every province except Kwangsi, Kansu, and Honan had primary military academies, with a total of 2,100 students. In addition, there was a variety of schools outside the standard primary school framework, such as schools for noncommissioned officers and for Manchu soldiers in Shansi and Shantung. Kwangsi joined the ranks with a military school at Kweilin in October 1905.[26]

The number and size of military primary schools increased with the abolition of the civil service examination system in September 1905. The schools had previously attracted students because they were free and provided a way for conscientious Chinese to help their country. Also, they were the only means for assured military promotion. But with the abolition of the civil service examinations, the traditional path to high civilian status, advancement through a military career seemed much more attractive. Robert Hart, the head of the Maritime Customs Bureau, wrote of the new acceptance of the military as a way of life:

> Militarism has taken root here and this new departure will not die out till a strong China shall have given "the king" "his own again." The last Edicts order the spread of military schools and call on Princes and Nobles to send their sons and brothers to them. Henceforth the soldier will be respected and petted, and, with her immense population and resources, the Chinese army of the future will count for something in the world's doings.[27]

In 1906 the Army Reorganization Commission was incorporated into the Ministry of the Army under T'ieh-liang, a Manchu.[28] At this time there was some central supervision over provincial academies by traveling inspectors. Favored provincial officials were recommended to the throne for their accomplishments in military education while officials who had "failed to do their duty and disobeyed" were denounced.[29] The court attempted in 1907 to consolidate further its control over the military academies when T'ieh-liang pressured Yuan Shih-k'ai to place the schools at Paoting under the direct supervision of the Army Ministry. Yuan agreed, apparently because of the depleted state of his Chihli provincial treasury. Running the complex of military schools at Paoting cost more than $1 million—a sum the governor-general's office was hard-pressed to raise.[30] Achieving control over the Paoting schools was also important because many of the students there were from other provinces.

With military schools in virtually every province by 1909, the central authorities were ready to implement the second stage of the 1904 plan for a hierarchy of schools. There were enough instructors who had been trained in Japan and at short-course officers' schools in China to supply the new schools. In the fall of 1909, two-year middle schools were established at Ch'ing-ho, Nanking, and Wuchang, and shortly thereafter in Sian. The next step in creating the hierarchy of schools—setting up an officers' academy in Paoting—would be taken in 1911 in order to accommodate the first graduates of the two-year middle school program. Each province had at least one of the twenty-seven military primary schools. Larger provinces enrolled up to 300 students, while smaller ones had a quota of 210. According to the 1904 plan, 2,000 students would enter the primary schools annually, and 90 percent of the graduates of these schools would be admitted to the four middle schools in Chihli, Kiangsu, Shensi, and Hupeh. About 1,500 middle school students were expected to graduate each year and be assigned to military units.[31] There were also more than 200 supplementary schools designed to train enlisted soldiers.[32] The officers' short-course academy was opened in 1911 at Paoting, with the full-term academy scheduled for completion the following year.[33] Thus, on the eve of the 1911 Revolution the Ch'ing court had carried out more than half of its original plan for a military education system and had laid the foundation for a national system to train a corps of officers.

Education was interrupted by the outbreak of revolution in October 1911. Many students joined in revolutionary activities, but others simply returned home when their schools closed. By the fall of 1912, however, the political situation had stabilized enough for most of the schools to reopen. Students were recalled and classes resumed where they had left off. At the elementary level, except for the change in name from *hsueh-hsiao* (school) to *hsueh-t'ang* (academy), in most respects the previous structure was retained. The middle schools at Sian and Nanking never reopened, and those at Ch'ing-ho and Wuchang were renamed, respectively, the First and Second Military Preparatory Schools.[34] Seventeen hundred graduates of the first and second classes of these two schools became the first class of the Paoting Army Officers' School.[35]

The central bureaucracy in charge of military education was reformed in 1912 when the Military Education Section of the Ch'ing merged with the Military Education Office of the south to become the

Department of Military Education, one of eleven departments in the new Army Ministry, under Tuan Ch'i-jui. The new department was assigned responsibility for formulating regulations, for textbooks and courses, and for discipline and examinations. Regulations were promulgated to provide a standard model to be followed in all schools. In October 1912, the department ordered that the school year run from December 1 to November 30. In-service training was to be integrated with classroom education. In 1915 the department became the Army Training Commission, incorporating the functions of the Military Education Publications Office, which had been in charge of standardizing textbooks.[36]

In January 1915, the first class of 1,114 cadets graduated from Paoting Academy; two groups, totaling 1,006, had graduated from Ch'ing-ho and 756 had finished the course at Wuchang.[37] Military education had reached an organizational peak, which was not sustained for long, however. The Second Revolution of 1913 had brought further disruption to the classrooms, and standards and control deteriorated even more after 1916. Many schools closed, including the one at Ch'ing-ho and several provincial academies. Others were kept in operation solely by provincial authorities; the quality of these depended on the care that individual leaders took in overseeing them. Yunnan's military academy was notable for its high level of instruction.[38] The ninth and final class of Paoting graduated in the early 1920s, and then the academy closed permanently, ending its turbulent history. The fourth-level military school, the General Staff College, continued to operate for several years, but it too fell victim to the internal strife of the warlord period. Remarkably, each stage of the 1904 organizational plan had been put into effect, providing a body of military personnel that was to play an instrumental role in China in the decades to come. Let us consider more closely the personnel, curriculum, and students of these military schools.

The Leadership of Military Academies

Provincial governors and governors-general were given responsibility for organizing and financing the new military academies after 1900, but not all provincial officials responded to the call with equal vigor. After the death of Liu K'un-i in 1901 and the eclipse of Chang Chih-tung, Yuan Shih-k'ai became the most active provincial governor in military reform.

Active provincial officials must have had mixed motives. Doubtless most wanted to strengthen China against foreign encroachment and realized that a strong army required competent officers. The Japanese victory over Russia in 1905 convinced these officials that they should follow the Japanese model in promoting military academies. Provincial loyalties may have dominated the motivations of others. Military primary schools often excluded nonprovincials and favored native instructors who had been educated abroad. Thus in some cases the schools became a means of counteracting Peking's centralizing pressures after 1900. Individual governors apparently used military academies to train officers responsive to their own needs.

Competition among provinces, as well as between the provinces and Peking, might also have affected the development of academies. Governors reportedly competed in offering returned students high positions in their own military academies.[39] Moreover, the failure to establish academies even after the imperial edicts of 1901 might be attributed to competition. Governors of outlying provinces, perhaps jealous of the funds Yuan received for building his divisions of the New Army, were slow to react when ordered to support military education out of their own provincial treasuries.[40] Shensi Governor Sheng-yun, for example, complained in 1904 that he lacked enough revenue for training new troops. And Ch'en Ch'ün-hsuan, governor-general of Kwangtung-Kwangsi in 1903-1906, refused to set up units for the New Army because of his dislike of Yuan and Prince Ch'ing, two powerful members of the Army Reorganization Commission. This is also a plausible reason why Kwangsi delayed the establishment of an academy, because Governor Ch'en had previously cooperated by setting up a school and sending students to Japan during his tenure as governor-general of Szechuan.[41]

Another obstacle to opening military schools was simply finding enough qualified teachers. Military schools were commonly staffed by a supervisor, a director, an inspector, and from four to fifteen instructors.[42] Scarcity of trained Chinese meant that instructors at the earliest academies were mostly foreigners—either German or Japanese. After 1900, teaching personnel fell into four categories: Japanese and other foreigners, Chinese trained by foreigners in Chinese academies, Chinese trained in Japan, and Chinese trained by Chinese in China. The last group eventually became the largest, but only after primary, middle, and short-course schools had been in operation for several years.

At the outset, instructors were mainly Japanese and Chinese who had been trained in Japan. Between 1900 and 1905, Japanese instructors were gradually replaced by trained Chinese. Some idea of the changing situation is evident in the rules drawn up in 1908 by the Ministry of Education to prevent disputes between Chinese authorities and foreigners employed at provincial schools. Permission of the Army Ministry and the Education Ministry was required before foreigners could be hired as military instructors, and three months' notice had to be given before a teacher could resign. Foreign instructors were allowed to teach only military subjects and foreign languages.[43]

A growing number of Chinese descended on Japan for military training between 1902 and 1907.[44] Equipped with degrees from the Shikan gakkō (Officers' school) or lesser military academies in Japan, graduates were immediately employed as instructors upon their return to China. After 1906 the majority of instructors was Chinese. But many also returned ready to propagate newly acquired revolutionary ideas. These Chinese for the most part were born in the early 1880s and studied in Japan in their early twenties.[45] Many had awakened to China's weakness after receiving a traditional education in the classics; some had had preliminary training in lower-level military academies in China. Hsu Ch'ung-chih and Chiang Tso-pin were typical instructors of these years. Hsu was born in Canton in 1887, the grandson of the governor-general of Fukien-Chekiang. After receiving a classical education, Hsu left for Japan where he enrolled in the second class of the Shikan gakkō, from which he graduated in 1907. Upon his return to China, Hsu was named chief instructor at the Fukien Military Primary School.[46] Chiang, born in Hupeh in 1884, was also educated in the traditional manner and attained the *sheng-yuan* degree. In 1902, he enrolled in a civil school offering military drill in its curriculum. While in Japan he joined the newly organized T'ung Meng Hui (Revolutionary Alliance or United League) in 1905, soon after he had registered at the Seijō gakkō, a preparatory school for military officers. He entered the fourth class of the Shikan gakkō, graduating in 1908. When he returned to China he took a special examination for military school graduates and was awarded a special *chü-jen* degree. In 1909 Chiang served as instructor at the Officers' Short-Course School in Paoting before transferring to an administrative post in the government. He was instrumental in the adoption of a proposal that called for graduates of modern military schools to replace old-style officers within five years.[47]

Provincial officials preferred to hire natives of the province to staff their academies. Between 1908 and 1910, for instance, more than twenty graduates of the Shikan gakkō from Yunnan returned to that province either as instructors or as field commanders.[48] This tendency

was even greater for a cadet whose stay in Japan was financed by his
provincial government. Li Ken-yuan and T'ang Chi-yao were two
such students. Both were aided by the Yunnan government. Li was
called home from Japan to accept an appointment as superintendent
and instructor in the Yunnan school; T'ang soon followed as an
instructor and became military governor of Yunnan five years later.[49]

The provincial orientation of the military academies is also
illustrated by the following incident in 1910:

> In the military college events have happened of late, the outcome of
> which does not promise well for the future of the Provincial Army.
> Despite the fact that Kwangsi is not noted for producing men of great
> talent, there seems to exist among the student class a strong feeling
> against the calling-in of extra-provincials as teachers. This feeling
> found vent a short time ago, when one of the masters had occasion to
> report some students who were ultimately expelled for their offence.
> On this more than half of the students marched out of the building, to
> be followed the next day by the rest. The whole school then went in a
> body to the yamen of the Governor to demand the reinstatement of their
> comrades and the dismissal of the master . . . the result was that there
> was evidently a complete victory for the boys, for almost the whole staff
> immediately resigned, from the director downwards.[50]

All of the instructors had been subject to a variety of influences
while in Japan. Foremost perhaps was their first-hand experience of
seeing Japan—a nation strengthened to the point of superiority over
both China and Russia—and realizing more than ever the impotence
of the Chinese government.[51] China's inability to keep the Russians
out of Manchuria in 1903 particularly provoked the students' rage at
their government.[52] Furthermore, students in Japan must have
noticed the high status accorded a soldier there, in sharp contrast to
their own status in traditional China. Nor could they have been
unreceptive to the debates ranging among Chinese reformers and
revolutionaries in Japan at the time—that they were is readily
apparent in the numbers who joined the T'ung Meng Hui after 1905.
The horizons of students were also broadened by their contacts with
nonmilitary students in Japan and with translations of Western
books and articles. Chiang Fang-chen, for instance, was active in
reformist debate in his capacity as editor of the *Tide of Chekiang*.
This journal and others like it broadened the awareness of their
readers by reports and opinions on scholarship, current events, and
literature.[53]

Military students in Japan were involved in controversies with the

Ch'ing officials sent to supervise them. In July 1902, students at the Seijō gakkō, irritated by a Ch'ing edict prohibiting unsponsored students from enrolling, staged a mass sit-in. The disturbance escalated to embrace broader political issues, giving the young cadets an experience in organized dissent.[54]

The revolutionary opinions that many Chinese students acquired in Japan were passed on to others when these students later assumed positions as instructors in Chinese military academies. Since the Japanese-trained students were employed nationwide, revolutionary thought infused academies throughout the country.

The number of Chinese studying in Japan dropped within a short time as more students elected to remain home to finish their military education. This choice became possible because of the gradual establishment of second- and third-stage academies. To find out what influenced Chinese military students after 1911, then, one must examine what was happening in China's own military academies.

Background and Selection of Military Students, 1901-1915

Students attending military academies in China between 1900 and 1910 had widely different family backgrounds. A general interest in military education permeated all levels of Chinese society, and there is evidence that the schools were well attended by people of scholar-gentry, rich and poor peasant, merchant, and military backgrounds.

Most higher class individuals entered the army only after military academies offered a more appealing route to top-echelon positions than mere enlistment. The prestige accorded education in traditional China may have contributed to the acceptance of military education as a proper career choice for young men of good families. Abolition of the civil examination system in 1905 removed the practical motivation behind classical studies, and graduation from a military academy assured cadets of lower-officer status at least, with opportunity to advance higher.[55] The risks were not so great as they would have been under the old enlistment and examination system. Further, a military career became even more respectable as China's weak international position became more widely acknowledged. Finally, many young students in civil schools were moved to apply to military schools by patriotic tracts, such as those by Liang Ch'i-ch'ao. Especially in the last years of the Ch'ing dynasty, young activists entered the military academies for revolutionary purposes.

It was not unusual for young people to be excited by the prospect of military education while their parents were not. Chu Teh is a case in point. Although the son of tenant farmers in Szechuan, Chu was fortunate enough to be sent to several schools for a traditional education. After the abolition of the civil service examinations in 1905, a teacher helped to convince Chu's skeptical parents that he should study at one of the newly established modern schools, and in 1906 he arrived at the new government civil college in Ch'i-fu. Apparently Chu was tempted to enter the military school that was also there "but feared to break entirely with his family who still shared the ancient contempt for soldiers." Chu's friend, Wu Shao-pei, faced the same problem, so Wu, Chu, and another friend decided to enroll in the military academy in the neighboring province of Yunnan.[56]

Li Tsung-jen's mother was similarly reluctant to have her son follow a military career because of its "unpredictable future." Li managed to gain his father's approval, however, and entered the Kwangsi Military Primary School in 1907.[57] Another cadet, Yang Sen, was able to persuade his father, a Szechuan landowner, to permit him to enter the province's military primary school only after he had secretly trained and excelled in military studies at an old-style private school.[58]

By 1911 observers were noting a dramatic reversal of the soldier's status in China. For example, G. E. Morrison wrote:

> The status of the soldier has been transformed. The relative ranks of civil and military have been reversed. The military now takes precedence over the civil. High commands have been given to the Imperial princes and prestige of the military service thereby raised. Good families now send their sons as officers.[59]

Entrants to military schools had to pass supposedly nondiscriminatory examinations of physical ability and basic literary skills. Ultimately, however, those who enrolled in the schools were drawn from landlord, rich peasant, and prosperous merchant families because only these could afford to send their sons to senior elementary schools—the unofficial prerequisites for taking the examinations.[60]

Many of the students admitted that the generous financial support offered by the academies was the main reason for their decision to enter military schools. Wan Yao-huang became an officer because his scholar-gentry family no longer could afford to send him to a civilian school; Chou Yung-neng was induced by the "attractive scholarships" offered at the Kiangsi Military Primary School; and Kung Hao, who had failed the examination for the *sheng-yuan* degree, enjoyed the "good rations" in the military schools. Yen Hsi-shan enrolled when his father's bank failed; Li Han-hun found expenses at the special class in law at Kwangtung University beyond his means and transferred to the Kwangtung Military Primary School; Liu Chih, who depended on his uncles for support, transferred from an English course at the Chi-an Christian School to the army primary school because the former required tuition and the latter did not.[61]

Despite rules stipulating that students at primary schools be between fourteen and seventeen years old, the ages of entering military students varied greatly. Half of the biographies studied reveal ages eighteen or over for pre-1905 entrants, with only a quarter falling within the specified age limit. After 1905, less than one-seventh were eighteen or older. A greater proportion was underage rather than overage. One reason for the shift was the abandonment of the civil service examinations in 1905. The increasingly important role a modern military education was given in China allowed students to decide upon a military career at a younger age. Also, the lower ages of students entering after 1905 may be attributed to stricter enforcement of the rules. Once the backlog of older students had been absorbed, the age standards could be more stringently maintained.

Throughout the last years of the Ch'ing and the early years of the Republic, the competition for admission to military academies was consistently intense. Applicants often numbered in the thousands for the 90 to 300 positions open at the provincial schools. In 1907 Li Tsung-jen, one of a thousand applicants, placed as one of ten alternates for the 130 positions at the Kwangsi school. He was told to go to Kweilin to sign up but was "ten minutes late" and was denied the opportunity to register. He returned home to await the following year's competition, in which he competed successfully against 3,000 others for one of 200 places in the class.[62] Following the 1911 Revolution, the new central government specifically encouraged provincial authorities to accept students from all parts of the province. Army Ministry regulations stipulated that if there were qualified candidates, each small *hsien* should be represented by one student and each large *hsien* by two.[63]

Curriculum and Student Life

Military Primary Schools

Once accepted and properly guaranteed, students entered a three-year course of general education, with only minor attention given to military training. The curriculum usually included Chinese classics, language, morals, mathematics, history, geography, nature studies, physical culture, drawing, and either physics, chemistry, foreign languages, or algebra. Li Tsung-jen recalled doing quadratic equations at the Kwangsi Primary School, an academy that emphasized physics and mathematics. In Szechuan, students could often choose one of five foreign languages to study, while in Kwangtung the provincial government assigned each class a language. Chang Fa-kuei's class studied German and the next class studied Japanese.[64] One observer attributed the emphasis on general education to the deficiency of the normal student's early education. The traditional emphasis on rote learning was also criticized. "The habit they have contracted of learning by heart without trying to comprehend, of taking as articles of faith the maxims of philosophy, and of replacing personal ideas by quotations, is a fatal cause of atrophy to the critical mind and reasoning faculty."[65]

Military training courses usually consisted of outdoor exercise, target practice, and rifle handling. The Yunnan Military Academy, comparable to but not actually part of the military primary school system, deemphasized general education in favor of military preparation and physical fitness. The Yunnan Academy was renowned for its fine instructors and well-trained cadets. Each day the cadets rose at dawn to do calisthenics, weight lifting, and group exercise. Each afternoon they trained with rifles and bayonets, engaged in gymnastics, and practiced military songs.[66]

Aside from the standardized textbooks issued by the Army Ministry, reading materials at the various schools differed greatly. The teachings of Sun Tzu, China's military sage, were widely discussed. Illegal copies of *Min pao*, smuggled into China from Japan, as well as the writings of Liang Ch'i-ch'ao and K'ang Yu-wei, were available to interested students. Chu Teh recalled reading about the life of George Washington and perusing Montesquieu's *Spirit of the Laws* in an instructor's office.[67] New students were often approached by teachers or older students to find if they were interested in joining revolutionary organizations such as the T'ung Meng Hui. At Yunnan there were two groups in the T'ung Meng Hui: students and teachers.[68] At Kwangsi in 1908, Governor Chang Ming-ch'i, though himself a modern reformer, feared that revolutionary influence was growing too strong in the military academy and brought in Ts'ai Ngo, a returned student from Japan, to try to control it. As related by Li Tsung-jen, "although Ts'ai was a member of the T'ung Meng Hui he was more careful and avoided exposing himself, which turned the aggressive young revolutionists against him."[69] Finally, as a result of student agitation, Ts'ai was forced to resign in 1909 and left for Yunnan. When Chang was subsequently promoted to governor-general and transferred to Kwangtung, the student revolutionaries were given a freer hand in promoting their cause. About sixty students at Kwangsi joined the T'ung Meng Hui during the tenure of the next two directors.[70]

Until the fad of cutting off the queue spread across China around 1909, cadets all wore their hair tightly secured under their hats. One student who cut his queue claimed that it was done for the sake of convenience and not as a revolutionary act.[71] Another was prompted to do it because of embarrassment—he had seen the queue called a "pigtail" in a revolutionary newspaper.[72]

Daily life at most of the academies consisted of hard work and strict discipline. Students rose early and retired late. If a student misbehaved, the punishment was one demerit on his record. For more serious offenses, the culprit was sent for a day or two to the "repentance room." In general, however, students were well behaved. As one observer evaluated the situation, "on the whole, the atmosphere in the Kwangsi Army Primary School was virtuous enough to command moral conformity. No other school in Kwangsi could compare . . . in curriculum and discipline."[73]

But discipline was not so strict as to eliminate protest entirely. In 1905 the *North-China Herald* reported the case of three students at the academy in Nanking who had secretly removed some training firearms from the storehouse. The students were discovered, arrested, and questioned personally by the governor-general, "who wished to make an example by summarily beheading them." Cooler minds prevailed, however, and the students were turned over to the Nanking prefect for punishment. The prefect found one innocent but kept the other two under guard while they awaited sentencing. The paper continued:

> In the meanwhile a great deal of discontent has arisen amongst the other students of the academy on account of the unreasonable severity of the Viceroy, and it culminated the other day in all of them resigning and leaving the academy. Upon this being reported to the Viceroy by the Director of the academy, Taotai Yu, the former replied that since this was so, he would allow them to resign without further concern, and the next day his excellency issued orders for proclamations to be posted calling for a new set of students for the academy. At the same time instructions were sent to the heads of the various Government schools of the Viceroyalty to keep strict watch upon the conduct of their students.[74]

Oral and written tests were given at regular intervals. Students were sometimes rewarded for good grades with an increase in their monthly stipend. At Kwangsi, for example, a first-year student whose grade average was less than "good" received only .8 ounces of silver, while those who were "good" or "excellent" received 1 and 1.2 ounces, respectively.[75] Tests during the academic year were administered and scored locally, but the final examinations were handled by a representative of the central government.[76] A successful performance on the final qualified the student for an army middle school.

Military Preparatory Schools

Since there were only four middle schools to serve the entire country, the student population at each came from several provinces. The campuses were large enough to accommodate the 1,000 cadets in attendance. The school at Wuchang was typical: it had several buildings in a stark, treeless setting, a dormitory for instructors, an auditorium, and a four-story building with rooms for students upstairs and classrooms and study rooms downstairs. The school was equipped with a barbershop, infirmary, laundry, stable, exercise field, and rifle range.[77] In their curriculum the middle schools placed more emphasis than the primary academies on military subjects, science, and mathematics. At Ch'ing-ho, students took courses in advanced physics, chemistry, plane and solid geometry, analytic geometry, and advanced trigonometry.[78]

Many of the students who later commented on their education at middle schools were less complimentary than they had been toward their primary schools. The larger size of the middle schools may have contributed to their dissatisfaction, but the main reason seems to have been the disruptive environment at most of the schools. Students who had finished their primary school in the relatively calm atmosphere before 1910 were caught up in the upheavals of the revolution during their middle school years. From the outset, revolutionary agitation was common at the middle schools, with the most serious incident being at the school in Wuchang in October 1911. When the uprising occurred, the schools were immediately closed, leaving students with the choice of returning to their homes or enlisting in a hastily organized fighting unit.[79]

A somewhat more stable political situation in 1912 allowed the schools to summon their students back by means of newspaper announcements and word of mouth. But the schools, renamed military preparatory schools, experienced further difficulties in 1915-1916 when opposition arose to Yuan Shih-k'ai. Tight restrictions were placed on all cadets in 1915 and periodic searches were conducted for revolutionaries.[80] The Second Military Preparatory School at Wuchang was again especially troubled. In early 1916 Yuan appointed General Sun Wu as its supervisor, ordering him to exact a loyalty oath from all instructors and students. Even so, about one hundred students joined the anti-Yuan organization, which held secret meetings at the school. Many cadets even withdrew from the school until 1916 when Yuan's death permitted them to return.[81]

Paoting Academy

Upon graduation from the two-year middle school course, cadets had to serve six months as student officers in the regular army before sitting for the examination to enter the officers' academy at Paoting. Paoting Military Academy was the highest-level school for most officers and a national meeting ground for future leaders of China. It was also a center of controversy for the nine classes that passed through its gates. The academy was located outside the east gate of Paoting, Chihli Province, in an open plain surrounded by aspen trees. The land around the academy was particularly suited for training soldiers. The campus consisted of a large rectangular area with a dining hall and lecture room at each end, flanked by two one-story buildings that served as dormitories and classrooms. A large exercise field, a stable, an arsenal, and various storehouses rounded out the facilities. This campus served as the focus of a one-and-one-half-year program in military techniques.[82]

Few general education courses were offered. Instead, the curriculum stressed battle tactics, weaponry, fortifications, and topography. Courses were also offered in military discipline, management, health, horsemanship, and foreign languages. Upon entering the academy, students would join a unit with a particular field of concentration—infantry, cavalry, artillery, engineering, or transport and supply—and would remain with this unit throughout the entire course. Infantry was by far the most popular: in 1914 there were six infantry companies, two each of cavalry and artillery, and one each of engineering and transport.[83] The 9,000 students who attended Paoting differed in educational background. Table 7.1 outlines these differences among the nine classes.[84]

The administration of Paoting was the center of much of the controversy that plagued the school. The first commandant, Chao Li-tai, had been director of the Army Short-Course School. Chao used his former students as instructors and was close to Army Minister Tuan Ch'i-jui, both of which aggravated the idealistic young cadets. The

TABLE 7.1
The Nine Classes of Paoting Academy

Number	Date Entered	Date Graduated	Number of Students	Previous Education
1	1912	1914	1,000	Graduates of first and second classes of military middle schools
2	Dec. 1914	May 1916	1,500	Graduates of first and second military preparatory schools
3	June 1915	Late 1916	1,500	Graduates of military preparatory schools
4	Dec. 1915?	--	500	Graduates of Hupei Officers School and Second Military Preparatory School
5	Early 1916	1918	800	Graduates of First Military Preparatory School
6	Dec. 1916	Spring 1919	1,000	Graduates of military preparatory schools and Ch'ing middle schools who participated in Second Revolution; students recommended by seven governors
7	?	?	1,000	Same as sixth class
8	1919	June 1922	700	Graduates of civil middle schools and students sent on recommendation of a military officer
9	1920?	?	700	Same as eighth class

Source: "Paoting chün-kuan hsueh-hsiao tsang sang shih,"
          Ch'un Ch'iu, No. 64 (1960), p. 4.

cadets went on strike, demanding Chao's ouster, better instructors, readmission of expelled students, and nondiscrimination against cadets with radical opinions.[85] But the central authorities would not back down; at Tuan's order, two regiments from the Peiyang Defense Garrison at Paoting surrounded the school. For over a month the situation was deadlocked, but finally, in October 1912, the students received an ultimatum from Tuan and marched en masse to Peking to arouse public support. In response, the governors of Hupeh,

Szechuan, Yunnan, Kiangsi, and Anhwei urged Tuan to compromise. In Peking the students won public sympathy and in the end Tuan was forced to give in, rescind his orders, fire Chao, and look for a new commandant. The thousand students who had marched on the capital returned in triumph to Paoting.

The individual suggested for the post was Chiang Fang-chen. Chiang was well trained in both traditional studies and modern military techniques, and had only recently returned to China after studying in Japan and Germany.[86] He was thirty years old when selected as head of Paoting, barely older than the cadets. He was enthusiastic about making Paoting into a first-rate training center. His inaugural speech to the cadets and staff stressed patriotism and unity as a means of catching up with the West.[87] He replaced the old short-course instructors with graduates of advanced Japanese military schools and other top officers. His dedication led him to hold frequent inspections and to teach courses himself for absent instructors. He also presented weekly lectures to the assembled student body on famous military men of the past.[88] Though regulations were lax when he took over, he soon restored discipline and order by such means as standardizing uniforms for each student. A mutual supervision system was instituted in which each unit of seven students was responsible for the misconduct of its individual members.

Chiang's reformist methods and ideas brought him into conflict with the Army Ministry. The disagreement between Chiang and the ministry mirrored the long-standing conflict between new and old army styles. The cadets Chiang trained were not likely to fit in with the old-style approach of the officers in charge of the system, who feared the influx of devoted, intelligent Paoting officers into the army. Chiang had no supporters within the army itself to defuse the situation.

The conflict was finally brought into the open by Chiang's repeated requests to the ministry for funds. Chiang needed money to improve the academy, but his applications were all denied by ministry officials who demanded that he economize. In June 1913, returning from a futile trip to Peking, Chiang called the students and staff into Paoting's main lecture hall. After a few remarks, he drew his pistol and shot himself. Although Chiang survived, his action shocked not only the spectators but leaders throughout the country. Provincial governors cabled their distress. Yuan Shih-k'ai sent his own physician to attend to Chiang, who never returned to Paoting.[89]

The incident occurred at the end of the school year. Influenced by the event and spurred by the outbreak of the Second Revolution, a number of students withdrew from the academy. When classes resumed in 1913, the new commandant was Ch'u T'ung-feng, a graduate of the Shikan gakkō and a personal friend of Tuan Ch'i-jui. Ch'u distrusted all those students who had gone south for the summer and expelled more than 500 of them, worsening relations between northerners and southerners at the school.[90] In the next ten years, Paoting saw three more commandants and then closed its doors permanently.

Careers after Graduation

What kind of position could students completing the three levels of military education expect to attain? Graduates of the early (pre-1900) schools tended to become instructors, while graduates of lower-level schools who did not finish their education at either Paoting or the Shikan gakkō were usually given a platoon or company command as their initial assignment. Students receiving higher-level training in Japan were generally named to responsible posts immediately upon their return to China, as military school instructors or as battalion or even regimental commanders. Paoting graduates had an excellent chance of winning top-echelon positions, especially in their home provinces. Many first served as junior officers and then moved up to company or battalion commands.

Recruitment and promotion were affected by several factors. First and foremost, a military school graduate's chances of getting a responsible post, and of being promoted quickly, were enhanced if he had some connection with his commander. In many cases this connection was a mutually attended school. Directors frequently hired instructors trained at the same school that they themselves had attended. For example, after Li Ken-yuan, a member of the sixth class of the Shikan gakkō, assumed the directorship of the Yunnan Military Academy in 1909, his Shikan gakkō classmates, T'ang Chi-yao and Li Lieh-chün, were hired as instructors. Also, Chao Li-tai, former director of the Peiyang Short-Course School, almost exclusively selected former Peiyang students and instructors when he became commandant at Paoting. And in turn, when Chiang Fang-chen, a graduate of the Shikan gakkō, assumed the post of commandant, he replaced Chao's selections with Japanese-trained soldiers.[91]

Li Tsung-jen was unable to find a decent army position after the school at which he was instructor closed, but in the spring of 1916 he was finally offered a position by a former colleague. On his way to take up his new post he encountered a division of the Yunnan Army, whose members included his former classmates at the Kwangsi Army Primary School—Liang Po-shan, Hsieh Shao-an, and Chu Liang-chi. The latter, a battalion commander, immediately offered Li a position as company commander. When that post proved unsatisfactory, Li resigned and accidentally ran across another schoolmate, Li Ch'i-chao. As a company commander Li Ch'i-chao was able immediately to secure a post for Li Tsung-jen under him. In the Thirteenth Regiment of the Sixth National Protection Army under Lin Hu, about 90 percent of the officers were graduates of the Kwangsi Military Primary School. In turn, when Li achieved a responsible position as an army commander he followed the same pattern—his chief of staff, Huang Hsu-ch'u, had been his classmate at Kwangsi.[92]

Paoting graduates had advantages in certain provinces. In Shansi, for example, candidates for high-ranking commissions in the provincial army had to attend the Paoting Military Academy in Hopeh or enlist in Yen Hsi-shan's own Military Instruction Corps.[93] Paoting's graduates also tended to be concentrated in the provincial armies of Hunan, Kwangsi, Kwangtung, and Szechuan.[94]

Personal, school, and provincial loyalties not only determined recruitment and promotion patterns but also formed the basis for rivalries in the military. Jerome Chen gives this description of the process in north China, where the

> warlords attempted to strengthen personal ties with each other instead of forging a coherent political programme for their provinces. They relied on ties between classmates. The Hsiaochan group not only furnished the leadership, but also marked the beginning of the two great cliques of northern warlords—the Anhwei and Chihli cliques. The inner circle of this group consisted of graduates of the Military School of Tientsin . . . who in the 1911 revolution showed remarkable unity in giving support first to the Manchu throne and later to Yuan Shih-k'ai.[95]

Commanders who attended late Ch'ing and early Republic military schools often cooperated against those who had not. Apparently, such was the case in Hunan in 1923, when a group of former Paoting students backed Chao Heng-t'i, then at odds with T'an Yen-k'ai. For his part T'an was supported by graduates of Japanese military academies.[96] In Szechuan, officers educated at Paoting tended to join forces against those educated in the province at the Szechuan Rapid-

Course School.[97] When Chiang Kai-shek, backed by his Whampoa Academy cadets, sought to expand his power during the Northern Expedition in 1926-1928, his main opposition surfaced among the Paoting group.[98] Finally, Donald Gillin has described the extensive use that Ch'en Ch'eng, a graduate of Paoting's eighth class, made of his Paoting connections in his efforts to win support for the central government in the 1930s.[99]

Conclusion

In 1901, with its abolition of the traditional military examination and its exhortation to provincial officials to establish military academies, the Ch'ing government took the first steps toward modernizing the Chinese officer corps. This policy won wide support throughout China, as shown by the large number of applicants to the academies. But central and provincial officials were not able to control the academies in the revolutionary atmosphere of the early twentieth century. Many returned students from Japan advocated revolution; as instructors, they influenced the cadets and, ultimately, the entire army as the academy graduates were assigned to various units.

Organizationally, while the military academy system devised in the Ch'ing period could only educate a limited number of students, in many ways it was well designed. The concept of provincial primary schools, supported and directed by the individual provinces but overseen by central inspectors, seemed to satisfy local needs and placate provincial officials. Although standards at the academies varied from province to province, the regional middle schools and national academy helped to build a national, uniformly trained officer corps. The deterioration of the primary school system after 1913 made an orderly progression of students through the hierarchy of academies virtually impossible, and the entire structure had collapsed by 1923.

Educationally, the academies were valuable in both military and nonmilitary terms. The curriculum of the military primary schools was devoted less to military training than to providing a rudimentary general education. Students who abandoned their military careers upon graduation from primary schools had in many cases acquired enough education to pursue civilian careers. A student enrolling in a military middle school was likely to follow a military career, particularly if he took the officer's training course at the Paoting

Military Academy. Although the system was often rocked by turmoil and was hampered by favoritism and provincialism, the late Ch'ing-early Republic military education program was significant, as illustrated by the number of military school graduates who played major leadership roles in later periods of Chinese history.

Warlordism and Educational Finances, 1916-1927

Ka-che Yip

On March 14 and 15, 1921, the faculty and staff of the eight government colleges and universities in Peking went on strike to protest the government of Peking's nonpayment of educational funds.[1] School representatives not only demanded the funds that were months in arrears, but they also insisted that the government guarantee future financial support by earmarking specific revenues for education. The Peking government, however, refused to yield to the demands. By early April, secondary and primary school students in Peking had decided to support the strike. They petitioned the government for immediate action and organized street lecture teams to denounce the government's alleged destruction of education. The antigovernment forces also broadened the campaign to focus on the failure of the Peking regime to provide adequate educational opportunities for the Chinese people. On June 3, about a thousand students together with faculty and staff representatives of the eight government schools staged a huge demonstration against the government's educational policy. The police quickly dispersed the crowd by force and several hundred demonstrators were wounded, some seriously.[2]

Although the crisis was temporarily resolved at the end of July when Peking agreed to divert other funds to meet the expenses of the schools, the incident dramatically brought to the fore the problem of the financing of public education in China during the warlord period (1916-1927). Warlordism, with its perennial internal wars and the disorderly conditions they created, had a damaging and inhibiting effect on the Chinese economy. Educational development was also seriously affected. The warlord governments' failure to support improvements in education meant that leadership in education passed largely to private educators. But the efforts of such educators as Hu Shih and Huang Yen-p'ei who actively promoted and experimented with new—mostly Western—ideas also suffered from lack of political and financial support. This chapter will study the relationship between warlordism and educational finance, and discuss the movement for educational fiscal independence and the impact that inadequate funding had on the development of education in modern China.

The Administration of Education

The public educational system underwent several changes in the period between 1921 and 1927. At the national level, the educational administrative structure, after minor modifications in 1914, remained in force until 1927. The Ministry of Education (Chiao-yü-pu) was headed by the minister of education (*chiao-yü chung-chang*), assisted by a vice-minister (*chiao-yü tz'u-chang*) who supervised various departments and agencies. The minister was appointed by the president and was a member of the cabinet. He was vested with the power to direct and control educational matters in the country and was responsible for securing educational funds.[3]

Throughout most of the warlord period, however, the education minister's authority was limited. First, the Peking government's effective control extended only to those provinces actually dominated by the warlord faction occupying Peking; individual warlords holding sway over other provinces had complete control over the regulation of educational matters in their respective provinces. As for the Peking government itself, the position of the education minister was by no means secure. The warlords' direct or indirect intervention in the formation of cabinets led to a high turnover of personnel. As Lucien Pye points out, with the rise of warlord politics, "the bureaucracy lost its freedom to make political decisions, for the power-holders were now located outside the formal organization"— the warlords' presence and their known views were sufficient to influence the actions of the responsible members of the bureaucracy.[4] An important criterion for the selection of cabinet ministers was to be their acceptability to the dominant warlord. From June 1916 to November 1924, twenty-four cabinets were successively appointed: each lasted for an average of about four months.

Under these circumstances, the Ministry of Education, like other ministries, was paralyzed by insecurity. In the years 1918-1928, the ministry had a total of twenty-one ministers.[5] Most were appointed without much deliberation and with little concern for qualifications. This absence of safeguards for the tenure of the education minister destroyed any continuity and discouraged initiative. The ministers would hardly want to risk their careers in fighting for educational fiscal independence. After all, they were political appointees dependent upon their political standing for whatever support—financial or otherwise—education might obtain.

In the provinces, the Department of Education (Chiao-yü-t'ing) was headed by the commissioner of education (*chiao-yü-t'ing-chang*) who was directly responsible to the minister of education. Yet the Department of Education was also within the jurisdiction of the governor who, through the so-called Third Section (Ti-san k'o) in his office, had taken over much of the power of the department. The governor also monopolized the right to appoint principals of schools supported by the province.[6] During this period, however, this administrative structure was at best a fiction since the development of education in the provinces depended ultimately on the individual warlord's policies.

Educational Policies of the Warlords

In general, warlords were not noted for their interest in the improvement of education. They were preoccupied first and foremost with their own political survival and the maximization of their personal power. At a time of shifting alliances and political instability, the establishment and maintenance of military supremacy was therefore far more urgent and important. Indeed, since the warlords' jurisdiction could be terminated at any time, there was no incentive for them to make any commitment to long-term projects such as the improvement of education. There was no educational planning, no blueprint for educational growth, and no assured support for schools that were already in existence.

At the same time, the warlords perceived a threat to their position from the intellectuals. The rise to power of the militarists had been accompanied by their direct assault upon the authority of the civil administration and the denial of political power to the educated elite. Yet the intellectuals were by no means subjugated and they continued to dominate most of the means of mass communication. The students' antiimperialist and antimilitarist activities in particular constituted a serious threat to the warlords' power. Indeed, throughout this period, the warlords constantly resorted to force and violence to suppress student activism.[7] They did not encourage the expansion or sanction the autonomy of education, which would have given the educated elite the power base to challenge their position.

Even when a warlord was active in promoting education, it was with the explicit aim of fashioning an instrument for the fostering of values and ideals supportive of the government. Feng Yü-hsiang and Yen Hsi-shan, for example, exhibited a keen awareness of the importance of ideological indoctrination through education. Feng's educational programs for his troops were designed to impart a new morality based on his interpretation of Confucianism and Christianity. Apart from classes for his soldiers, Feng also set up a secondary school for the sons of his officers in 1917. While he was at Nan-yuan, each regiment operated a School for the Common People in which qualified military and noncombatant officers acted as teachers; after he assumed control of Honan in 1922, he assigned to education revenues derived from certain specified taxes and invited Ling Ping, the dean of Nankai University, to become the commissioner of education for Honan.[8]

Yen Hsi-shan, who ruled Shansi virtually unopposed for two decades, launched a campaign in 1918 to eradicate illiteracy. He built more than 26,000 "people's schools" operated by provincial authorities and largely maintained out of the proceeds of an income tax paid by the residents of each district. Fiscal statistics in 1923 showed that education was the largest single item in the Shansi provincial budget. But the principal function of these schools was ideological rather than pedagogical. As Donald Gillin puts it, "What he [Yen] wanted from his school system was an army of trained farmers and workers able to read his propaganda, yet not educated enough to question it." Because he was fearful of student radicalism in institutions of higher learning, Yen allocated to colleges and universities less than a seventh of the money he spent each year on education.[9]

The Financing of Public Education

Faced with the need to maintain vast standing armies and to meet the mounting cost of fighting wars, the warlords were forced to divert most of the resources they could command to military activities. Although the amounts devoted to education had indeed steadily increased since 1913, military expenses had escalated even more rapidly during the same period. Paul Monroe estimated that the number of soldiers in China increased from about 1,370,000 in 1920 to around 1,600,000 during 1926-1927, with an average cost of about $375 per soldier per year.[10] The cost of fighting had also soared. One day's fighting in 1922 cost about as much as one month's fighting in 1918, and in the 1920s wars were taking place almost without interruption.[11] Between 1922 and 1930, an average of ten major wars erupted in China each year.[12]

The low emphasis placed upon education by most of the warlords was clearly revealed in the budgetary allocations for education. In the fiscal year 1914-1915, the proposed appropriation for education in the Peking government's budget was $3,276,904, slightly less than 1 percent of the total budget. On the other hand, military appropriations constituted about 40 percent of the budget. In 1919-1920, military allocations accounted for 42 percent of the total budget, and education, with an allotment of $6,763,518, amounted to only 1 percent. The percentages for military and education allocations rose to 71 percent and 3 percent, respectively, in 1923-1924. In fact, yearly expenditures for education, whether budgeted or in fact, never exceeded 3 percent of the total annual expenditures of the Peking government between 1912 and 1927.[13] With military and other expenditures soaring, the impoverished Peking government resorted to foreign and domestic borrowing. Still, the government incurred huge arrears. For education alone, they amounted to almost $3 million during the period from 1916 to 1922.[14] The discontent and frustration of educators, teachers, and school personnel were hardly surprising. The limited financial support for education was not even adequate for the few provinces over which the Peking regime had effective control, let alone for the whole country.

Educational expenditures varied from province to province. On the whole, as in the case of the Peking government, budgetary allocations for military purposes far exceeded those for education. In Kiangsu, for example, 39.2 percent of the 1916-1917 budget was earmarked for military uses, and 10.2 percent for education. In 1919-1920, the percentages for the military and for education were 70 and 1.1, respectively.[15] Half of Hopeh's expenditure in 1923 went for military activities while in Shantung the amount was 59 percent.[16] Aggravating the situation was the fact that in the 1920s, the number of provinces affected by wars increased considerably. From six in 1923, the number rose to thirteen in 1925 and fifteen in 1926.[17] The accompanying destruction further weakened the financial capabilities of the provinces and reduced the likelihood of any significant increase in educational expenditures.

For both the central and provincial government, the budgeting of funds for education did not mean that educational authorities would actually receive the amounts allocated. First, the minister of education and the commissioner of education had no control over government revenues. Unlike, for example, the Ministry of Communications, which ran the railways and received revenues from them, the Ministry of Education had no independent source of revenue and remained one of the least solvent government departments. The finance minister was in theory in charge of the disbursement of funds, although the warlord had the final say in all matters. Very often, money earmarked for education was diverted to other—especially military—uses without prior consultation with educational officials. The finance minister would also delay, or even stop, the release of funds. Indeed, one of the objectives of the movement to attain educational fiscal independence was to eliminate the capricious manner in which money for education was disbursed. In 1920, a resolution adopted by the National Education Association (Ch'üan-kuo chiao-yü lien-ho-hui) described the problem very well:

> Education is the basis for building the nation, and regular funding is its life blood. However, with regard to the educational funds of the provinces and districts, the officials in charge of finance often arbitrarily delay the release of funds and [the payments] are frequently not made on time. [The officials] would stop the disbursement of funds altogether on the slightest pretext. Consequently, many schools that have been established for many years can no longer be maintained. It is such a pity![18]

A major obstacle to the realization of educational fiscal autonomy was the way in which educational funds were raised and the nature of their sources. The central government derived its revenue mainly from various taxes and from provincial contributions that could no longer be counted upon as a reliable source of income. Indeed, after 1918, most provinces were able to keep the revenue that should have been remitted to the central government. Educational funds came mostly from the customs service; the salt gabelle; tobacco, wine, and stamp taxes; taxes on rolled tobacco, flour, and mines; and miscellaneous income from administrative fees. In reality, the bulk of revenues from the most important items, such as the customs service and salt gabelle, were used for the payment of foreign and domestic loans, while those from the taxes on wine and tobacco were, except for the provinces directly under Peking's control, retained by the provincial warlord governments. There was thus a recurring deficit that had to be reduced somehow by additional borrowing. Most educators maintained that the crux of the problem was that there were no specific sources of income tax that were committed for education. In December 1920, the Ministry of Education declared that 70 percent of the revenue from personal income taxes would be used for the development of national and local education. But there is no evidence that this measure was carried out.[19] For almost a year—between June 1926 and June 1927—when Peking was run by the regency cabinets, the minister of education had to close most of the government schools because the teachers had not been paid for months, and the schools had neither light nor water because of unpaid bills.[20] Without control over a stable and readily available source of revenue, education planners were subject to the whims of bureaucrats in other branches of government and educational programs were sacrificed for military and political expediencies.

Educational revenues on the provincial level were derived mainly from land taxes (with their multifarious surtaxes), title deed taxes, business or sales taxes, business brokerage taxes (*ya-shui*), and likin, as well as miscellaneous and unclassified taxes. The proceeds from these, in whole or in part, would be assigned to public education. Some provinces also had "school lands" owned by the government, the revenue from which was earmarked for education at the *hsien* level. But the funds from the aforementioned sources were not always available. In January 1926, the Szechuan government decreed that the revenue from the salt gabelle be used as Chengtu University's operational fund, but the money was soon appropriated by the military.[21] There were some attempts by various provincial governments to guarantee the autonomy of educational finances. The Honan government promised in July 1922 to use the proceeds from title deed taxes for education. But it was not until August 1925 that a special committee was set up to supervise the collection and disbursement of funds. Other provinces, such as Kiangsu and Chekiang, began in the early 1920s to allocate the income from rolled tobacco for educational activities.[22] Some of these measures, however, met with strong opposition. In 1924, monasterial authorities in Kiangsu vigorously objected to the introduction of a special surtax to aid education on donations to monasteries; and tea merchants in Chekiang, Fukien, Anhwei, and Kiangsi protested the use of the revenues from a special levy on their businesses for educational purposes.[23] Finally, the unstable nature of some taxes, such as the business brokerage tax, reduced their usefulness as sources of income for educational undertakings.

The Movement for Educational Fiscal Independence

Against this background of mounting fiscal difficulty and confusion, a movement for educational fiscal independence emerged in the late 1910s and continued throughout most of the next decade. Participants in the movement included educators, school officials, and students. Educators demanded the assured financial support of the schools and their faculties as well as the restructuring of the system of public educational finance so as to guarantee fiscal independence. At the same time, students launched a far more vigorous and often openly antiwarlord campaign to reduce, and indeed to eliminate entirely, the militarists' control over education. The students were joined by some of their elders and the campaign became part of the general antiwarlord and antiimperialist movement of the 1920s.

In their arguments for educational fiscal independence, educators stressed the importance of education in the modernization and strengthening of China. One educator termed education "the only hope for China."[24] The educators insisted that education should receive top priority in national planning and be given generous financial support by the government. The problem of Chinese education, they claimed, was not simply one of introducing and implementing the most up-to-date educational ideas. It was, more importantly, one of how the educators could assume direct and independent control over the planning and financing of education. Politicians and warlords, they maintained, were both insensitive and unqualified to deal with educational matters. They insisted that educational fiscal autonomy would guarantee the freedom of action necessary for the development of education.[25] Such arguments presupposed the primacy of education in the modernization of China as well as the leading role that the educated elite should play in this process. Moreover, most educators of the 1910s and 1920s believed that education was a correlate, if not a requisite, of a democratic order. The prospect for a modern and democratic China, therefore, rested on the success of educational planning and development.

To realize their objectives, educators tried to mobilize public opinion to exert pressure on the warlord governments. They publicized their ideas in newspapers and journals and through their activities in the many educational associations hoped to influence government policy. Some of them also put forth concrete proposals for educational reform. Li Shih-ch'en, a prominent educator, urged the decentralization of the educational administrative structure. He suggested that educational associations and educational executive committees at the provincial, *hsien,* city, and town levels replace the Ministry of Education and the Department of Education. The local educational bodies, composed of people knowledgeable in educational matters, should prepare the annual budget for education and be responsible for the collection and safeguarding of the funds.[26] Another educator, Chuang Tse-hsuan, proposed the creation of a National Endowment for Education to provide for a stable and steady source of income. The trustees of the endowment, mostly educators, would be empowered to raise, manage, and distribute the money.[27] Both proposals therefore stressed the independent control and oversight of education by educators.

On February 12, 1922, the National Association for Educational Autonomy was founded in Peking. In its first declaration, the association pledged to work for the separation of education from politics and the setting up of an independent source of revenue for education.[28] Other organizations, such as the National Education Association, also adopted resolutions urging educational fiscal autonomy.[29] And in August 1925, the Association for the Advancement of Chinese Education recommended to the Peking government a constitutional amendment that would guarantee a minimum of 20 percent of the national and provincial budgets for educational development.[30]

However, the mere adoption of resolutions in educational conferences or the drafting of proposals for reforms proved not very effective in solving the financial crisis. Many teachers resorted to the drastic step of going on strike or resigning if their demands went unheeded. Such strikes were usually supported by students. Shu Hsin-cheng has described one teacher strike in Changsha in 1920; the account illustrates very well the pattern of confrontation between teachers and the warlord government as well as the warlords' attitude toward education.[31]

In November 1920, T'an Yen-k'ai, the *tu-chun* of Hunan, proclaimed self-government for his province. He appointed Chao Heng-ti as military commander and Lin Chih-yü as acting governor. His professed aim was to convert Hunan into a "model self-governing province." Public school teachers in the province hoped that this expressed desire to improve conditions in Hunan would mean, among other things, the release of educational funds in arrears. When this did not take place, teachers in the First Normal School in Changsha went on strike. The school, with many renowned scholars from other parts of the country on its faculty, had a national reputation of being a progressive institution. The strike was an embarrassment to the government.

The development of the strike followed a pattern common to similar events in the 1910s and 1920s. First, the teachers petitioned the government for money. When the funds were not forthcoming and after the ensuing negotiations had proved fruitless, they went on strike. At the same time they issued manifestos to solicit the backing of students and the public. Students then threw in their support and organized their own campaign. Chao Heng-ti and Lin Chih-yü were unwilling to be blamed for tainting the "progressive" image of the province and reluctantly agreed to provide the needed money.

But as the clash between students, teachers, and the Peking police in June 1921 showed, not all these protests ended peacefully. Indeed, frustrated teachers might sometimes resort to violence, as in October 1924 when government teachers in Fukien wrecked the office of the finance minister after their demands for funds were not met.[32]

Throughout the 1920s there were teacher protests and strikes in cities such as Peking, Tsinan, Wuchang, and Canton and in provinces such as Kiangsu, Anhwei, Fukien, and Szechuan.[33] Except for a few cases such activities proved to be futile. For instance, despite the settlement in July 1921, the financial troubles of the eight government colleges and universities in Peking were far from over. In November 1923, the faculty and staff of these schools again went on strike because the government had once more failed to provide them with the necessary funds. In the final analysis, as one educator claimed, the problem of educational finance was a political problem and the solution to the problem was political reform.[34]

Students and the Educational Crisis

Unlike their elders, students were far more radical in their reaction to the crisis in education. Disgusted with the continual deterioration of the political situation, most students became convinced of the need for direct political action in bringing about national unification and the modernization of China. For them, educational problems such as the absence of planning and the chronic shortage of funds were but symptoms of a larger malaise. They argued that, ultimately, the warlords were responsible for the failure of Chinese education because they had either neglected it or had exploited it for personal gains. The students therefore asserted that the problems of educational finance, and indeed of the entire educational system, could be solved only after the warlords had been eliminated. Many went even further and maintained that meaningful and lasting changes, whether in education, society, or economy, had to be accompanied by a fundamental political reconstruction.[35]

As a first step to the reorganization of education, students concurred with their elders that there should be educational autonomy. The students insisted that inadequate financial support not only demoralized both teachers and students but also led to a deterioration in the quality of education. Besides supporting their teachers' protests, students were also active in initiating their own campaigns for educational fiscal independence. A noted example of such a campaign took place in Kiangsu in 1923. In early January the provincial legislature decided to trim the educational budget by about $10,000. This action provoked immediate opposition from the students. The Nanking Student Union petitioned the government to reconsider the decision, and on January 10 about a thousand students held a rally to protest the budget cut. Seven days later, representatives of the newly founded Kiangsu Student Association passed resolutions calling for educational fiscal independence. In Shanghai, approximately 1,400 students demonstrated their displeasure in a huge parade on January 29. But despite these protests, there is no evidence to indicate that the Kiangsu government agreed to restore the original allocations.[36]

Students were also concerned with the ill effects that the shortage of funds had on conditions in the schools. Many school facilities were in a state of disrepair and in order to meet the mounting expenses, some school authorities increased tuition and other fees. Such actions were the direct causes of numerous incidents of student unrest, commonly known as *hsueh-ch'ao*, during the 1910s and 1920s. In March 1922, when the administration of Kiangsu Sixth Middle School raised the prices in the cafeteria, the students set up a special food committee to negotiate with school authorities. The negotiations, however, broke down and the students organized a series of campus disturbances. The unrest ended after three months with the appointment of a new principal.[37] Indeed, during 1922 there were at least eighteen cases of *hsueh-ch'ao* related to the problem of school finances, involving such issues as the lowering of tuition, the disclosure of school finances, and the sanctity of educational funds.[38]

Many students directed their wrath at the school authorities, whom they accused of colluding with the warlords in the destruction of education. They therefore demanded greater student control over the administration of school affairs and insisted on their "right" to intervene in such matters as the planning and design of the curricula, the use of school funds, the hiring and dismissal of personnel, and the improvement of school facilities. The students considered such control vital to the realization of student self-government (*hsueh-sheng tzu-chih*), an idea that was extremely popular with students at the time.[39]

But as the decade of the 1920s wore on, many students became disenchanted with the possibility of reforming the educational system. Increasingly, they interpreted the failure of the system within the larger context of the collapse of the political order and intensified their attempts to revivify education within the framework of the burgeoning antiwarlord movement. Antimilitarist sentiment was also prompted by the Chinese Communist Party and the Kuomintang through their activities and propaganda. The Communists had raised the banner of antiwarlordism and antiimperialism as early as 1922. By 1924, these two themes were equally important in the platform of the Kuomintang after the collaboration with the Communists had been agreed upon. In sharp contrast to the apathy and indecisiveness that characterized the warlords' attitudes toward education, the Manifesto of the First National Congress of the Kuomintang contained several important policy statements on education. They included pledges to promote the principle of equality of the sexes in education, to enforce the sanctity and independence of educational funds, and to advance the equality of educational opportunities.[40] This and other programs of the Kuomintang and the Chinese Communist Party helped to convince many students that a basic revolution involving the fundamental reconstruction of Chinese society, politics, and education was the key to the salvation of China.

Warlordism and Modern Chinese Education

The chronic shortage of funds during the warlord period had grave consequences for the development of education in modern China. For the teachers and staff in public schools, nonpayment of salaries often caused economic hardships. According to a nationwide survey of incomes and expenditures of 1,228 middle school teachers in China in 1924, median annual income was $706.45, and the median annual expenditure for their families amounted to $659.66, leaving a yearly balance of $46.79.[41] Any delay in the payment of salaries would therefore have serious consequences. The financial insecurity not only demoralized the teachers but also discouraged other qualified persons from entering the teaching profession. Indeed, a common complaint of students during this period was the incompetence of their teachers. Preoccupied with their own problems, many teachers showed little interest in the life of their students, which, in turn, undoubtedly contributed to the growth of student discontent.

An even more serious consequence was the inequality of educational opportunities. The above discussion has shown that educational funds were derived almost entirely from taxation, and unfortunately the tax burden fell mostly on those least able to shoulder it. One educator cynically remarked in 1924: "In foreign countries, the wealthy people pay money to [educate] the poor. It is only in China that the poor pay money to [educate] the wealthy."[42]

Moreover, since there was not enough money to maintain even the existing schools, programs designed to promote universal education and mass literacy were never carried out to any significant extent. In fact, many schools increased their academic and nonacademic fees in an attempt to reduce the deficits, and thus education became increasingly expensive. It has been estimated that by 1930 the completion of six years of primary school, four years of middle school, and four years of college would require a minimum of $508, $1,120, and $1,891, respectively. Poor peasants and urban workers could hardly afford to send their children to school. A study of 2,866 farming families conducted between 1921 and 1925 in north and central China showed that landlords had received an average aof 4.3 years of education while the average for tenant farmers was 2.9.[43] Also, since the majority of the high schools, colleges, and universities were located in the cities, the poor peasants were further deprived of educational opportunities. Indeed, such opportunities had been monopolized by the propertied classes, whether in the city or in the countryside. Many educators had hoped that the development of education would produce a literate and enlightened populace to act as the basis for the development of a democratic China. However, the actual result was a sharpening of the division in Chinese society, especially between the educated elite—most of them congregating in urban areas—and the laboring masses.

Finally, although many factors impeded China's modernization, there is no doubt that the warlords' neglect of education contributed to the failure of efforts in this direction. The failure was not simply one of not educating and training a pool of competent personnel needed for the technological development of China. More seriously, it was a failure to educate the general population, which would have supported and helped to promote China's progress toward modernity. To accomplish these goals would have required, among other things, the broadening of educational opportunities and the diversion of a large portion of the national wealth to the development of education. Unfortunately, the warlord system, with its insatiable demand for money, made the rational allocation of resources impossible.

Revolution, Nation-building, and Chinese Communist Leadership Education During the Sino-Japanese War

Jane L. Price

During the Sino-Japanese War (1937-1945), the Chinese Communist Party (CCP) constructed an extensive educational complex for Party and non-Party members throughout its border regions. The profusion of educational institutions in Yenan and outlying areas can be taken as a measure of the gains the Communists had made. What started out as a tiny band of disaffected intellectuals in 1920 had swelled by late 1945 into a powerful political movement controlling 149 million people and one-fourth of the population of China. Thus, by the end of the Sino-Japanese War, the Chinese Communist movement had become a major political force that could claim to speak for all of China, and the Communists began to face the problems of a major political force—problems of modernization and political integration that any group hoping to reunify China would have to solve. This essay will show how the Chinese Communists tackled their nation-building problems in their policies for leadership education and how they built the leadership core for victory in 1949.

Well before the Sino-Japanese War the Chinese Communist Party had paid close attention to the preparation of its leaders. From infancy the Party had relied on an array of institutions to train the men and women who guided its military and mobilization work. But as the Chinese Communist movement expanded into large units of territory, the Party's leadership requirements grew more complex. Besides political activists and military leaders, the Communists were in desperate need of scientists, administrators, technicians, medical workers, and educators who could form the backbone of a modern society. These needs were addressed by Chinese Communist leadership education during the Yenan period.

By 1942 more than twenty full-time schools for leadership training were operating in the city of Yenan alone. Most of these institutions prepared various types of high-level leaders for positions of authority above the local level. They were classified either as "united front" schools, which trained both Chinese Communist Party and non-Party cadres for the war of resistance, or as "Party schools," exclusively for Communist Party members. Many "united front" schools were set up to accommodate the massive influx of intellectuals from outside the border regions who streamed into Yenan after the outbreak of the Sino-Japanese War. Such institutions facilitated the absorption of intellectuals into the Chinese Communist movement and helped win commitment to Communism from an influential group in Chinese society.

K'ang-ta, the "Revolutionary Crucible"

In number of graduates and impact on Chinese Communist educational policy and philosophy, the most influential institution for leadership education during the Sino-Japanese War was "K'ang-ta," the Anti-Japanese Military and Political University. It was an outgrowth of earlier Chinese Communist schools—such as the Red Army Academy in Juichin—that prepared political commissars and command personnel for the Red Army. After the outbreak of war with Japan, this school changed its orientation to united front mobilization work, and added non-Communist intellectuals and border region peasants to its student body.

The name of Anti-Japanese Military and Political University was applied officially on January 20, 1937, to a Red Army academy that had opened in 1936 in Wayaopao, then Paoan, then Yenan in Shensi. K'ang-ta operated until the end of the Sino-Japanese War, with a main campus in Yenan and about twelve branches in outlying Chinese Communist base areas.[1] Altogether the main and branch schools of K'ang-ta were reported to have graduated 100,000 students.[2]

A significant portion of these graduates were not veteran Chinese Communist Party members or military personnel but students from former enemy areas assigned to united front mobilization work. They came to dominate the composition of the K'ang-ta student body in the late 1930s and early 1940s. The first session of K'ang-ta took place in 1936 while it was still the Red Army Academy in Paoan. Most of the first class, numbering 140, consisted of high-level Red Army cadres, with the school's principal, Lin Piao, and its educational director, Lo Jui-ch'ing, concurrently students and teachers.

With the move to Yenan and reorganization into the Anti-Japanese

Military and Political Academy in early 1937, the second class enrollment jumped to 1,200. Eighty percent were cadres from the Second and Fourth Front armies, but the remainder included local Communists from the northwest and a group of students from outside the Communist border regions. This class graduated in July 1937 and left immediately for the front. The third class, in residence from September 1937 to April 1938, showed the effects of the united front on the Chinese Communist movement. Forty percent of its total enrollment of 1,800 had previously been students from outside the border regions. Students from the "white areas" dominated the fourth class of 4,500, in session from April to October 1938, and the fifth class of 8,000, which ran from October 1938 to January 1940.

Due to the tightening Nationalist blockade of the Communist base areas, few students managed to reach Yenan thereafter. Subsequent K'ang-ta classes found few intellectuals in their midst. Just before the graduation of the fifth class, the main K'ang-ta campus moved to Wuhsiang, Shansi, and had resettled by January 1941 in the Shansi-Hopei-Shantung-Honan border region. There is little information on the remaining K'ang-ta classes of the main school or its branches, but most appear to have trained primarily Eighth Route or New Fourth Army officers who had reached the command level of company, battalion, or regiment.[3]

It was during the period when the main K'ang-ta campus was in Yenan that it had its greatest impact on Chinese Communist educational policy for the Sino-Japanese War. On its instructional and administrative staff were some of the most outstanding leaders of the Chinese Communist Party—testimony to the Party's concern with leadership and educational questions. Lin Piao was nominal principal of K'ang-ta at this time but spent most of these years commanding the 115th Division of the Eighth Route Army or taking medical treatment in Moscow. Under these circumstances, daily management of the school fell to Lo Jui-ch'ing, who became vice-principal and political commissar in 1938 and served as acting head. Mao Tse-tung assumed the chairmanship of the Education Department in the first half of 1937 and was assisted by Chang Wen-t'ien, Ch'en Po-ta, Ch'eng Fang-wu, Ho Kan-chih, and Ai Ssu-ch'i. Tung Pi-wu served as political commissar for students from "white areas," who were under the general supervision of Nieh Ho-t'ing. Other Communist luminaries on the faculty and staff included Chu Teh, Ch'in Pang-hsien, Wu Liang-p'ing, Wang Chia-hsiang, Lo Jung-huan, and Liu Ya-lou.[4]

In curriculum, the school placed priority on united front issues and basic military knowledge. All students took both military and political courses, with the ratio of military to political subjects determined by the nature of each student's future work assignment. Military cadres who entered K'ang-ta from the army or faced military assignments upon graduation devoted 70 percent of their time to military subjects and 30 percent to political and cultural subjects. The ratio of military to political subjects was reversed for political cadres expecting to work in the army, mass organizations, or official administrative positions.[5]

To date, there are no detailed descriptions of the content of K'ang-ta courses and available accounts differ somewhat in their version of what was taught. The Wuhan Mobilization Society's report on "The Situation at K'ang-ta" divided courses into three categories: (1) political courses, consisting of Chinese problems, general discussion of social science, general discussion of Sun Yat-sen's Three People's Principles, political common knowledge, and philosophy; (2) military courses, such as guerrilla warfare, strategy and infantry tactics, and drill and deportment; and (3) "cultural" courses, including common knowledge of history and geography, basic natural science, arithmetic, and Japanese language.[6]

A wartime Japanese report classified the K'ang-ta curriculum into courses for Red Army cadres and other CCP organizations and courses for students working in "white areas." Both groups took courses in dialectics, history of the Chinese revolution, political economy, Leninism, guerrilla warfare, and military affairs. The all-Communist "cadre companies" were assigned additional work in strategy and tactics of the Red Army, history of the founding of the Red Army, tactics and strategy of the Chinese revolution, and materialism.[7]

While much of the course content and study materials dealt with Chinese problems, there was considerable emphasis on Marxist-Leninist theoretical issues.[8] This aspect of the study program may have been designed to appeal to non-Communist intellectuals in the student body. Courses on political economy, dialectical materialism, or the Marxist theory of history, as related to Chinese concerns, furnished an intellectual framework for students to use in translating nationalism into Communism.

One can see how this conversion process might have operated in descriptions of the course work on social science, Chinese problems, and the united front. In the course on Chinese problems, students were taught that Chinese society was "semifeudal, semicolonial." Instructors presented the "correct" revolutionary viewpoint as "antifeudal and antiimperialist" and enjoined students to fight Japanese imperialism to achieve national independence. The course attempted to show the historical roots of the Three People's Principles and their realization through the united front. Along similar lines, the social science course tried to demonstrate the theoretical basis for the eventual collapse of Japanese imperialism and the success of the national revolution in China.[9]

Other courses on wartime political work and guerrilla warfare introduced Communist organizational principles and Maoist military strategy. Students of wartime political work learned the significance of political work among regular army units and guerrilla bands; how to inspire troops for both offensive and defensive combat; how to plan retreats; and how to conduct propaganda among local peasants and enemy troops. The guerrilla warfare course defined guerrilla activity as a positive offensive form of combat involving unity with the common people.[10]

Military classes at K'ang-ta were conducted in the open air. To bring training as close to actual combat as possible, the school frequently staged large-scale maneuvers. Every company simulated military operations daily through diagrams in a sandpan. Among the military lessons at K'ang-ta were instruction in night combat, close-range combat, bayonet fighting, shooting, and hurling grenades.[11]

The military as a source of organizational inspiration pervaded many aspects of student life at K'ang-ta. Student conduct was regulated by military codes of behavior to develop such qualities as discipline, efficiency, and endurance for a crisis environment. In organization the student body adopted military lines of division, subdividing into "battalions" (*ta-tui*), then "companies" (*tui*), "district companies" (*ch'ü-tui*), and "small groups" (*hsiao-tsu*). Although the size of each division changed periodically, the small groups remained constant at ten persons each. An instructor for military and political education was assigned to each battalion and company. Some of the companies also had cultural instructors.[12]

Qualities nurtured through the militarization of student life were part of a distinct "school style" articulated at K'ang-ta as "unified, tense, lively, and serious."[13] Linked to endurance and discipline was the determination to "overcome difficulties in the face of immense hardship" and "turn liabilities into assets." These qualities were prized throughout the history of the Chinese Communist movement but found special reinforcement at K'ang-ta.

From its inception the school was in constant struggle with a hostile environment. For the first class there were only three full-time instructors and a staff largely inexperienced in educational work. To compensate, students turned to teaching themselves. They used their knees for desks and fashioned classrooms and sleeping quarters from caves dug in the hills outside Paoan. The second class in its new Yenan location in January 1937 found itself swamped with an enrollment of 1,200, inducing severe shortages of facilities, personnel, and teaching materials. The student mix—Red Army fighters, local peasant cadres, and non–border region students—posed certain social and pedagogical difficulties. School authorities, however, came to view this disparity in knowledge and experience as potentially beneficial. Accentuating the positive, they encouraged students to pool their experiences and learn from one another.

In the third class of 1,800 this trend continued. Students pooled their own books to form a "circulating library" and dug more than 170 caves in the loess cliffs outside Yenan between November 1 and 15, 1937. One participant observed:

> The work was not very heavy, but it was a stern test to the majority of the young students who had never worked with a pick before. After a day of work, we were all sweaty and our hands were studded with blisters. Everybody had sore legs and an aching back. However, it was precisely such labor which steeled and educated us and transformed our way of thinking. It gave us even greater courage and strength to overcome difficulties.[14]

The educational value of physical labor took on new dimensions in the fourth K'ang-ta class. Its 4,500 students began to participate actively in production campaigns.[15] These campaigns enabled K'ang-ta to become self-sufficient in food and were another means of teaching students the dignity of manual labor. Production activities were conducted with local peasants and helped teach students from elite backgrounds how to relate to the common people—an important mobilization skill and Communist idea. Physical labor, as an activity for character building, became enshrined in combined work and study programs for other Communist leadership training schools as a basic tenet of Chinese Communist educational philosophy. Daily trials "steeled" cadres for future hardship on the revolutionary battleground. Such challenges also reinforced dialectical thought patterns—the ability to see things in terms of their opposites—and voluntaristic attitudes—greater confidence in the human will as a force shaping history.

Other pedagogical principles articulated at K'ang-ta also took inspiration from the material shortages and crisis environment of the Kiangsi and Yenan years. One cardinal principle was called the *ch'i-fa*, or mind-opening method, and had evolved during the Kiangsi period. At K'ang-ta the *ch'i-fa* method was contrasted to the traditional lecture format, rote memorization, or simple questions and answers. It was defined as "a method of investigation moving from induction to deduction." A practitioner of *ch'i-fa* proceeded "from near to far, from concrete to abstract, from part to whole," thereby grasping from one incident or example the law of development of a complex phenomenon.

To employ *ch'i-fa*, a topic would be first dissected into its main points. Then, through questions and answers each major point would be broken down into minor points that illustrated facets of the main issue. For example,

> in discussing how feudal society was able to develop into capitalist society, the internal contradictions of feudal society and the process and outcome of their development must be explained, which leads to an investigation of the laws of development of society based on private ownership as well as speculation on its future.[16]

This learning method was found to have ideological as well as pedagogical value. It too encouraged dialectical thinking supportive of Marxist-Leninist analysis and was another means of bringing K'ang-ta trainees one step closer to Chinese Communism.

Another outcome anticipated of the *ch'i-fa* procedure was the ability to apply abstract principles to specific situations in real life. Students who had mastered this technique were expected to use it in the future when faced with no specific instructions from higher authorities. In other areas of K'ang-ta education as well, the "unity of theory and practice" was consistently underlined. In the words of former student Niu K'o-lun:

> Whatever was taught was done. When the lesson dealt with weapons, we promptly dismantled a rifle and learned to shoot. When the lesson dealt with attack or defense by a battalion or company, a field exercise was held. Things were studied for application.[17]

To prevent both teachers and students from digressing from the key points of each lesson, the *hsiao-erh-ching* ("small but essential") principle governed curriculum and course content. Instructors conscientiously planned ahead to teach students essential points in a minimal amount of time. They tailored topics of lectures and discussions to the time limit of each class period and each student's thought span. Students were taught to evaluate the essential points of reading materials.[18]

Streamlined curriculum and pedagogical practices at K'ang-ta were spurred on by the dictates of revolution and war and the perennial shortage of qualified teachers. Top Party leaders, responsible for many of the lectures, were often too pressed with other duties to adhere to a regular class schedule. Through careful planning, the principles of *ch'i-fa* and *hsiao-erh-ching* were combined with group study so that students under supervision could largely educate themselves. The school began to rely on a type of paraprofessional corps called the "education staff."

"Mutual help and collective study" was another school ideal. Each company selected several students to tutor illiterate or semiliterate students of worker or peasant background. The educationally disadvantaged were also encouraged to participate actively in discussion sessions to clarify anything they could not understand.[19] Group study and tutoring efforts thus upgraded student performance at K'ang-ta while developing human relations skills for future mobilization work.

In addition to group study sessions, the values prized at K'ang-ta found reinforcement in other forms of collective activity: "sit and talk" meetings, "current events discussion meetings,"[20] "revolutionary competition"[21] events, and Salvation Room[22] programs. The most heavy-handed approach to ideological remolding occurred at "life investigation and discussion" meetings that took place in the Salvation Room. Its procedures were similar to "criticism and self-criticism" sessions that have been basic to Chinese Communist Party political education since the 1930s. An individual's entire life history was dissected to measure his conduct against school principles[23] in the hope of checking potentially deviant behavior or unorthodox beliefs.

This picture of K'ang-ta life is an ideal one, and there is evidence that K'ang-ta education did not always live up to its slogans. School authorities did not refrain from pointing out shortcomings. Lo Jui-ch'ing believed that despite impressive gains in the size and quality of his staff, some cadres continued to show weak teaching and leadership abilities. Lo found that the coordination of work and study did not always proceed smoothly and that funds for operating expenses were perennially scarce.[24]

It would appear that the students from non-Communist areas were the most disappointed with K'ang-ta education. The K'ang-ta setting exposed the tensions involved in absorbing large numbers of outside intellectuals into the Chinese Communist movement. Youthful emigrés to Yenan displayed a number of motives for attending K'ang-ta besides the call of pure patriotism. Many fled to Yenan in pursuit of a "university" diploma and release from the strictures of traditional family life. Hostile accounts of K'ang-ta are replete with vignettes of "free love between the sexes" and condemnations of the school's socially permissive atmosphere. Some students found the life of recurrent hardship too much to bear. Others resented restraints on individual self-expression in study groups and the steady diet of Marxist-Leninist analysis. There were still others disappointed in the quality of military and political instruction at the school.[25] One senses that a number of intellectuals at K'ang-ta became disenchanted with the Chinese Communist Party's commitment to relentless class struggle and feared its threat to national unity.

This did not mean that all of K'ang-ta's students had the same reaction, and many of the thousands who flocked to Yenan stayed on as political workers for units of the New Fourth and Eighth Route armies or leaders of the "united front" mobilization activities behind the lines. Propaganda teams prepared at K'ang-ta moved into villages, challenged local gentry, and organized mobilization committees to funnel manpower and resources to the front. K'ang-ta alumni were among those supervising village-level guerrilla, logistical, and personnel replacement groups that stood in for regular Communist army units.[26]

It should be pointed out that the features of K'ang-ta's educational program were not innovations of the Yenan era, but drew heavily from Chinese Communist experiments in leadership education in the 1920s and 1930s. However, K'ang-ta brought together various educational practices from diverse sources in earlier periods and systematized them into a "revolutionary pedagogy" that has inspired Chinese Communist educational practice and philosophy from the Yenan period to the present day.

"United Front" Schools

Other leadership training institutions that produced personnel for "united front" mobilization work tried to emulate the K'ang-ta model. The North Shensi Public School in Yenan maintained close ties to K'ang-ta and opened under similar circumstances. It appealed to patriotic intellectuals seeking training for national salvation work.

Headed by Ch'eng Fang-wu, with Shao Shih-p'ing as director of the Education Department, Shen-pei (as it was commonly called) offered two- and later three-month courses with intellectuals specifically in mind.[27]

Most of the students matriculated at the North Shensi Public School had received a middle-school to university-level education and included artists, musicians, writers, military men, and self-employed individuals between the ages of seventeen and forty. An entrance examination, consisting of ten simple questions, favored enthusiasm and commitment to the "united front" over educational achievement or political persuasion as criteria for admission.[28]

Once enrolled, students spent 70 percent of their time on political subjects and 30 percent on military subjects. There were four basic courses: (1) general introduction to the social sciences; (2) united front and people's movement work; (3) guerrilla warfare and basic military knowledge; and (4) lectures on current events. The teaching staff has been described as consisting of experienced "revolutionary fighters," such as Mao Tse-tung, Chang Wen-t'ien, K'ang Sheng, Li Fu-ch'un, Ho Kan-chih, Wang Jo-fei, Li Fan-fu, Hsu Ping, Yang Sung, Ai Ssu-ch'i, Ho Ting-hua, Li Wei-i, Principal Ch'eng Fang-wu, Lo Mai (Li Wei-han), Chou Ch'ün-ch'uan, Ch'en Ch'ang-hao, and Wu Liang-p'ing.[29] Since quite a few of these individuals also lectured at K'ang-ta, one can assume some overlap in course content between the two institutions.

Suffering from the same teacher and material shortages as K'ang-ta, the North Shensi Public School tried to emulate K'ang-ta's organizational and study principles. Students were arranged in companies, platoons, and sections, with each section numbering ten to twelve persons. Every company was assigned a "study representative" for each subject to guide "study life." Study plans issued by school authorities were developed through a series of discussion meetings of students and instructors.[30] As at K'ang-ta the group discussion format governed most of the study life at Shen-pei under the "educational principles" of (1) "the unity of theory and practice," (2) *hsiao-erh-ching*, and (3) "unity of students and teachers." Shen-pei likewise boasted a slogan for its "school style"—"devotion and unity, tenseness and liveliness"—and valued material hardship as a "compulsory course for participating in the front-line resistance war or people's movement work." Other aspects of student life, including "revolutionary competition" and "criticism and self-criticism" sessions, followed the K'ang-ta pattern.[31]

By June 1938 the North Shensi Public School had produced five classes totalling 3,000 graduates. Upon termination of studies, males were usually dispatched to the front lines to organize guerrilla bands or mass agitation activities. Female graduates generally undertook mobilization work behind the lines.[32] Some outstanding students were sent on to K'ang-ta or another Chinese Communist Party school for further training.

Some united front schools catered to particular mobilization needs. Chinese Women's University in Yenan, set up in March 1939, trained only female cadres to head mobilization work involving other women. Much of its top leadership came from the former "Twenty-eight Bolshevik" faction of the Chinese Communist Party. Below Principal Ch'en Shao-yü (Wang Ming) and Vice-principal Hsun Li-chih were ex-"Bolsheviks" Ch'en Ch'ang-hao, heading the Instructional Affairs Office, and Meng Ch'ing-shu (Mme. Ch'en Shao-yü), in charge of the General Affairs Office.[33]

Although Chinese Women's University gave preference to "worker-peasant women," anti-Japanese activists, and students from military-political training schools behind Japanese lines, the majority of those enrolled were non-Communist intellectuals in their twenties. On the basis of results from preliminary examinations students were either assigned to one of six general classes, to one high-level research class, or to one "special class." The research class trained "theoretical cadres" with a university education or its equivalent, or two years of study in other Communist institutions. Graduates were assigned to lead war work, political work in enemy areas, teaching, medical work, propaganda work, or cooperative organizing. The "special class" furnished basic literacy skills to "worker-peasant" students with some experience in the women's movement.[34] Very little study time was allocated to issues concerning the Chinese women's movement alone. Instead, Women's University, in accord with the Chinese Communist Party's traditional position on women's problems, tried to tie in female emancipation with more general revolutionary goals. The Chinese Communist Party continued to argue that the interests of women would be served best through measures to eliminate an exploitative social and economic system. Feminist concerns were thus subordinated to the general mobilization strategy of the Chinese Communist Party during the Sino-Japanese War period. In the address to the opening ceremony of Chinese Women's University, Principal Ch'en Shao-yü cautioned his students to remain "steadfast wives, good mothers, and filial daughters" for the sake of maximizing support for the Chinese Communist movement in its conservative peasant milieu. The curriculum and other aspects of Women's University, then, attempted to acclimate independent-minded women intellectuals to conditions in the border regions and to convert their feminism to Marxism.

Like K'ang-ta and the North Shensi Public School, Chinese Women's University embraced an educational philosophy of the "unity of theory and practice" and the combination of collective and independent study. An observer described all of the courses as "salted with Marxist philosophy, including the Chinese Communist Party's own interpretation of the Three People's Principles."[35] Women's University students also participated in the production campaigns and the majority of graduates went into rural education work. A portion returned to their homes in guerrilla districts to lead mass organizations, and a few pursued further military training at K'ang-ta.[36]

United front schools sponsored by the Chinese Communist Party proliferated outside of Yenan as well, the most notable being the National Revolutionary University in Linfeng, Shansi.[37] But even the "spirit of overcoming obstacles" was insufficient to guarantee the longevity of Women's University and the North Shensi Public School. The Chinese Communist educational authorities criticized their course content as "too abstract" and remote from the daily problems of cadre work. Course coverage also suffered from continuing shortages of teachers and texts (especially introductory theoretical materials) and short matriculation periods. The critical factor, however, may have been a shortage of students, especially the non-Communist intellectuals, after the Nationalists cut off access to the border regions in mid-1939. Deprived of their raison d'être, the North Shensi Public School and Chinese Women's University disappeared several years after their founding.[38]

Specialist Schools

Throughout the 1940s, the Chinese Communist Party continued to train a sizable portion of intellectuals in its "specialist schools." These schools appear to have been less heavily influenced by the K'ang-ta educational model than schools preparing mobilization workers. The variety of training institutions for specialists is evidence of the growing responsibilities of administration, education, and modernization facing the Chinese Communist Party in the border regions.

For example, a Natural Sciences Research Institute, founded in

Yenan in July 1939, trained scientific and technical personnel and operated a center for scientific research. Under the leadership of Principal Hsu T'e-li and Vice-principal Ch'en K'ang-po, the institute consisted of two departments, each with a two-year period of matriculation. A "standard" department concentrated on pure research and offered courses in chemistry, biology, physics, and geology. In the "preparatory department," courses were more elementary (mechanical drawing, basic physics, mathematics, and chemistry) and included subjects such as Chinese problems, Marxism-Leninism, political economy, and Russian and English language. To link scientific theory to practical border region problems and meet operating expenses, the institute ran three factories: a machine factory, which manufactured various tools, looms, carts, and agricultural implements; a glass factory; and an alcohol factory.[39] Middle-level technicians and staff personnel were trained at a Worker's University outside Yenan. An institution called Motor University, founded on June 1, 1937, prepared cadres for motorized transport and communications work in the Chinese Communist armed forces.[40]

Specialists in artistic and cultural work were nurtured at the Lu Hsun Academy of Arts, founded in Yenan in February 1938. The school had departments in drama, art, music, and literature and sponsored an experimental drama troupe. During a six-month training period students could choose from an array of offerings in language, dancing, phonetics, singing, musical instruments, folk music, study of famous compositions, rehearsal and practice, folk drama, famous plays, composition and study, present situation of the art movement, Chinese literature, practical writings, present situation in literature, writing and practice, journalism, border region education, and selections from world literature. Most of the students were from the "white areas." Required courses in the theory of art and contemporary political theory helped transform them into revolutionary artists promoting "a New Democratic art and culture" with "the standpoint of Marxist-Leninist theory."[41]

There were also schools to train "specialists" in Party work in Yenan and the border regions. The most prominent was the Central Party School in Yenan, headed by Li Wei-han between 1937 and 1940; Teng Fa between 1940 and 1942; Mao Tse-tung between 1942 and 1944; and P'eng Chen after 1944.[42] The student body, which grew from approximately 300 in 1938 to about 5,000 in 1944, was composed almost exclusively of high- and middle-level Chinese Communist Party cadres.[43] Most were either peasants or former students, with a sizable portion from the "white areas" enrolled in a short-term program.[44] Visitors to the Central Party School also observed national minorities receiving basic literacy training, and administrators and other experts undergoing remedial political education.[45]

The bulk of the Central Party School curriculum was oriented toward the immediate problems of Party workers. Twenty-five percent of the total study time was devoted to problems of current events; 17 percent to the Chinese situation and Chinese revolutionary strategy; 30 percent to Party construction; 23 percent to Marxism-Leninism; and 5 percent to group research. Mao Tse-tung was the principal lecturer in the areas of philosophy, the history of the modern Chinese revolution, and the "theory of New Democracy." Other instructors included Chinese Communist Party theorists Fan Wen-lan, Ai Ssu-ch'i, and Ch'en Po-ta. There is evidence of some K'ang-ta influence in reports of independent study combined with group discussion, and of students from diverse backgrounds trading knowledge and experiences.[46]

Yenan also housed a Border Region Party School, renamed the Northwest Party School in 1941. It was headed by Kao Kang and prepared Party personnel with special competence in the problems of the Shensi-Kansu-Ningsia border region.[47]

For high-level theoretical work, the Chinese Communist Party operated the Central Research Institute. It had been founded in 1938 in Yenan and was called the Academy of Marxism-Leninism before reorganization in 1941. This institute was strictly research oriented and boasted a highly selective admissions policy. It had only three departments—philosophy, political economy, and research on Chinese problems—and its staff included some of the most outstanding Chinese Communist Party theorists. Graduates usually staffed various levels of Chinese Communist Party schools or high-level Party posts.[48]

The trend toward specialization, as manifested by the institutions discussed in this essay, received impetus from the Chinese Communist Party's evaluation of leadership policy in late 1941. Its "resolution on the Yenan Cadre Schools" of December 17 of that year strengthened the position of education specialists over Party branches at the major cadre schools.[49] Especially in "united front" specialist schools open to non-Communists, policy shifted away from political studies in favor of technical studies. This did not mean, however, that the Chinese Communist leadership wished technical specialization to be divorced from political objectives, and it called for strengthening the study of Chinese history, local conditions, and Party history and policy.[50]

The most well known specialized training institution to emerge from the 1941 reforms was Yenan University. After its opening in September 1941 it underwent two reorganizations, in April 1943 and May 1944.[51] In the process the university absorbed other ranking specialist schools, such as the Natural Sciences Research Institute, Lu Hsun Academy of Arts, and the Administration Academy. This school aimed at applying skilled personnel to specific border region problems.

Prior to reorganization, Yenan University was headed by Wu Yü-chang, and after April 1943 by Chou Yang, with Wang Tzu-i as vice-principal and Sung K'an-fu as secretary. Along with personnel, the number of departments, curriculum, and student composition changed with each reorganization, following trends toward increased specialization and concentration on local border region problems. After 1943 most of the student body and teaching staff consisted of border region locals, especially those active in war and production work. Few students came from proletarian and poor peasant backgrounds and 60 percent had at least a middle-school educational background. One can presume that Yenan University continued in the tradition of processing intellectuals for leadership positions in the Chinese Communist movement. Records on university staff and students in 1944 show more than half the student body being trained for administrative positions in the border regions.[52]

Following reorganization in 1944, Yenan University consisted of five major divisons: (1) an Administration Academy, with departments in administration, law, education, and finance and economics; (2) the Lu Hsun Academy of Arts, with departments in drama and music, art, and literature; (3) the Natural Sciences Academy, with departments of engineering, chemistry, and agriculture; (4) a Medical Department; and (5) a special "Female Section," probably meeting the same leadership requirements as Chinese Women's University. Each division offered general and specialized courses in its field, and matriculation periods ranged from one to two years at the Medical School, two years at the Administration and Lu Hsun academies, and three years at the Natural Sciences Academy.

Offsetting specialization at each division was a core curriculum required of all students that involved 30 percent of total study time. All students thus took courses in (1) general principles of border region construction; (2) history of the Chinese revolution; (3) revolutionary philosophy; (4) methods of thought; and (5) current events.[53] Student political consciousness was also developed through features of student life evocative of K'ang-ta. Both faculty and students were exhorted to "join in every kind of relevant practical work and research into every kind of practical question." Each course was tied to the administrative or production organs of the border region dealing with the task under study. A considerable portion of course content dealt with the policies, directives, and operations of these organs. In many instances, study time was divided between the classroom and on-the-job training. Students also spent 20 percent of their time in physical labor outside the classroom.[54]

Leadership Education and the *Cheng-feng* Movement

In effects on the Chinese Communist leadership structure the institutions discussed in this essay were both a blessing and a curse. They had upgraded the quality of tens of thousands of leaders for diverse functions in the Chinese Communist movement. At the same time, however, specialization threatened to pit different leadership types against each other—commanders versus Party representatives in the military; bureaucrats versus peasant organizers; Party theorists versus "practical workers." These were early hints of the "red-expert" controversy that has continued to haunt the Chinese Communist Party.

In addition, "united front" institutions had not adequately dealt with the problems raised by the rising proportion of intellectuals in the Chinese Communist movement. The early 1940s still saw the processing of intellectuals as a major issue in Chinese Communist leadership policy. Those drawn to Communism through nationalism and the "united front" still remained to be reconciled with the peasant cadres committed to local interests served by the land revolution. All of these fragmenting tendencies threatened Chinese Communist control over the base areas and the viability of the Communist "alternative" for China.

Education was again invoked as the principal corrective for this new crop of problems. The *cheng-feng* rectification movement, launched officially on February 1, 1942, attempted to tackle the crises of the 1940s by strengthening the Party chain of command without sacrificing local flexibility. Its major thrust was ideological rather than organizational and relied on systematic exposure to study to remold Party members' outlook and behavior. This rectification movement defined clearly and comprehensively—in a manner unprecedented in Party history—the basic goals of the Chinese Communist movement and a common denominator of actions, attitudes, and beliefs expected of all Communist leaders.

It is beyond the scope of this essay to take up the *cheng-feng* movement in detail, and my discussion will focus on those aspects of rectification related to the concerns of leadership education. First of all, the *cheng-feng* movement aimed at bridging gaps between leadership types that had widened from increased specialization in leadership functions during the Sino-Japanese War. Study materials for the rectification campaign set forth a basic core of knowledge to be mastered by every cadre associated with the Chinese Communist movement, regardless of work specialty. The Chinese Communist Party Central Propaganda Department issued a standard set of twenty-two documents as the content of rectification study for cadres of all levels. These documents dealt with essentially three questions: (1) intra-Party organizational behavior;[55] (2) ideological tendencies;[56] and (3) proper work style toward the non-Party community.[57] A composite of qualities desirable from all three categories outlined the "ideal" leadership model for all Chinese communities.

The "model Communist" depicted in the *cheng-feng* study documents was one who could show both obedience to the Party and individual initiative; steer a narrow course between "commandism" and "tailism";[58] reconcile particular work problems with "universal" principles of Marxism-Leninism; relate the details of "investigation and research" to the general revolutionary goals of Chinese Communism; and show closeness to the masses yet place loyalty to the Chinese Communist movement above personal ties. Of course this "ideal-typical" model of a revolutionary leader did not match any one person but set a standard for all Party cadres to emulate. It was not expected that every leader working under the Chinese Communist Party would meet the ideal. The hope was for the general quality of Party membership to be uplifted as individuals strove toward that end.

It is not difficult to discern potential gains for the Chinese Communists' organizational unity and revolutionary mobilization work if each Party cadre set out to improve himself along the lines suggested by the *cheng-feng* documents. But the *cheng-feng* movement also had far-reaching implications for the Chinese Communists' claim to speak for all of China, in the areas of elite values and their relationship to nation building. One factor in the political, economic, and cultural trials faced by China since the mid-twentieth century has been an "elite-mass gap"[59] produced by modernization. Education may be the handmaiden of modernity, but it often separates leaders in developing societies from their people.

Modern scientific and technical education, as imported from the West, has been criticized for creating a Chinese elite that was divorced in orientation and outlook from the vast majority of the Chinese people, especially those in the countryside.[60] Reintegrating an elite that was highly Westernized and urban in orientation was one of the major problems of the national government's bid for leadership in China. Through experimentation in the institutions discussed in this essay the Chinese Communists attempted to devise an educational system that could promote modernization while furthering integration of Party leaders and society at large. Glorification of physical labor, "mutual help and collective study," and curricula tailored to local problems are among the features of Chinese Communist leadership education addressed to this issue.

One creation of the *cheng-feng* architects was a system of values that could be shared by both leaders and followers. Although the Chinese Communist movement had arisen in response to Chinese problems, its ideological outlook and operational guidelines were drawn from foreign sources. The survival and eventual success of Communism in China depended on its ability to apply Marxism-Leninism to a backward agrarian society. The "sinification of Marxism" received a great boost from the *cheng-feng* movement and the accompanying *hsia-hsiang* ("to the village")[61] movement initiated in July 1941.

An outstanding theme of the *cheng-feng* study materials was the need for the Chinese Communist Party leadership to penetrate the countryside effectively. Mao Tse-tung's writings in the *cheng-feng* collection in particular made forceful arguments for detailed studies of local conditions and Chinese history as the basis for revolutionary theory and practice. Foreign revolutionary models, applied uncritically in China, were assailed for promoting "dogmatism," "sectarianism," and "formalism" in Party work. The *cheng-feng* documents defined "real leadership" as "correct and concrete understanding of the actual conditions of the various social classes of China," which in turn depended on the ability "to investigate society and the conditions of each class's livelihood."[62] The *cheng-feng* movement thus furnished guidelines to make Chinese Communism, as a political movement, "China-centered." The formula advanced for integrating Chinese Communist elites with society during the *cheng-feng* movement has characterized nation building in China since 1949.

The *cheng-feng* movement also functioned as a sifting process for Chinese Communist leadership evaluation. It helped determine the most effective study methods for producing cadres and disseminated them throughout the Communist leadership structure. Cadre training programs at lower levels of the Chinese Communist Party had traditionally tried to emulate practices at high-level schools such as those in Yenan. However, only a small portion of the entire Chinese Communist Party membership had been exposed to study on a formal basis. A basic "rectification methodology"—consisting of reading the standard study materials, note taking, directed group discussions, "struggle" over major issues raised by the documents, "criticism and self-criticism," and investigation of individual life histories and work performance—was distilled from pedagogical practices at the high-level schools discussed in this essay. Through the rectification campaigns, these learning practices were infused to lower levels of the Chinese Communist Party and eventually became regular features of Chinese Communist Party life.

While there were certain universal objectives in the *cheng-feng* movement, the procedures and outcome showed considerable variation throughout the Chinese Communist Party, including its high-level training institutions. The Central Party School served as a transmission belt for the *cheng-feng* movement to the entire Chinese Communist Party. It had traditionally coordinated cadre activities in scattered base areas by providing periodic training to their ranking leadership personnel. At the time the *cheng-feng* movement was launched, 1,000 high-level Chinese Communist Party leaders were concentrated at this institution.[63] Because of its impact on the entire Chinese Communist Party, the Central Party School found its rectification activities the source of much criticism from the top Communist leadership. Rectification work lasted three years and the school underwent two reorganizations.[64]

The Central Research Institute was the center for the Party's drive against intellectuals and left-wing writers. There were two areas of controversy: (1) the degree of Westernization tolerable in literary works; and (2) the extent to which practitioners of "literary realism" could criticize the policies of the Chinese Communist Party. These questions also dominated *cheng-feng* activities at the Lu Hsun Academy of Arts.[65]

The *cheng-feng* movement may have been a factor in the merger of the Academy with Yenan University in 1943, and Yenan University's interest in linking specialized studies with practical border region problems. Yenan University from April to September 1942 took up its educational philosophy and the issues of ideological and Party controls in a "united front" school as its principal rectification problems. After September, *cheng-feng* activities turned toward investigation of the life histories of individuals. Faculty and students participated in a "confession movement," or "sincerity campaign" (*t'an-pai yun-tung*) that lasted until the following July.[66] Stepped-up ideological and organizational controls at Yenan University and other "united front" schools were another means to test intellectuals' commitment to Chinese Communism.

Very little is known about the rectification program at K'ang-ta, and few published descriptions of the school are available for this period of time. By early 1941 the main school had moved behind enemy lines and, with its branches, had become increasingly oriented toward the production of military cadres. Their functions, in contrast to those of intellectuals, may have been too vital to sacrifice several months to rectification work. A report on rectification at the Fifth, or Central China, branch of K'ang-ta, headed by Ch'en I and Feng Ting, suggests precisely this conclusion.[67]

During most of 1942 the *cheng-feng* campaign remained concentrated at the higher-level cadre schools and upper administrative organs of the Chinese Communist Party. Due to difficulties in clarifying the basic issues for rectification and finding suitable personnel to supervise study programs, the movement spread very slowly to the local level. By 1943 special *cheng-feng* training classes were common at the district and subdistrict levels of the Chinese Communist Party. Study methods were flexible and tried to serve local needs. The rectification movement trailed into 1944 and, as at higher-level training institutions, had mixed results.

In the eyes of the Chinese Communist Party leadership, the rectification campaign had succeeded in articulating the goals of the Communist movement. It helped draw together diverse elements in the Chinese Communist leadership structure and widely scattered segments of the Party's organization. It is likely that the *cheng-feng* movement strengthened the Chinese Communist Party's communications system and facilitated the absorption of intellectuals into the Communist movement. Through improvements in leadership quality, the Chinese Communists were able to overcome tendencies that had fragmented and paralyzed their rivals. By the close of the *cheng-feng* movement the Chinese Communist Party had produced a leadership group that was united and sophisticated enough to put it at the helm of China.

Part 4

Retrospect: Chinese History
as Written

On the "Rediscovery" of the Chinese Past: Ts'ui Shu and Related Cases

Joshua A. Fogel

What is meant by the "rediscovery" of some old text, heritage, or person? A whole span of differing circumstances surrounds each of the various entities that we include in this term. For instance, the rediscovery par excellence was Tun-huang, where for centuries texts had been preserved in a Kansu cave apparently without a soul having ever seen them. A less perfect though still exemplary case involves the works of Wang Fu-chih (1619-1692), the brilliant proto-nationalist hermit from Hunan, whose writings were supposedly unknown for 150 years until Tseng Kuo-fan (1811-1872) sponsored their republication. Wang's works were not totally unknown throughout the eighteenth and early nineteenth centuries, however; in fact, from the research of Chinese scholars in the late 1950s and early 1960s, we know that more than a handful of scholars saw Wang's writings in manuscript form and commented on them in their own essays throughout this lengthy hiatus.[1] As one eminent sinologist explained it to me: "It took a big shot like Tseng Kuo-fan to sponsor the publication of so sensitive a writer as Wang."

This essay is concerned with several even less perfect cases of those phenomena nevertheless heralded by their promoters as "rediscoveries" (Chinese *tsai fa-hsien*; Japanese *sai hakken*), particularly that of the remarkable eighteenth-century historian and classical scholar Ts'ui Shu (1740-1816). Ts'ui's works were never lost or sealed in a cave, nor were they remotely anti-Manchu, but the importance of his ideas had simply been ignored for a century. Thus, his "rediscovery" involved the resuscitative efforts of twentieth-century scholars who found contemporary meaning in his works that had been missed by other readers for many years. What is especially interesting about the

The author would like to thank James Polachek, John Langlois, and William Rowe, all of whom read earlier drafts of this essay.

case of Ts'ui Shu is that his rediscovery occurred twice (once in China and once in Japan) under entirely different circumstances, and as such provides us with a fascinating case of comparative sinology. Thus, this essay has the following aims: (1) to present several cases of "rediscovery" of earlier historians by both Chinese and Japanese historians of this century; (2) to ask why Ts'ui and others were seen as so vital by their revivers; (3) to interpolate possible Sino-Japanese connections; and (4) to discuss the importance of the rediscovery effort.

For nearly half a century the historiographical output of the Republican period has been shielded from critical evaluation by two connected forces: (1) a pervasive nationalism, which among other things teaches students of modern Chinese history that the foreign powers and Japan in particular were monstrous ogres at virtually every turn (this can greatly distort one's perception of events in twentieth-century history and can emotionally charge terms like "imperialist"); and (2) the research of a handful of men, like Hu Shih and his group of students, whose overwhelming intellects have made serious criticism of their work, or in fact their whole intellectual project, extremely difficult. This essay will concentrate on the latter of these forces, which was itself heavily influenced by Chinese nationalism. In recent years historians have begun to liberate themselves from this influence and have slowly gained a better understanding of scholarship in (and the history of) the Republican period. Much work remains to be done; much needs to be reassessed. Furthermore, while we know something about political ties in this period between the Chinese and Japanese (e.g., Sun Yat-sen, Li Ta-chao, China *rōnin*, anarchism), we know little of the intellectual or scholarly ties, or, for that matter, little about late nineteenth- and early twentieth-century Japanese sinology. I hope here to contribute somewhat to a better understanding of these two traditions of scholarship.

Ts'ui Shu's Dual Rediscovery

In the April 1923 issue of *Kuo-hsueh chi-k'an* [Journal of national studies], Hu Shih (1891-1962) introduced Ts'ui Shu, a then little-known scholar from Chihli, to a large segment of the Chinese scholarly world. Several years before, Hu's pupil Ku Chieh-kang (b. 1895) had begun a laborious process of editing and punctuating Ts'ui's writings; the final product appeared fifteen years later in 1936, the *Ts'ui Tung-pi i-shu* [Collected works of Ts'ui Shu] in sixteen string-bound volumes (*ts'e*). In his biography of Ku, Laurence Schneider writes that "of all the obscure scholars that he resuscitated . . . none had been more obscure than Ts'ui Shu, nor did any receive more lavish treatment and studied reverence."[2] Schneider suggests that Hu learned of Ts'ui from Chang Hsueh-ch'eng's writings, but, as the late Arthur Hummel pointed out in his superb essay on Ts'ui, there is in fact "no evidence" that Chang knew of Ts'ui Shu's existence.[3] The information came from elsewhere.

The *Ts'ui Tung-pi i-shu* contains not only an edited and punctuated text of Ts'ui's writings but numerous essays by those who collaborated with Ku in the project (Ch'ien Mu, Ch'ien Hsuan-t'ung, Hu Shih, William Hung, Chao Chen-hsin, and others), reprints of portions of many essays that touch on Ts'ui, a complete punctuated edition of the extant writings of Ts'ui's younger brother Mai (*Ts'ui Te-kao hsien-sheng i-shu* [Collected works of Ts'ui Te-kao]) and of four of his ancestors, several in-laws, and close relatives, maps of Ts'ui's travels, and more. In the following year William Hung and others prepared an index, the *Ts'ui Tung-pi i-shu yin-te*, as part of the Harvard-Yenching index series.[4] In much of the introductory sections to the *Ts'ui Tung-pi i-shu*, thanks and praise are traded among the editors with great delight over their completed project.[5] Perhaps the most revealing of these sections, however, is Ku Chieh-kang's own prefatory comments in which he explains in detail how he found various Ts'ui materials and who helped at which points of the project. This is interesting less for its content than for the fact that Ku here makes no mention that Ts'ui's works had been edited, punctuated, and published thirty-two years earlier in Japan.[6] We shall return to this omission shortly.

In the case of Ts'ui Shu, something closer to the ordinary usage of the term "rediscovery" had occurred at the turn of the century with a group of Japanese sinologists.[7] In 1900 one of the founders of the Kyoto school of sinology, Kano Naoki (1868-1947), was performing some research in Peking when the Boxer Rebellion erupted. He is said to have gone to "great risks" in carrying out with him twenty-five *chüan* in manuscript form of Ts'ui Shu's most famous work, the *K'ao-hsin lu* [Record of investigating beliefs]. When he arrived in Japan, he showed them to Naka Michiyo (1851-1908), generally considered the father of modern sinology in Japan, and in fact the man who coined the term *Tōyōshi* ("East Asian history").[8] Naka was quickly convinced that Ts'ui was someone of intellectual import and set out to prepare an edited and punctuated (with Kambun *kariten*) edition of Ts'ui's writings. In December 1900, an announcement of the project in the main Japanese historical journal of the day, *Shigaku zasshi* [Journal of historical studies], said that Naka's edition would appear as the second item in the *Shigakkai sōsho* [Series of the Historical Association]. The notice concluded by reiterating that Ts'ui Shu's work was extremely important and that it expressed the realization of the idea of "anticipating [clouds and] rainbows in the midst of a great drought" (*taikan ni gei o nozomu*), a kind of awkward allusion to the "Liang Hui-wang" chapter of *Mencius*.[9]

Naitō Konan (1866-1934), the other principal founder of the Kyoto school, read this notice while in Osaka on the staff of the *Ōsaka asahi shimbun* and wrote an article, "Dokusho gūhitsu" [Random notes on books read], which *Nihon* published on January 2, 1901. He had apparently known of Ts'ui before Kano found the Peking texts, for in his lectures at Kyoto University, which were later turned into the *Shina shigaku shi* [History of Chinese historiography], he said that Naitō Chisō (no relation), an eminent historian of Japan, had read of Ts'ui in the *Kuo-ch'ao hsien-cheng shih-lüeh* [Biographies of prominent Chinese of the Ch'ing dynasty],[10] was impressed, and mentioned it to Konan. Chisō had already died, and Konan already owned his own set of Ts'ui's works by the time of the first *Shigaku zasshi* notice. Naitō's edition was almost certainly a text that had been in Japan since late Tokugawa times. As he personally communicated to his student, Kanda Kiichirō, this edition had come over from China and was held in the library of Tōdō-*han* in Ise, which is odd considering that Ts'ui's works are not listed among the Chinese books that made their way to Japan in the Edo period.[11] In his response to this notice, Naitō reported that his own copy of the *Ts'ui Tung-pi hsien-sheng i-shu* had fifty-five *chüan* and that the Kano-Naka edition was not even the complete *K'ao-hsin lu*. He went on to suggest strongly that Ts'ui Shu's works be published as a *zenshū* (collected works) for the benefit of future readers and cheerfully offered his copy to the *Shigakkai sōsho* editors. Naitō then moved briefly to a discussion of Ts'ui's life by his disciple and original compiler, Ch'en Lü-ho, and to the entry on Ts'ui in the *Kuo-ch'ao hsien-cheng shih-lüeh* of which Naitō then translated a large portion.[12] Naitō concluded with a veiled tone of slight disgust for the way *Shigaku zasshi* reporters had ended their first notice about "long droughts"; he worded it in such a way as to defend Ch'ing scholarship of the Chia-ch'ing (1796-1821) and Tao-kuang (1821-1851) periods against the idea that this had been a thoroughly arid era in serious historical research.[13]

In the next issue of *Shigaku zasshi*, only a month later, the editors fell all over each other in apologizing for their errors in the earlier notice and in gratitude to "Naitō Konan's great kindness . . . and genius." They also reported that Naitō had lent his edition to Naka Michiyo.[14] Naka spent the next three years poring over these texts, punctuating, correcting errors, and preparing them for publication. In the midst of his work he published an article on the critical importance of Ts'ui Shu's *K'ao-hsin lu*,[15] and by 1903 three of four volumes were published; by April 1904 the entire project had been completed.[16] So excited was Naka with this Ts'ui Shu find that in his more popular work, *Naka Tōyō ryakushi* [Naka's brief history of East Asia], published in December 1903, while still engaged in his Ts'ui Shu research, he devoted a full half page of praise to Ts'ui and the *K'ao-hsin lu*, more space than was allotted to Huang Tsung-hsi, Ku Yen-wu, Wang Yang-ming, Ssu-ma Ch'ien, or virtually any other figure in East Asian history.[17]

This extremely high estimate of Ts'ui was not limited to Naka Michiyo. Kano seems to have retained a measure of objectivity with respect to Ts'ui;[18] Naitō, aside from a considerable number of references to Ts'ui's judgments about the validity of certain ancient texts—to which he referred in his own history of ancient China— seemingly wrote nothing else about Ts'ui of an evaluative nature.[19] On the other hand, many others wrote extremely adulatory things about Ts'ui, including Naka's biographer and famous historian in his own right, Miyake Yonekichi (1860-1929), who in commenting on Naka's edition of Ts'ui's works compared Ts'ui to Motoori Norinaga (1830-1901)—Motoori's *Kojiki den* and Ts'ui's *K'ao-hsin lu* both being exemplary criticisms of biased views of the true meaning of the classics[20] (albeit an entirely different set of classics). The general enthusiasm for Ts'ui must have been remarkable, for seventy years later, in his history of the Ch'ing dynasty, Masui Tsuneo introduced him as "Nihon no gakusha konomi no Sai Jutsu" [Ts'ui Shu whom Japanese scholars (so) like].[21]

The excitement that greeted Ts'ui Shu's rediscovery in Japan found a parallel twenty years later in China. It is difficult to assess how aware of the Japanese edition of Ts'ui's works Chinese intellectuals were, and even harder to say how much use Ku, Hu, and the others made of the Naka edition. Arthur Hummel, who translated Ku's introduction to the *Ku-shih pien* [Symposium on ancient history] as *The Autobiography of a Chinese Historian*, states without a trace of doubt that "in 1921 Dr. Hu Shih came across a Japanese edition" of Ts'ui's works, surely the Naka reprint.[22] "Though this is an excellent reprint," wrote Hummel elsewhere, "it attracted little notice in China" except for an occasional mention, often with glaring errors or misunderstandings.[23]

Yet, the Chinese editors clearly knew of Naka's work and even praised it here and there. In his 1923 article, Hu Shih stated plainly that, as a result of Naka's work, "Chinese gradually came to know that such a man as Ts'ui Shu has lived."[24] Hu pointed out then that Liu Shih-p'ei (1884-1919) had seen the Japanese text and been influenced by it to write a short biography of Ts'ui for the journal *Kuo-ts'ui hsueh-pao* [Journal of the national essence] as early as 1907. This essay was punctuated and included in the Chinese edition of Ts'ui's works. Similarly, Chao Chen-hsin, who proofread the original *Ts'ui Tung-pi hsien-sheng i-shu* for errors, remarked in a preface that Ts'ui was not at all well known in China until Naka's edition was published.[25] Near the very end of the Chinese edition were selections from a number of Chinese works relevant to Ts'ui and translations of several Japanese writings, and Ku pointed out in his introduction to this section (one of the few times Ku had anything to say of the Japanese edition) that the Naka reprint had led to Ts'ui Shu's first recognition by Chinese scholars such as Liu Shih-p'ei and Ko Hsiao, a recognition that spread slowly. Other references to the Japanese text in the Ku edition included several paragraphs in translation from Miyake Yonekichi's biography of Naka as well as an excerpted translation by the eminent historian Chou I-liang of an essay on Ts'ui by Okazaki Fumio, which had appeared in 1927 in *Shinagaku,* the journal of the Kyoto school of sinology.

Ts'ui Shu and the Uses of History

As Schneider points out, Ts'ui Shu's writings were "the single body of thought most influential on Ku Chieh-kang's study of antiquity."[26] Let us scrutinize this influence a little more closely. Ku learned from Ts'ui an historiographic method of unveiling the layers of spuriousness in successive treatments of antiquity. While Confucius spoke of antiquity going back no further than sage-kings Yao and Shun, by the Han dynasty Ssu-ma Ch'ien began his *Shih-chi* with the Yellow Emperor (Huang-ti); and later historians went still further back to Fu-hsi. In Ts'ui's language this process is called *pu-shang* or *pu-shang ku,* meaning "adding on to antiquity," and, in explicating this process by which fabricated strata of history were added on backwards in successive periods, Ts'ui was performing an act of Confucian reverence; in Schneider's words, "with each new discovery of a layer of counterfeit history over the authentic classical stratum, Ts'ui became more assured that he was performing his calling to 'protect the *Tao*, protect the Sages, and protect the canon.'"[27] Ku Chieh-kang used and developed this approach in a more secular form to brilliant ends in his own studies of ancient Chinese history.

As in the case of Ts'ui's "rediscovery" itself, however, we find a slightly earlier, parallel development in Japanese historiographic circles. Naitō Konan, one of the central figures in the Japanese rediscovery of Ts'ui Shu, had in 1897 published one of his first book-length works, *Kinsei bungaku shiron* [An historical discussion of modern Japanese scholarship],[28] from a series of articles he had previously published in the *Ōsaka asahi shimbun*. It was essentially an intellectual history of the Tokugawa period; however, Naitō selected as "absolutely the most original and enlightening scholars in the three hundred years" of the Tokugawa era: Tominaga Nakamoto (1715-1746), Yamagata Bantō (1748-1821), and Miura Baien (1723-1789),[29] an extraordinarily unorthodox selection when one considers that these three figures were barely known at that time. Naitō was particularly impressed by Tominaga, a virtual unknown until the publication of Naitō's work, and Tominaga's book *Shutsujō kōgo* [Historical survey of Buddhism].[30] Tominaga (like Yamagata and Miura) had been a nonsamurai, nonprofessional scholar from an Osaka *chōnin* background; Naitō was especially pleased by his commoner origins. It appears Naitō first heard of Tominaga, interestingly enough, from the same Naitō Chisō, as evidenced by Konan's first essay concerning Tominaga, "Choin sango" [Scattered words in the shade of a tree of useless wood], published in 1893.[31]

In the *Shutsujō kōgo*, Tominaga presented his theory of *kajō* (Chinese *chia-shang*, "accumulation" or "adding on to antiquity") in debunking the development of Buddhism. He demonstrated that as each new Buddhist sect preached the superiority of its heaven to all those preceding it, there accumulated a hierarchy of heavens, created backwards. Naitō Konan employed this theoretical conception to study ancient Chinese history. He showed that while Confucius generally cited the Duke of Chou (or T'ang) as the essential beginning of Chinese history and institutions, Mo-tzu went back to King Yü of the Hsia dynasty. Mencius went back even further to Yao and Shun who abdicated the throne to men of virtue, not to their own sons as had Yü—hence Mo-tzu's ideal was not as good as the earlier Yao-Shun paradigm. Somewhat later the Taoists went back as far as the Yellow Emperor, before Yao and Shun; the *nung-chia* school made Shen-nung the beginning, and the divination school went still further back to Fu-hsi; finally the Taoist alchemists (*fang-shih*) spoke of the *san-huang* ("three deities")—*t'ien-huang* ("heavenly deity"), *ti-huang* ("earthly deity"), and *t'ai-huang* ("great diety")—as the start of it all.[32] Professor Miyazaki Ichisada, one of Naitō's most famous disciples, has remarked of this inverse development: "A lineage of saints was formed in a direction opposite to the chronological order, a lineage generated by different schools successively vying for superiority."[33]

Clearly Ts'ui Shu's *pu-shang* and Tominaga Nakamoto's *kajō* are extremely similar ideas, if not methodologically identical. Ku draws directly from Ts'ui, and Naitō directly from Tominaga. Miyazaki has suggested that Ku Chieh-kang's work on ancient China may have been influenced by Naitō, but he frankly admits that he cannot say for sure.[34] And nowhere does Ku make reference to such an influence. While he certainly knew of Naitō through the Ts'ui Shu project (although neither he nor any other of the Chinese editors ever mention Naitō's contribution) or through many other possible links, according to Ku his source was always Ts'ui. Similarly, we know that Naitō Konan was intimately aware of Ts'ui Shu's historical theories; however, citations to Ts'ui's works in Naitō are always to corroborate this or that exegetical point and, aside from the instances mentioned above, not of an overall historiographic nature; for that Naitō had Tominaga.

One might suggest that we have here a dual case of scholarly nationalism, with each twentieth-century historian explicitly deriving his source of inspiration from the eighteenth-century scholar of his own nation. This view does not adequately describe Naitō, however, because, although firmly nationalistic, his vision was much broader and he often relied on the writings and theories of Chinese scholars past and present. For Naitō the overall East Asia sphere centered on China, whose culture he considered the most advanced in the world. Witness, for instance, his admiration for the works of Ssuma Ch'ien (135?-93? B.C.), Chao I (1727-1812), Ch'ien Ta-hsin (1728-1804), Ku Yen-wu (1613-1682), and particularly his close friends, Lo Chen-yü (1866-1940) and Wang Kuo-wei (1877-1927), among many others. It would sound strange indeed to hear Naitō echo the kind of sentiments we will soon hear Hu Shih and Lo Chen-yü utter. Yet, Ku does not seem to reflect this kind of eclecticism; and, by the same token, Naitō did not have to contend with numerous brilliant Chinese Japanologists.

Why Ts'ui Shu?

This is indeed the crucial question. The simple answer, that Hu and Ku made a remarkable rediscovery for China of one Ts'ui Shu, a forgotten eighteenth-century man of great historiographic talents, seems no longer sufficient to explain their selection of this figure. Schneider's answer takes us a little further into this problem, but is still just the tip of the iceberg: "Ts'ui was a perfect subject for the scholar's hall of fame because of the range and brilliance of his critical thought, his charming style of writing, and, of course, his mistreatment by the Chinese scholar-official world."[35] The Ts'ui find may have been happily unexpected (although I have serious doubts about this possibility), but the general scheme into which Ts'ui was either placed or forced must be brought into clearer focus.

We should first bear in mind the continuing search by late nineteenth- and early twentieth-century Chinese intellectuals for precedents in their own culture for views and attitudes deemed "modern" in their own day. Scholars of all political persuasions took part in this search, which at times seems to have taken on the air of a parlor game. In due course we find Huang Tsung-hsi being dubbed "China's Rousseau" (by Ch'en T'ien-hua), Kuan-tzu "the first Chinese materialist" (by Feng Yu-lan and others), and K'ang Yu-wei "China's Luther" (by Liang Ch'i-ch'ao). Wang Fu-chih was alternatively seen as China's answer to the eighteenth-century French materialists, to Kant, to Hegel, and was even portrayed as a proto-Marxist (by many different scholars).

In such a context we can see that Ts'ui was a fortuitous find indeed. To scholars of the early Republican era it was clear that one of Western scholarship's superior points was its reliance on the scientific method and its use of proof in the discipline of history. The numerous fallacies and contradictions and the political conservatism inherent in Western positivistic thought[36] were disregarded. Ts'ui appeared as an early paragon of Western-style historical research, while his methodology demonstrated that China's tradition of hard critical historians had proudly survived into the Chia-ch'ing reign. This theme is self-evident in the title of Hu Shih's inaugural article, "K'o-hsüeh te ku-shih-chia Ts'ui Shu" [Ts'ui Shu, a scientific historian of ancient China]. Interestingly, Hu admitted thirteen years later, in an introduction to Ku's edition of Ts'ui's works, that he may have overestimated Ts'ui's greatness in this 1923 essay, now that much new material had been uncovered in the past century for the study of ancient China (specifically mentioned are oracle bones and bronze inscriptions), but he adamantly maintained that Ts'ui's scientific spirit of "investigate and only then believe" (*k'ao erh hou hsin*) would never die.[37]

Science (or in fact scientism) was a magic word in early twentieth-century China, as to a certain extent it remains, and its forced entrance into the methodology of modern humanistic studies betokened another magic word, progress. This attitude lay behind Hu Shih's practice of proudly counting the number of proofs supplied by various Ch'ing *kao-cheng* scholars proving the authenticity or spuriousness of sections of the classics, and then pointing to this as evidence of an indigenous scientific strain in Chinese scholarship.

This line of argument, however, reflects only one part of the overall picture. As we have seen, Ts'ui had been rediscovered much earlier in Japan and was known in China considerably before Hu and Ku began to work on his writings and to lionize his spirit. To a large extent, the zeitgeist of early Republican intellectual circles lent to Ts'ui the aura of a "pioneer" in their eyes, a view that could not be mustered thirty years earlier in China when the Naka edition first appeared, but could be in mid-Meiji Japan. The idea that someone can be ahead of their time is of course as ahistorical as it is meaningless; nonetheless certain figures of the past do seem to us more "modern" than others. This appearance or illusion, however, is due entirely to the concerns of the present, and in the 1920s Ts'ui was for the first time perceived in China as a forerunner of critical, scientific historical research. Similarly, Wang Fu-chih even after being rediscovered was not actively republished and circulated until the 1900s and 1910s when men perceived his peculiarly irreverent attitudes and his contempt for the influence of state orthodox Confucianism on conceptions of history and certain historical figures. Perhaps most important in Wang's case was the realization that he advocated a developmental, progressivistic, protomaterial-istic theory of history and an anti-Manchu nationalism (theoretical as well as emotional) with extraordinarily "modern" (ca. 1900-1911) applicability. His historicism had Chinese roots—Tu Yu (735-812) of the T'ang had argued along similar (although not widely accepted) lines—but his nationalism and indeed his conception of China as a "nation" seem to have had little meaning until the late Ch'ing–early Republican era. In this way "rediscovery" may be possessed of a largely self-serving objective totally unrelated to the normal usage of the term. It is vital that we understand that the cluster of names that we associate with an historical period or incident has not fallen from the sky but has been supplied to us by former scholars. Hu Shih and his group of students and colleagues did significant groundwork, particularly with the *Ts'ui Tung-pi i-shu,* and we have not as yet transcended them.

Finally, it appears that there was a great deal more conscious effort at work in the Chinese "rediscovery" of Ts'ui Shu than in the Japanese. More than an act of scholarship (as it seems was the case with Naka Michiyo), Ku Chieh-kang and Hu Shih were engaged in such enormous labors, much of which had already been done, virtually as an act of nationalism. While Naka seems never to have had any intention that his edition be widely consumed by people other than scholars, Ku's and Hu's work was intended clearly as a popularization of Ts'ui Shu, to make him known to as wide an audience of Chinese readers as possible. This kind of nationalistic scholarship shines through in a comment made by Hu Shih in his 1923 essay: "That such a great scholar with such impressive writings should have been buried for a hundred years [sic] is indeed a great shame to the Chinese intellectual community."[38] This same attitude is reflected in a comment made in 1899 by Lo Chen-yü in an introduction to his edition of Naka Michiyo's *Shina tsūshi* [Comprehensive history of China], written in Kambun: "Alas, it is shameful [indeed] that the history of our country cannot be written by our own kinsmen but must be written by one of another country."[39] And, despite fifteen years of work preparing the *Ts'ui Tung-pi i-shu* for publication, with a certain amount of time to reflect on Ts'ui's real importance, Ku Chieh-kang noted in a letter to Ch'ien Hsuan-t'ung that regretfully Ts'ui was only a "Confucianist criticizing ancient history; not an historian criticizing ancient history."[40] Of course, one should not necessarily be held accountable by the scholarly community for comments made in private (or semiprivate) letters, but it is clear that Ku was dismayed here because Ts'ui could not fully jump from the eighteenth century into the twentieth: Ts'ui must remain a creature of his time. In a more level-headed moment, Ku fully understood this dilemma:

> I could not minimize his [Ts'ui's] limitations, the work being marred by traditional prejudices and by excessive faith in the classics and the doctrines of Confucius and Mencius. It would be unfair, however, to reproach him for this; he was born in a home that reverenced the Sung philosophy, and his purpose in writing was to brush aside everything that stood in the way of an understanding of the ancient sages. He employed the critical method primarily to further this end. Our duty is to go a step further and overthrow his preconceptions, reconstructing classical study upon new foundations.[41]

Our task now is to take one more step than Ku's generation.

Two Further "Rediscoveries"

Several other "rediscovery" efforts of the twentieth century may elaborate on and perhaps elucidate this problem. Naitō Konan is generally accorded the honor of being the first person to have recognized anew the value of Chang Hsueh-ch'eng's (1738-1801) historiographic insights.[42] Naitō began reading Chang's major works, the *Wen-shih t'ung-i* [General principles of literature and history] and the *Chiao-ch'ou t'ung-i* [General principles of bibliography] in 1902 and later through connections in China was able to obtain a manuscript copy of Chang's writings, the *Chang-shih i-shu,* in eighteen *ts'e.* Naitō relates that he was so excited about reading Chang's works that he read all that he possessed straight through to the end, and then gave part of them to Kano Naoki; later, Chang was to become something of a rage at Kyoto University. Yet despite all the praise others have accorded him, Naitō admitted that Chinese such as Chang Erh't'ien (1869-1945) and Sun Te-ch'ien (1869-1935) had known of and been reading Chang for some time; and we know that Chang Ping-lin (1869-1936) and perhaps even Kung Tzu-chen (1792-1841) were aware of Chang Hsueh-ch'eng's ideas.[43]

A native of eastern Chekiang and *landsmann* of Chang Hsueh-ch'eng, Chang Er-t'ien was the author of *Shih-wei* [The little things in history], published in 1911, in which he actively attempted to revive the historiographic approach of his fellow native. [44] However, I do not believe that his was the connection to which Naitō Konan's praise of Chang Erh-t'ien and Sun Te'ch'ien referred. Naitō knew of Chang Hsueh-ch'eng well before 1911 and in that year, probably before he knew of the *Shih-wei,* gave a lecture in Hiroshima on Chinese historical scholarship in which he said that "the most famous figure of the Eastern Chekiang school was Chang Hsueh-ch'eng. It was he who made the general differentiation of schools between Eastern and Western Chekiang; and his work, the *Wen-shih t'ung-i,* is a brilliant comprehensive discussion of writings on history (*shiron*) or historiography (*shigaku*)."[45]

Naitō was friendly with Shen Tseng-chih (1850-1922), author of *Meng-ku yuan-lu chien-cheng* [Notes on the origins of the Mongols], and considered him an exceptionally gifted scholar. Shen's "disciples," whom Naitō also personally knew and for whom he was also full of praise, were Chang Erh-t'ien (who later compiled the *Meng-ku yuan-lu chien-chang* and added his own "chiao-pu" or addendum) and Sun Te-ch'ien, author of the *Han-shu i-wen-chih chü-li* [Selections from the bibliographic treatise of the Han history], *T'ai-*

shih-kung shu-i-fa [How Ssu-ma Ch'ien wrote (the *Shih-chi*)], and *Liu Hsiang chiao-ch'ou-hsüeh tsuan-wei* [On Liu Hsiang's editorial methodology]. Naitō, in fact, requested that Chang be asked to contribute an essay to a festschrift dedicated to him; he was asked and complied. However, the man who Naitō always claimed, but never it seems wrote down, was the real rediscoverer (or recognizer) of Chang Hsueh-ch'eng was T'an Hsien (1830-1901). The recognition of Chang's genius appeared in T'an's diary, the *Fu-t'ang jih-chi*, a work that Naitō not only regarded highly but often firmly "advised his students to read." He had obtained a copy of it at the very end of the Meiji or the beginning of the Taishō era (ca. 1912).[46] Thus, while T'an was not the source of Naitō's own interest in Chang Hsueh-ch'eng, Naitō sought to give him the recognition that he felt T'an deserved. We can only guess that Naitō may have initially learned of Chang Hsueh-ch'eng from Sun Te-ch'ien or Chang Erh-t'ien (or possibly Shen Tseng-chih, whom he met in China in 1902), and it is equally possible that they in turn learned of Chang from T'an Hsien, whom it seems Naitō never met.

In 1920 Naitō published in *Shinagaku* a brief biographical sketch of Chang Hsueh-ch'eng, which he prepared from his own copy of the *Chang-shih i-shu*, under the title but without the intent of being a full-fledged *nien-p'u*.[47] Shortly thereafter, Hu Shih published a much longer, full-fledged *nien-p'u*, which, as Paul Demiéville has remarked, was "a form contrary to all the theories of Chang Hsueh-ch'eng."[48] In his introduction to the *Chang Shih-chai hsien-sheng nien-p'u*, Hu echoed a by then familiar lament: "What is most shameful for us [Chinese] is that the first scholar to prepare a chronological biography of Chang Shih-chai [Hsueh-ch'eng] was a foreigner."[49]

Hu had only intended to write a kind of corrigenda to Naitō's 1920 piece, but he found so many errors and omissions that he wrote his own, much more detailed *nien-p'u*. Naitō almost immediately wrote a response to Hu, indicating that he was happy to have been the instrument of Hu's recharged interest in Chang Hsueh-ch'eng. Naitō explained that he did not believe in long *nien-p'u* as a viable way to discuss a man's work and intellectual development, but rather a short, simple *nien-p'u*, more like a *lü-li* (*rireki* or "personal résumé"), to complement a larger investigation of a subject's ideas. Naitō also pointed out in this response doubtful spots in Hu's *nien-p'u*, important facts missing from both of their efforts, and the vital sources he had discovered since 1920 of writings by Chang's friends and acquaintances (principally Wang Tsung-yen).[50] Naitō later provided this promised larger discussion of Chang in his brilliant

"Shō Gakusei no shigaku" [Chang Hsueh-ch'eng's historiography], written shortly after the response to Hu Shih.

Why Chang Hsueh-ch'eng? The Chinese canonization of Chang Hsueh-ch'eng by Hu Shih provides material for us to enhance our picture of "rediscovery" built around Ts'ui Shu. If we trace Naitō's proposed pedigree for the recognition of Chang Hsueh-ch'eng's import back to T'an Hsien, then there really is no reason to speak of rediscovery at all in this case, and even less so if the Kung Tzu-chen connection to Chang is accurate. Just over a generation separated Chang's death from T'an (and Kung's life overlapped Chang's for almost a decade); at best we can say that Chang's genius was not recognized by his contemporaries or their immediate successors. Yet once Hu Shih gleaned the contemporary relevance of Chang's ideas, inspired by reading Naitō's *Shinagaku* piece, Chang became another "significant" but ignored figure who required active resuscitation so that Chinese scholars could be proud of their own heritage.

One puzzling question then is why Chang and Ts'ui were both used by the Hu Shih group of early Republican scholars in this fashion. The answer to this problem is probably simple. The marked differences between Chang and Ts'ui were topics for specialized research and thus irrelevant to the overall project of revival. In the view of Hu's group, Chang and Ts'ui shared the dubious distinction of having been shamefully forgotten and ignored—that they had this in common superseded any philosophical or methodological differences and rendered them source material not for a better approach to the study of history but for election into the pantheon of great Chinese scholars, a pantheon enriched by their belated entrance. Similarly, Hu (and one assumes his students in the early Republic) prided himself on the distance he maintained from political affairs; his "liberalism" surely supported the acceptance for revival of two or more dissimilar men.

Closely related to the case of Chang Hsueh-ch'eng was that of Cheng Ch'iao (1104-1162), the Sung historiographer and author of the *T'ung-chih* [Comprehensive record]. The latter writer was also resuscitated in China by Hu and his circle well after having gained renewed attention in Japan through the work of Naitō Konan, who made Cheng's ideas central to his own *Shina shigaku shi*. Cheng had been forgotten soon after his death until Chang Hsueh-ch'eng realized the great importance of his conception of the way historical works need be written, i.e., in a comprehensive (*t'ung-shih*) fashion, not broken into individual periods (*tuan-tai shih*). However, as Chang was "forgotten," so Cheng went into his second decline. When

Naitō and others began to work on Chang, Cheng Ch'iao was un-
earthed in the process.[51]

A Different Kind of Rediscovery

One final case illustrates strikingly the degree to which historiographical currents, and ideological currents as well, followed a two-
way course between China and Japan. This case, documented by
Shimada Kenji of Kyoto University, is that of the "rediscovery" by
Naitō Konan and others of the late Ming eccentric philosopher, Li
Chih (1527-1602). In the Ming section of Naitō's *Shina shigaku shi*,
given as lectures around 1915, the largest space is reserved for an
explication of Li Chih's view of history, which is extremely
surprising considering that Li was still a virtual unknown in 1915. In
China, Li did not return to the scholarly limelight until Wu Yü's 1916
essay, "Ming Li Cho-wu pieh-chuan" [A biography of Li Cho-wu
(Chih) of the Ming], was published.[52] Even this 1915 reference to Li
was not Naitō's first, however, for in a 1901 article entitled "Dokusho-
ki sansoku" [Notes on three books read], published in *Nihonjin*, the
third entry is "Ri-shi *Sōsho*" [Mr. Li's *Ts'ang-shu*].[53] Yet, as Shimada
makes clear, this whole "rediscovery" becomes murky at this
point for a number of reasons.

The first actual modern mention of Li in a Chinese publication
came in two short pieces in the journal *Kuo-ts'ui hsueh-pao*, late in
1905.[54] Chinese overseas students in Japan, though, undoubtedly
knew of Li earlier because while in Japan many of them had become
intimately aware of and reverential toward the great *bakumatsu
shishi*, Yoshida Shōin (1830-1859). Shōin had been reading Li Chih's
works in prison shortly before his execution in 1859 and was greatly
impressed with Li's spirit and individuality.[55] Li's suicide also
apparently gave Shōin courage for his own imminent decapitation.
In turn, so impressed was Liang Ch'i-ch'ao (1873-1929) with stories
he heard of the sacrifice and bravery of Japanese *shishi*, that he took
the name Yoshida Shin, from Shōin and Takasugi Shinsaku (1839-
1867, a prominent disciple of Shōin's), respectively, when in Japan in
1898 to escape execution after the failure of the Hundred Days
Reform.[56]

The Japanese scholar and political figure Miyake Setsurei (1860-
1945) had once employed Naitō as his assistant, and the latter had in
fact ghostwritten several of Miyake's most famous works, including
Shin-zen-bi Nihonjin [Truth, goodness, beauty—the Japanese]. In
Miyake's 1893 book *Ō Yōmei* (Wang Yang-ming), there is an

epilogue by Miyake's colleague, Kuga Katsunan (1856-1907), lauding Li Chih. The influence of Wang Yang-ming and his school on the Meiji Restoration *shishi* is well known; in this epilogue, Kuga pointed out that Li Chih (a follower of Wang Yang-ming) was deeply revered by Shōin, and with this Kuga presented the very first Meiji period honoring of Li Chih—three years later Chinese students first came to study in Japan and twelve years later the *Kuo-ts'ui hsueh-pao* articles appeared. Shimada suggests strongly that Naitō Konan's 1901 article in *Nihonjin* was seen by Chinese overseas students in Japan and triggered Li's revival; as evidence he cites the notice in the inaugural issue of *Kuo-ts'ui hsueh-pao*, which states that the editors were in touch with the "journal of Miyake Yūjirō [Setsurei] and Shiga Shigetaka,"[57] none other than *Nihonjin*.

Concluding Remarks

It should be clear that, short of a Tun-huang, "rediscovery" as the term has been used by historians in the past has various connotations in various settings. Perhaps *tsai fa-hsien* and *sai hakken* are misnomers; they are certainly misleading if taken literally. The actual linkages by which a great figure from the past was brought back to the fore seem to have relied to a considerable extent on the politics, concerns, biases, and changing interests of contemporary scholars as well as the exigencies of the times in which the latter lived; this may ultimately be more revealing to us as historians than the "rediscovered" person or persons. We have seen how this revival project in the hands of Hu Shih and his colleagues has virtually provided us with our present curriculum for the study of modern Chinese intellectual history. One would like to know why, for example, the cluster of eighteenth-century figures we read about is always the same. Why do we always talk about Chang Hsueh-ch'eng and Tai Chen (also popular with the Hu Shih group), and not Ch'ien Ta-hsin, Chao I, Chu Yun, Shao Chin-han, or Wang Ming-sheng? Largely responsible for this, I believe, is the work of Liang Ch'i-ch'ao (and K'ang Yu-wei before him), Hu Shih, the early Ku Chieh-kang, Ch'ien Mu, William Hung, and a handful of other towering intellects who in the late Ch'ing and early Republic did an enormous service to our field in bringing into popular focus a number of men forgotten or ignored by earlier generations of Chinese. As scholars, however, it is our responsibility not merely to accept this legacy, but to criticize it vigorously and point to its flaws.

It is especially interesting to note the style of reintroduction by which the principals of this essay reemerged on the twentieth-century scholarly agenda. In Japan, where these men were first rediscovered for the most part, the intended audience was limited to academic circles. Neither was there concern to popularize these men's work nor, more significantly, can we detect any signs of defensiveness or nationalistic pride. Of course, the rediscovered figures were Chinese, but not even in the case of Naitō's work on Tominaga do we see this massive sales campaign touting the newly found figure.[58] At least, this reveals the greater sense of self-assuredness on the part of Japanese scholars, which in turn was a reflection of the comparative firmness of China's and Japan's respective international positions in the early twentieth century. It is clear that Hu Shih and his group were, however unconsciously, using scholarship in an attempt to bolster China's national self-esteem. As I hope I have shown, these scholars were, like everyone else, products of their age, and their concerns reflect that age, just as this author's concerns reflect our own irreverent times. It should not be surprising that Chang Hsueh-ch'eng and Li Chih continue to fascinate contemporary students of history and philosophy in the West, whereas Ts'ui Shu seems to have gone into a second eclipse. We live in a time when a probing philosophy of history (Chang) and a life-style reflecting a noncon-formist philosophy (Li) are far more popular than textual exegeses shallowly (in a philosophical sense) informed only by Confucian classical truth.

Perhaps the best heuristic device for understanding this idea of "rediscovery" may be found in E. H. Carr's paradigm for election into the realm of "historical facts." An event must first be nominated by one historian, seconded by another, and after several votes are cast in its favor by other historians, it can properly be deemed "historical fact."[59] However, this model only describes the act of rediscovery without an indication of causation. Here Croce's observations of over a generation ago on historical judgments can be of service: one always draws on present experience and needs, and in so doing, one lends any period (or personality) under study the character of "contemporary history."[60] In the final analysis, what is history as we know it other than historiography?

The Vicissitudes of Chinese Communist Historiography: Ch'ü Ch'iu-pai from Martyr to Traitor

Li Yu-ning

Ch'ü Ch'iu-pai (1899-1935) is well known to students of modern Chinese history as a leader of the Chinese Communist Party (CCP) during one of its bleakest periods and as a pioneer exponent of proletarian literature and the latinization of written Chinese. Like almost all of the early leaders of the CCP, Ch'ü has been the subject of conflicting interpretations. Unlike most others, however, he was long viewed in a favorable light in official Communist historiography. For three decades after his execution by the Kuomintang (KMT) in 1935, he was extolled as a revolutionary martyr. Then, in the mid-1960s, the verdict was reversed, and he was denounced as a shameless traitor. The course of the changing interpretations, and the reasons underlying them, are the subjects of this paper.

Ch'ü Ch'iu-pai: A Brief Life

Ch'iu-pai's early childhood was passed in his hometown of Ch'angchou, Kiangsu, in the comfortable circumstances befitting a household with a grandfather and uncle in official service. He early showed a bent for art and literature and in his youth read voraciously works on philosophy and religion, particularly Buddhism. In all probability, he never engaged in any manual labor.[1]

In his teens, Ch'iu-pai experienced a series of misfortunes, which contributed to the formation of his rather melancholic character and his hostility toward Chinese society. His father, though talented and well educated, lacked financial acumen and was an opium smoker incapable of sustained effort. Eventually, he left his wife and six children without support. Poverty compelled Ch'iu-pai to leave high school in 1914 when he was fifteen, a year before graduation, and to become the principal of a primary school in an isolated village of neighboring Wusih District. As the eldest son of his mother, he began to assume responsibilities for his family, but his small salary was insufficient to support the whole family. In addition to economic problems, his well-educated mother, whom Ch'iu-pai loved dearly, was an opium smoker. In 1915, financial stress and family discord caused her to commit suicide. This was a traumatic experience for Ch'iu-pai, and a major cause for his grievances against traditional Chinese society.

After his mother's death, the family broke up, and Ch'iu-pai went to live with a cousin, Ch'ü Ch'un-pai, in Wuchang. In 1916, he moved to Peking, following the family of Ch'un-pai, who had been transferred to a minor post in the Peiyang government. In the summer of 1917, Ch'iu-pai was admitted to the National Institute of Russian Language. Established under the auspices of the Ministry of Foreign Affairs, the institute offered a tuition-free, five-year study program with professional prospects after graduation—service with either the Chinese consulates in Russia or the Chinese Eastern Railway. Ch'ü proved to be an outstanding student at the institute.

During these trying years, Ch'ü was perhaps as much concerned with finding a personal meaning for his own life as with the larger problems of China, for he was reading the great Taoist classics, *Tao-te ching* and *Chuang Tzu*, as well as representative writings of Mahayana Buddhism and Neo-Confucianism. And though he very soon was to become a political activist, Ch'ü was to continue to feel an attraction toward contemplation and tranquility throughout his life.

The May Fourth Movement of 1919 saw the beginning of Ch'ü's active involvement in Chinese political life. He led students from the Russian Language Institute in demonstrations, and he represented the school in the newly formed Peking Student Union. The year 1919 also marked the beginning of Ch'ü's career as a writer. He organized two short-lived magazines, *Hsin-she-hui* [New society] and *Jen-tao* [Humanity] and in this and the years immediately following wrote extensively on a wide range of topics of the day, such as the evils and the hypocrisy of the Confucian family system, the liberation of women from the oppression of the traditional family, national self-determination, the labor question, and various schemes for the total reform of society. Under the influence of Tolstoy, Ch'ü at this time believed love of one's fellow human beings to be the ultimate source of happiness. This may very well have been one of the ideas that led him toward socialism, and to join the Society for the Study of Socialism, whose membership included such current and future luminaries as Ch'en Tu-hsiu (1879-1942), Li Ta-chao (1888-1927), Chang Kuo-t'ao (1897-   ), Chou En-lai (1899-1976), and Mao Tse-tung (1893-1976). In 1919-1920, however, Ch'ü's thinking was eclectic and he was not yet fully committed to any single school of thought. A discontented and idealistic youth, he was in search of a solution to problems facing China.

In the autumn of 1920, Ch'ü was sent to Moscow as a correspondent for *Ch'en pao* [Morning post], a well-known Peking newspaper belonging to the Research Clique, a group of intellectuals and others who advocated a relatively conservative brand of constitutional democracy. His decision to go to Russia was spurred by his "inner demand," a spirit of self-denial derived in part from the Buddhist concept of bodhisattvahood. He viewed his departure from his country as equivalent to a "renunciation of the world" in order to achieve an understanding of higher truth for the sake of his compatriots. In effect he visualized himself as a kind of compassionate bodhisattva—in the world, but not of it—although his inspiration was humanistic, not religious.

Ch'ü reached Moscow on January 25, 1921. During his two-year stay in Russia he published forty-four articles (amounting to some 160,000 Chinese characters) in *Ch'en pao*, providing Chinese readers with one of the earliest and most sympathetic accounts of Soviet Russia. He also wrote his first autobiographical accounts, *O-hsing chi-ch'eng* [Journey to hungerland] and *Chih-tu hsin-shih* [Impressions of the red capital]. While in Russia he taught at the Communist University of the Toilers of the East and, in early 1922, through the sponsorship of Chang T'ai-lei (1898-1927), joined the infant Chinese Communist Party.

In January 1923, Ch'ü returned to Peking as a journalist, his Party membership as yet unknown to outsiders. He applied for a teaching post in the department of Russian literature at Peking University, but was rejected. In that spring, he moved to Shanghai, where he associated freely with literary figures and joined the Literary Research Society, founded in 1920 by his friends Cheng Chen-to (1897-1958), Keng Chi-chih, and others. He started writing, under several pen names, for *Hsiang-tao chou-pao* [The guide weekly], the organ of the CCP, and was entrusted by Ch'en Tu-hsiu, head of the CCP, to edit the reorganized *Hsin ch'ing-nien* [New youth]. Ch'ü's commitment to Marxism is immediately apparent in his writings from this period, for he applied Marxist theory to the analysis of Chinese society and was a vigorous advocate of class struggle and the seizure of power by revolutionary means. Through these writings he gradually established a reputation as a Party publicist.

At the Third Congress of the CCP, held in Canton in June 1923,

Ch'ü was elected to the Central Committee. He was then twenty-four years old, the youngest member of the committee. Under Comintern pressure the congress resolved that all CCP members should join the KMT. From the start Ch'ü favored this united front policy.

In the autumn of 1923, Ch'iu-pai became the dean of the recently founded Shanghai University and concurrently chairman of the sociology department. Yü Yu-jen (1878-1963), a veteran KMT journalist, poet, and a distinguished calligrapher, was the president of the university. Ch'ü invited a number of other young Communists to serve on the faculty, and for the next few years of the united front period the university became a hotbed of Communist propaganda and activities.

Ch'ü had joined the KMT by December 1923 and played an important role in its reorganization. Not only was he an author, together with Mikhail Borodin (1884-1951) and Wang Ching-wei (1883-1944), of the draft "Kuomintang Manifesto," he was also Borodin's collaborator in preparing many other documents pertaining to the reorganization of the KMT. At the First Congress of the KMT, held in Canton in early 1924, Ch'ü was elected an alternate member of the KMT Central Executive Committee along with other Communists, including Mao Tse-tung.

At the CCP's Fourth Congress held in Shanghai in January 1925, Ch'ü was reelected to the Central Committee and also became a member of the newly created Political Bureau, the Party's top policymaking body. He continued to identify himself with the policies of the Comintern despite the misgivings of some other leaders, especially Ch'en Tu-hsiu and P'eng Shu-chih. Ch'ü's constant call for active Communist participation in the KMT applied to the Northern Expedition, which in his view was the "armed revolutionary war" and the "direct continuation of the May 30th Movement" of 1925. The Communists should, he urged, following the Moscow line, strive for hegemony within the KMT during the expedition.

From April to July 1927, the CCP, whose rapid growth of influence was unparalleled in Comintern annals, was decimated by the purges carried out by Chiang Kai-shek and other military leaders. With Wuhan as their main base, the Communists tried desperately to regain their strength but internal disunity and external pressure rendered their task impossible. In mid-July, the Communists withdrew from the Wuhan government of the so-called Left KMT. Ch'en Tu-hsiu resigned from the post of CCP Secretary General and relinquished his function of presiding over the Politburo. The new leaders, including Ch'ü, decided to pursue a policy of insurrection and staged the Nanchang Revolt on August 1. At the August 7th conference of the Central Committee of the CCP, held in Wuhan on the demand of the Comintern, Ch'ü was placed in charge of the CCP's Politburo, a responsibility he retained until April 1928. Under Ch'ü's leadership, the conference officially laid down the insurrectionist line, which was considered by some to be "left adventurism," and paved the way for the so-called Li Li-san line in the following years.

In April 1928, Ch'ü left Shanghai to attend the Sixth Congress of the CCP, held in Moscow in June 1928. He was reelected to the Politburo, entrusted with the drafting of the congress' political resolution, and appointed the Party's representative to the Comintern. In July he led the Chinese delegation at the Sixth Comintern Congress, where he sat on the Presidium and worked on the Program Commission. In early September he became a member of the Presidium of the Comintern's Executive Committee (ECCI), being the only Chinese to hold office in that supreme Comintern organ. In addition, he was appointed to the Political Secretariat, the executive body of the ECCI, and its Presidium. His knowledge of the Russian language and his long identification with Comintern policies presumably were important considerations in his selection for such prominent positions.

In the summer of 1930, Ch'ü Ch'iu-pai returned to China under Comintern orders to put an end to the insurrectionist policy at the Third Plenum held in September in Lushan. Once again he presided over the Party's Politburo until the Fourth Plenum in Shanghai in January 1931, when he in turn was expelled from the Politburo by a group of young men led by Wang Ming (Ch'en Shao-yü, 1905-1974), known as the Russian returned students, on the grounds that Ch'ü had been compromising toward the Li Li-san line. This event, which effectively terminated Ch'ü's political career, led to a new series of factional disputes within the CCP.

From early 1931 to late 1933, Ch'ü Ch'iu-pai returned to literary work, translating and interpreting Soviet literature and Marxist literary theories, tasks that made him the first notable Chinese exponent of proletarian literature. He was also actively involved in the activities of the League of Left-Wing Writers. Ch'ü was critical of Chinese literature in the post–May Fourth period, which he felt had not truly broken with the literature of the past. He demanded a complete break in both style and content and advocated that the written language be identical with the common spoken language of the average person. He was a major exponent of "Latinxua," using the Latin alphabet for writing Chinese. And he was the first prominent Chinese Communist to apply Marxist theory to the problem of reforming the Chinese language.

In January 1934, Ch'ü became the commissar of education of the Chinese Soviet Republic in Kiangsi. When the Communists set out on the Long March in October 1934, he was ordered to remain in Juichin with the remaining troops, which were to fight a rearguard action against the KMT armies in Kiangsi and Fukien. By mid-February 1935, the KMT's encirclement campaigns and economic blockade had made it impossible for the Communists to hold the Juichin area. Ch'ü was ordered by the Party to go to Shanghai, by way of Fukien; en route he was arrested by KMT troops in Fukien. During his imprisonment, while awaiting his fate, he displayed poise and calm and wrote poems in the traditional style and an autobiographical account, *To-yü te hua* [Superfluous words]. Conscious of an obligation to present his version of his career for the historical record, Ch'ü reviewed his life. Calling himself a "kind of traitor," he stated his desire not to pretend to be a martyr. He wrote that his participation in political work for the past fifteen years had been reluctant and that he had not performed any task very well. He was really a useless, half-baked "man of letters [*wen-jen*]," and as such, it had been a "historical misunderstanding" for a man of his temperament and abilities, who was incapable of being a true revolutionary fighter, to become a leader of the CCP. He accepted responsibility for the policies of adventurism and the Li Li-san line. Then, indulging in what he termed the "petit bourgeois intelligentsia's habit of self-analysis," he questioned whether his views were truly Marxist and confessed that his thinking contained "viewpoints contrary to Marxism-Leninism" and had always been "intersected by non-Marxist crooked ways." Reviewing what he had learned from rereading Chinese and Western classics in recent years, he stated the belief that neither political nor moral categories were adequate to capture the full richness of any human being. "Reading these works," he wrote, "you understand people as being of various types of character, not in general terms such as 'good people,' 'bad people,' or 'bureaucrats,' 'commoners,' 'workers,' 'rich peasants,' etc. Before you stand flesh and blood human beings, with individual characteristics, even though they are in certain relations of production and in certain classes." Finally, as if to confirm and perhaps in some metaphorical way summarize this repudiation of much of what he had been known to stand for, and his more eclectic view of life, Ch'ü concluded with the words, "Chinese *tou-fu* is delicious—nothing better in all the world. Farewell.''

Ch'ü Ch'iu-pai was executed by the KMT on the morning of June 18, 1935, in Ch'angt'ing, Fukien, and buried late that afternoon in a cemetery at the foot of Coiled-Dragon Hill (P'an-lung kan), situated to the west of the Mountain of Buddha's Disciples (Lo-han ling).

Evaluations of Ch'ü from His Death to 1949

Ch'ü's death was widely reported in the Chinese press. An interview that Ch'ü had had with reporter Li K'e-ch'ang during his imprisonment was published in *Kuo-wen chou-pao* [National news weekly] on July 8, 1935.[2] Part of *Superfluous Words* first appeared in three installments in a pro-KMT journal *She-hui hsin-wen* [Social news] in August and September 1935.[3] Later, in 1937, *I-ching*, a literary and historical bimonthly, published a more complete version of *Superfluous Words*, along with several sympathetic articles on Ch'ü's life and writings.[4] Ch'ü's last letter to Kuo Mo-jo (1891-1978) was first published in a Chinese journal in New York City called *Hsien-feng* [Vanguard], probably in 1936.[5] The publication of these materials in the non-Communist press reflects a general rather than an exclusively political interest in him at the time. One reader thought that his last poem was "sad, elegant, mournful, and ghostly," and added: "I think that anyone who reads his *Superfluous Words*, in particular the so-called bourgeois type *wen-jen* of our generation, who have experienced so many vicissitudes, cannot but shed tears of sympathy."[6]

Lu Hsun, long a close friend of Ch'iu-pai, expressed his grief over Ch'ü's death by publishing some of his writings in book form. In early 1934, when he was departing for Kiangsi, Ch'ü had left a copy of some manuscripts with Lu Hsun for safekeeping. After Ch'ü died, Lu Hsun, although already quite ill, devoted much time and effort to editing and publishing his late friend's translations from Russian of literary theories of Marx, Engels, Lenin, Laforgue, and Gorky, and Lunarcharsky's drama, *The Liberated Don Quixote,* among others. It took Lu Hsun an entire year, beginning in October 1935, to prepare the publication of two thick volumes. Although he lived to see the publication of only the first volume of *Hai-shang shu-lin* [Writings done in Shanghai], he completed proofreading the second volume a few days before his death. The work was typeset in Shanghai and printed in Japan.[7]

Hsieh Tan-ju, Ch'iu-pai's Shanghai landlord during 1931-1933, also preserved part of Ch'ü's writings. It was Ch'ü's habit, under constant threat of being arrested by the police, to make two carbon copies of his writings. Usually he sent the original copy to editors of magazines or newspapers and kept the carbon copies for himself. Before his departure for Juichin, he had entrusted one copy of his manuscripts to Lu Hsun and asked Hsieh Tan-ju to keep the other. The two copies are almost identical, although there are some minor differences due to revisions made by Ch'ü. The manuscripts can be divided into two main categories: translations and essays on literature, and random essays (*tsa-wen*) that are mostly short commentaries on social and literary topics. Some of these writings had already been published in various journals and newspapers in Shanghai. Ch'ü's translations and essays on literature were included in the two-volume *Hai-shang shu-lin,* but his *tsa-wen* remained unavailable in book form at the time of Lu Hsun's death in 1936. Many of these were later collected by Hsieh Tan-ju, who arranged their publication in 1938 as *Luan-t'an chi ch'i-ta* [Vulgar music and others]. This work, which consisted mostly of Ch'ü's *tsa-wen* written during 1931 and 1933, was issued in the name of Hsia She. The publication date was given as May 5, Karl Marx's birthday. *Luan-t'an chi ch'i-ta* seems to have enjoyed great popularity, for a second printing was released on December 1, 1938, a third on November 20, 1939, and a fourth on July 15, 1940, all by the same Hsia She in Shanghai. In 1940, Hsia She also published a collection of Ch'ü's essays on literature for the masses, under the title *Chih-t'ou chi* [Streetcorner writings]. The publication of Ch'ü's writings in Shanghai reflects the relative freedom of the press in that city at the time. Later, during the Sino-Japanese War, *Hai-shang shu-lin, Luan-t'an chi ch'i-ta,* and other collections of Ch'ü's writings were reprinted several times in Shanghai, Manchuria, and Communist-controlled areas. All this suggests a broad interest in his writings.[8]

Ch'ien Hing-ts'un (better known by his pen name Ah Ying), a leftist writer and literary historian, intended to publish a complete collection of Ch'ü's writings, and an advertisement for "Ch'ü Ch'iu-pai ch'üan-chi" [Complete works of Ch'ü Ch'iu-pai] appeared in a journal called *Wen-hsien* [Documents] in January 1939.[9] For reasons unknown, the intended collection was never published.

Contrary to Ch'ü's last wishes expressed in *Superfluous Words,* after his death he was praised by the Communists as a valiant fighter and heroic martyr. In August 1935, the English edition of *Communist International* carried an article about him and Ho Shu-hen (1874-1935).[10]

At the time of Ch'ü's death, the Communists were still on the Long

March, but the following year they commemorated the first anniversary of his death in at least two memorial volumes. One was entitled *Chi-nien wo-men te min-tsu ying-hsiung ho jen-min chan-shih* [In memory of our national heroes and fighters of the people], mimeographed and distributed by the underground Communist headquarters in Shanghai. It included seven articles on Ch'ü the "martyr" in addition to several other essays on other martyrs.[11] The second volume was entitled *Hsun-kuo lieh-shih Ch'ü Ch'iu-pai* [Ch'ü Ch'iu-pai: A martyr for his country].[12] The preface extolled Ch'ü for his role in the revolution:

> Comrade Ch'ü Ch'iu-pai was not only one of the greatest leaders of the Chinese Communist Party, but also one of the most outstanding leaders of the Chinese people. He devoted his entire life to the struggle for the liberation of the Chinese people and of Chinese society. On the occasion of the first anniversary of his sacrifice, not only members of the Chinese Communist Party, but all the people of China should commemorate this outstanding leader.[13]

The volume includes a eulogy to Ch'ü, a biographical sketch of him, an article entitled "In memory of our dear comrade in arms Ch'ü Ch'iu-pai," a joint article by Wang Ming and K'ang Sheng (1898-1976), telegrams of condolence from various foreign Communist parties, and an article by Mao Tse-tung on culture and education in the soviet areas. The inclusion of Mao's essay, which praises educational advances in the soviet areas but does not mention Ch'ü's name, was meant as a tribute to Ch'ü's work as the commissar of education during the Kiangsi period. The article "In memory of our dear comrade in arms Ch'ü Ch'iu-pai," signed by one Tu Ning and dated May 10, 1936, charged that the KMT had forged Ch'iu-pai's writings in prison in order to defame him:

> After the death of Comrade Ch'iu-pai, the fascists ... forged his notes in prison, and revised and imitated his letters from prison in order to vilify and slander him after having cruelly slaughtered him. For instance, *Superfluous Words* published in the fascist *She-hui hsin-wen*, the interview with a reporter published in *Kuo-wen chou-pao*, the letter to Kuo Mo-jo printed in *Hsien-feng* in America, all came from one and the same reactionary source and are intended to insult and humiliate Comrade Ch'iu-pai.[14]

Thus, the first published Chinese Communist response to Ch'ü's writings in prison, in which he had expressed second thoughts about

his political activities, was to deny their authenticity, in order to
retain the image of Ch'ü's revolutionary purity.

Various collections of biographical sketches of revolutionary
martyrs published by the Chinese Communists in the 1940s almost
invariably included highly laudatory articles on Ch'ü. Usually, these
articles stressed his participation in the May Fourth Movement, his
contribution to introducing Marxism-Leninism-Stalinism into
China, his Party leadership role in 1925-1928, his opposition to
"Ch'en Tu-hsiu–ism," his work on the latinization of the Chinese
language, his literary activities during the early 1930s, and his
contributions to educational advances in the soviet areas. Rarely, and
then only briefly, did they mention his involvement in the Li Li-san
line or his expulsion from the Politburo in early 1931. In an article
written in 1946 by Hsiao San, for example, Ch'iu-pai was
characterized as

> a participant and leader of the May 4th patriotic parades and
> demonstrations, an activist in the new culture movement, a truthful
> reporter of the October Revolution and the New Russia, one of the
> finest leaders of the Chinese Communist Party, an outstanding talent
> of the Party, an early publicist of Marxism-Leninism in China, a
> faithful activist and a leader of the Chinese people.

Hsiao San also noted that

> Comrade Ch'iu-pai was very respectful to Comrade Mao Tse-tung.
> After inspecting the peasant movement in Hunan, Comrade Mao Tse-
> tung wrote his famous "Report on an investigation of the peasant
> movement in Hunan" and sent it to *Hsiang-tao chou-pao*. Having
> published a few paragraphs [of the report], P'eng Shu-chih, then the
> editor of *Hsiang-tao chou-pao*, would not publish the remainder, and
> *Chung-yang jih-pao* [Central daily news] of Wuhan could reprint only
> those paragraphs already published in *Hsiang-tao chou-pao*. Comrade
> Ch'ü Ch'iu-pai, then in Wuhan, not only published the full text of
> Comrade Mao Tse-tung's report as a book, but also wrote a preface to
> it.[15]

The praises heaped on Ch'ü by Chinese Communists in the 1940s
and 1950s were in general conformity with the official Party
evaluation of him, which was reflected in the "Resolution on
Questions on the History of the Party," adopted by the enlarged
session of the Party Central Committee on April 20, 1945. Since the
main targets of censure in this resolution were Ch'ü's political foes,

the so-called Russian returned students led by Wang Ming, it is not surprising that Ch'ü was favorably treated. While criticizing the Party leadership for "adventurism" following emergency conference on August 7, 1927, and for taking a "compromising attitude" toward the Li Li-san line at the Third Plenum of the Sixth Party Congress in September 1930, the resolution does not single out Ch'ü as being responsible for these "mistakes." According to this resolution, Ch'ü's expulsion from the Politburo at the Fourth Plenum in January 1931 by Wang Ming and his followers was "misdirected." Referring to that event, the resolution stated that "both that plenary session and the Central Committee after it promoted 'left' doctrinaire-sectarian comrades to leading posts on the one hand, and, on the other, dealt excessively severe blows to comrades who had committed mistakes along the Li Li-san line, and misdirected blows at comrades headed by Ch'ü Ch'iu-pai who had allegedly committed 'mistakes along the line of conciliation.' " In evaluating the Party cadres who were demoted by the "left doctrinaire-sectarians" and later arrested and executed by the KMT, the resolution said: "Comrade Ch'ü Ch'iu-pai, who allegedly committed 'mistakes along the line of conciliation,' was a prestigious Party leader; he did much useful work (mainly cultural) even after he was attacked, and he died a hero's death in June 1935 at the hands of Kuomintang executioners. The memory of the proletarian heroism of all these comrades will be kept fresh forever."[16] Thus, although the resolution was not concerned with giving an official overall evaluation of Ch'ü's role in the history of the Party and had little of a positive nature to say about him, it did single him out as one of the few former Party leaders exempted from severe condemnation. Ch'ü continued to be depicted as a martyr for the revolution.

Changing Evaluations in the People's Republic

Ch'ü's official reputation remained high after the establishment of the People's Republic. Indeed, special measures were taken to honor his memory. In the summer of 1951 the local government of Ch'angt'ing, having located his grave, removed his remains and placed them in an earthenware jar, which was kept on display in the district government office. Afterwards, a stone monument and a memorial tomb were erected on the former burial site. West Gate Road, where Ch'ü had been imprisoned, was renamed Ch'iu-pai Road, and later a broadcasting station built on this road was also named after him.[17]

In 1954 Ch'ü's remains were transferred from Ch'angt'ing to Peking. On the occasion of the twentieth anniversary of his death, June 18, 1955, his remains were interred in Martyrs' Cemetery at Papao-shan, Peking. Chou En-lai presided over the ceremony, which was also attended by such Party notables as Tung Pi-wu, K'ang Sheng, P'eng Chen, Lu Ting-i, as well as Chou Chien-jen, Yeh Shao-chün, Hsu Kuang-p'ing, and Yang Chih-hua (Ch'iu-pai's widow). At the ceremony, Lu Ting-i, director of the CCP's Central Committee Propaganda Department gave a brief account of Ch'ü's life, which may be taken to represent the CCP's evaluation of Ch'ü in the 1950s:

> Comrade Ch'ü Ch'iu-pai was an outstanding political activist and propagandist of the Chinese Communist Party. . . . In 1920, as a newspaper reporter he visited Soviet Russia, and was one of China's earliest progressive intellectuals to report on this socialist country. . . .
>
> During the period of the First Revolutionary War in our country, between 1924 and 1927, Comrade Ch'ü Ch'iu-pai, together with Comrades Mao Tse-tung and Jen Pi-shih [1904-50], in order to protect the Party's correct policy concerning the united front, carried out resolute struggles, repudiated the erroneous anti-Soviet, anti-Communist arguments of the bourgeois right-wing, and criticized the mistake of abandoning proletarian leadership committed by the right deviation opportunists within the Party, represented by Ch'en Tu-hsiu. In 1927, at the most critical juncture of the Chinese revolution, he, together with other comrades, took charge of convening the August 7th Emergency Conference of the Central Committee of the Chinese Communist Party, criticized the opportunism of the right deviationists, and established the correct principles of land revolution and armed resistance against the Kuomintang's counterrevolutionary rule. . . . In September 1930, he presided over the Third Plenum of the Sixth Congress of the Chinese Communist Party and corrected the mistakes of the adventurist line within leading organs of the Party.
>
> In the years from 1931 to 1933, Comrade Ch'ü Ch'iu-pai and Mr. Lu Hsun led the left-wing cultural movement in Shanghai. During this period, he devoted himself to the introduction of Marxist literary theories and of Russian and Soviet literary works, and made important contributions to the Chinese revolutionary cultural movement. . . .
>
> At 10 A.M., June 18, 1935, outside the West Gate of Ch'angt'ing, Fukien, he courageously died for his cause. Comrade Ch'ü Ch'iu-pai was a fighter of the Chinese proletariat with boundless loyalty. To his last breath, he devoted himself to the revolution. His noble qualities and the merits and accomplishments of his entire life will live forever in the people's hearts.[18]

Here, Ch'ü is praised for a wide range of activities: Party leader,

Party propagandist, translator, literary critic, and contributor to the movement for a revolutionary culture. It is also significant to note that no mention was made of Ch'ü's involvement in the Li Li-san line or his writings in prison. The next day, June 19, this short account by Lu Ting-i and a news item on Ch'ü's reburial at the Martyr's Cemetery appeared on the front page of the official CCP newspaper, *Jen-min jih-pao* [People's daily].

Although Ch'ü was accorded the highest honor for a dead Communist, his political past was not made fully known. The carefully compiled and handsomely printed *Ch'ü Ch'iu-pai wen chi* [The writings of Ch'ü Ch'iu-pai], which was published in four thick volumes in 1953-1954, included only literary writings. The preface to this collection, which represents the contemporary CCP evaluation of his literary activities, began as follows:

> An unbending Communist Party member, an immortal martyr, Comrade Ch'ü Ch'iu-pai gave his entire life to the task of the liberation of the people of our country. His revolutionary activities were mainly in Party work and actual political struggles. He left us a very large quantity of writings, most of which are essays and translations concerning political and social questions. But Comrade Ch'ü Ch'iu-pai was also a celebrated, talented revolutionary writer, critic, and literary translator. Although he did not have much time to engage in literary activities, he still left a not inconsiderable quantity of literary essays and translations, which are undoubtedly a most precious treasure of contemporary Chinese literature.
>
> These works are precious because, first of all, their author was as unbending a fighter in literary activities as in actual revolutionary activities. These works clearly show that their author took from beginning to end a challenging, attacking attitude toward old culture, old China, and enemies of the people. These works, whether creative writings, critiques, researches, or even introductions and translations, all sharply reflect the significance of their times, all possess a clear and correct purpose of social struggle. . . . The traditional spirit of the cultural revolution and literary revolution of May 4th was no other than the fighting spirit of revolutionary democratic ideology and Communist ideology; Comrade Ch'ü Ch'iu-pai was an important representative of this very spirit, and his works can explain completely this significance.
>
> In the past, during the dark age of reactionary rule, these works once carried forward the struggle of charging with bayonets and breaking through the enemy's lines on the revolutionary cultural front, and they produced a momentous, ineradicable impact on literary thought. Even today, they still have their military functions.

> In particular, for youth and literary workers, Comrade Ch'ü Ch'iu-pai's literary legacy possesses profound educational significance.
>
> Furthermore, these works themselves, whether in their ideological content, or in their artistry, all have constructive achievements, and all vividly manifest their author's talent and creativity.[19]

Thus Ch'ü Ch'iu-pai was praised as a talented representative writer in the revolutionary tradition of the May Fourth Movement, and his literary works were regarded as possessing not only historical significance but also contemporary relevance. Nevertheless, his works were seen to contain some "shortcomings." When the compilers of the collection wrote the following paragraphs, they summed up a representative view, which can be found in various articles and books on Ch'ü written in the 1950s.

> Of course, when we read and study these precious works, we must pay attention to the author's deviations [*p'ien-hsiang*] in particular arguments. For example, the author's evaluation of the achievements and significance of the May 4th literary revolution is obviously too low. Related to this is his evaluation of the linguistic achievements [*pai-hua*] of the new literature after May 4th, which is also somewhat too low. Furthermore, in his discussion of the question of language in "Mass Literature," there are individual sentences that can mislead people into thinking that language possesses a class nature. And in his analysis of the process of the development of a unified language of the nationalities (the language of the Hans), there are deviations in individual places.[20]

These criticisms did not seriously affect the compiler's positive evaluation of Ch'ü's place in modern Chinese history:

> However, these individual shortcomings cannot diminish the glorious value possessed by Comrade Ch'ü Ch'iu-pai's literary legacy itself. The chief significance of these writings of battles is that they once fulfilled the function of opening up an age. Furthermore, views contained in these works on important and major issues, such as the role of literature in class struggle, the popularization of literature, questions concerning literary language and others, are fundamentally Marxist and conform to Comrade Mao Tse-tung's directives. As to the above-mentioned deviations in particular arguments, when we study them, we can differentiate [the correct from the incorrect] by basing ourselves on the writings of Comrade Stalin (*Marxism and the Questions of Linguistics*) and of Comrade Mao Tse-tung (*On New Democracy* and others).[21]

The collection did not contain any of Ch'ü's writings on purely political matters, and in their preface the compilers passed over this part of his career without comment. Needless to say, *Ch'ü Ch'iu-pai wen-chi* did not include any of Ch'ü's writings during his imprisonment.

Thus, in the 1950s, Ch'ü's position in the official historiography of the Chinese Communist movement appeared secure. Hundreds of articles—mostly personal reminiscences and discussions of his literary writings—were published in various newspapers and journals, and several books were compiled to facilitate research on his writing.[22] On the anniversaries of his birth (January 29) and death (June 18), it was usual for various newspapers, including *Jen-min jih-pao*, to publish articles in honor of his memory.

The year 1959, when Ch'ü would have reached age sixty if alive, was the last year in which Ch'ü's official reputation was so high. Since 1960, as far as we know, no articles have appeared in any major publication in the People's Republic of China to commemorate either his birth or his death. In the early 1960s, although his name still appeared in some works, articles devoted primarily to him became increasingly infrequent. It is difficult to ascertain the reason for this change, but it may very well be related to the Sino-Soviet rift. Ch'ü was well known for his Russian orientation in both his political and literary activities, and it seems understandable that the esteem in which he had been held should decline as the official attitude toward Russia and Russian influences on China cooled.

As relations between Moscow and Peking became increasingly exacerbated, the Party's attitude toward Ch'ü altered even more drastically, and, by the mid-1960s, in place of qualified praise there was harsh condemnation. In order to understand the reasons for this reversal, which was interrelated with Chinese domestic politics as well as Sino-Soviet relations, it is necessary to take a look at one of the major historiographic controversies of the early 1960s, the debate over the proper evaluation of Li Hsiu-ch'eng (1823-1864).

In 1963, Ch'i Pen-yü, who later was to play an important role during the early phase of the Cultural Revolution, published an article entitled "P'ing Li Hsiu-ch'eng tzu-shu" [Evaluation of Li Hsiu-ch'eng's autobiographical account] in the leading historical journal *Li-shih yen-chiu* [Historical research].[23] Li Hsiu-ch'eng, an important leader of the Taipings, had been captured in 1864 by an army led by Tseng Kuo-ch'üan (1824-1890). During his imprisonment and before his execution, Li wrote an account of himself, which became an important source on Taiping history and the subject of much scholarly controversy. In the 1950s an annotated version was published by the noted historian Lo Erh-kang, who praised Li Hsiu-ch'eng. According to Lo, Li's writing of the autobiographical account was a "painful strategy designed to gain by delay" (*k'u-jou huan-ping chi*) and therefore could not be considered as an act of betraying the Taiping revolution.[24] Before the publication of Ch'i Pen-yü's essay, Li had been extolled as a national hero in both academic and popular historical works. Ch'i's essay challenged this positive evaluation and argued that Li's autobiographical account was tantamount to a confession to the enemy, and that Li should therefore be criticized as a "traitor" who had capitulated to the enemies of the revolution, instead of being glorified as a hero.[25] According to a Red Guard paper published in 1967, Ch'i's essay was written "under Chairman Mao's personal direction."[26] Although Red Guard newspapers are not necessarily reliable sources, other evidence, as we shall see, tends to corroborate this assertion.

The publication of Ch'i Pen-yü's article initially met strong disapproval from the CCP Central Committee's Propaganda Department, which, under the control of Liu Shao-ch'i, wielded a wide range of power in many areas, including the press and cultural affairs. On September 14, 1963, Chou Yang (1908-   ), then a deputy-director of the Propaganda Department, called a meeting of representatives of various academic organizations and newspapers, at which he declared that it was a mistake to brand Li Hsiu-ch'eng a traitor. Chou also told the journalist Teng T'o (ca. 1911-   ) and the eminent historian Chien Po-tsan to write refutations of Ch'i Pen-yü's article. This move was blocked by an order from Mao himself.[27] There was no response to Ch'i's argument in the Chinese press until July 1964, after Chou Yang had lost control of the Propaganda Department and had himself become a target of criticism. During the late summer, numerous articles on Li Hsiu-ch'eng were published in various journals and newspapers. At first, there was a vigorous debate over the issue, with articles both for and against Li. But eventually only articles condemning Li Hsiu-ch'eng were published.[28]

In the broader political context, Ch'i's article was merely one of many on the theme of the errors, the evils, and the ultimate futility of any policy of capitulation. Nikita Khrushchev, the leader of the Soviet Communist Party, was at this time continually criticized for his policy of coexistence with the capitalist world, which Peking proclaimed to be capitulation to the threat of atomic war. And, less directly, those unnamed Chinese leaders who advocated making compromises with Moscow to resolve the Sino-Soviet dispute were also seen as advocates of capitulation.

With the approach of the Cultural Revolution, the emphasis in attacks on enemies of the revolution shifted from Russian "revisionists" to domestic "traitors," those whose domestic policies were said to betray the high ideals of the Chinese revolution. Ch'ü Ch'iu-pai was now named as one who had betrayed the Party and the revolution. Sometime during 1964, Chou En-lai made a report to a Politburo meeting, saying that, like Li Hsiu-ch'eng, Ch'ü Ch'iu-pai should also be considered a "traitor," because of the autobiographical account, *Superfluous Words,* he had written while in prison. According to Chou, his report, which was not published until 1966, was inspired by Ch'i Pen-yü's article on Li Hsiu-ch'eng. Two years later, on August 30, 1966, in a talk to representatives of the Chinese Academy of Sciences, Chou explained his position.

> Good family background is a good thing; good behavior is another good thing. It is also a good thing if one's family background is not good but his behavior is good. Bad family background and bad behavior make two bad things. With two bad things, one should die, or should be called a restorationist. This depends mainly on one's behavior and one's fidelity near the end of one's life. Ch'ü Ch'iu-pai came from the bureaucratic big bourgeoisie. Toward the end of his life he wrote *Superfluous Words.* His behavior was bad, and at the end of his life he betrayed [the Party]. I made a report about this to the Politburo. Before it was published, Red Guards learned about it. They went to the Pa-pao-shan Martyrs' Cemetery and smashed Ch'ü's tombstone. . . . Ch'ü Ch'iu-pai, who came from an intellectual, bureaucratic family, lost his fidelity at the end of his life, just like Li Hsiu-ch'eng. We should learn from the young historian Ch'i Pen-yü. . . . Ch'ü Ch'iu-pai was captured by the enemy, debased himself, and bowed on his knees [to his captors]; yet in the end he nevertheless was killed by the KMT.[29]

It is doubtful that prior to 1964 Chou En-lai or many other Chinese Communist leaders were unaware of the existence of *Superfluous Words.* Although official biographies of Ch'ü either rejected the authenticity of the document or simply ignored it, Ch'ü's widow, in her reminiscences written in 1958, had mentioned it.[30] The reasons why Chou chose to make an issue out of it in 1964 are not clear. He may have been motivated as much by a desire to use Ch'ü's case to side with Mao against Mao's opponents on domestic issues as by a desire to criticize those who favored reaching a compromise accommodation with the Russians. In any event, within a few short years, denouncing so-called traitors came to mean repudiating Liu Shao-ch'i and his followers. Among the many charges made against Liu during the Cultural Revolution was one closely related to the new evaluation of Ch'ü Ch'iu-pai. Liu was accused of having advocated a "philosophy of surviving" (*huo-ming che-hsueh*). For example, an editorial of *Chieh-fang chün pao* [Liberation Army newspaper] in 1967 said:

> During the period of democratic revolution, he [Liu] repeatedly promoted the line of surrender to the bourgeoisie. As early as the eve of the outbreak of the war of resistance against Japan, he wildly propagated the philosophy of surviving, directing certain arrested "Communist Party members" to surrender to the class enemy. Later, he further shielded them, invited defectors and recruited traitors, built his own faction for selfish purposes, and permitted them to steal high positions.[31]

Among Liu's followers who had once been arrested by the KMT was An Tzu-wen (ca. 1904-   ), head of the CCP's Organization Department. In a talk to a group of Red Guards on February 8, 1967, Chou En-lai blended together criticisms of Li Hsiu-ch'eng, Ch'ü Ch'iu-pai, Lu Ting-i, and Liu Shao-ch'i:

> I suggested that we should pay attention to investigation and research. During my meeting with leading members of X faction of Nankai University, I told them to do more investigation. They decided to penetrate into many libraries. After several months' investigation, one student found that An Tzu-wen was a member of the black gang. Nankai University discovered materials dating back over twenty years. It was Liu Shao-ch'i who had given approval to An Tzu-wen's betrayal and collective defection to the KMT. After entering the city referring to the establishment of the P.R.C., as head of the Organization Department of the CCP's Central Committee, An Tzu-wen would not make these materials available. Before his death, Ch'ü Ch'iu-pai also wrote an autobiographical account, just like Li Hsiu-ch'eng; and yet, in the end he nevertheless was killed by Chiang Kai-shek. This account was hidden by Lu Ting-i. These are major events, materials written in black and white. These materials are worthwhile.[32]

Six weeks later, in another talk with a group of Red Guards on March 21, Chou En-lai further associated the appraisal of Ch'ü with criticisms of not only Liu Shao-ch'i and An Tzu-wen, but also Teng Hsiao-p'ing (ca. 1902-   ):

Due to the Red Guards, this movement has exposed a great many traitors. Before his death, Ch'ü Ch'iu-pai wrote *Superfluous Words*, which was the confession of a traitor. Inspired by Comrade Ch'i Pen-yü's essay [on Li Hsiu-ch'eng], I brought up this question in a Politburo meeting [in 1964]. Young people have inspired we older folk. Recently, it has been further discovered that before his execution Ch'ü Ch'iu-pai wrote a letter to the authorities begging for pardon. He was a traitor. These were mistakes of the organizational line of Liu Shao-ch'i and Teng Hsiao-p'ing. An Tzu-wen was in charge of the Organization Department for over twenty years. On the surface, they seem to be even more "left" than us; actually, they are opposed to Mao Tse-tung's thought.[33]

In 1967-1968, the "movement to punish Ch'ü" (*t'ao Ch'ü yun-tung*) reached many parts of China. Not only were his tomb and corpse in Peking smashed, but memorial halls and museums in his honor, for example, in Ch'angchou, Ch'angt'ing, and Shanghai, were demolished, and materials about him were burned or destroyed. Ch'ü was branded a "traitor," an "anarchist," and a "passivist," and was posthumously stripped of his Party membership. Although these activities were most vociferously performed by young Red Guards, they were encouraged by Chou En-lai, Ch'en Po-ta (1904-   ), K'ang Sheng, and others who had sided with Mao in attacking Liu Shao-ch'i and his followers. Chou, Li Fu-ch'un (1899-1975), and Ch'i Pen-yü all issued directives concerning "criticism of Ch'ü Ch'iu-pai."[34]

Since the Cultural Revolution, Ch'ü Ch'iu-pai has continued to be condemned as a "traitor." During the recent anti-Confucius movement, he, along with such other prominent figures in the history of Chinese Communism as Ch'en Tu-hsiu, Wang Ming, Liu Shao-ch'i, and Lin Piao, was designated a "Confucian disciple." For example, in a pamphlet published in 1974, Ch'ü was described in these terms:

Like all reactionaries in history and chiefs of various opportunist lines in the Party, Ch'ü Ch'iu-pai was a 100 percent disciple of K'ung Lao-erh [derogatory name for Confucius].

During the era of the fierce antiimperialist and antifeudal great revolution, Ch'ü Ch'iu-pai talked about neither class struggle, nor national contradictions, nor armed seizure of political power. He hoisted the broken Confucian flag of "Peace is valuable," he did everything he could to peddle the "benevolent way" of "loving people," shouted "everyone needs love," tried in vain to use K'ung Lao-erh's "way of the mean" to oppose the proletarian revolution.

During the early phase of the Second Civil War, Ch'ü Ch'iu-pai promoted a "left" adventurist line. After he had been criticized for his line, not only did he refuse to accept the lesson and to reform his own bourgeois world outlook, but, on the contrary, he became passive and pessimistic, even attacked the people's revolutionary movement. He published articles to propagate the Confucian way, attacked the May 4th movement, negated the struggle of "Down with Confucius and Company" of the May 4th period, branded the May 4th movement as "almost equivalent to no revolution," which sufficiently exposed his pessimism and disillusionment with the revolution. He gave up struggle, and advocated regressive, opportunist viewpoints. . . .

In order to save his own life, Ch'ü Ch'iu-pai wrote a confession—*Superfluous Words*. He bowed on his knees to Chiang Kai-shek and surrendered, and became a shameful traitor. In his confession, he tried hard to show to the enemy that he was taking "the most frank, most sincere attitude" to say "words from his heart." He confessed to the enemy that he "understood Confucius' way of loyalty and reciprocity," and that he possessed "Chinese gentry consciousness." The confession of this traitor clearly exposed his treacherous features of betraying Marxism-Leninism and the proletarian revolution.

Ch'ü Ch'iu-pai inherited in total K'ung Lao-erh's "way of loyalty and reciprocity." . . . Like K'ung Lao-erh, Ch'ü Ch'iu-pai stubbornly stood on the same ground as the declining class, advocating regression and opposing progress and revolution. In order to save his base life, he bowed on his knees and surrendered to the enemy. While maliciously attacking the Chinese Communist Party, he knelt at Chiang Kai-shek's feet and begged: "If you'll graciously release me, I shall be loyal to the Party-State." In order to achieve this base purpose, he exposed himself without any reservation to show to the enemy that he "understood Confucius' way of loyalty and reciprocity," that he could conform to not only [the way of] "Do not do to others what you do not wish others to do to you" but also the [way of] "Do not do to others what others do not wish." He attempted in vain to connect himself with Chiang Kai-shek by the black line of the Confucian way. He thought that since he had expressed his intention to be "loyal" to Chiang Kai-shek, Chiang Kai-shek would definitely treat him with "the way to reciprocity." But the KMT reactionaries did not "preserve" his "life" because he "understood Confucius' way of loyalty and reciprocity." They sent him to the guillotine. This was the shameful end he came to by extolling K'ung [Lao-erh] and betraying the revolution.[35]

In *Superfluous Words*, in the context of discussing his "cowardly" character, Ch'ü had indeed written "I seem to understand Confucius's way of loyalty and reciprocity. So in the end I became a leader of the compromisers."[36] But nowhere in this document, or in any other published material from his last weeks, did Ch'ü beg Chiang Kai-shek to release him, say that he could conform to the Confucian principles of "Do not do to others what you do not wish others to do to you" or "Do not do to others what others do not wish." The source of these accusations is not indicated; they may perhaps have been taken from the recently discovered letter to which Chou En-lai referred in his talk with Red Guards on March 21, 1967. Unfortunately, this letter has not yet been published.

Other accusations in this condemnation more clearly lack substance. As we have seen, Ch'ü had from an early time repeatedly advocated class struggle and the armed revolutionary seizure of power. He had indeed been critical of the literature of the May Fourth era, but his criticism had been that it had not been truly revolutionary, a judgment which could not fairly be interpreted as disillusionment with the revolution. Nor did Ch'ü ever use Confucianism to oppose the proletarian revolution, for he had been a critic of the evils of Confucian society from an early point in his political life. It is true that parts of *Superfluous Words* can and have been interpreted as offering to abandon his revolutionary career in return for a reprieve. A more careful reading of the entire work, however, reveals it as the thoughts of a complex person about the significance of his own life, as he waited with resignation for the execution he knew was soon to come.

Conclusions

From Ch'ü's death to the present the ultimate criterion for Chinese Communist interpretations of Ch'ü's life has been its meaning for the history of the Chinese revolution and the Chinese Communist Party. And the chief criterion for determining the framework for that meaning seems clearly to have been contemporary political circumstances at the time of each interpretation.

In general, no distinction is drawn between Ch'ü's public persona and Ch'ü as an individual human being. The editors of *Ch'ü Ch'iu-pai wen-chi* do distinguish between Ch'ü's positive contributions to modern Chinese literature and his political activities and opinions, which they state were not without error. But they see literature in political, not aesthetic, terms. The trend is in the direction of increasingly exclusive political criteria, and toward increasing simplification and even distortion of a complex life. One may not agree with all the views expressed in the 1945 "Resolution on Questions on the History of the Party" or in the preface to *Ch'ü*

Ch'iu-pai wen-chi of 1953, but one can still see that, within the prescribed political context, some balance in interpretation is maintained. By the time of the anti-Confucian campaign in 1974, however, Ch'ü's life, character, and ideas have become merely one more virtually undifferentiated instance of a stereotyped formula. The possibilities of doubt, of shifts in feelings or beliefs as a result of self-reflection, of ambivalence, or of making a positive contribution to the revolution in spite of holding currently unacceptable beliefs, are all implicitly precluded. The standard is political, and politics is the realm of the absolute.

As of August 1977, the evaluation of Ch'ü Ch'iu-pai remained entirely negative. But, given the vicissitudes in Chinese Communist historiography in the past, and the likelihood that Mao's death will be followed by significant changes in cultural and intellectual life in the People's Republic, it would not be surprising if new interpretations of Ch'ü Ch'iu-pai, and perhaps new materials relevant to understanding his life, are published in the future.

Notes

An Appreciation

1. For an example of the utility of the Oral History Project to present and future historians of modern China, see the paper by Ms. O'Brien in this volume.

Chapter 1

1. Yegor F. Timkovskii, *Puteshestvie v Kitai cherez Mongoliu* [Travels to China over Mongolia], 3 volumes, St. Petersburg, 1824. Translated into English, French, and German in the 1820s.

2. Danilevskii's biographer, Sergei Trubachev, said that some of the *Christmas Fantastic Stories* to which "Life One Hundred Years After" belongs were written "in 1879 or later." See his "Biographical Sketch," in *Sochinenii G. P. Danilevskogo* [Works of G. P. Danilevskii], eighth posthumous edition, 24 volumes (St. Petersburg, 1901), 1:86. All subsequent references to Danilevskii's story are to this edition.

3. P. N. Sakulin, *Iz istorii russkogo idealizma: knias V. F. Odoevskii, myslitel', pisatel'* [From the history of Russian idealism: Prince V. F. Odoevskii, thinker and writer] (Moscow, 1913), 1, parts 1 and 2. (These two parts are referred to hereafter as Sakulin 1, 1, and Sakulin 1, 2.) This account of the life and work of Odoevskii is brought up to the end of the 1840s, and thus embraces the time when *The Year 4338* was written. A list of utopias preceding Odoevskii's is in Sakulin 1, 1, pp. 181ff.

4. The biography of Odoevskii is based mainly on Sakulin. Also consulted were the entries on Odoevskii by Ivan Kubasov in *Russkii biograficheskii slovar'* [Russian biographical dictionary] (St. Petersburg, 1905), volume "Obesianov–Ochkin," pp. 124-50; and by A. F. Koni in *Novyi entsiklopedicheskii slovar'* [New encyclopedic dictionary] (St. Petersburg, 1916), 29, columns 294-300.

5. "Odoevskii is one of the best contemporary Russian writers," wrote V.

G. Belinskii in his 1844 survey of Russian literature. V. G. Belinskii, *Sobranie sochinenii v triokh tomakh* [Collected works in three volumes] (Moscow, 1948), 2:691.

6. I have used the Munich 1967 edition of *Russian Nights*, which is an exact copy of the Moscow 1913 edition.

7. N. Kotliarevskii, *Starinnye portrety* [Ancient portraits] (St. Petersburg, 1907), p. 197.

8. Odoevskii, *Russian Nights*, pp. 340-42.

9. Ibid., p. 344.

10. Ibid., p. 423.

11. Odoevskii, unpublished notes pertaining to *Russian Nights* cited in Sakulin 1, 1, p. 595.

12. The Slavophiles were opposed chiefly by the "Westernizers," who argued that "Russia is a part of Europe and its new civilization is European," and that Russia must learn from Europe because "everything great, noble, human, and spiritual arose, grew up, blossomed profusely, and brought forth luxurious fruit in the soil of Europe." So wrote one of the movement's outstanding figures, V. G. Belinskii. *Polnoe Sobranie sochinenii* [Complete collected works] (Moscow, 1953-59), 8:472 and 5:105.

13. Odoevskii, *Russian Nights*, pp. 335-36.

14. This idea was perhaps suggested to Odoevskii by Timkovskii (see Timkovskii 1:145). He certainly did not get it from Father Iakinf, who even after the occupation of Canton in 1842 still refused to believe in the British victory.

15. Perhaps suggested by Timkovskii 2:359; or by the superficial docility with which the Chinese appeared to bear subordination to the Manchus.

16. Odoevskii, *4338 god. Fantasticheskii roman* [The year 4338. A fantastic novel], edited with notes and introduction by Orest Tsechnovitser (Moscow, 1926). The text cited in this essay is from Odoevskii, *Povesti i rasskazy* [Long and short stories], introduction and notes by E. Iu. Khin (Moscow, 1959), pp. 416-18 (text) and 490-93 (notes). This is an exact copy of Tsechnovitser's Moscow 1926 edition.

17. Sakulin 1, 2, p. 170.

18. Sakulin 1, 2, p. 184, quoting Odoevskii's notes.

19. Odoevskii, *The Year 4338*, text, p. 426.

20. Ibid., notes, p. 448.

21. Sakulin 1, 1, pp. 574ff.

22. Odoevskii, *The Year 4338*, text, p. 422.

23. Ibid., fragments, pp. 440-41.

24. Preface to Tsechnovitser edition, pp. 4-5. The notes and fragments were in many cases written several years later than the published text, and thus sometimes contradict it.

25. This summarizes Odoevskii, *The Year 4338*, text, pp. 414-17.

26. Odoevskii, *The Year 4338*, text, p. 420.

27. Ibid., text, p. 422. This total denigration of Chinese history and culture could not have been suggested to Odoevskii by Father Iakinf, who

appreciated the old culture highly.

28. Ibid., text, pp. 421-22.

29. Odoevskii's conception of an International Union was perhaps derived from the ideas of the Abbé Castel St. Pierre, as expressed in his two proposals: *Projet pour rendre la paix perpetuelle en Europe* [A plan for everlasting peace in Europe] (1713), and *Projet de traité pour rendre la paix perpetuelle entre les souverains chrétiens* [Draft treaty for the establishment of everlasting peace among the Christian sovereigns] (1717). These proposals for a sort of League of Nations were realized in the alliance of great powers founded in 1815 at the Congress of Vienna, becoming identified with the autocratic system of Metternich. St. Pierre's ideas became widely known in Russia probably because J.-J. Rousseau wrote a critical summary of them. His proposals were discussed in Russian intellectual circles in the 1820s. See Pushkin, *Complete Works* (Moscow, 1949), 7:531 and 718n.

30. Odoevskii, *The Year 4338*, text, p. 421.

31. "Galvanostate—a balloon brought into action with galvanism" (Odoevskii's note), *The Year 4338*, fragments, p. 439.

32. Ibid., text, p. 420.

33. Ibid., text, p. 425.

34. Ibid., text, p. 425.

35. Ibid., fragments, p. 442.

36. Ibid., fragments, pp. 442-43.

37. Ibid., text, p. 435.

38. Ibid., text, pp. 433-34.

39. For discussion of a similar institution in late imperial China, see the Rowe article in this volume.

40. Odoevskii, *The Year 4338*, text, p. 434.

41. Ibid., text, pp. 426-27.

42. Ibid., text, p. 431.

43. Ibid., text, p. 432.

44. Ibid., text, p. 433.

45. Ibid., text, pp. 417-18.

46. Ibid., text, pp. 427-28.

47. Ibid., text, pp. 8, 422-23.

48. The story "Zhizn cherez sto lot" [Life one hundred years after] is included in the collection of fantastic stories *Sviatochnye rasskazy* [Christmas stories], and appears in Danilevskii's *Works*, 19:12-34.

49. The biography of Danilevskii is based on accounts of his life by Sergei Trubachev in Danilevskii's *Works*, 1:1-91; by S. Vengerov in *Novyi entsiklopedicheskii slovar'* [New encyclopedic dictionary] (St. Petersburg, 1916), 15, columns 491-92; and by A. Cherkas in *Russki biograficheskii slovar'* [Russian biographic dictionary] (St. Petersburg, 1905), volume "Dabelov–Dal'kovskii," pp. 63-66.

50. For information on the "Jewish problem," I have relied mainly on Simon Dubnov, *Weltgeschichte das judischen Volkes* [World history of the Jewish people], translated from the Russian by A. Steinberg, ten volumes

(Berlin, 1925-30), 9:174-262, 395-451, 263-318, and 452-459, respectively. On the Jewish population in 1848, see pp. 174-75n.

51. This mood had evidently erased from his mind his first encounter with a Jew, which was most friendly. A Jewish artisan who came frequently to his father's and grandfather's estates was the person who first tutored him in the Russian alphabet when he was five years old. Trubachev, in Danilevskii's *Works*, 1:21.

52. Father Iakinf, *Kitai: ego zhiteli, nravy, obychai, i prosveshchenie* [China: its inhabitants, mores, customs, and education] (St. Petersburg, 1840), p. 389.

53. Nicholai A. Polevoi (1796-1846) was a brilliant, self-made man. The son of a tradesman, he received no formal education but read extensively on his own. Beginning in 1825, he edited a journal called *Moskovskii Telegraf* [Moscow telegraph], which was outspokenly liberal and supported the new literary trend toward romanticism. He wrote the widely popular *Istoria russkogo naroda* [History of the Russian people] (1829). His journal was suppressed in 1834. After that Polevoi was inwardly broken, and during the last years of his life he earned his living by contributing to reactionary journals and writing tawdry patriotic plays popular with the average theater-goer, but dismissed with contempt by the progressive intellectuals. *The Chinese War of Theodosia Sidorovna*, a work of this sort, was published in the journal *Dagerotip* [Daguerrotype], nos. 9, 10, and 11 (St. Petersburg, 1842).

54. O. Senkovskii was a complicated man, and the designation "conservative" characterizes him only approximately. His interesting reviews of Father Iakinf's books were published in *Library for Reading*, nos. 49 and 50 (1841-42) and no. 91 (1848). They were reprinted in Senkovskii's *Sobranie sochinenii* [Complete works] (St. Petersburg, 1858-59), 6:344-479.

55. "Russian Literature," in the journal *Sovremennik* [Contemporary], no. 1 (1848), p. 49. This review by Belinskii, expressing a negative view not only of Iakinf's book but of China and the Chinese in general, was not included in the 1953-59 edition of Belinskii's complete works—this was the time of Sino-Soviet friendship.

56. *Trudy chlenov rossiskoi dukhovnoi missii v Pekine* [The works of the Russian Ecclesiastical Mission in Peking], 4 volumes (St. Petersburg, 1852-57).

57. I. A. Goncharov, *Fregat Pallada* [The frigate *Pallas*], volumes 6 and 7 of Goncharov's complete works (St. Petersburg, 1896), 7:135.

58. Sakulin 1, 2, p. 184n.

59. Data about Vasiliev are taken from *Istoria i kultura Kitaia* [The history and culture of China, a symposium in memory of Academician V. P. Vasiliev] (Moscow, 1974), pp. 7-110. The quotation is from p. 15.

60. V. P. Vasiliev, "Kitaiskii progres" [Progress in China], in *Otkrytie Kitaia* [The discovery of China] (St. Petersburg, 1900). This article was first published in 1883, but there is reason to believe that the author expressed his ideas earlier in intellectual circles where he and Danilevskii could have met. I

have the strong impression that the ideas of Vasiliev were in fact reflected in those of Danilevskii. The paragraphs quoted are from "Progress in China," pp. 148, 159, 150, 155, 162-63, 163, 158, and 163, respectively.

61. "Droshkies" (*dolgushi* in Russian) were long vehicles in which passengers could sit on two sides.

62. In the real 1968 the great-grandchildren of Poroshin could have seen a picture no less startling: large crowds of young Frenchmen carrying portraits of a Chinese and holding in their hands little red books containing aphorisms of that man—Mao Tse-tung.

63. A *Calendar* in nineteenth-century Russia and elsewhere in Europe was a book of reference providing information about various problems of life, adapted to certain days and arranged chronologically. See *Slovar' sovremennogo russkogo iazyka* [Dictionary of the contemporary Russian language] (Moscow, 1936-65), 5 (1956), column 705.

64. Danilevskii uses the word *monitor* after the vessel *Monitor* used by the Union forces during the American Civil War against the Confederate *Merrimac* in 1862.

65. Summarized from Danilevskii, "Life One Hundred Years After," pp. 23-25.

66. Danilevskii attributes these words to Bismarck, but the famous Russian poet Tiutchev, who for many years was in the diplomatic service, quoted them as said by the Austrian Minister of Foreign Affairs von Beist. F. I. Tiutchev, *Polnoe sobranie sochinenii* [Complete collected works] (St. Petersburg, 1913), pp. 208, 411-12.

67. Danilevskii wrote his story in an atmosphere of great resentment by Russian nationalists, and especially by the Slavophiles, against the Western European Great Powers, who had taken the side of Turkey during the Russian-Turkish war of 1877-78. Russia declared war on Turkey on April 24, 1877, to aid the insurrection of the Balkan Slavs who had been dominated and cruelly treated by Turkey, but also to promote its own interests in the area. The Treaty of San Stephano (March 23, 1878), concluded after the Russian victory, secured great advantages for the Balkan Slavs and for Russia. On the initiative of Austria and Britain, who opposed the growth of Russian influence on the Balkan peninsula, the Berlin Congress (June 13–July 13, 1878) was convened, with Russia, Turkey, Austria, Britain, Italy, and Germany participating, and German chancellor Bismarck playing the role of "honest broker." The Congress deprived the Slavs and Russia of a great part of the gains won after the Russian victory.

It is obvious that on this occasion Danilevskii recalled also the Russian war with Turkey in 1853-56, when Turkey was very effectively assisted by France under Napoleon III and by England under the prime ministership of J. T. Palmerston (1855-58). At that time Russia was defeated and forced to sign the humiliating Treaty of Paris (March 30, 1856).

68. The exclusion of Turkey from Europe, the Russian conquest of Constantinople, and the creation of a Slavic state on the Balkan peninsula was still an aim of Russian nationalists during World War I. As for the

Russian conquest of India, this idea had very few supporters in the nineteenth century.

69. Throughout this passage, Danilevskii makes too many mistakes even for the writer of a fantastic story. Writing at the end of the 1870s or later he should have known that since 1871 when the German empire (*Reich*), a federation of single German states (*Länder*), was founded as a constitutional monarchy, its legislative assembly was known as the *Reichstag* ("house of representatives"). The *Landtag* ("diet") was the legislative body operating within each of the separate states. See *Brockhaus Enzyclopedie* ("encyclopedia"), 17th edition (Wiesbaden, 1966-76), 11:105 and 15:588. The popedom was and is an institution ruling all Roman Catholics of the world, not only Italians; moreover, the Kingdom of Italy was founded in 1861 against the will of the pope. No Gambetta was ever a president of France.

70. The Rothschild family became a great financial power in various European countries in the 1830s. The joke about Rothschild I was launched in France at that time. See Dubnov 9:273.

71. It seems that Danilevskii unknowingly predicts something that is now taking place in the administration of justice in his native land.

72. No Rothschild or any other Jew ever became president of the French Republic in the more than one hundred years of its existence. Danilevskii could not imagine that in 1968 all Frenchmen, and Frenchwomen, would have the right to vote.

73. Danilevskii, "Life One Hundred Years After," p. 31.

74. This was hardly a fair characterization on Poroshin's (or Danilevskii's) part. Justus von Liebich (1803-73) was a famous German chemist whose introduction of mineral fertilizers brought about a great enlargement of the basis of human nourishment (*Brockhaus Enzyclopedie*, 11:452). Rudolf Virchov was a famous German chemist and an outstanding liberal of the time (ibid., 19:685).

75. Odoevskii, *The Year 4338*, p. 448n. See the amusing article in the New York *Village Voice*, 21, no. 45 (November 8, 1976): "Important Sale—Great Britain, Including All Assets and Dependencies. By Public Auction, the Ballroom, Buckingham Palace."

Chapter 2

1. Cheng Hsiang-hsin and Hai Hsi-yen, "A-pa t'u-chai chih hsien-kuang chi ch'i she-chih wen-t'i" [The present situation in the native villages of A-pa and the problem of their administration], *Pien-cheng kung-lun* [Frontier Affairs] (hereafter FA) 1, nos. 9 and 10 (1942):35.

2. Ho Ming-kuo, "Shen-pi chih Sung-p'an ts'ao ti" [The mysterious Sung-p'an grassland], part 2, FA 4, nos. 2 and 3 (1945):50.

3. Cheng and Hai, "Present situation in A-pa," p. 39.

4. Liu En-lan, "The social customs of the tribes people as affected by their climatic and geographical environment," *Journal of the West China Border Research Society* (hereafter JWCBRS), 15, series A (1944):12-13.

5. Chiang Chih-ang, "The Black River communal politics," JWCBRS 15, series A (1944):22.

6. Liu En-lan, "Tribes of Li-fan county in northwest Szechuan," JWCBRS 15, series A (1944):4.

7. Ho Ming-kuo, "Mysterious Sung-p'an grassland," part 2, p. 55.

8. Ibid.

9. Yu Shih-yu, "Ma-wo Ya-men" [The Ma-wo government], FA 3, no. 6 (1944):36.

10. Chiang Chih-ang, "Black River communal politics," pp. 25-26.

11. Yu Shih-yu, "Ma-wo government," pp. 36-37.

12. Chiang Chih-ang, "Black River communal politics," pp. 26-27.

13. Ibid., pp. 29-31.

14. Liu En-lan, "Social customs of the tribes people," p. 16.

15. Hu Chien-min, "Ch'iang-tsu ti hsin-yang yu hsi-wei" [The beliefs and customs of the Chiang people], *Pien-chiang yen-chiu lun-tsung* [Frontier studies] (Chengtu, 1941), pp. 2-10.

16. David C. Graham, "The Customs of the Ch'iang," JWCBRS 14, series A (1942):97.

17. Albert Tafel, *My Tibetan Trip: A Trip through Northwestern China and through Inner Mongolia into Eastern Tibet* (Stuttgart, 1914), translated by Carol Cerf for the Human Relations Area Files (New Haven, 1956), pp. 377-80.

18. Lin Yueh-hua, "Ch'uan K'ang Chia-yung ti chia-tsu yu hun-yin" [Family and marriage among the Giarong of Szechuan and Sikang], *Yenching Journal of Social Sciences* 1 (1948):136.

19. Tafel, *My Tibetan Trip*, pp. 363-68.

20. Lin Yueh-hua, "Family and marriage among the Giarong," pp. 137-38.

21. T'ang Ying-hua, "K'ang-jen nung-yeh chia-t'ing tsu-chih ti yen-chiu" [A study of the Khamba peasant family organization], part 1, FA 3, no. 6 (1944):46.

22. Li Yi-jen, *Hsi-k'ang tsung-lan* [A comprehensive view of Sikang] (Shanghai, 1947), p. 121.

23. Eric Tiechman, *Travels of a Consular Officer in Eastern Tibet* (Cambridge, 1922), pp. 3-4.

24. Pedro Carrasco, *Land and Polity in Tibet* (Seattle, 1959), pp. 141-52. Chen Han-sheng, *Frontier Land System in Southernmost China* (New York, 1949), pp. 81-85.

25. K'o Hsiang-feng, *Hsi-k'ang she-hui chih niao-k'an* [A bird's eye view of the Sikang society] (Chungking, 1941), pp. 60-62.

26. Chen Han-sheng, *Frontier Land System*, p. 85.

27. Carrasco, *Land and Polity in Tibet*, p. 218.

28. Chen Han-sheng, *Frontier Land System*, pp. 87-89; T'ang Ying-hua, "Khamba peasant family organization," part 1, p. 47.

29. Chen Han-sheng, *Frontier Land System*, pp. 89-90.

30. K'o Hsiang-feng, pp. 47-48; T'ang Ying-hua, "Khamba peasant family

organization," part 3, FA 3, no. 9 (1943):39. Tafel, *My Tibetan Trip*, p. 193.

31. T'ang Ying-hua, part 5, FA 4, nos. 4, 5, 6 (1945):34-35.

32. F. Kingdon Ward, *The Riddle of the Tsangpo Gorges* (London, 1926), pp. 8-9.

33. Ibid., pp. 187-89, 252-53, 303-11.

34. Alan Winnington, *Tibet: Record of a Journey* (London, 1957), p. 63. Also, Fu Sung-lin, *Hsi-k'ang chien sheng chi* [The establishment of Sikang Province] (Chengtu, 1911), p. 196.

35. Chiang Ying-liang, "Hsi-nan pien-chu ti t'e-chung wen-tzu" [The distinctive scripts of the southwestern frontier], FA 4, no. 1 (1945):26-27.

36. Hsu I-t'ang, *Lei-po Hsiao-liang-shan chih Lo-min* [The Lolos of Hsiao-liang-shan in Lei-po] (Chengtu, 1944), pp. 71-104.

37. Lin Yueh-hua, "Ta-liang-shan lo-lo ti chieh-chi chih-tu" [The class system of the Lolos of Ta-liang-shan], FA 3, no. 9 (1944):23-24.

38. Hsu I-tang, *Lolos of Hsiao-liang-shan*, pp. 54-55.

39. Ibid., pp. 51-52.

40. Ibid., pp. 57-64.

41. Ibid., p. 52. Also, Lin Yueh-hua, "Class system of the Lolos," pp. 22-24; Winnington, *Tibet*, pp. 29-32. Hsu quoted a survey that estimated that commoners contributed 98 percent of the Hsiao-liang-shan population; nobility, 1.67 percent; and slaves, .33 percent. Lin's own estimate of the Ta-liang-shan population was commoners, 60-70 percent; nobility, 10 percent; and slaves, 20-30 percent. Winnington quoted a Communist report of an official investigation of a district in Ning-lang which revealed that in 1955 the population was composed of nobility, 2 percent; commoners, 60 percent; and slaves, 38 percent. For the Ning-lang region as a whole, the percentages were: nobility, 6 percent; commoners, 47 percent; and slaves, 47 percent. The total population of the district was 56,000. If the various estimates quoted above were accurate, they seem to indicate that the areas nearest to the centers of effective Chinese rule and also the older Yi settlements had a greater proportion of commoners because the newly captured slaves were sold as far away from their original homes as possible and that many slaves and their descendants having lived a long period in the Yi territory had been permitted to join the ranks of the commoners.

42. Hsu I-t'ang, *Lolos of Hsiao-liang-shan*, pp. 52-53. Also, Lin Yueh-hua, "Class system of the Lolos," pp. 25-26; Winnington, *Tibet*, pp. 32-35.

43. Jen Nai-ch'iang, *Hsi-k'ang t'u-ching* [An illustrated study of Sikang] (Nanking, 1933).

44. Wu Tse-lin, "Mo-hsieh-jen chih she-hui tsu-chih yü tsung-chiao hsin-yang" [The social organization and religious beliefs of the Moso people], part 1, FA 4, nos. 4, 5, 6 (1945):30-31.

45. Ibid., p. 30.

46. Ibid., part 2, 4, nos. 7, 8 (1945):9-10. Also, Joseph F. Rock, *The Ancient Na-khi Kingdom of Southwest China* (Cambridge, 1947), 2:391.

47. Rock, *Ancient Na-Khi Kingdom*, p. 391.

48. Hsu Fang-kan, "Li-tai ch'a-yeh pien-i shih lueh [A brief history of

frontier tea trade], FA 3, no. 11 (1944):25-26. Also, T'ang Fang-chih, "T'ien ch'a Ts'ang hsiao" [Yunnan tea in the Tibetan trade], FA 3, no. 11 (1944):48-49.

49. William W. Rockhill, *The Land of the Lamas* (London, 1891), p. 282.

50. H. R. Davies, *Yunnan: The Link between India and the Yangtse* (Cambridge, 1909), p. 251. Also, Rockhill, *Land of the Lamas*, pp. 207-8, 258, 284; Li Yi-jen, *View of Sikang*, p. 342.

51. Cheng Ho-sheng, "Ch'ing-tai tui yu Hsi-nan tsung-tsu chih fu-sui" [The pacification of the southwestern tribes in the Ch'ing period], FA 2, nos. 6, 7, 8 (1943):4.

52. *Sze-ch'uan t'ung-chih* [Gazetteer of Szechuan province] (hereafter ST), *chüan* 92, p. 28a.

53. Ibid., *chüan* 92, pp. 15-26. A total of 5,115 Chinese families and 2,167 Giarong families were resettled in the region after the Giarong war ended. In 1908, according to Tafel, there were about 2,500 Chinese families in Rarden and an equal number of Giarong families; the same situation prevailed in Chanla. If his estimates were accurate, the Chinese population had hardly increased at all. Tafel, *My Tibetan Trip*, p. 365.

54. Li Yi-jen, *View of Sikang*, p. 42. According to Jen Nai-ch'iang, during the early Ch'ing period, 1650-1750, there were about 3,000 Chinese immigrants, mostly soldiers, in Kham; during the middle period, 1750-1850, there were about 16,000 soldiers, traders, and miners in that area; and during the last period, 1851-1911, the total number of immigrants was about 21,000. If these estimates were correct, the number of agricultural settlers could not have been more than a few thousand. See Jen Nai-ch'iang, *Study of Sikang*, p. 242.

55. Chen Han-sheng, *The Frontier Land System*, p. 75. According to Wei Yuan, because of the abundance of land in Chinghai, Gushi Khan decided to make it the home of the Khosote Mongols. Kham was relegated to the role of a revenue-producing province. Wei Yuan, *Sheng-wu chi* [An account of imperial campaigns], *chüan* 3, p. 40a.

56. Hsiao I-shan, *Ch'ing-tai t'ung-shih* [History of the Ch'ing dynasty] (Shanghai, 1927), p. 679.

57. *Ta Ch'ing i-t'ung chih* [The imperial domain of the Ch'ing dynasty], Chia-ch'ing edition, *chüan* 546, p. 4a.

58. Rock, *Ancient Na-khi Kingdom*, pp. 134-35. This information was obtained from the family chronicle of the Mu *t'u-ssu* as translated by Rock. Chinese history usually stated that these districts were ceded to the Tibetans by Wu's grandson and successor.

59. *Tung-hua lu* [Tung-hua chronicle] (hereafter THL), K'ang-hsi reign, *chüan* 15, pp. 19a-20a.

60. Wei Yuan, *Account of imperial campaigns*, *chüan* 5, p. 4.

61. ST, *chüan* 90, pp. 43a-45a.

62. ST, *chüan* 92, pp. 2, 14b-15a. THL, K'ang-hsi reign, *chüan* 64, p. 1; *chüan* 65, p. 22a. Also, Jen Nai-ch'iang, *Study of Sikang*, p. 62.

63. Arthur W. Hummel, *Eminent Chinese of the Ch'ing Period, 1644-1911*

(Washington, D.C.: U.S. Government Printing Office, 1943), 2:760.

64. THC, K'ang-hsi reign, *chüan* 104, p. 7a.

65. ST, *chüan* 92, p. 4.

66. Wang Ngo-shih, "Ts'ang lu tsung-chi" [Notes on Tibet and Kham], in *Hsiao-fang-hu-chai yü-ti ts'ung-ch'ao* [Collection of geographical studies from the Hsiao-fang-hu-chai], third series, p. 26a. Wang was a member of the 1726 border demarcation team that divided Kham between Szechuan and Tibet.

67. Li Tieh-tseng, *Tibet, Today and Yesterday* (New York, 1960), p. 40.

68. Wei Yuan, *Account of imperial campaigns, chüan* 3, pp. 40b-42a.

69. THL, Yung-cheng reign, *chüan* 4, p. 10b. Also, Jen Nai-ch'iang, *Study of Sikang*, p. 64. The court had discussed the feasibility of recovering these lost districts in 1681. The governor-general of Yunnan-Kweichow, however, pointed out in a 1682 memorial that to reoccupy them would involve the expulsion of the Mongol governor. He suggested instead the sending of a Moso emissary to the Dalai Lama to effect the peaceful return of these formerly Moso lands. See THL, K'ang-hsi reign, *chüan* 28, p. 7. In 1720, the governor-general of Yunnan-Kweichow reported that the native chiefs and monk officials of Chung-tien and nearby districts had petitioned the government for permission to be put back under Chinese jurisdiction. The governor-general proposed that these areas as well as Li-tang and Ba-tang be put under the administration of the Li-chiang *t'u-ssu*. The proposal was opposed by Nien Keng-yao on the ground that military necessity dictated that they should be controlled by the Szechuan government. The court agreed with Nien. THL, K'ang-hsi reign, *chüan* 105, pp. 4b-5b.

70. THL, Yung-cheng reign, *chüan* 4, pp. 42b-43a.

71. Ibid., *chüan* 7, p. 22.

72. Jen Nai-ch'iang, *Study of Sikang*, pp. 111-13.

73. *Wei Ts'ang t'ung-chih*, pp. 392-96.

74. ST, *chüan* 92, pp. 26b-27a.

75. Wei Yuan, *Account of imperial campaigns, chüan* 7, pp. 15a-20a.

76. ST, *chüan* 87, pp. 12b-15a.

77. Wei Yuan, *Account of imperial campaigns, chüan* 7, pp. 20a-26a.

78. ST, *chüan* 87, pp. 24b-25a.

79. ST, *chüan* 95, pp. 86b-87b.

80. Jen Nai-ch'iang, *Study of Sikang*, p. 218. Also *Ch'ing-shih kao, chüan* 126, pp. 4a-5a; Lu Ch'uan-lin, *Ch'ou-chan shu-kao* [Memorials on the Chan-tui Incident], *chüan* 1, p. 21. Jen stated that the Tibetans asked for 200,000 taels. Both the *Ch'ing-shih kao* and Lu's preface reported the sum to be 160,000 taels. In Lu's memorial to the court, however, he put it at 300,000 taels. It was possible that the Tibetans had demanded different sums at different times during the negotiations. In any case, the officials in charge at that time had glossed over the entire incident in their reports to the court.

81. *Ch'ing-shih kao, chüan* 126, p. 5.

82. Lu Ch'uan-lin, *Memorials on the Chan-tui Incident, chüan* 1, pp. 1a-3b, 15a-16a, 23a-25a; *chüan* 3, pp. 20a-21a.

83. A provision in the Chefoo Convention of 1876, which stipulated that the Chinese government should provide proper protection for a British mission of exploration from China to India via Tibet, was violently opposed by the Tibetans and caused a great deal of embarrassment to frontier officials who had to uphold it against the wishes of the Tibetans.

84. Ting Pao-chen, *Ting Pao-chen tsou-tu* [Memorials and letters of Ting Pao-chen], in *Ch'ing-chi Ch'ou-Ts'ang tsou-tu* [Memorials and letters on the management of Tibetan affairs at the end of the Ch'ing dynasty], 1:50-54.

85. Ibid., pp. 46-48.

86. Lu Ch'uan-lin, *Memorials on the Chan-tui Incident, chüan* 2, pp. 19a-20b; *chüan* 3, p. 4. For an earlier indication of Russian ambitions toward India, see Olga Lang's discussion of the work of G. P. Danilevskii in this volume.

87. Ibid., *chüan* 2, pp. 2a-3b.

88. Ibid., *chüan* 3, pp. 40b-41b.

89. Wu Feng-p'ei, "Chi Kuang-hsü San-shih-i-nien Pa-tang chih luan" [The 1905 Batang riot], *Yü kung*, [Historical geography], 6, no. 12:43-52. See also the biography of Feng-ch'uan in Ting Shih-ch'uan, *Ch'ing-tai chu-Ts'ang ta-ch'en k'ao* [Imperial commissioners for Tibet during the Ch'ing dynasty] (Nanking, 1943), pp. 127-28.

90. Fu Sung-lin, *Hsi-k'ang chien sheng chi* [The establishment of Sikang Province] (Chengtu, 1911), pp. 5b-6b.

91. Ting Shih-ch'uan, *Imperial Commissioners for Tibet*, pp. 143-45.

92. Ting Shih-ch'uan, *Imperial Commissioners for Tibet*, pp. 141-42. Also Fu Sung-lin, *Establishment of Sikang*, pp. 6b-8a.

93. Fu Sung-lin, *Establishment of Sikang*, p. 17b.

94. Ibid., pp. 17b-18b.

95. Ting Shih-ch'uan, *Imperial commissioners for Tibet*, pp. 146-47.

96. Fu Sung-lin, *Establishment of Sikang*, pp. 19b-20a.

97. *Ch'ing-shih kao, chüan* 126, pp. 6b-7a.

98. K'o Hsiang-feng, "Hsi-k'ang chi hsing" [Diary of a Sikang journey], FA 1, nos. 9, 10 (1942):86-87.

99. Chou Tz'u-yu and Li Te-sen, "K'ang-pa p'an-luan ti chen-hsiang" [The real story of the Khamba rebellion], *Hsi-k'ang wen-t'i ti chen-hsiang* [The truth of the Tibetan question] (Hong Kong, 1959), pp. 51-55.

Chapter 3

1. Ping-ti Ho, *The Ladder of Success in Imperial China* (New York: John Wiley and Sons, 1964); E. A. Kracke, Jr. "Family vs. Merit in Chinese Civil Service Examinations under the Empire," *Harvard Journal of Asiatic Studies* 10 (1947):103-23.

2. Robert M. Marsh, *The Mandarins* (New York: The Free Press, 1961); Robert M. Marsh, "Bureaucratic Constraints on Nepotism in the Ch'ing Period," *Journal of Asian Studies* 19, no. 2 (February 1960):117-33; Robert M. Marsh, "The Venality of Provincial Office in China in Comparative

Perspective," *Comparative Studies in Society and History* 4 (July 1962):454-66; Robert M. Marsh, "Formal Organization and Promotion in a Pre-industrial Society," *American Sociological Review* 26, no. 4 (August 1961): 547-56.

3. Seymour M. Lipset and Reinhard Bendix, *Social Mobility in Industrial Society* (Berkeley: University of California Press, 1966); Herbert Goldhamer, "Social Mobility," *International Encyclopedia of Social Sciences,* edited by Edward C. Sills (New York: The Macmillan Co. and The Free Press, 1968); Otis D. Duncan and Peter M. Blau, *The American Occupational Structure* (New York: John Wiley, 1967); Leonard Plotnicov and Arthur Tuden, eds., *Essays in Comparative Social Stratification* (Pittsburgh: University of Pittsburgh Press, 1970).

4. By lineage, I refer to a consanguineal unilateral descent group whose members trace themselves from a known common ancestor. The relations of the members are definable by precise familial terms.

5. Ts'ao Hsueh-ch'in and Kao Ngo, *Hung-lou meng* [Dream of the Red Chamber] (Peking: Jen-min wen-hsueh chu-pan she, 1973), 4 vols. Also see Chou Ju-ch'ang, *Hung-lou meng hsin cheng* [New verification of *The Dream of the Red Chamber*] (Peking: Jen-min wen-hsueh ch'u-pan she, 1967), 2 vols.; Shih Ta-ch'ing, *Hung-lou meng yü Ch'ing-tai feng-chien she-hui* [*The Dream of the Red Chamber* and the feudal society of the Ch'ing dynasty] (Peking: Jen-min ch'u-pan she, 1967).

6. I wish to express my thanks to Richard G. Fox of Duke University who called my attention to such a unit at the ACLS Workshop on "Elites and Political Decision-making in Chinese History," organized by Robert M. Hartwell, June 12-25, 1976.

7. For a short description of the *lü-li* or career record, see term no. 95 in E-tu Zen Sun, *Ch'ing Administrative Terms* (Cambridge: Harvard University Press, 1961), p. 14.

8. Sometimes members from collateral branches are all included at the end.

9. For example, great-grandmother, Surname X, granddaughter of A; eldest daughter of B, sister of C, D, E; and aunt of F.

10. For example, aunt, married Surname X, son of Y.

11. Except Shangtung 1859. The *Shantung t'ung-kuan lu* (1859) [The Shantung official directory] does not contain information on officials higher than the rank of circuit intendant.

12. For instance, *Chiangsu t'ung-kuan lu* (1880).

13. See *Honan t'ung-kuan lu* (1837), *Shantung t'ung-kuan lu* (1859), *Anhui t'ung-kuan lu* (1871), *Chiangsu t'ung-kuan lu* (1880), *Honan t'ung-kuan lu* (1898), and *Chifu t'ung-kuan lu* (1904).

14. Marion J. Levy, *Modernization and the Structure of Society* (Princeton: Princeton University Press, 1966), see part 3, chapter 1: "Kinship and Family Structure," pp. 375-435.

15. Sometimes the common unilineal ancestry of a clan may not be traceable genealogically even though all members of the clan accepted the

line of common descent.

16. Maurice Freedman, *Lineage Organization in Southeastern China* (New York: The Athlone Press, 1958); Francis L. K. Hsu, *Under the Ancestor's Shadow* (New York: Doubleday, 1967); Marion J. Levy, *The Family Revolution in Modern China* (Cambridge: Harvard University Press, 1949).

17. For the *wu-fu*, see Maurice Freedman, *Lineage Organization*, pp. 41-45; Chao Feng-chieh, *Min fa ch'in shu pien* [Kinship in the Republican judicial system] (Taipei: Kuo-li pien-i kuan, 1974), pp. 1-31.

18. Maurice Freedman, *Lineage Organization*, pp. 73-77; Marion J. Levy, *The Family Revolution*, pp. 208-31.

19. Madeleine Chi, "The Law of Avoidance during the Han Dynasty," *The Journal of the Institute of Chinese Studies* 6, no. 2 (Hong Kong: The Chinese University of Hong Kong, December 1973):547-60.

20. *Ta-Ch'ing hui-tien shih-li* [Statutory amendments to the collected institutes of the great Ch'ing dynasty], edited by Li Hung-chang (Shanghai: Shang-wu yin-shu-kuan, 1908), 1220 *chüan*.

21. This was the temporary residence set up by migrants in an area away from their native district. According to the Chinese Regulations for Residence (*hu-chi fa*), one who set up a residence for six months or more in a district or town outside his native district would have to report that district or town as his temporary residence. This law also applied to those having resided in a place for more than six months who had no native district or whose native district was unclear.

22. Hsu Tao-lin, *Chung-kuo fa-chih shih lun-lüeh* [An outline history of Chinese legal institutions] (Taipei: Cheng-chung shu-chü, 1953), pp. 129-31. *Ta-Ch'ing hui-tien shih-li*, *chüan* 47, Board of Civil Appointment, 31 Appointment of Han officials, section on Avoidance of Relatives.

23. *Ta-Ch'ing hui-tien shih-li*, idem.

24. Ibid.

25. Wu Ching-tsu, *The Scholars* (Peking: Foreign Languages Press, 1973), pp. 114-19.

26. Liu T'ieh-yun, *The Travels of Lao-Ts'an*, translated by Harold Shadick (Ithaca, N.Y.: Cornell University Press, 1966), pp. vii-xv.

27. Kenneth E. Folsom, *Friends, Guests and Colleagues* (Berkeley: University of California Press, 1968), pp. 68-69.

28. *Ta-Ch'ing hui-tien shih-li*, *chüan* 84, Board of Civil Appointment, Regulations for Punishment, see section on Official Avoidance.

29. *Chung-chou t'ung-kuan lu* (1898), 1st *tse*.

30. The deceased progenitors were identified by the word "confer." To "confer" posthumously a distinction is *"tseng"* in Chinese, as distinguished from the word "to confer," *"shou,"* to a living official. But not all of one's progenitors had distinctions. We have no way of finding out exactly how many of them were deceased.

31. *Chiangsu t'ung-kuan lu*, Kuang-hsu 6th year (1880).

32. *Chung-chou t'ung kuan lu* (1898), 1st *tse*.

33. Titles of honor were frequently conferred by the government upon the officials themselves or their wives or were granted posthumously to their deceased progenitors for the service they rendered or because of particular merit. Similar to official ranks, titles of honor were divided into nine rankings, each subdivided into two classes. See H. S. Brunnert and V. V. Hagelstrom, *Present-Day Political Organization of China*, translated from the Russian by A. Beltchenko and E. E. Moran (Shanghai: Kelly and Walsh, 1912), pp. 495-97.

34. Our impression of the proliferation of purchasers in the period usually comes from the statistics on official degree holders. There may be more nonofficial degree holders who obtained their degrees through the civil examination, which would thus decrease our percentage. This percentage therefore has to be cross-checked with other sources in the future.

35. Hsu Ta-ling, *Ch'ing-tai chüan-na chih-tu* [The purchase system in the Ch'ing period] (Hong Kong: Lung-men shu-tien, 1968), pp. 159-61.

36. For a list of ranks and classes, see Robert Marsh, *The Mandarins*, pp. 206-35. Also see H. S. Brunnert and V. V. Hagelstrom.

37. Robert M. Marsh, "Formal Organization and Promotion in a Pre-industrial Society," pp. 553-54.

Chapter 4

1. Hsiao Kung-ch'uan, *Rural China: Imperial Control in the Nineteenth Century* (Seattle: University of Washington Press, 1960), p. 66. Other works of this category, all of which treat *pao-chia*, include Ch'ü T'ung-tsu, *Local Government in China under the Ch'ing* (Cambridge, Mass.: Harvard University Press, 1962); Sybille van der Sprenkel, *Legal Institutions in Manchu China* (London: Athlone, 1962); and, of more recent vintage, John R. Watt, *The District Magistrate in Late Imperial China* (New York: Columbia University Press, 1972).

2. Philip Kuhn, "Local Self-Government under the Republic: Problems of Control, Autonomy, and Mobilization," in Frederick Wakeman and Carolyn Grant, eds., *Conflict and Control in Late Imperial China* (Berkeley and Los Angeles: University of California Press, 1976). Among other recent English-language treatments of *pao-chia* and related systems are Alan Richard Sweeten, "The Ti-pao's Role in Local Government as Seen in Fukien Christian 'Cases,' 1863-69," and David Faure, "Land Tax Collection in Kiangsu Province in the Late Ch'ing Period," both in *Ch'ing-shih wen-t'i*, 3, no. 6 (December 1976).

Curiously, while general treatments of *pao-chia* in English have usually appeared in the context of studies of Chinese formal administration, in Chinese and Japanese works the context is frequently a critique of local autonomy in China. See, for example, Li Tsung-huang, *Chung-kuo ti-fang tzu-chih kai-lun* [A general treatise on local autonomy in China] (Taipei: Cheng-chung, 1949), and Wada Sei, *Shina chihō jichi hattatsu shi* [History of the development of local autonomy in China] (Tokyo: Chūka Minkoku hōsei kenkyūkai, 1939). Kuhn's work seems to have introduced this perspective into English-language scholarship.

3. *Shen-pao,* Kuang-hsu 4th year/9th month/1st day. Subsequent citations follow this format. The Shanghai daily *Shen-pao,* first published in 1872, maintained a reporter in Hankow and is a major source for this chapter. While owned by a foreigner, it was managed by a Chinese and in my opinion reflected a thoroughly Chinese point of view. I have used the forty-volume reprinted edition prepared by Wu Hsiang-hsiang (Taipei: Hsueh-sheng shu-chü, 1964).

4. Hu Lin-i, *Hu-wen-chung-kung i-chi* [Collected works of Hu Lin-i], *chüan* 14: page 2. Subsequent citations follow this *(chüan*:page) format. A typical Western impression in this regard was recorded in the 1850s by the Abbé Huc, *A Journey through the Chinese Empire* (New York, 1859), 2, p. 142.

5. Yeh Tiao-yuan, *Han-k'ou chu-chih ts'u* [Hankow song of the bamboo branches] (1850) (hereafter HKCCT), 5:9.

6. See, for example, the collective roughhousing of sedan-chair bearers in Hankow (HKCCT, 2:5), and the local antagonisms generated by groups of Anhwei and Kwangtung natives in the city (*Shen-pao,* Kuang-hsü 2/4/2; *North-China Herald,* June 29, 1872).

7. Lin Tse-hsu, *Lin-wen-chung-kung cheng-shu* [Political writings of Lin Tse-hsu], reprinted in *Chin-tai Chung-kuo shih-liao tsung-k'an* [General edition of historical materials on modern China] (Taipei: Wen-hai, 1965), 51:588-89.

8. HKCCT, 5:5-6; Japanese investigators cited in Joseph W. Esherick, *Reform and Revolution in China: The 1911 Revolution in Hunan and Hubei* (Berkeley and Los Angeles: University of California, 1976), p. 109.

9. HKCCT, 1:9.

10. HKCCT, 5:20; *Shen-pao,* Kuang-hsü 4/6/20.

11. Esherick, *Reform and Revolution in China,* p. 7 and passim.

12. Charles Alabaster, in Great Britain, Foreign Office, *China, No. 4 (1884): Commercial Reports of Her Majesty's Consuls in China, 1883,* p. 86.

13. *Hsia-k'ou hsien-chih* (1920) (hereafter 1920 HC), 15:6.

14. 1920 HC, 15:28.

15. Tōa Dōbunkai Chōsa Hensambu, *Shina kaikō jōshi* [A gazetteer of the open ports of China], 2 (Shanghai?, 1924), pp. 475-77; Hu Lin-i, 14:4.

16. The 1883 revamping of security systems in Hankow included devotion of much attention to local *pao-chia* operations, and to this extent the present essay concerns chiefly conditions prior to that year. Most conclusions reached here, however, are equally applicable to the later period.

17. *Han-yang fu-chih* (1747) (hereafter 1747 FC), 12:2. For excerpts and a discussion of this important edict, see Hsu Ping-hsien, *Ch'ing-tai chih-hsien chih-ch'ang chih yen-chiu* [A study of the powers of the *hsien* magistrate in the Ch'ing dynasty] (Taipei: Ssu-li tung-wu ta-hsüeh, 1974), pp. 214-15.

18. Joint memorials of Yü-t'ai and Shao Ping-yen, Tao-kuang 21/12/23, Tao-kuang 22/12/23, etc., Ch'ing palace archives, National Palace

Museum, Taipei.

19. Hsiao, *Rural China*, p. 45. For an opposing view, see Hsu, *Powers of the* hsien *magistrate*, p. 218.

20. *Shen-pao*, Kuang-hsu 2/3/21.

21. *Han-yang hsien-chih* (1818) (hereafter 1818 HC), 12:18.

22. Some of the requirements for native place registration in Hanyang *hsien* are listed in *Shen-pao*, Kuang-hsu 1/10/16. One of a vast number of possible examples of individuals who were for all intents and purposes Hankow natives, but who for reasons of business maintained registration elsewhere, may be found in the biography of the Shensi merchant Hung Hsi-lu, *Han-yang hsien-shih* (1884) (hereafter 1884 HS), 3 *hsia*:7.

23. *Shen-pao*, Kuang-hsu 2/3/21.

24. 1818 HC, 12:17.

25. 1818 HC, 12:10.

26. Memorial of Hukuang Governor-general Na-erh-ching-o and Hupeh Governor Chou Chih-ch'i, Tao-kuang 17/2/3, Ch'ing palace archives, National Palace Museum, Taipei.

27. 1818 HC, 12:10.

28. *Shen-pao*, Kuang-hsu 2/3/21.

29. Thomas Taylor Meadows observed of Canton city in 1847 that while the *pao-cheng* were still to be found, these lower-level headmen had been consigned fully to the realm of legal fiction. Meadows, *Desultory Notes on the Government and People of China, and on the Chinese Language* (London, 1847), pp. 120-21.

30. 1818 HC, 12:9; 12:19.

31. Ibid.; 1920 HC, 3:1.

32. Ho Ch'ang-ling, ed., *Huang-ch'ao ching-shih wen-pien* [Essays on statecraft in the Ch'ing dynasty] (reprinted Taipei, 1963), p. 1031, cited in Dwight Perkins, *Agricultural Development in China, 1368-1968* (Chicago: Aldine, 1969), p. 153n.

33. Laurence Oliphant, *Narrative of the Earl of Elgin's Mission to China and Japan in the Years 1857, '58, '59* (New York, 1860), p. 560.

34. W. F. Mayers, N. B. Dennys, and C. King, *The Treaty Ports of China and Japan: A Complete Guide* (London, 1867), p. 446.

Despite the generally negative portrayal of *pao-chia* by Hsiao Kung-ch'uan, and my own findings for Hankow presented here, it would be a mistake to underestimate the presence of the system's enrollment mechanisms in nineteenth-century urban China. We have seen that in Hankow they were consistently employed to produce census figures, however unreliable. Moreover, Professor Imahori Seiji has presented concrete evidence of an enrollment system effectively in force in Pa-hsien, Szechuan (incorporating Chungking) in 1827. The enrollment process there differentiated between residential (*min-hu*) and commercial (*p'u-hu*) households, and in the case of the latter clearly sought to bring under *pao-chia* control the urban population's mobile merchant elements. To this end the chronologically senior investing partner was arbitrarily designated "head of household," regardless of that individual's native place or actual residence. Enrollment certificates were submitted to the administration upon the opening of the business, and the form of this certificate survives today. In addition to the "head of household's" name, age, and residence, the names of all employees and partners, the location of the business by *pao*, *chia*, and *p'ai*, and the name of the local *pao-cheng*, the form called for the names of the cognizant *pao*, *chia*, and *p'ai* level functionaries of the county's *li-chia* system. Imahori, "Shindai ni okeru gōka no kindaika no hasu—toku ni tōka bukateki keitai ni tsuite" [The slant of modernization of partnerships in the Ch'ing dynasty, especially as regards the shape of the separation of *tung* and *huo*], *Tōyōshi kenkyū*, 17, no. 1 (1956):5.

Nevertheless this does not demonstrate (nor does Imahori maintain) that the originally intended collective responsibility principles underlying *pao-chia* were in force, or even that the frequently absentee proprietor who was thus enrolled had any idea who his fellow *p'ai* or *chia* members were. In light of the prominent inclusion of *li-chia* personnel on the enrollment form, it is likely that this procedure's chief utility was in aiding the tax-collection process. It is particularly noteworthy that while the terminology of "household" was maintained, it was clearly the physical premises that were being enrolled (see below, note 40 and related text).

35. *Shen-pao*, Kuang-hsu 2/3/21.

36. *Han-yang hsien-chih* (1867) (hereafter 1867 HC), 8:35.

37. My evidence here is inferential. Lin used these tactics (notably the registration of transients at all inns, etc.) in Kwangtung, where he almost certainly was imitating those he had employed so successfully in his immediately preceding tenure in Hukuang. See Frederick Wakeman, *Strangers at the Gate* (Berkeley and Los Angeles: University of California Press, 1966), p. 35.

38. Rowe, "A Note on *Ti-pao*," *Ch'ing-shih wen-t'i* (December 1977). On the separate origins of these two institutions, the most persuasive analysis is Saeki Tomi, "Shindai no kyōaku-chihō ni tsuite—Shindai chihō gyōsei hitokusari" [On the *hsiang-yüeh ti-pao* in the Ch'ing dynasty—a scene of Ch'ing local administration], *Tōhōgaku*, 28 (July 1964):91-100.

39. *Shen-pao*, Kuang-hsu 3/4/23, Kuang-hsu 3/11/21, Kuang-hsu 3/12/13, etc.

40. The assignment to *pao-chia* units of territorial rather than human parameters was probably of necessity demanded in all of nineteenth-century urban China. A Hankow native's lengthy description of Nanking in the 1860s, for example, repeats the formula, "The 8th *chia* is (such and such a) street. . . . The 15th *chia* is (such and such an) alley. . . . etc." Wang Pao-hsin, *Hsu Han-k'ou tsung-t'an* [The Hankow compendium, continued] (1932), *chüan* 2. In Hankow itself, by at least the beginning of the Tao-kuang reign, a marginal strip of urban area outside the four formally constituted wards of the city was referred to administratively as the "five outer *chia*," leading one to suspect that division into *chia* was maintained throughout the town. Fan K'ai, *Han-k'ou tsung-t'an* [The Hankow compendium] (1822), 2:2.

41. *Shen-pao*, Kuang-hsu 4/7/19, Kuang-hsu 4/6/26, Kuang-hsu 2/4/2. Mr. Chang Wei-jen of the Academia Sinica, Taipei, who has collected and analyzed several thousand Ch'ing dynasty criminal cases, informed me that in his materials from all parts of China, it was nearly universally true that the crime had first been brought to official attention through the medium of a local headman.

42. Hukuang Governor-general Pien Pao-ti to Tsungli Yamen, Kuang-hsu 10/10/5, Tsungli Yamen archives, Academia Sinica, Taipei (hereafter TLYM).

43. Hukuang Governor-general Li Han-chang to Tsungli Yamen, Kuang-hsu 5/3/21, TLYM.

44. Hukuang Governor-general Hsu Ts'ung-ying to Tsungli Yamen, T'ung-chih 9/3/5, TLYM; *Shen-pao*, Kuang-hsu 3/11/21, Kuang-hsu 3/12/13, etc.

45. *Shen-pao*, Kuang-hsu 4/11/17.

46. Hukuang Governor-general Lu-shen and Hupeh Governor Yang Tse-ts'eng memorial of Tao-kuang 11/?/?, in Wang Yun-wu, ed., *Tao-Hsien-T'ung-Kuang ssu-ch'ao tsou-i* [Selected memorials from four reigns] (Taipei: National Palace Museum, no date), 1:232-35.

47. *Shen-pao*, Kuang-hsu 3/4/23; Tung Kuei-fu, ed., *Han-k'ou tzu-yang shu-yuan chih-lüeh* [Abridged history of the Tzu-yang Academy of Hankow] (1806), 8:57, 8:62-63; Hou P'ei-chün, ed., *Han-k'ou Shan-Shen-hsi hui-kuan chih* [History of the Shansi-Shensi provincial association of Hankow] (1896), 1:10, etc.

48. *Shen-pao*, Kuang-hsu 2/8/17; Lin Tse-hsu, *Lin Tse-hsu chi: kung-tu* [Documents on Lin Tse-hsu: correspondence with subordinates] (Peking, 1963), p. 19.

49. *Shen-pao*, Kuang-hsu 4/5/25.

50. Those cases cited here are drawn from reports of Hukuang governors-general to the Tsung-li Yamen dated Kuang-hsu 8/8/1, T'ung-chih 11/5/4, T'ung-chih 13/10/20, T'ung-chih 6/1/29, and T'ung-chih 7/12/15, TLYM. Many others could also be cited. Sweeten describes similar cases culled from Tsungli Yamen materials on Fukien Province.

A bizarre example of the Hankow headman's responsibility as "knower" of his neighborhood may be seen in the 1885 case of the flogging of one such functionary as punishment for the suicide of a local man who had been falsely accused by his employer of embezzlement. It would appear that, in the same way that the county magistrate was personally liable for losses of life or property by fire, *pao-chia* personnel were held personally accountable for the lives and security of their charges. In this case, for example, the accusing employer was not similarly punished—no criminal action had occurred. The headman was simply being "sanctioned" for his negligence in allowing the situation to deteriorate so far without intervention and proper investigation. See Thomas Gillison, *Report of the London Missionary Hospital at Hankow, for the Years 1883-1885* (Hankow, 1885), p. 11.

51. Meadows, *Desultory Notes*, p. 117.

52. Hukuang Governor-general Li Han-chang to Tsungli Yamen, T'ung-chih 13/10/20, TLYM.

53. Li to Tsungli Yamen, Kuang-hsu 3/10/28, Kuang-hsu 5/14/4, TLYM.

54. 1884 HS, *kung-k'uan-pu*, p. 5.

55. *Chiu-sheng-chü t'iao-kuei* [Lifeboat bureau regulations] (Hanyang, 1839), in China, Imperial Maritime Customs, *Special Series: Lifeboats* (Shanghai: Inspectorate General of Customs, 1893) (hereafter *Lifeboats*), Chinese enclosures, pp. 31-33.

56. Hukuang Governor-general Weng T'ung-chüeh to Tsungli Yamen, Kuang-hsu 1/11/13, TLYM.

57. Faure, "Land Tax Collection," pp. 64-65.

58. 1747 FC, 12:2.

59. *Shen-pao*, Kuang-hsu 3/6/16.

60. Meadows, *Desultory Notes*, pp. 119-20.

61. Faure, "Land Tax Collection," p. 56.

62. *Shen-pao*, Kuang-hsu 2/3/21.

63. 1747 FC, 12:2. I am grateful to Mr. Su Yun-feng for bringing this passage to my attention.

64. Hsiao, *Rural China*, pp. 79-82.

65. 1747 FC, 12:2.

66. All nine appear in Tsungli Yamen archives on Hankow, reports of Hukuang governors-general dated T'ung-chih 3/5/24, T'ung-chih 6/1/29, T'ung-chih 8/7/5, T'ung-chih 13/10/20, Kuang-hsu 7/11/8, Kuang-hsu 8/8/1, T'ung-chih 9/3/5, Kuang-hsu 3/10/28, Kuang-hsu 5/3/21, TLYM.

67. This same phenomenon, that of lineage connections within *pao-chia* and other types of subadministrative local leadership, is noted by Philip Kuhn in the early Republican period. Kuhn, however, apparently considers it a new development of that time. Kuhn, "Local Self-Government," pp. 293-94.

68. *Shen-pao*, Kuang-hsu 2/3/21.

69. *Shen-pao*, Kuang-hsu 5/7/1.

In another front-page editorial from the following year, *Shen-pao* draws a general distinction between the practices of local headmen in urban and rural areas. In contrast to the views cited above of the Hanyang local historian (writing in the mid–eighteenth century), this later writer holds that the proximity of the yamen forces headmen in the city to be more circumspect, and consequently *poorer* than their rural counterparts. He further notes the influence of the city-dwelling gentry: "An urban *pao-cheng* has merely to hear the complaints of a gentry member and he scampers [to rectify the cause of the complaint] like a running dog." Note that in spite of such colorful language, gentry dominance of local headmen is considered by this writer to be wholly within the public interest. *Shen-pao*, Kuang-hsu 6/11/3.

70. *Shen-pao*, Kuang-hsu 4/11/16.

71. *Lifeboats*, Chinese enclosures, pp. 31-33.

72. 1884 HS, 2:22.

73. For a catalog of the *pao-cheng's* formal duties within the Ch'ing

political order, see Hsu, *Powers of the* hsien *magistrate*, p. 216ff.

74. *Shen-pao*, Kuang-hsu 3/11/21, Kuang-hsu 4/11/17; Meadows, *Desultory Notes*, p. 119.

75. *Shen-pao*, Kuang-hsu 8/12/20.

Chapter 5

1. Thomas L. Kennedy, "Chang Chih-tung and the Struggle for Strategic Industrialization: The Establishment of the Hanyang Arsenal 1884-1895," *Harvard Journal of Asiatic Studies* 33, (1973):154-82.

2. Recent studies dealing with the establishment of the Hanyang Ironworks include: Albert Feuerwerker, "China's Nineteenth-Century Industrialization: The Case of the Hanyehping Coal and Iron Company Limited," *The Economic Development of China and Japan*, C. D. Cowan, ed. (London: George Allen and Unwin, 1964), pp. 79-110; Ch'uan Han-sheng, *Han-yeh-p'ing kung-ssu shih-lüeh* [A brief history of the Hanyehping Iron and Coal Company] (Hongkong: The Chinese University of Hongkong, 1972), pp. 1-78; *Wen-hsiang-kung ch'üan-chi* [Collected works of Chang Chih-tung] (hereafter CWHK) (Taipei: Wen-hai ch'u-pan-she, 1963), *kung-tu* [official documents], 20:30-31; *Hu-pei ping-kung kang-yao-ch'ang t'iao-shuo piao-tse* [Itemized discussions and charts of the Hupeh Arsenal and the Steel and Powder Works] (hereafter HPKC), 13 vols. (Hanyang: Hupeh Arsenal, 1910), held by the Academia Sinica Institute of History and Philology, Taipei, "Hu-pei ping-kung kang-yao-ch'ang ke-hsiang hsiang-hsi ch'ing-hsing" [Detailed conditions of the Hupeh Arsenal and Steel and Powder Works]: "1. Yuan-shih yen-ke ch'ing-hsing" [Establishment and development]; Ralph Powell, *The Rise of Chinese Military Power, 1895-1912* (Princeton: Princeton University Press, 1955), pp. 172-99; Liu Chin-tsao, ed., *Ch'ing-ch'ao hsu wen-hsien t'ung-k'ao* [Ch'ing dynasty continuation of the general study of literary remains] (Taipei: Hsin-hsing shu-chü, 1965), 133: *k'ao* 8923; *North China-Herald and Supreme Court Gazette* (hereafter NCH) (Shanghai, 1872-1941), May 27, 1911.

3. HPKC, "ke-hsiang hsiang-hsi ch'ing-hsing": "yuan-shih yen-ke ch'ing-hsing"; "yao-ch'ang ping fu-shu ke-ch'ang chien-tsao chi chi-ch'i ch'ing-hsing" [construction and machinery of the powder works and its subordinate plants]; "kang-ch'ang chien-tsao chi chi-ch'i ch'ing-hsing" [construction and machinery of the steel refinery]. "Hu-pei ping-kung kang-yao-ch'ang tzu k'ai-pan ch'i chih Hsuan-t'ung yuan-nien chih shou-chih ke-k'uan ssu-chu ch'ing-tse" [Income and expenditure tables for the Hupeh Arsenal and Steel and Powder Works through 1909], "shou-k'uan hsiang-hsia" [income]: "te-kuan hsiang-hsia" [regular income]; "shou Hu-pei mi-k'o li-chin" [Hupeh grain likin]; "shou I-ch'ang kuan-shiu" [Ichang customs]. CWHK, *tsou-i* [memorials], 47:11-15. Sun Yu-t'ang et al., eds., *Chung-kuo chin-tai kung-yeh-shih tzu-liao* [Materials on China's modern industrial history] (hereafter CCKT), 4 vols. (Peking: San-lien shu-tien, 1957), 1:543.

4. CCKT, 3:234-35; 1:544.

5. HPKC, "ke-hsiang hsiang-hsi ch'ing-hsing": "ping-kung-ch'ang ch'üan-ch'ang pu-chih ch'ing-hsing" [layout of the whole arsenal].

6. CWHK, memorials, 47:11-15. HPKC, "shou-chih ke-k'uan ssu-chu ch'ing-tse": "shou-k'uan hsiang hsia": te-k'uan hsiang-hsia": "shou I-chang kuan-shui," "shou Hu-pei t'u-yao kuo-ching-shui" [Hupeh domestic opium border-crossing tax].

7. HPKC, "shou-chih ke-k'uan ssu-chu ch'ing-tse": shou-k'uan hsiang-hsia": "huo-k'uan hsiang-hsia" [unfixed income]. CWHK, memorials, 63:19-22. Hosea Ballou Morse, *The International Relations of the Chinese Empire*, 3 vols. (Taipei: Wen-hsing shu-tien, 1963), 3:350. Meribeth E. Cameron, *The Reform Movement in China, 1898-1912* (Stanford: Stanford University Press, 1931), pp. 136-59. H. S. Brunnert and V. V. Hagelstrom, *Present Day Political Organization of China* (Taipei: Wen-hsiang shu-tien, 1963), pp. 194-95.

8. HPKC, "shou-chih ke-k'uan ssu-chu ch'ing-tse": shou-k'uan hsiang-hsia": "huo-k'uan hsiang-hsia."

9. CWHK, *tien tu* [telegrams] 17:31b; 18:33b; 19:4b-5a, 21b, 36a, 37b-38a; 23:12a; 25:10a, 10b-11a, 14b-15a; 25:17b-18a; 31:4b-5a, 23b, 28a, 29a; 32:9a. HPKC, "ke-hsiang hsiang-hsi ch'ing-hsing": "yuan-shih yen-ke ch'ing-hsing"; "p'ao-ch'ang ke-hsiang ch'ing-hsing" [conditions at the gun factory], "ping-kung-ch'ang Kuang-hsu erh-shih-i-nien chih Hsuan-t'ung i-nien nien-ti tsao-cheng chun-huo" [munitions produced at the Hupeh Arsenal 1895 through 1910]. CCKT, 1, 535-540, Liu Chin-tsao, ed., *Ch'ing-ch'ao hsu wen-hsien t'ung-k'ao* [Ch'ing dynasty continuation general study of literary remains], 239: *k'ao* 9846. Sidney R. Freemantle, "Ordnance," *Encyclopedia Britannica*, 1910-1911, 20:214, 223.

10. HPKC, "ke-hsiang hsiang-hsi ch'ing-hsing": "yuan-shih yen-ke ch'ing-hsing," "p'ao-tan-ch'ang ke-hsiang ch'ing-hsing" [conditions at the gun ammunition plant], "ch'ou-tan-ch'ang ke-hsiang ch'ing-hsing" [conditions at the projectile casting shop], "p'ao-tan t'ung-ke-ch'ang ke-hsiang ch'ing-hsing" [conditions at the cartridge plant], "p'ao-chia-ch'ang ke-hsiang ch'ing-hsing" [conditions at the gun carriage plant].

11. HPKC, "ke-hsiang hsiang-hsi ch'ing-hsing": "yao-ch'ang ping fu-shu ke-ch'ang chien-tsao chi chi-ch'i ch'ing-hsing" [construction and equipment of the powder works and subordinate plants]; "chih-tsao mien-hua-yao chi wu-yen-yao ke-chung yuan-liao ch'ing-hsing" [materials for production of gun cotton and smokeless powder].

12. Su Yun-feng, *Chang Chih-tung yü Hu-pei chiao-yü kai-ke* [Chang Chih-tung and education reform in Hupeh] (Taipei: Chung-yang yen-chiu-yuan chin-tai-shih yen-chiu-so, 1976), pp. 143-48, 246; William Ayers, *Chang Chih-tung and Educational Reform in China* (Cambridge: Harvard University Press, 1971), pp. 100-254.

13. HPKC, "ke-hsiang hsiang-hsi ch'ing-hsing": "ping-kung kang-yao liang-ch'ang yung-jen ch'ing-hsing" [personnel conditions in the arsenal and steel and powder works].

14. British Public Record Office: Foreign Office Files 371/34, 16763, May 16, 1906.

15. CCKT, 3:244-245. HPKC, "ke-hsiang hsiang-hsi ch'ing-hsing": "yung-jen ch'ing-hsing." In the spring of 1906 there were reported to be twenty Japanese in the arsenal employed as foremen and in other positions. Effective control was alleged to rest with Colonel Ikata of the Imperial Japanese Army, Chang's artillery advisor. *National Archives Microfilm Publications* M862, Numerical and minor files of the Department of State 1906-10, Roll 217, numerical file case nos. 2106-2108/89, "The Chinese Army," September 21, 1906, pp. 336-38.

16. CCKT, 1:543. CWHK, telegrams, 32:5b-6a. HPKC, "ke-hsiang hsiang-hsi ch'ing-hsing": "yuan-shih yen-ke ch'ing-hsing."

17. W.H.B. Smith, *Mauser Rifles and Pistols* (Harrisburg, Pa.: The Stackpole Company, 1954), pp. 81-83, 109-12. CCKT, 1:541. CWHK, telegrams, 25:25b-26a, memorials, 37:26. Kennedy, "Chang Chih-tung and the Struggle for Strategic Industrialization," p. 177.

18. CWHK, telegrams, 32:5b-6a, official documents, 15:29-34. Chou Wei, *Chung-kuo ping-ch'i shih-kao* [A draft history of Chinese weapons] (Peking: San-lien shu-tien, 1957), 316. Smith, *Mauser Rifles and Pistols*, p. 89.

19. CWHK, telegrams, 37:3b-4a, 8b, *shu-cha* [letters], 5:28-29. Thomas L. Kennedy, "The Kiangnan Arsenal in the Era of Reform, 1895-1911," *Chung-yang yen-chiu-yuan chin-tai shih yen-chiu-so chi-k'an* [Bulletin of the Institute of Modern History Academia Sinica], 3, part 1 (1972), pp. 297-99.

20. Henry Seton-Karr, "Rifle," *Encyclopedia Britannica*, 1910-1911, 23:327-328. CWHK, official documents, 16:8-11. HPKC, "ke-hsiang hsiang-hsi ch'ing-hsing": "Ke-tz'u fang-she ch'ing-hsing" [the conduct of test-firing].

21. CWHK, memorials, 33:19-22, official documents, 33:37-38. HPKC, "ke-hsiang hsiang-hsi ch'ing-hsing": "ch'iang-ch'ang ke-hsiang ch'ing-hsing" [conditions at the rifle factory], "shou-chih ke-k'uan ssu-chu ch'ing-tse," "shou-k'uan hsiang-hsia," "li-nien chi hsuan-t'ung yuan-nien tsao-ch'eng po-chieh shih-tsun ke-hsiang chün-huo piao-tse" [tables of production, distribution, and storage, 1895-1909]. Kennedy, "The Kiangnan Arsenal in the Era of Reform 1895-1911," pp. 304, 317-18, 328, 331.

22. HPKC, "ke-hsiang hsiang-hsi ch'ing-hsing": "ch'iang-ch'ang ke-hsiang ch'ing-hsing": "kung-tso" [operations]. Seton-Karr, "Rifle," p. 328.

23. HPKC, "ke-hsiang hsiang-hsi ch'ing-hsing": "ch'iang-ch'ang ke-hsiang ch'ing-hsing."

24. HPKC, "ke-hsiang hsiang-hsi ch'ing hsing": "ch'iang-tan-ch'ang ke-hsiang ch'ing-hsing," "ke-tz'u fang-she ch'ing-hsing."

25. HPKC, "ke-hsiang hsiang-hsi ch'ing-hsing": "ch'iang-tan-ch'ang ke-hsiang ch'ing-hsing."

26. HPKC, "shou-chih ke-k'uan ssu-chu ch'ing-tse": "chih-kuan hsi anghsia" [expenditures].

27. HPKC, "ke-hsiang hsiang-hsi ch'ing-hsing": "ch'iang-ch'ang ke-

hsiang ch'ing-hsing": "liao-wu" [matériel], British Public Record Office: Foreign Office files 371/34, 16763 (May 16, 1906).

28. HPKC, "ke-hsiang hsiang-hsi ch'ing-hsing": "yao-ch'ang ping fu-shu ke-ch'ang chien-tsao chi chi-ch'i ch'ing-hsing."

29. HPKC, "ke-hsiang hsiang-hsi ch'ing-hsing": "yung-jen ch'ing-hsing."

30. HPKC, "ke-hsiang hsiang-hsi ch'ing-hsing": "ch'üan-ch'ang ching-fei ch'ing-hsing" [financial data for the whole arsenal].

31. HPKC, "shou-chih ke-k'uan ssu-chu ch'ing-tse": "chih-k'uan hsiang-hsia."

32. CWHK, telegrams, 37:26, official documents, 16:8, memorials, 51:27-29, *shu-cha* [letters], 4:32-33. Li Kuo-ch'i, *Chang Chih-tung te wai-chiao cheng-t'se* [Chang Chih-tung's foreign policy] (Taipei: Chung-yang yen-chiu-yuan chin-tai-shih yen-chiu-so, 1970). H. B. Morse, *The International Relations of the Chinese Empire*, 3:350.

33. HPKC, "li-nien chi hsuan-t'ung yuan-nien tsao-ch'eng po-chieh shih-tsun ke-hsiang chun-huo piao-tse" [various types of munitions produced, distributed, and stored through 1909], British Public Record Office: Foreign Office file 405/126 No. 28, 405/120 No. 8, 405/12 No. 33, 405/128 No. 60, 405/122 No. 29. NCH, November 20, 1903, January 15, 1904, February 25, 1904.

34. HPKC, "li-nien chi hsuan-t'ung yuan-nien tsao-ch'eng po-chieh shih-tsun ke-hsiang chun-huo piao-tse."

35. NCH, October 14, October 21, December 2, and December 9, 1911.

36. H. B. Morse, *The Trade and Administration of the Chinese Empire* (Shanghai: Kelly and Walsh, 1907), p. 347. Hsiao Liang-lin, *China's Foreign Trade Statistics 1864-1949* (Cambridge: Harvard University, East Asian Research Center, 1974), pp. 168-80.

37. For a discussion of political factors that influenced Chang's role as a reformer particularly in the years from 1898 to 1900, see Daniel H. Bays "Chang Chih-tung after the '100 Days': 1898-1900 as a Transitional Period for Reform Constituencies," in *Reform in Nineteenth Century China*, edited by Paul A. Cohen and John E. Schrecker (Cambridge: Harvard Univesity, East Asian Research Center, 1976), pp. 317-25.

Chapter 6

1. Mao Tse-tung, *Xin minzhu zhuyi* [On New Democracy] (Peking: Renmin Chubanshe, 1966), p. 49.

2. It may be noted in passing that Mao uses the archaic term *yanyu* for "language" or "speech" instead of the modern term *yuyan*.

3. For the material in the three preceding paragraphs, see John DeFrancis, *Nationalism and Language Reform in China* (Princeton, N.J.: Princeton University Press, 1950), pp. 129-31.

4. Dayle Barnes, "Language Planning in Mainland China: A Sociolinguistic Study of *P'u-t'ung-hua* and *P'in-yin*," Ph.D. dissertation, Georgetown University (1974), p. 250, quotes Du Zijing, *1949 nien Zhongguo wenzi*

gaige lunwen ji [Essays on Chinese writing reform in 1949] (Shanghai, 1950), p. 265, who in turn quotes Zheng Dobin, *1940-1942 Shen-Kan-Ning bianqu Xin Wenzi Yundong da shiji* [Great events in the New Writing movement in the Shen-Kan-Ning border region in 1940-42].

Note that the term "New Writing" was written as "Sin Wenz" in the latinization transcription of the 1930s and 40s, and is now written as "Xin Wenzi" in the Pinyin system used in the People's Republic.

5. Ma Hsu-lun, "Zhongguo wenzi gaige yanjiu weiyuanhui chengli hui kaihui ci" [Opening remarks at the inaugural meeting of the Committee for Research on Chinese Writing Reform], *Zhongguo Yuwen* (July 1952), p. 4.

6. Ibid.

7. Wu Yü-chang, "Zai Zhongguo wenzi gaige yanjiu weiyuanhui chengli hui shang de jianghua" [Speech at the inaugural meeting of the Committee for Research on Chinese Writing Reform], *Zhongguo Yuwen* (July 1952), p. 5.

8. Kuo Mo-jo, "Zai Zhongguo wenzi gaige yanjiu weiyuanwei chengli hui shang de jianghua [Speech at the inaugural meeting of the Committee for Research on Chinese Writing Reform], *Zhongguo Yuwen* (July 1952), p. 3.

9. J. V. Stalin, *Concerning Marxism in Linguistics* (London: Soviet News, 1950), pp. 3-8 and passim. For a discussion of how Stalin's (and Mao's) views were used in the retroactive criticism of an early Chinese Communist writer on language reform problems, Ch'ü Ch'iu-pai, see Chapter 11 in this volume.

10. Wu Yü-chang, "Speech at the Inaugural Meeting."

11. "Zhongguo wenzi gaige yanjiu weiyuanwei juxing di-sanci quanti huiyi" [Third Plenary meeting of the Committee for Research on Chinese Writing Reform], *Zhongguo Yuwen* (May 1953), p. 33.

12. "Zhongguo wenzi gaige yanjiu weiyuanwei juxing di-sanci quanti huiyi" [Third Plenary meeting of the Committee for Research on Chinese Writing Reform], *Zhongguo Yuwen* (June 1953), p. 34.

13. Li Chin-hsi, *Wenzi gaige gaishuo* [Sketch of writing reform] (n.p., 1972), pp. 8-9. I am indebted to Constantin Milsky for drawing my attention to this work and kindly providing me with a copy.

In the scheme advanced by Li Chin-hsi, who in the 1920s had participated in the creation of the system of tonal spelling known as Gwuoyeu Romatzyn, this idea was advanced again in a particularly bizarre form, that of indicating tones by the varied use of capital and small letters, e.g., 1st tone MA, 2nd tone mA, 3rd tone ma, 4th tone Ma. Viviane Alleton has reported that when she visited the PRC in the summer of 1977 she was informed by linguists whom she questioned about the system that it was a private initiative by Li Chin-hsi that received little support. See "La transcription alphabetique du chinois: forme et pedogogie du pinyin en République populaire de Chine" *Cahiers de linguistique, d'orientalisme et de slavistique*, no. 10 (1978), note 3.

14. Constantin Milsky, *Préparation de la réforme de l'écriture en République populaire de Chine 1949-1954* (La Haye: Mouton, 1974), p. 367.

15. Chou En-lai, *Dangqian wenzi gaige de renwu* [Current tasks in writing

reform] (Peking: Renmin chubanshe, 1958), pp. 11-12.

16. *Mao Zedong wansui* [Long live Mao Tse-tung], p. 31. Although this work has no indication of where, when, or by whom it was published, it was apparently produced in Taiwan from documents smuggled out of mainland China. I am indebted to Helmut Martin for drawing my attention to this work and kindly providing me with a copy of the talk from which my quotation is derived.

17. Alain Peyrfitte, *Quand la Chine s'éveillera . . . le monde tremblera* (Paris: Fayard, 1973), p. 153.

18. See note 10.

19. See note 11.

20. John DeFrancis, "Language and Script Reform," in Thomas A. Sebeok, ed., *Current Trends in Linguistics* (The Hague: Mouton, 1967), pp. 136-38.

21. *Jianhuazi zongbiao jianzi* [General index of simplified characters] (Peking, 1964), and *Jianhuazi jianzi* [Index of simplified characters] (Peking, 1974).

22. *Di-yi pi yitizi zhenglibiao* [First group of variant forms] (Peking, 1955).

23. Chang Su-chen, "Reduction in Number of Chinese Characters," *Journal of the Chinese Language Teachers Association* 11, no. 3 (October 1976):187-91.

24. See note 17.

25. Sally M. Ng, "The Phonetic Aspect of Character Simplification," *Journal of the Chinese Language Teachers Association* 11, no. 3 (October 1976):179-86.

26. For a discussion of this complex sociolinguistic problem before 1949 see DeFrancis, *Nationalism and Language Reform in China*, chapters 6, 11, and passim.

27. Stalin, *Marxism and Linguistics*, p. 10. Emphasis in the original.

28. DeFrancis, "Language and Script Reform," pp. 139-41.

29. This directive is quoted much more often than the other instructions forming part of a statement on language policy presented by Mao as item 46 in his "Sixty Points on Working Methods," submitted to the Politburo on January 31, 1958. The whole of item 46, as given in Jerome Ch'en, *Mao Papers* (London: Oxford University Press, 1970), is as follows (bracketed material added by Ch'en):

> A cadre from another place should learn the dialect of the place [where he works]; all cadres should learn the *p'u-t'ung-hua* [the standard Han-Chinese]. We must draw up a five-year plan, aiming at a certain linguistic standard. Han cadres who work in a minority area must learn the language of that minority. Likewise cadres of a minority must learn Han-Chinese.

30. In this connection it may or may not be significant that Lu Hsun's declarations made in the 1930s in support of dialect romanization were

included in a 1974 reprint of his scattered writings, in which he came out strongly for the replacement of Chinese characters by a latinized system of writing. (*Lu Xun lun wenzi gaige* [Lu Hsun on writing reform], (Peking: Wenzi gaige chubanshe, pp. 23-24 and passim.)

31. Even Cantonese refugees opposed to the P.R.C., perhaps motivated by nationalistic sentiments that cut across conventional political orientations, have expressed approval of receiving their education from the earliest grades in Putonghua. See Dayle Barnes, "Language Planning in China," in Joan Rubin et al., eds., *Language Planning: A Cross-National Survey*, (The Hague: Mouton, 1977).

32. Wang Boxi, "Kong lao-er shi fandui Hanzi geming de zu shiye" [Old man Confucius is the granddaddy of opposition to the revolution in Chinese characters], *Shenru pi-Lin pi-Kong cujin wenzi gaige* [Deeply enter into criticism of Lin Piao and Confucius and promote writing reform] (Peking: Wenzi gaige chubanshe, 1974), pp. 22-23. These allegations against Liu Shao-ch'i were made after his fall from power. Before that, in his report to the Eighth Congress of the CCP in 1958, Liu is quoted as having summoned everyone "to promote actively the reform of Chinese characters," Zhou Youguang, *Hanzi gaige gailun* [Sketch of reform of Chinese characters], revised edition (Peking: Wenzi gaige chubanshe, 1964), p. 15.

33. The last complete citation of Mao's remarks that I have seen was made by Kang Lang, an opponent of the use of Latin letters, in 1957. (*Hanyu pinyin fangan cao'an taolun ji II* [Volume 2 of discussions on the draft scheme of Chinese orthography] (Peking: Wenzi gaige chubanshe, 1957), p. 141.

34. BBC Summary of World Broadcasts, June 5, 1975, p. FE/4921/15. I am indebted to Helmut Martin for drawing my attention to this item, which is reproduced in his *Chinas Sprachplanung 1588-1975 aus komparativer perspektive* (in press), p. 377.

35. *New York Times*, September 7, 1975, p. 7.

36. Beverly Hung Fincher, personal communication, February 10, 1977.

37. Harald Richter, personal communication, January 9, 1977.

38. Constantin Milsky had noted that "the militants of the Cultural Revolution, while showing their hostility towards *pinyin*, appeared as defenders of script reform, so far as simplification of characters was concerned." "New Developments in Language Reform," *The China Quarterly*, no. 53 (January-March 1973), p. 126.

39. I am indebted to Helmut Martin for drawing my attention to the two *Guangming Daily* items.

Chapter 7

1. Quoted in Chiu-sam Tsang, *Nationalism in School Education in China* (Hong Kong: 1967), p. 35.

2. "Paoting chün-kuan hsueh-hsiao tsang-sang shih" [The convulsive history of the Paoting Academy], *Ch'un Ch'iu*, no. 63 (1960), p. 2.

3. Li Shou-k'ung, "Ch'ing-chi hsin-chün chih pien-lien chi ch'i yen-pien" [The molding of the New Armies in the Ch'ing and their evolution], *Chung-kuo li-shih hsueh-hui shih-hsueh chi-k'an,* no. 2 (April 1970), p. 85.

4. Knight Biggerstaff, *The Earliest Modern Government Schools in China* (Port Washington, New York: Kennikat Press, 1972), pp. 62-63.

5. William Ayers, *Chang Chih-tung and Educational Reform in China* (Cambridge: Harvard University Press, 1971), pp. 108-10.

6. Ibid., p. 111.

7. Biggerstaff, *Earliest Modern Government Schools,* p. 63.

8. Conflicting reasons have been put forth for the demise of the early academies. Li Shou-k'ung notes that the Tientsin Academy was a victim of the Sino-Japanese War of 1894-1895, while Biggerstaff says it continued to operate until being destroyed in the Boxer uprising. Chang's academy closed in the early 1890s, only to be reopened and divided in 1902 into separate naval and military establishments (Biggerstaff, *Earliest Modern Government Schools,* pp. 63-64).

9. Li Shou-k'ung, "Molding of the New Armies," p. 86.

10. Ayers, *Chang Chih-tung and Education Reform,* pp. 117-18.

11. Li Shou-k'ung, "Molding of the New Armies," p. 91.

12. F. Negrier, "Les Forces Chinoises en 1910," *Revue des Deux Mondes* 5, no. 58 (August 1910):508.

13. C. Gadoffré, "Vallée du Yangtze: les Troupes Chinoises et leurs Instructeurs," translated by James Rockwell, *Journal of the United States Infantry Association* 1 (July 1904):114.

14. Ibid., p. 115.

15. Biggerstaff, *Earliest Modern Government Schools,* p. 72.

16. J. Schrecker, *Imperialism and Chinese Nationalism* (Cambridge: Harvard University Press, 1971), pp. 7-11.

17. Gadoffré, "Vallée du Yangtse," p. 111.

18. Ayers, *Chang Chih-tung and Educational Reform,* p. 215.

19. *North-China Herald,* hereafter NCH (September 18, 1901), p. 556.

20. NCH (February 19, 1902), p. 547.

21. NCH (September 11, 1901), p. 514.

22. Li Shou-k'ung, "Molding of the New Armies," p. 113; and Ralph Powell, *The Rise of Chinese Military Power, 1895-1912* (Princeton: Princeton University Press, 1955), p. 145.

23. NCH (February 18, 1903), p. 334.

24. Powell, *Rise of Chinese Military Power,* p. 166.

25. Ibid., p. 181.

26. NCH (September 8, 1905), p. 544.

27. Robert Hart, "Letters to J. D. Campbell" (October 22, 1905), 12:2861-62. Unpublished manuscript at East Asian Institute, Columbia University.

28. Li Shou-k'ung, "Molding of the New Armies," p. 123.

29. NCH (September 14, 1906), p. 635.

30. NCH (January 4, 1907), p. 17; and NCH (March 8, 1907), p. 504.

31. Chu Wu, "Wo kuo chih lu-chün" [The army of our country], *Kuo-feng*

pao 1, no. 21 (1910):68-70.

32. "Paoting," p. 2.

33. Chu, "The Army of our Country," p. 67; and *The China Yearbook* (London: George Routledge, 1912), p. 246.

34. Lu-chün pu, ed., *Lu-chün hsing-cheng chi-yao* [A brief account of army administration] (Peking, 1916), pp. 296-303.

35. "Paoting," p. 3.

36. Lu-chün pu, "Army administration," pp. 291-309; and *The China Yearbook* (1913), p. 275.

37. Lu-chün pu, "Army administration," pp. 308-09.

38. *The China Yearbook* (1925-1926), p. 1139.

39. Ch'en Hsu-lu and Lao Shao-hua, "Ch'ing-mo ti hsin-chün yü hsin-hai ko-ming" [The New Armies of the late Ch'ing and the Revolution of 1911], *Hsin-hai ko-ming wu-shih chou-nien lun-wen chi* [Symposium on the fiftieth anniversary of the Revolution of 1911] (Peking, 1962), 1, p. 159.

40. Stephen Mackinnon, "The Peiyang Army, Yuan Shih-k'ai, and the Origins of Modern Warlordism," *Journal of Asian Studies* 32, no. 3 (May 1973):408-9.

41. Paula Harrell, "The Years of the Young Radicals: the Chinese Student in Japan, 1900-1915," (Ph.D. dissertation, Columbia University, 1970), p. 67; and Chang Chung-lei, "Ch'ing-mo min-ch'u ssu-ch'uan ti chün-shih hsueh-t'ang chi ch'uan chun-p'ai hsi" [Military academies and military cliques in Szechuan in the late Ch'ing and early Republic], in *Hsin-hai ko-ming hui-i lu* [Memoirs of the Revolution of 1911] (Peking, 1962), 3.

42. H. S. Brunnert and V. V. Hagelstrom, *Present Day Political Organization of China* (Shanghai: Kelly and Walsh, 1912), p. 313; and Wan Yao-huang, "Wan Yao-huang hsien-sheng fang-wen chi-lu" [Record of interviews with Wan Yao-huang] (Taipei: Institute of Modern History, Academia Sinica, n.d.), p. 12.

43. NCH (September 5, 1908), p. 602.

44. Li Shou-k'ung, "Molding of the New Armies," p. 135.

45. This discussion is based for the most part on information from Howard Boorman et al., eds., *Biographical Dictionary of Republican China* (New York: Columbia University Press, 1967 et seq.), 4 volumes.

46. Boorman, *Biographical Dictionary*, 2:124.

47. Ibid., 1:358.

48. Ibid., 3:288.

49. Ibid., 2:305 and 3:223.

50. NCH (March 11, 1910), p. 541.

51. See for example Yen Hsi-shan's comment in Li Shou-k'ung, p. 136.

52. Harrell, "Years of the Young Radicals," p. 111.

53. Ibid., pp. 48-49.

54. Ibid., pp. 67-94.

55. Edward Fung, "Military Subversion in the Chinese Revolution of 1911," *Modern Asian Studies* 9, no. 1 (February 1975):103-23.

56. Agnes Smedley, *The Great Road* (New York: Monthly Review Press,

1956), pp. 36-80.

57. Li Tsung-jen, "Memoirs," Columbia University Chinese Oral History Project, p. 3-1.

58. Boorman, *Biographical Dictionary*, 4:8.

59. Quoted in Fung, "Military Subversion," p. 104.

60. Y. Hatano, "The New Armies," in *China in Revolution: The First Phase*, edited by Mary C. Wright (New Haven: Yale University Press, 1968), p. 373.

61. Wan Yao-huang, "Interviews," p. 1; Chou Yung-neng, "Chou Yung-neng hsien-sheng fang-wen chi-lu" [Record of interviews with Chou Yung-neng] (Taipei: Institute of Modern History, Academia Sinica, 1964), p. 1; Kung Hao, "Kung Hao hsien-sheng fang-wen chi-lu" [Record of interviews with Kung Hao] (Taipei: Institute of Modern History, Academia Sinica, 1962), p. 24; Donald Gillin, *Warlord: Yen Hsi-shan in Shansi Province, 1911-1949* (Princeton: Princeton University Press, 1967), p. 9; Li Han-hun, "The Reminiscences of Li Han-hun," Columbia University Chinese Oral History Project (1962), p. 2; and Liu Chih, *Wo ti hui-i* [My recollections] (Taipei: 1966), p. 2.

62. Li Tsung-jen, "Memoirs," p. 3-3.

63. Chang Fa-k'uei, "The Reminiscences of Chang Fa-k'uei," Columbia University Chinese Oral History Project (1970); Li Lieh-chun, *Li Lieh-chun chiang-chun tsu-chuan* (n.p., 1944), p. 2.

64. Ch'in Te-shun, "Ch'in Te-shun hsien-sheng fang-wen chi lu" [Record of interviews with Ch'in Te-shun] (Taipei: Institute of Modern History, Academia Sinica, 1960-61), p. 8; Chang Chung-lei, "Military Academies and Military Cliques," pp. 347-48; Chang Fa-k'uei, "Reminiscences"; and Li Tsung-jen, "Memoirs," p. 3-3.

65. Gadoffré, "Vallée du Yangtze," p. 122.

66. Chu Hung-chi, "Lu-chün ti shih-chiu chen chi Yun-nan chiang-wu-t'ang" [The Nineteenth Division of the New Army and the military academy of Yunnan], *Hsin-hai ko-ming hui-i lu* [Recollections of the 1911 Revolution] (Peking: 1962), 3:392.

67. See for example Chang Fa-k'uei, "Reminiscences"; Wan Yao-huang, "Interviews," p. 11; Smedley, *The Great Road*, pp. 85-86; and Chou Yung-neng, "Record of Interviews," p. 1.

68. Smedley, *The Great Road*, p. 86.

69. Li Tsung-jen, "Memoirs," p. 3-7.

70. Li Pin-hsien, "Li Pin-hsien hsien-sheng fang-wen chi-lu" [Record of interviews with Li Pin-hsien] (Taipei: Institute of Modern History, Academia Sinica, 1963).

71. Liu Shih-i, "Liu Shih-i hsien-sheng fang-wen chi-lu" [Record of interviews with Liu Shih-i] (Taipei: Institute of Modern History, Academia Sinica, 1963), p. 1.

72. Ch'in Te-shun, "Interviews with Ch'in Te-Shun," p. 10.

73. Li Tsung-jen, "Memoirs," pp. 3-4, 3-5.

74. NCH (April 28, 1905), p. 183.

75. Li Tsung-jen, "Memoirs," p. 3-5.

76. Lu-chün pu, "Army administration," p. 314.

77. Wan Yao-huang, "Interviews," pp. 13-14.

78. Ch'in Te-shun, "Interviews with Ch'in Te-shun," p. 11.

79. Liu Chih, "My Recollections," p. 4.

80. Boorman, *Biographical Dictionary*, 1:373.

81. Li Han-hun, "Reminiscences," p. 4.

82. "Paoting," no. 64, p. 5.

83. Liu Chih, "My Recollections," p. 7; and Ch'in Te-shun, "Interviews with Ch'in Te-shun," p. 14.

84. "Paoting," no. 64, p. 4.

85. See for example Liu Chih, "My Recollections," p. 7; Hu Tsung-to, "Hu Tsung-to hsien-sheng fang-wen chi-lu" [Record of interviews with Hu Tsung-to] (Taipei: Institute of Modern History, Academia Sinica, 1962), p. 6; Tao Chu-yin, *Chiang Po-li hsien-sheng chuan* [Biography of Chiang Po-li] (Shanghai: Chung-hua, 1948), p. 36; and Kung Hao, "Interviews with Kung Hao," p. 26.

86. Boorman, *Biographical Dictionary*, 1:313.

87. "Paoting," no. 63, p. 3.

88. Kung Hao, "Interviews with Kung Hao," p. 127; and Tao Chu-yin, *Biography of Chiang Po-li*, p. 38.

89. "Paoting," no. 63, pp. 3-6; and Tao Chu-yin, *Biography of Chiang Po-li*, pp. 38-43.

90. "Paoting," no. 64, p. 4.

91. Chu Hung-chi, "The Nineteenth Division," p. 390.

92. Li Tsung-jen, "Memoirs," chapters 4, 5, and 7.

93. Gillin, *Warlord*, p. 26.

94. Jerome Ch'en, "Defining Chinese Warlords and Their Factions," *Bulletin of the School of Oriental and African Studies* 31, no. 3 (1968):576.

95. Ibid., p. 575.

96. Kung Hao, "Interviews of Kung Hao," p. 5.

97. Chang Chung-lei, "Military Academies and Military Cliques," p. 351.

98. See Ch'en, "Defining Chinese Warlords," p. 576.

99. Donald Gillin, "Problems of Centralization in Republican China: The Case of Ch'en Ch'eng and the Kuomintang," *Journal of Asian Studies* 29, no. 4 (August 1970):845-50.

Chapter 8

1. The eight government colleges and universities were: National Peking University, Peking Higher Normal School, Peking Women Higher Normal School, College of Law and Politics, College of Industry, College of Agriculture, College of Medicine, and College of Art.

2. For documents on this incident, see Shu Hsin-cheng, *Chin-tai Chung-kuo chiao-yü shih-liao* [Historical materials of modern Chinese education] (Shanghai, 1928), pp. 146-76.

3. Chang Chi-hsin, *Chung-kuo chiao-yü hsing-cheng ta-kang* [An outline of the Chinese educational administrative structure] (Shanghai, 1934), pp. 88-94.

4. Lucien Pye, *Warlord Politics: Conflict and Coalition in the Modernization of Republican China* (New York: Praeger, 1971), p. 134.

5. For the names and tenure of the ministers, see Ch'en Hsi-chang, *Hsi-shuo Pei-yang* [A detailed discussion of the Peiyang period] (Taipei, 1971), 3:541-60.

6. Chang Chi-hsin, *Educational Administrative Structure*, pp. 115-17.

7. For a discussion of student activism in the 1920s, see my article, "The Chinese Student Movement, 1920-1928: A Preliminary Study," in *The Montclair Journal of Social Sciences and Humanities* 3, no. 1 (Spring 1974):42-54.

8. James E. Sheridan, *Chinese Warlord: The Career of Feng Yü-hsiang* (Stanford: Stanford University Press, 1966), pp. 79-83, 115-16, 120-24.

9. Donald Gillin, *Warlord: Yen Hsi-shan in Shansi Province, 1911-1949* (Princeton: Princeton University Press, 1967), pp. 59-78. The quotation is from p. 71.

10. Paul Monroe, *China: A Nation in Evolution* (New York, 1928), p. 174.

11. Hsi-shen Ch'i, *Warlord Politics in China, 1916-1928* (Stanford: Stanford University Press, 1976), p. 168.

12. *Chung-kuo chin-tai nung-yeh shih tzu-liao* [Historical materials on modern China's agriculture] (Peking, 1957), 2:609.

13. Ronald Cheng (Ch'eng Yu-sung), *The Financing of Public Education in China* (Shanghai, 1935), pp. 78-79.

14. Ibid., p. 180.

15. Ibid., p. 82, table 34.

16. Ramon H. Myers, *The Chinese Peasant Economy: Agricultural Development in Hopei and Shantung, 1890-1949* (Cambridge: Harvard University Press, 1970), p. 271.

17. Ku Mou, *Hsien-tai Chung-kuo chi ch'i chiao-yü* [Modern China and its education] (Shanghai, 1934: Hong Kong, 1975 reprint), 2:7.

18. Ibid., 2:367.

19. Ting Chih-p'in, *Chung-kuo chin ch'i-shih nien lai chiao-yü chi-shih* [A chronological record of Chinese education in the last seventy years] (Shanghai, 1935), p. 89.

20. Franklin W. Houn, *Central Government of China, 1912-1928. An Institutional Study* (Madison: The University of Wisconsin Press, 1959), p. 158.

21. Ting Chih-p'in, *Record of Chinese Education*, p. 128.

22. Ibid., p. 98; and Ch'eng Ch'i-pao, "Chung-kuo chiao-yü ching-fei wen-ti" [The problem of Chinese educational funds] in Li Shih-ch'en, ed., *Chiao-yü tu-li wen-ti chih t'ao-lun* [A discussion of the problem of educational autonomy] (Shanghai, 1925), p. 97.

23. Ting Chih-p'in, *Record of Chinese Education*, p. 157; and *Chung-hua chiao-yü chieh* [Chinese educational review], 15:9 (March 1926), section on

educational news in China, p. 4.

24. Chuang Tse-hsuan, "Chiao-yü chi-chin-t'uan ho chiao-yü tu-li [The national endowment for education and the autonomy of education] in Li Shih-ch'en, ed., *Problem of Educational Autonomy*, p. 67.

25. These arguments were summed up well in a memorandum submitted to the Ministry of Education by the National Educational Association in 1925. See *Chung-hua chiao-yü chieh*, 15:6 (December 1925), section on educational news in China, p. 1.

26. Li Shih-ch'en, "Chiao-yü tu-li chien-i" [A suggestion for educational autonomy] in Li Shih-ch'en, ed., *Problem of Educational Autonomy*, pp. 1-16.

27. Chuang Tse-hsuan, "National Endowment for Education," pp. 67-83.

28. Hsin chiao-yü [New education], 4, no. 5 (May 1922), pp. 901-3.

29. *Chung-hua chiao-yü chieh* 15, no. 6 (December 1925), p. 7.

30. Ibid., 15, no. 4 (October 1925), section on educational news in China, pp. 4-5.

31. Shu Hsin-cheng, *Wo ho chiao-yü* [Education and me] (Shanghai, 1945), pp. 167-68.

32. Ting Chih-p'in, *Record of Chinese Education*, p. 116.

33. Ibid., pp. 108, 116-17, 134, 137, 150; and *Hsin chiao-yü* 8, no. 3 (April 1924), p. 466.

34. Ch'eng Ch'i-pao, "Problem of Chinese Educational Funds," p. 86.

35. See, for example, Ch'en Wei-jen, "Hsien-tai hsueh-sheng so shou-yü cheng-chih ho chin-chi ti ying-hsiang chi ch'i chieh-chueh feng-fa" [How students of today are affected by political and economic forces and the method to solve these problems], *Hsueh-sheng tsa-chih* [Students magazine] (August 1923), p. 4; and Hsiung Pao-feng, "Hsueh-sheng yü cheng-chih" [Student and politics], ibid. (September 1923), pp. 1-4.

36. *Hsueh-sheng tsa-chih* (March 1923), pp. 1-2.

37. Ch'ang Tao-chih, "Hsueh-hsiao feng-ch'ao yen-chiu" [The study of school storms] (Shanghai, 1925), p. 53.

38. I have identified eighteen such cases from Ch'ang Tao-chih's study; Yang Chung-ming's article, "Min-kuo shih-i-nien chih hsüeh-ch'ao" [Student storms in 1922], *Hsueh-sheng tsa-chih* (February 1923); and other contemporary sources.

39. See "Ts'an-yü hsiao-wu yun-tung" [The movements to participate in school affairs], *Chung-kuo ch'ing-nien* [China's youth] (September 1925), pp. 632-37.

40. *Ko-ming wen-hsien* [Collected documents of the revolution] (Taipei, 1953-), 8:128.

41. Ku Mou, *Modern China and Its Education*, 2:371-72, and 375.

42. Quoted in Ronald Cheng, *Financing of Public Education*, p. 119.

43. Ku Mou, *Modern China and Its Education*, 2:435.

Chapter 9

1. On the origins of K'ang-ta see T'ung-i ch'u-pan she, ed., *Chung-kung*

chih chiao-yü [Chinese communist education] (n.p., 1944), p. 3; Warren Kuo, *Analytical History of the Chinese Communist Party*, 3 (Taipei: 1968-1971), pp. 6, 232; and Wang Hsueh-wen, "Chinese Communists' Yenan Spirit and Educational Tradition," *Issues and Studies*, 7, no. 5 (February 1971):50-63. Many of the K'ang-ta branches were set up by the Eighth Route or New Fourth armies and trained primarily military cadres. A list of branches and their heads can be found in *Chung-kung chih chiao-yü*, pp. 54-55; Chalmers A. Johnson, *Peasant Nationalism and Communist Power: The Emergence of Revolutionary China, 1937-1945* (Stanford, Calif.: Stanford University Press, 1962), p. 153 and note 76, p. 233; *Ta shih-tai ti yung-lu* [Crucible of a great period] (n.p.: Hua-tung chun-shih cheng-chih ta-hsüeh cheng-chih pu, 1950), p. 6; and the biographies of Hsieh Fu-chih and Shao Shih-p'ing in Donald W. Klein and Anne B. Clark, *Biographic Dictionary of Chinese Communism, 1921-1965* (Cambridge, Mass.: Harvard University Press, 1971).

2. James P. Harrison, *The Long March to Power* (New York: Praeger, 1973), p. 321.

3. *Chung-kung chih chiao-yü*, pp. 50-51; and Wang Chien-min, *Chung-kuo kung-ch'an-tang shih-kao* [Draft history of the Chinese Communist Party] (Taipei, 1965), 3:278.

4. Tung-yuan she [Mobilization society], *K'ang-ta tung-t'ai* [The situation at K'ang-ta] (Hankow, 1939), p. 9; and Klein and Clark, *Biographic Dictionary*, p. 642. Other descriptions of the K'ang-ta faculty list Chang Ju-hsin, Chang Hao, Wang Li, Chang Chen-han, Liu Tung, Chang Wu-yuan, Wu Hsin-hsien, Li T'e, Ting Ling, Keng Piao, Chang Chi-ch'ien, Chang Kuo-t'ao, Chang Ai-p'ing, Li Wen-ling, Wu Hsi-ju, Chang Hsiang-fu, K'ai Feng, Ts'ai Shu-fan, and Wu Hsi-kung as on the school teaching staff at one time. See Kusano Fumio, *Shina henku no kenkyū* [A study of the Chinese border regions] (Tokyo: Kokumin sha, 1944), pp. 81-82; Kang P'ing, "K'ang-Jih ta-hsueh hsun-li," *K'ang-chan chiao-yü tsai Shen-pei* [Education for the Resistance War in North Shensi], edited by T'ien Chia-ku (Hankow: Ming-jih ch'u-pan she, 1938), pp. 43-46; Nym Wales, *My Yenan Notebooks* (Madison, Conn.: Helen F. Snow, 1961), p. 39, and Agnes Smedley, *The Great Road: The Life and Times of Chu Te* (New York: Monthly Review Press, 1956), p. 243.

5. *K'ang-ta tung-t'ai*, p. 96.

6. Ibid., p. 97. See also *Chung-kung chih chiao-yü*, p. 49; and Wang Chien-min, *Draft History of the CCP*, 3:280.

7. Kusano Fumio, *Chinese Border Regions*, pp. 81-82.

8. For example, the principal study materials for political and economic subjects were *Political Common Knowledge* (a Soviet translation); *Outline of Politics* by Lin Po-ch'ü; *Political Economy* by Ch'en Chih-yuan; *The February Revolution and the October Revolution* (a Soviet translation); *History of the Development of Human Society; Imperialism;* and *People's United Front* (all edited by the K'ang-ta Education Committee); Lenin's *Left-wing Communism: An Infantile Disorder; Inevitability of Proletarian Revolution* (a Soviet translation); and *Party Principles* by Chang Wen-t'ien.

For philosophy, materials consisted of a piece by Marx under the Chinese title of *Dialectical Materialism* and one by Mao called *Outline of New Philosophy*.

9. *K'ang-ta tung-t'ai*, pp. 102-3.

10. Ibid., p. 103.

11. Ibid., p. 85; and *K'ang-ta tung't'ai*, p. 7.

12. Wang Chien-min, *Draft History of the CCP*, 3:280 and *K'ang-ta tung-t'ai*, p. 96. The proper Chinese words for "battalion" and "company" are *ying* and *lien*, respectively. *Tui* is a general term for "unit," "group," or "corps." However, this essay will employ the terms "battalion," "company," and "district company" to distinguish various student groupings.

13. *K'ang-ta tung-t'ai*, p. 124.

14. Niu K'o-lun, "The Smelting Furnace," translated and reprinted from *Jen-min jih-pao*, August 23, 1965, in *Current Background*, no. 777 (November 18, 1965), p. 32.

15. Production campaigns were a response of the Communist border regions to the reimposition of the Nationalist blockade in May 1939 and the Japanese "Three-All" campaigns launched in 1941. See Harrison, *March*, pp. 316-17. On the trials of the various K'ang-ta classes and their solutions see *K'ang-ta tung-t'ai*, pp. 18-22, 40-42.

16. *K'ang-ta tung-t'ai*, pp. 88-90.

17. Niu K'o-lun, "The Smelting Furnace," p. 34. As evidence of the length to which this principle was carried, Niu cited Liu Ya-lou's class on the element of surprise in guerrilla warfare and night attacks. In the middle of the following night, students were mustered out of bed to take up positions on a ridge outside Yenan.

18. *K'ang-ta tung-t'ai*, pp. 86-87, 104-6.

19. Ibid., pp. 206-8, 213.

20. On supplementary forms of discussion meetings, see ibid., p. 111.

21. "Revolutionary competition" involved students competing in groups rather than individually for first place in academic work, discipline, or cultural activities. It had been a feature of CCP political education since the Kiangsi period.

22. Salvation Rooms were Soviet-inspired culture and entertainment centers for Communist army troops. Before the Sino-Japanese War they were called Lenin Clubs.

23. *K'ang-ta tung-t'ai*, pp. 209-10.

24. Ibid., p. 33. See also Agnes Smedley, *Battle Hymn of China* (New York: Knopf, 1943), p. 165.

25. See Ch'en Lien-hua *K'ang-ta yü ch'ing-nien* [K'ang-ta and youth] (Chungking, 1940), pp. 5-8, 20-21, 27-29.

26. William Whitson, with Chen-hsia Huang, *The Chinese High Command* (New York: Praeger, 1973), pp. 157-59.

27. Kuo, *Analytical History*, 3:234. Wang Chien-min, *Draft History of the CCP*, 3:281. Lu P'ing, "Yen-an ti szu-ko hsüeh-hsiao [Four Yenan schools], *Sheng-huo tsai Yen-an* [Life in Yenan], edited by Lu P'ing (n.p., 1938), p. 129.

28. Hsu Hsing, "I-ko K'ang-chan ti hsueh-hsiao" [A school for the resistance war], *K'ang-chan chiao-yü tsai Shen-pei*, p. 30.

29. On courses and teachers see Shao Shih-p'ing, "Shen-pei kung-hsueh shih-shih kuo-fang chiao-yü ti ching-yen yü chiao-hsün" [Experience and lesson of the North Shensi Public School implementing national defense education], *Chieh-fang* [Liberation], no. 37 (May 6, 1938), p. 13.

30. Hao Chung, "Tse-yang chin Shen-pei kung-hsueh" [How to enter the North Shensi Public School], *Shen-pei ti ch'ing-nien hsueh-sheng sheng-huo* [Life of young students in North Shensi], edited by Lo Jui-ch'ing and Ch'eng Fang-wu (Shanghai: Chien-she ch'u-pan she, 1940), p. 5.

31. Shao Shih-p'ing, "Experience of the North Shensi Public School," pp. 12, 14.

32. Ma Chun, "Shen-kung, K'ang-ta ho tang-hsiao" [North Shensi Public School, K'ang-ta, and the Party School], *K'ang-chan chiao-yü tsai Shen-pei*, p. 18. Wang Chien-min, *Draft History of the CCP*, 3:281.

33. On the staff and organization of Women's University, see Kusano Fumio, pp. 87-88; Ma Chi-ling, *Shen-pei niao-k'ao* [A bird's eye–view of North Shensi] (Chengtu: Cheng-chih, 1941), p. 91; and Edgar Snow, *Scorched Earth*, 2 (London: Victor Gollancz, Ltd., 1941):263-64.

34. Ibid., p. 263 and Ch'en Shao-yü, "Tsai Yen-an Chung-kuo nü-tzu ta-hsueh tien-li ta-hui shang ti pao-kao" [Report on the opening ceremony of Chinese Women's University in Yenan], *Kung-fei fan-tung wen-chien hui-pien* [Collection of reactionary Communist bandit documents], Yushodo Microfilms, reel 18, p. 128.

35. Snow, *Scorched Earth*, 2:264. See also Ch'en Shao-yü, "Opening Ceremony," p. 129.

36. Ch'en Shao-yü, "Opening Ceremony," p. 129. Kusano Fumio, *Chinese Border Regions*, p. 89. Snow, *Scorched Earth*, 2:262 and 265.

37. Headed by Communist P'eng Hsueh-feng, this institution was set up by the Eighth Route Army in cooperation with Shansi warlord Yen Hsi-shan. It trained "national salvation cadres" to work with Yen's New Army and in enemy areas. Its curriculum and learning format were similar to K'ang-ta and other CCP united front schools. See T'ao Fen, "Ch'i-t'a kuan-yü Min-tsu ko-ming ta-hsueh" [Another concerning the National Revolutionary University], *K'ang-chan chiao-yü tsai Shen-pei*, pp. 92-105; Evans F. Carlson, *Twin Stars of China* (New York: Dodd, Mead, 1940), pp. 61-63; and Donald Gillin, *Warlord: Yen Hsi-shan in Shansi Province, 1911-1949* (Princeton: Princeton University Press, 1967), p. 274.

38. The North Shensi Public School merged with the Youth Training Class and Work School of the Lu Hsun Academy of Arts in 1939 to form North China United University. Chinese Women's University merged with the Tse-tung Youth Cadre School and parts of other schools to form Yenan University in September 1941. It is likely that the struggle between Ch'en Shao-yü and Mao Tse-tung, which resurfaced during the *cheng-feng* movement, also had some bearing on the closing of the school. See *Chung-kung chih chiao-yü*, p. 68.

39. On the institute, see idem. Enrollment figures for 1943 show 180

students in the "preparatory" department and 80 in the "standard" department.

40. On Worker's University see ibid., p. 69; and Wang Chien-min, *Draft History of the CCP*, 3:282. On Motor University, see Ma Chun, "North Shensi Public School," p. 22.

41. On the Lu Hsun Academy see *Chung-kung chih chiao-yü*, p. 70; Wang Chien-min, *Draft History of the CCP*, 3:283; and Kuo, *Analytic History*, 3:234 and 243.

42. This school had been set up after the Long March at Wayaopao and later Paoan and was headed prior to 1937 by Tung Pi-wu. On the leadership of the Central Party School, see ibid., p. 38; Kuo, *Analytic History*, 4:576; and Nym Wales, *Red Dust* (Stanford: Stanford University Press, 1952), p. 43.

43. In other words, cadres above the local committee level if civilian, and above the regimental level if military.

44. On the student composition and enrollment at the Central Party School, see *Chung-kung chih chiao-yü*, p. 38; Ma Chun, "North Shensi Public School," p. 22; Lu P'ing, "Four Yenan Schools," p. 131; Kuo, *Analytic History*, 3:233; and Wales, *Yenan Notebooks*, p. 104.

45. See Wales, *Yenan Notebooks*, pp. 104 and 106; and Gunther Stein, *The Challenge of Red China* (New York: Whittlesey House, 1945), pp. 152-53 and 258.

46. Lu P'ing, "Four Yenan Schools," p. 131, and Stein, *Challenge of Red China*, pp. 151-52; *Chung-kung chih chiao-yü*, p. 38.

47. On the Border Region Party School, see *Chung-kung chih chiao-yü*, pp. 38-39 and *Hsueh-hsi sheng-huo* [Study life], edited by Wen-hua chiao-yü yen-chiu hui (n.p., 1941), pp. 129-30.

48. *Chung-kung chih chiao-yü*, p. 39.

49. In other words, Party branch leaders could no longer interfere directly with school administration as in the past. They were restricted to recommendations or criticisms within regular Party channels and an auxiliary role in implementing the schools' education plans.

50. "Resolution of the Central Committee of the Chinese Communist Party on the Yenan Cadre Schools," December 17, 1941, reproduced in Boyd Compton, *Mao's China: Party Reform Documents, 1942-1944* (Seattle: University of Washington Press, 1966), pp. 74-79.

51. It was first formed via a merger of Chinese Women's University, the Tse-tung Youth Cadre School (founded in May 1940), and part of the North Shensi Public School. In 1943 it combined with the Natural Sciences research Institute, Lu Hsun Academy of Arts, Nationalities Academy (founded July 1941), and New Character Cadre School (founded April 1941). The 1944 reorganization involved incorporation of the Administration Academy (founded July 1940). On the history of Yenan University, see *Yen-an ta-hsueh kai-k'uang* [General situation at Yenan University] (n.p., mimeo, June 1944), p. 1.

52. Only thirty students were identified as of proletarian background and 163 of poor peasant background. The largest groups came from "small

property owners" (330), middle peasants (303), and landlords (270). There were 773 enrolled in the Administration Academy; 314 in the Lu Hsun Arts Academy; 72 in the Medical Department; 49 in the Natural Sciences Academy; and 74 in a special "Female Section." See ibid., pp. 13-14.

53. For details on the curriculum at Yenan University, see "Yenan University Educational Line and Temporary Regulations," May 21, 1944, reproduced in Michael Lindsay, *Notes on Educational Problems in Communist China, 1941-47* (New York: Institute of Pacific Relations, 1950), pp. 133-39.

54. Ibid., p. 138. According to Harrison Forman in *Report from Red China* (New York: Henry Holt and Company, 1945), p. 86, Yenan University raised 60 percent of its own food supply.

55. The most noteworthy on intraorganizational behavior were Ch'en Yun's "How to Be a Communist Party Member" (1939), and Liu Shao-ch'i's "Training of the Communist Party member" (1939) and "On the Intra-Party Struggle" (1941). All are reproduced in Compton, *Mao's China.*

56. On ideological tendencies see in particular Mao Tse-tung, "Reform in Learning, the Party, and Literature" (February 1, 1942), "In Opposition to Party Formalism" (February 8, 1942), "The Reconstruction of Our Studies" (May 5, 1941), "In Opposition to Liberalism" (September 7, 1937), and "In Opposition to Several Incorrect Tendencies within the Party" (December 1929). All are available in Compton, *Mao's China.*

57. The most noteworthy pieces for this area are the CCP Central Committee's "Resolution on Methods of Leadership" (June 1, 1943) and "Resolution on Investigation and Research" (August 1, 1941), and Mao Tse-rung's "Second Preface to Village Investigations" (March 17, 1941). All are available in Compton, *Mao's China.*

58. "Commandism" and "tailism" are terms employed by the Chinese Communist Party to describe deviations from proper cadre work style. "Tailism" is defined as the practice of blindly following popular demands and "commandism" is one of the terms for overly arrogant and authoritarian behavior.

59. See James S. Coleman, ed., *Education and Political Development* (Princeton: Princeton University Press, 1965), pp. 355-57.

60. The leading exponent of this point of view is Y. C. Wang. See especially his preface to *Chinese Intellectuals and the West, 1872-1949* (Chapel Hill: University of North Carolina Press, 1966).

61. This campaign involved the transfer of a large number of outside activists to local areas.

62. Mao Tse-tung, "Second Preface to Village Investigations," Compton, *Mao's China,* p. 55.

63. Chang Ting-ch'eng, "Cheng-feng tsai Yen-an Chung-yang tang-hsiao" [Rectification at the Yenan Central Party School], *Hsing-huo liao-yuan* [A single spark can start a prairie fire], 6 (Peking: Jen-min wen-hsueh ch'u-pan she, 1962):15. See also Kuo, *Analytic History,* 4:566, 575.

64. Chang Ting-ch'eng, "Rectification," p. 7; Kuo, *Analytic History*

4:573-76; Kusano Fumio, *Chinese Border Regions,* p. 116. See also "Hsin ti chiao-yü fang-chen ch'e-ti kai-tsu" [Thoroughly reorganize a new educational line], *Chieh-fang jih-pao,* January 28, 1942.

65. Merle Goldman, *Literary Dissent in Communist China* (Cambridge, Mass.: Harvard University Press, 1967), pp. 38-42; and Kuo, *Analytic History,* 4:617-18.

66. *Yen-an ta-hsueh,* p. 2.

67. See Hsueh Mu-ch'iao, "Cheng-feng hsueh-hsi tsai K'ang-ta" [*Cheng-feng* study at K'ang-ta], *Cheng-feng,* no. 1 (September 1942), pp. 39-44, Yushodo Microfilms, reel 12.

Chapter 10

1. See T'ang Ming-pang, "Wang Ch'uan-shan shih-chi fang-wen-chi" [A record of visits to historical spots relating to Wang Fu-chih], in *Wang Ch'uan-shan hsueh-shu t'ao-lun chi* [A symposium on the learning of Wang Fu-chih], edited by Hunan-Hupei-sheng che-hsueh she-hui k'o-hsueh hsueh-hui lien-ho-hui (Peking: Chung-hua shu-chü, 1965), 2:574-91.

2. Laurence A. Schneider, *Ku Chieh-kang and China's New History: Nationalism and the Quest for Alternative Traditions* (Berkeley and Los Angeles: University of California Press, 1971), p. 93.

3. Arthur Hummel, "Ts'ui Shu," in *Eminent Chinese of the Ch'ing Period (1644-1912),* edited by Hummel (Washington: Government Printing Office, 1943), p. 773. This short essay on Ts'ui is the best I have seen in any language. Hummel was apparently really taken with Ts'ui. Professor Chaoying Fang, who did a great deal of work on the *Eminent Chinese of the Ch'ing Period* project, told me that he added to or touched up virtually every entry in that volume except Hummel's on Ts'ui, to which he made no alterations whatsoever. See also Hummel, "Portrait of a Scholar," in *There is Another China: Essays and Articles for Chang Poling of Nankai* (New York: King's Crown Press, 1948), pp. 131-50.

4. Hung Yeh (William Hung) et al., eds., *Ts'ui Tung-pi i-shu yin-te* (Index to the collected works of Ts'ui Shu) (Peiping: Harvard-Yenching Institute Sinological Series, no. 5, 1937). Considering all the truly seminal works in Chinese culture that still have no indexes, this index for Ts'ui's works stands out remarkably; it reflects the kinds of concerns surrounding this whole project, which I shall discuss presently.

5. Ch'ien Mu's introduction deserves special mention for its typically brilliant command (even forty years ago) of all sorts of materials; and his conclusion that Ts'ui Shu, like Chinese people and thinkers in general, always suffered from an overabundance of reverence for antiquity, is the hallmark of his famous *Chung-kuo chin san-pai-nien hsueh-shu shih* [Chinese intellectual history over the past three hundred years] (Shanghai: Commercial Press, 1936). Ch'ien Mu, "Hsu [Introduction] to *Ts'ui Tung-pi i-shu,* edited by Ku Chieh-kang (Shanghai: Ya-tung t'u-shu-kuan, 1936), 1:15-17. Every subsection of this work has its own pagination.

6. Ku Chieh-kang, "Hsu" [Introduction] to *Ts'ui Tung-pi i-shu,* 1:1-4.

Ku reveals later in other prefatory notes, comments, and by the inclusion of various essays that he was fully aware of the Japanese edition, and Hu Shih knew of it many years before, but Ku chose to ignore it here.

7. This side of the story has yet to be told straight through with full accuracy. For partial accounts, see: Hashimoto Masayuki, "Sen-Shin jidai shi" [History of the pre-Ch'in period], in *Meiji igo ni okeru rekishigaku no hattatsu* [The development of historiography from the Meiji period], edited by Rekishi kyōiku kenkyūkai (Tokyo: Shikai shobō, 1933), pp. 407-09; Tam Yue-him, "In Search of the Oriental Past: The Life and Thought of Naitō Konan" (Ph.D. dissertation, Princeton University, 1975), pp. 171-74; Naitō Konan, *Shina shigaku shi* [History of Chinese historiography], in *Naitō Konan zenshū* [Collected works of Naitō Konan], edited by Naitō Kenkichi and Kanda Kiichirō (Tokyo: Chikuma shobō, 1969-76), 9:393-94. This last source is the most accurate.

8. Miyake Yonekichi, "Bungaku hakase Naka Michiyo-kun den" [Biography of Professor of Literature Naka Michiyo], in Naka Michiyo, *Naka Michiyo isho* [The remaining (i.e., as yet unpublished) works of Naka Michiyo], edited by the Ko-Naka Michiyo hakase kōseki kinenkai (Tokyo: Dai Nihon tosho, 1915), pp. 32-33; and Goi Naohiro, *Kindai Nihon to Tōyoshigaku* [Modern Japan and East Asian studies] (Tokyo: Aoki shoten, 1976), p. 52. The story goes that at a meeting in 1894 of middle and upper normal school teachers, Naka proposed a division of the generic course, "Gaikoku rekishi" [History of foreign countries], into "Seiyōshi" [Western history] and "Tōyōshi" [East Asian history]. His proposal was accepted and so the term *Tōyōshi* was born. For Naka it meant all East Asian nations (except Japan) with China at the center. By 1897 the Mombushō had recognized Naka's proposal and a textbook bearing the title *Tōyōshi* soon followed. The terms *Seiyō* and *Seiyōshi* predate this episode, as does the expression *Tōyō*.

9. "*Kōshinroku* no honkoku" [Reprinting of the *K'ao-hsin lu*], *Shigaku zasshi* 11, no. 12 (December 1900):127. *Mencius*, "Liang Hui wang," *hsia*, 11, no. 2. James Legge, *The Chinese Classics, Vol. II: The Works of Mencius* (London: Trübner and Co., 1861), p. 47. In this passage, Mencius referred to an incident from the *Shu-ching* to illustrate how anxiously and excitedly the people viewed the great work being done by T'ang—later, in the same section, Mencius says, "it was like rain falling at the right time, the people were ecstatic" (*jo shih yü hsia, min ta yüeh*).

10. This account of Ts'ui's ideas is fascinating and oddly never previously attracted anyone's attention (so far as we now know). It describes Ts'ui's distinctive historiographic approach, which we shall examine shortly, and goes into considerable detail. See Li Yuan-tu, *Kuo-ch'ao hsien-cheng shih-lüeh* (Taipei reprint: Wen-hai ch'u-pan-she, n.d.), 36:1651-61. As an aside there is also an entry (from two sources) on Ts'ui in the *Kuo-ch'ao ch'i-hsien lei-cheng ch'u-pien* [Biographies of Ch'ing venerables and worthies, arranged by categories], compiled by Li Huan (Taipei reprint, 1966), 14:8232; this predates all rediscovery efforts by at least a decade, the whole collection having been completed in 1890. I have rapidly gone through the works of Naitō Chisō that I could locate and have found no reference to Ts'ui Shu; my

guess is that the comunication to Konan was either in a letter or done orally. For a brief introduction to Naitō Chisō, see Takasu Yoshijirō, "Kaidai" [Explanatory preface], in *Mitogaku taikei* [Compendium of the Mito school] (Tokyo: Ida shoten, 1941), 7:15. Chisō was a Kangaku scholar from Edo-*han* who lived into the mid-Meiji era. His principal work was the multivolume *Tokugawa jūgodai shi* [A history of the fifteen generations of the Tokugawa].

11. Kanda Kiichirō, "Naitō Konan to Shina kodaishi" [Naitō Konan and ancient Chinese history], in *Tonkōgaku gojūnen* [Fifty years of the study of Tun-huang] (Tokyo: Chikuma shobō), p. 90. Oba Osamu, *Edo jidai ni okeru Tōsen mochiwatarisho no kenkyū* [A study of books brought over from China in the Edo period] (Suita: Kansai daigaku tōsai gakujutsu kenkyūjo, 1967).

12. Hashimoto and Tam, following Hashimoto, say that Naitō prepared a biography of Ts'ui (in this essay), which was based on rare works (Tam, "In Search of the Oriental Past," p. 173), and explicated the *K'ao-hsin lu* (Hashimoto, "History of the Pre-Ch'in Period," p. 408). In actuality, Naitō merely translated the Ts'ui section of the *Kuo-ch'ao hsien-cheng shih-lüeh*, not at all a rare source. Implicit in his doing such a translation, I believe, is criticism of the *Shigakkai sōsho* project, because there are sections in the source translated that refer to works by Ts'ui that the *Shigakki sōsho* people did not have.

13. Naitō Konan, "Dokusho gūhitsu," in *Naitō Konan zenshū*, 7:16-17, 21. Originally published in *Nihon* on January 2, 1901.

14. "Futatabi *Kōshinroku* no honkoku ni tsuite" [Again on the reprinting of the *K'ao-hsin lu*], *Shigaku zasshi* 12, no. 2 (February 1901):125-26.

15. Naka Michiyo, "*Kōshinroku* kaidai" [Explication of the *K'ao-hsin lu*], *Shigaku zasshi* 13, no. 7 (July 1902):51-61.

16. *Sai Tōheki isho* [The collected works of Ts'ui Tung-pi], edited by Naka Michiyo, four volumes (Tokyo: Meguro shoten, 1903-4).

17. Naka Michiyo, *Naka Tōyō ryakushi* [Naka's brief history of East Asia] (Tokyo: Dai Nihon tosho, 1903), pp. 170-71.

18. Kano Naoki, *Chūgoku tetsugaku shi* [History of Chinese philosophy] (Tokyo: Iwanami shoten, 1975), pp. 604-8.

19. From his lecture notes for the *Shinchō shi tsūron* [General history of the Ch'ing dynasty], we can see that he had planned to discuss Ts'ui, but simply overlooked this note during the lecture: "Wang Fu-chih, Fang Pao, Ch'en Hou-yao, Ku Lien-kao, Wang Mao-hung, and Ts'ui Shu: they came out of the Sung school and later became followers of the Han school," *Naitō Konan zenshū*, 8:459. See also Naitō Kenkichi, "Atogaki" [Afterword] to *Naitō Konan zenshū*, 8:493.

20. Miyake Yonekichi, "Biography of Naka Michiyo," p. 37. A scholar of Japanese history and contemporary of Naka, Miyake was famous for his innovative use of an interdisciplinary approach to the study of history, and as such is considered along with several others to have set down the roots of a modern historiography and pedagogy in Meiji Japan. He was also a

phenomenal linguist. See Kadowaki Teiji, "Miyake Yonekichi," in *Nihon rekishi daijiten* [The great encyclopedia of Japanese history] (Tokyo: Kawade shobō shinsha, 1975), 9:107; and Yamane Tokutarō, "Miyake Yonekichi," in *Ajia rekishi jiten* [Encyclopedia of Asian history] (Tokyo: Heibonsha, 1961), 8:408.

21. Masui Tsuneo, *Shin teikoku: saigo no kyodai teikokū* [The Ch'ing empire: last of the great empires], volume 7 of *Chūgoku no rekishi* [The history of China] (Tokyo: Kōdansha, 1974), pp. 316-17.

A brief comparison of the original *Ts'ui Tung-pi hsien-sheng i-shu* compiled by Ch'en Lü-ho (with an afterword dated 1825) with the Naka edition and the Ku Chieh-kang edition seems in order at this point. I was fortunate enough to have the opportunity to look through a rare copy of one of the original editions at Kyoto University library and to make use of Professor Kuwabara Jitsuzō's (1870-1931) own copy of the Naka edition, replete with Kuwabara's red-penciled notes and place markers throughout the text (his *Tōyōshi* collection was donated to the Bungaku-bu library at Kyoto University by his son, Professor Kuwabara Takeo). Naka Michiyo's work entailed a reprinting on excellent paper of the contents of the original Ch'en edition with the addition of punctuation and a certain amount of textual analysis for errors. In essence, Ku Chieh-kang did the same. Aside from general clause and sentence breaks, however, the punctuation systems differ. Naka, of course, inserted Kambun *kariten*, which usually indicate the precise order in which a given clause is to be read in Japanese and thus may specify subjects, objects, verbs, and even particles. On the other hand, Ku used Western punctuation with periods, commas, even adding question marks, exclamation points, and most significantly indications of place names, text names, and personal names. (Compare *Ts'ui Tung-pi hsien-sheng i-shu*, compiled by Ch'en Lü-ho, 55 *chüan*, afterward dated 1825; Naka Michiyo, editor, *Sai Tōheki isho;* and Ku Chieh-kang, main editor, *Ts'ui Tung-pi i-shu*). The major difference between these two editions, aside from numerous prefaces and reprinted material not by Ts'ui himself in the Chinese one, was the discovery by William Hung of a lengthy poetry collection of Ts'ui's, the *Chih-fei chi* [The knowing fallacy collection], which he found in the Yenching University library in 1931, over a decade into Ku's project. It had been listed in Ts'ui's own original table of contents, but, when Ch'en Lü-ho later compiled this edition of Ts'ui's writings, the *Chih-fei chi* was not included and thus was supposedly lost. It and several other bits and pieces presumed lost were similarly punctuated, edited, and included in the thirteenth *ts'e* of the Chinese edition. (See Ku, "Hsu" [Introduction] to Ts'ui's *Chih-fei chi*, in *Ts'ui Tung-pi i-shu*, 13:2-3 and 16. Hu and Ku did discover several other hitherto "lost" Ts'ui poems and essays, also inserted in this volume of the collected works. This is the major contribution of the Chinese edition.)

22. Ku Chieh-kang, *The Autobiography of a Chinese Historian*, translated by Arthur Hummel (Leyden: E. J. Bryll Ltd., 1931), p. 82, note 4.

23. Hummel, *Eminent Chinese of the Ch'ing Period*, p. 776.

24. Hu Shih, "K'o-hsueh te ku-shih-chia Ts'ui Shu," reprinted in *Ts'ui Tung-pi i-shu*, 2:3.

25. Chao Chen-hsin, in *Ts'ui Tung-pi i-shu*, 1:55.

26. Schneider, *Ku Chieh-kang*, p. 94.

27. Laurence Schneider, "From Textual Criticism to Social Criticism: The Historiography of Ku Chih-kang," *Journal of Asian Studies* 28, no. 4 (August 1969), p. 777; Schneider, *Ku Chieh-kang*, pp. 197-98.

28. For an explanation of why the title of this work is to be translated in this way, see Ojima Sukema, quoted by Naitō Kenkichi, "Atogaki" [Afterword] to *Naitō Konan zenshū*, 1:687.

29. Naitō Konan, *Kinsei bungaku shiron*, in *Naitō Konan zenshū*, 1:58.

30. A beautifully annotated and punctuated edition of the *Shutsujō kōgo* with readings provided has been prepared by Mizuta Norihiza, in *Tominaga Nakamoto-Yamagata Bantō, Nihon shisō taikei* [Compendium of Japanese thought], 43 (Tokyo: Iwanami shobō, 1973). For more on Tominaga, see Ishihama Juntarō, *Tominaga Nakamoto* (Tokyo: Sōgensha, 1942). For other discussions of Tominaga by Naitō see: "Ōsaka no chōnin to gakumon" [Osaka merchants and their scholarship], originally a lecture presented in Osaka in 1921, later included in *Nihon bunkashi kenkyū* [Studies in the history of Japanese culture], in *Naitō Konan zenshū*, 9:149-57; "Ōsaka no chōnin gakusha Tominaga Nakamoto" [Tominaga Nakamoto, a scholar from the Osaka merchant class], in *Sentetsu no gakumon* [The knowledge of former wise men], in *Naitō Konan zenshū*, 9:370-93, esp. 377-78 on *kajō*; "Tominaga Nakamoto no 'Okina no fumi' ni tsuite" [On Tominaga Nakamoto's "Letter of an old man"], originally in *Chūgai nippō* (March 11, 1924), in *Naitō Konan zenshū*, 6:227-29; and "Ōsaka no ichi ijin" [One great man of Ōsaka], originally in *Ōsaka asahi shimbun* (January 22, 1905), in *Naitō Konan zenshū*, 4:408-11.

31. See Naitō Konan, "Choin sango," collected in *Ruishu dashu* [Tears and saliva], in *Naitō Konan zenshū*, 1:380-400; the reference to Naitō Chisō is on p. 380.

32. This is laid out much more elegantly in Naitō Konan, *Shina jōkoshi* [Ancient Chinese history], in *Naitō Konan zenshū*, 10:19-23, 145-46. For a slightly different rendition, see Naitō Konan, "Ōsaka no chōnin gakusha Tominaga Nakamoto," in *Naitō Konan zenshū*, 9:387-88. Naitō also used this *kajō* methodology in his studies of the *Shang-shu*, *Erh-ya*, and *I-ching;* all are included in his *Kenki shōroku* (Short essays for clarification), in *Naitō Konan zenshū*, volume 7. They are: "Shōsho keigi" (Pondering doubtful spots in the *Shang-shu*), 7:9-23; "Jiga no shin kenkyū" (A new study of the *Erh-ya*), 7:24-37; and "Eki gi" (Doubts about the *I-ching*), 7:38-47.

33. Miyazaki Ichisada, "Dokusoteki na Shinagakusha Naitō Konan hakase" [An innovative sinologist, Professor Naitō Konan], in *Chūgoku ni manabu* [Studying China] (Tokyo: Asahi shimbunsha, 1971), p. 257. This essay has been rather badly translated as "Konan Naito: An Original Sinologist," *Philosophical Studies of Japan* 7 (1967):93-116.

34. Miyazaki Ichisada, "Naitō Konan to Shinagaku [Naitō Konan and sinology], in *Kindai Nihon o tsukutta hyakunin* [One hundred men who made modern Japan], 2 (Tokyo: Mainichi shimbunsha, 1966):412. Kanda Kiichirō, a scholar of ancient China, has also noted the striking similarity between Ku's and Naitō's methodology—see Kanda, "Naitō Konan," p. 88. For other intellectual connections between Ku and Japanese sinology, see an essay on Ogura Yoshihiko, "Ko Ketsugō to Nihon" [Ku Chieh-kang and Japan], in *Ware Nyūmon ni ari* [I stood at the Dragon Gate] (Tokyo: Ryūkei shosha, 1974), pp. 3-31, originally published in *Shisō* (January 1972).

35. Schneider, *Ku Chieh-kang*, p. 93.

36. This theme has been brilliantly treated by Herbert Marcuse in his *Reason and Revolution: Hegel and the Rise of Social Theory* (London: Routledge & Kegan Paul, 1963).

37. Hu Shih, "Hsu" (Introduction) to *Ts'ui Tung-pi i-shu*, 1:4 and 6-7.

38. Hu Shih, "K'o-hsueh te ku-shih-chia Ts'ui Shu," *Ts'ui Tung-pi i-shu*, 2:5.

39. Quoted in Miyake Yonekichi, "Biography of Naka Michiyo," p. 27. Naka Michiyo's *Shina tsūshi* was the first modern comprehensive history of China. It has been translated into classical Japanese by Wada Sei as volumes 418-20 in the Iwanami bunko series (Tokyo: Iwanami shoten, 1975), three volumes, originally published in this translation in 1938-41.

40. Quoted in Schneider, "From Textual Criticism," p. 777.

41. Ku, *Autobiography*, p. 83.

42. Paul Demiéville, "Chang Hsueh-ch'eng and his Historiography," *Historians of China and Japan*, edited by W. G. Beasley and E. G. Pulleyblank (London: Oxford University Press, 1961), pp. 176-77; Mitamura Taisuke, *Naitō Konan* (Tokyo: Chūō kōron, 1972), p. 127; David Nivison, *The Life and Thought of Chang Hsueh-ch'eng (1738-1801)* (Stanford: Stanford University Press, 1966), pp. 2 and 284; Miyazaki, "Dokusōteki na" p. 263; Momose Hiromu, "Chang Hsueh-ch'eng," *Eminent Chinese of the Ch'ing Period*, p. 40; Shimada Kenji, *Chūgoku kakumei no senkushatachi* [Pioneers of the Chinese revolution] (Tokyo: Chikuma shobō, 1970), p. 240.

43. Naitō Konan, "Shō Gakusei no shigaku" [Chang Hsueh-ch'eng's historiography], appended to *Shina shigaki shi*, in *Naitō Konan zenshū*, 11:472. Chang Erh-t'ien and Sun Te-ch'ien are mentioned by Naito but not by Nivison. Chang Ping-lin's reference to Chang Hsueh-ch'eng is cited by Nivison, *Life and Thought*, p. 283. Kung Tzu-chen is listed for discussion by Naito but never discussed in this context because no student notes from this lecture existed at the time this work was compiled; see *Shina shigaku shi*, in *Naitō Konan zenshū*, 11:447; however, Nivison makes this possible connection elegantly clear, *Life and Thought*, pp. 281-82. Naito provides elaboration of Sun's and Chang's ties to Chang Hsueh-ch'eng in the field of bibliographic studies (*mu-lu-hsueh* or *moku rokugaku*) in which Chang Hsueh-ch'eng made important innovations. See Naitō, *Shina mokuroku-gaku* [Bibliographic study in China], originally lectures at Kyoto University from April to June of 1926, in *Naitō Konan zenshū*, 12:437. This book

provides much information on Chang's contributions to this field.

44. See Teng Chih-ch'eng, "Chang-chün Men-ch'ü pieh-chuan" [A biography of Mr. Chang Meng-chu'u Erh-t'ien], *Yen-ching hsueh-pao* 30 (June 1946):323-25. Chang's interests were widespread although he is perhaps most famous for his role in the writing and compiling of the *Ch'ing-shih kao* [Draft history of the Ch'ing dynasty].

45. Naitō Konan, "Shina gakumon no kinjō" [The present state of Chinese scholarship], originally presented as a lecture in Hiroshima on August 8, 1911, in *Naitō Konan zenshū*, 6:56. In the *Shinchōshi tsūron*, given as lectures in the summer of 1915, Naitō had virtually adulatory things to say about Chang: "no one who came after him could compare with so rare a genius" as seen particularly in the *Wen-shih t'ung-i*. See *Naitō Konan zenshū*, 8:368.

46. Kanda Kiichirō and Mitamura Taisuke, in "Sengaku o kataru: Naitō Konan hakase" [A discussion of a past wise man: Professor Naitō Konan], roundtable discussion by Kaizuka Shigeki, Mitamura Taisuke, Kanda Kiichirō, Miyazaki Ichisada, Naitō Kenkichi, Nagata Hidemasa, and Yoshikawa Kōjirō, *Tōhōgaku* 47 (January 1974):157-59; this transcribed discussion has been reprinted along with five similar ones previously published in *Tōhōgaku* as *Tōyōgaku no sōshishatachi* [The founders of East Asian studies], edited by Yoshikawa Kōjirō (Tokyo: Kōdansha, 1976), pp. 94-96 and 98. On T'ang Hsien, see Morohashi Tetsuji, editor, *Dai Kan-Wa jiten* [Great Chinese-Japanese dictionary] (Tokyo: Taishūkan shoten, 1957-60), 9:11034; T'ang was a *chü-jen* of the T'ung-chih period. Recently in the mainland journal *Li-shih yen-chiu* a letter from Chang Ping-lin to T'an Hsien dated 1897 was republished; and it was explained that Chang considered T'an to be his teacher. The content of the letter was to attack K'ang Yu-wei and his group of reformers. See "Chin-tai-shih tzu-liao chieh-shao: Chang T'ai-yen gei T'an Hsien te i-feng hsin" [Introduction of source materials on modern history: A letter from Chang T'ai-yen to T'an Hsien], *Li-shih yen-chiu* 3 (1977):124-25. For the Naitō *festschrift*, see *Shigaku ronsō: Naitō hakase shōju kinen* [Essays in historiography presented to Professor Naitō on his sixty-fifth birthday], edited by Nishida Naojirō (Kyoto: Kōbundō shobō, 1930); Chang's essay appears on pp. 273-74.

47. Naitō Konan, "Shō Jitsusai sensei nempu" [A chronological biography of Chang Shih-chai (Hsueh-ch'eng)], *Shinagaku* 1, no. 3-4 (October 1920), in *Naitō Konan zenshū*, 7:67-79.

48. Demiéville, "Chang Hsueh-ch'eng," p. 177.

49. Hu Shih, *Chang Shih-chai hsien-sheng nien-p'u* [A chronological biography of Chang Shih-chai] (Taipei: Commercial Press, 1968), p. 1. K'ang Yu-wei is often credited with making Chang known to the Chinese intellectual world; I have been unable to see just where K'ang fits in this particular "rediscovery" effort. As with other K'ang endeavors, I suspect it may have been largely a self-professed achievement.

50. Naitō Konan, "Ko Tekishi no shincho Shō Jitsusai nempu o yomu" [On reading Hu Shih-chih's recently written chronological biography of Chang Shih-chai], *Shinagaku* 2, no. 9 (May 1922), in *Naitō Konan zenshū*,

12:80-90; Naitō, *Shina shigaku shi*, in *Naitō Konan zenshū*, 11:447.

51. On Cheng, see Naitō Konan, "Gisaku ichidō" [One strand of a draft idea], written in Kambun, *Naitō Konan zenshū*, 14:78-84, first published in *Shinagaku* 6, no. 4 (August 1931); see also Naitō, *Shina shigaku shi*, in *Naitō Konan zenshū*, 11:450; Naitō, *Shina Mokurokugaku*, in *Naitō Konan zenshū*, 12:407, 411-14, 420, 425, 430-31, 433-34. Also of value is an essay by Naitō's son which provides information on this rediscovery in China and Japan, Naitō Shigenobu, "Tei Shō no shiron ni tsuite" [On Cheng Ch'iao's historiography], *Tōyōshi kenkyū* 1, no. 2 (September-October 1936), pp. 1-13. See also Suzuki Shun, "Tei Shō" (Cheng Ch'iao) *Tōyō rekishi daijiten* [Great Encyclopedia of East Asian history] (Tokyo: Heibonsha, 1938), 6:285. For Ku Chieh-kang's work on Cheng, published in *Kuo-hsueh ts'ui-pao* as early as 1923, see Schneider, *Ku Chieh-kang*, passim.

52. Wu Yü, "Ming Li Cho-wu pieh-chuan," *Chin-pu tsa-chih* 9:3-4 (1916), reprinted in *Wu Yü wen-lü* [The writings of Wu Yü] (Shanghai: Ya-tung t'u-shu-kuan, 1921), 2:20-51. See Shimada Kenji, "Watakushi no Naitō Konan" [Naitō Konan for me], *Naitō Konan zenshū geppō* 6 (June 1970):6. For a discussion of Li Chih in English, see Wm. Theodore deBary, "Individualism and Humanitarianism in Late Ming Thought," in deBary, ed., *Self and Society in Ming Thought* (New York and London: Columbia University Press, 1970), pp. 145-247.

53. Naitō Konan, "Dokusoki sansoku," in *Naitō Konan zenshū*, 12:28-30.

54. "Ta Chiao Jo-hou shu" [Reply to Chiao Jo-hou's letter] and Chiao Jo-hou, "Li-Shih Ts'ang-shu hsu" [An introduction to Mr. Li's *Ts'ang-shu*], *Kuo-ts'ui hsueh-pao* 1, no. 11 (1905), pp. 1a-2b of the "chuan-lu" section; see Shimada, "Watakushi no Naitō Konan," p. 7.

55. Yoshida Shōin, "Ri-shi Funsho sho" (A summary of Mr. Li's *Fen-shu*), in *Yoshida Shōin zenshū*, edited by Yamaguchi-ken kyōiku-kai, (Tokyo: Iwanami shoten, 1934-36), 9:1-24; and Yoshida Shōin, "Ri-shi Zoku sōsho sho" (A summary of Mr. Li's *Hsu Ts'ang-shu*), ibid., 9:25-53. See also K. C. Hsiao, "Li Chih," *Dictionary of Ming Biography (1368-1644)*, edited by L. Carrington Goodrich and Chaoying Fang (New York: Columbia University Press, 1976), 1:817; and Shimada Kenji, "Ri Shi" [Li Chih], in *Ajia rekishi jiten*, 9:211-12.

56. Kitayama Yasuo, *Chūgoku kakumei no rekishiteki kenkyū* [Historical studies of the Chinese revolution] (Kyoto: Minerva shobō, 1972), p. 81.

57. Shimada, "Watakushi no Naitō Konan," p. 8.

58. Naitō Konan comes closest to this in his *Kinsei bungaku shiron*, and in his essay "Ōsaka no ichi ijin," cited above.

59. E. H. Carr, *What is History?* (Middlesex: Penguin, 1976), pp. 8-30, especially pp. 12-13.

60. Benedetto Croce, *History as the Story of Liberty*, translated by Silvia Sprigge (London: George Allen and Unwin, 1962), p. 19.

Chapter 11

1. This brief biographical sketch of Ch'ü is based on my manuscript "A

Biography of Ch'ü Ch'iu-pai" and my dissertation "A Biography of Ch'ü Ch'iu-pai: from Youth to Party Leadership (1899-1928)" (Columbia University, 1967).

2. Volume 12, no. 26.

3. Volume 12, no. 6 (August 21, 1935), no. 7 (September 1), and no. 8 (September 11). The journal was published in Shanghai.

4. Volumes 25, 26, and 27 (March 5, March 20, and April 15, 1937).

5. It is quoted in full by Cheng Hsueh-chia in his article "Ch'ü Ch'iu-pai te i-sheng" [Ch'ü Ch'iu-pai's life], *Tung-ya chi-k'an* [East Asia quarterly], 4, no. 4 (April 1, 1973):25-26.

6. Hsueh-hua, "To-yü te hua yin-yen" [An introduction to *Superfluous Words*], *I-ching* 25, p. 17.

7. Ting Ching-t'ang, *Hsueh-hsi Lu Hsun ho Ch'ü Ch'iu-pai tso-p'ing te chao-chi* [Notes from studying works by Lu Hsun and Ch'ü Ch'iu-pai] (Shanghai: Shang-hai wen-i ch'u-pan she, 1961), pp. 20-22.

8. Ibid., pp. 186-95. The word *hsia* was chosen both to commemorate Ch'ü's stay at Tzu-hsia Road and because it refers to the rosy light of dawn.

9. Ibid., p. 212.

10. "In Memoriam of Two Fiery Revolutionaries and Old Members of the Chinese Communist Party, Comrades Tso Tsu-bo (Strachov) and Ho Su-hin," *Communist International* 12:15 (August 5, 1935), pp. 752-54. The article was signed "Wan Min [Wang Ming], Kon-sin [K'ang Sheng] and a group of Chinese Comrades." Ho Shu-heng accompanied Ch'ü during the retreat from Kiangsi to Shanghai. The group was discovered by the KMT local militia in Wu-p'ing hsien, Fukien. Ho was killed during an exchange of fire, while Ch'ü and others were captured.

11. Ting Ching-t'ang, *Notes from Studying Works*, pp. 210-11.

12. The name and place of the publisher were not given.

13. *Hsun-kuo lieh-shih Ch'ü Ch'iu-pai*, mimeographed for distribution, p. 7.

14. Ibid., p. 31.

15. "Chi-nien Ch'ü Ch'iu-pai t'ung-chih hsun-nan shih-i chou-nien" [Commemorating the eleventh anniversary of Comrade Ch'ü Ch'iu-pai's martyrdom], in Hua Ying-shen, ed., *Chung-kuo kung-ch'an-tang lieh-shih chuan* [Biographies of Chinese Communist martyrs] (Hong Kong: Hsin min-chü ch'u-pan she, 1949), pp. 67-70.

16. *Mao Tse-tung: Selected Works* (New York: International Publishers, 1956), 4:182-83, with minor modifications.

17. T'ang T'ieh-hai, *Chung-yang lao ken-chü ti yin-hsiang chi* [Impressions of the former central base areas] (Shanghai: Lao-tung ch'u-pan she, 1952), p. 54; Ts'ao Ching-hua, "Lo-han ling ch'ien tiao Ch'iu-pai ping i Lu Hsun hsien-sheng" [Mourning for Ch'iu-pai at Lo-hang Ling and remembering Mr. Lu Hsun], *Ta-kung pao*, December 2, 1952.

18. *Jen-min jih-pao*, June 19, 1955.

19. Ch'ü Ch'iu-pai wen-chi pien-chi wei-yuan-hui, eds., *Ch'ü Ch'iu-pai*

wen-chi, 4 volumes (Peking: Jen-min wen-hsueh ch'u-pan she, 1953-54), 1: preface, 1-2.

20. Ibid., preface, p. 4. On the controversy regarding the class nature of language, see the article by John DeFrancis in this volume.

21. Ibid., preface, p. 5. Stalin's *Marxism and the Question of Linguistics* was first published in 1950.

22. For a listing of works on Ch'u up to 1959, see Ting Ching-t'ang, *Notes from Studying Works,* pp. 208-31.

23. Ch'i's article appeared in no. 4, 1963, pp. 27-42.

24. For Lo's interpretation, see his *Chung-wang Li Tzu-ch'eng tzu-chuang kao chien-cheng* [Commentaries on the manuscript of the Loyal Prince Li Hsiu-ch'eng's autobiography], enlarged edition (Peking: Chung-hua Bookstore, 1957); "Chung-wang Li Hsiu-ch'eng te k'u-jou huan-ping chi" [The Loyal Prince Li Hsiu-ch'eng's painful strategy designed to gain by delay], *Kuang-ming jih-pao,* July 28, 1964; and "Chung-wang Li Hsiu-ch'eng k'u-jou huan-ping chi k'ao" [An investigation into the Loyal Prince Li Hsiu-ch'eng's painful strategy designed to gain by delay], *Li-shih yen-chiu,* 4 (August 1964).

25. For a discussion of the debate on Li Hsiu-ch'eng, see Stephen Uhalley, Jr., "The Controversy over Li Hsiu-ch'eng: An Ill-timed Centenary," *Journal of Asian Studies,* 25, no. 2 (February 1966):305-17. Also relevant is *Taiping Rebel: The Deposition of Li Hsiu-ch'eng,* edited by C. A. Curwen (New York: Cambridge University Press, 1977).

26. *T'ao Ch'ü chan-pao* (Militant paper to punish Ch'ü), published in Peking, May 6, 1967.

27. Chao Ts'ung, *Wen-ke yun-tung li-ch'eng shu-lüeh* [A brief account of the Cultural Revolution], 4 volumes (Hong Kong: Union Research Service, 1971), 1:61.

28. Some articles on Li Hsiu-ch'eng, published during 1964-65, were collected in *Li Hsiu-ch'eng p'ing-chia wen-t'i hui-pien* [A collection of articles on the question of the evaluation of Li Hsiu-ch'eng—from the Shanghai *Wen-hui pao* in 1964], 2 volumes (Hong Kong: O. K. Newspaper Agency, publication date not indicated); and Ts'un-ts'ui hsueh-she, ed., *T'ai-p'ing t'ien-kuo yen-chiu lun-chi* [Collected essays on the study of the Taipings], 2 volumes (Hong Kong: Ch'ung-wen Bookstore, 1972). For an excellent analysis of intellectual trends at this time, see Merle Goldman, "The Chinese Communist Party's 'Cultural Revolution' of 1962-64," in Chalmers Johnson, ed., *Ideology and Politics in Contemporary China* (Seattle: University of Washington Press, 1973), pp. 219-54.

29. *T'ao Ch'ü chan-pao,* May 6, 1967.

30. Yang Chih-hua, "I Ch'iu-pai" [Recollections about Ch'iu-pai], *Hung-ch'i p'iao-p'iao* [Red flags are flying], 8 (Peking: Chung-kuo ch'ing-nien ch'u-pan she, 1958):55.

31. Quoted in *Wen-ke yun-tung li-ch'eng shu-lüeh,* 1:61.

32. *T'ao Ch'ü chan-po,* May 6, 1967.

33. Ibid.

34 A Moscow Chinese Language Broadcast on July 16, 1967, monitored in Taipei. The Soviet press has been consistently favorable to Ch'ü, regarding him as a Marxist publicist, an outstanding revolutionary, and a friend of the Russian people. There is available in the Russian language a literary biography of him and a collection of his literary writings. The Chinese criticisms of Ch'ü have been regarded by the Russians as defamation and slander with the purpose of revising the history of the Chinese revolutionary movement in order to depict Mao as its sole leader.

35. *I-ch'ieh fan-tung p'ai tou-shih tsun K'ung-pai* [All reactionaries were Confucius's worshippers], compiled by the History Department at Chi-lin University (Peking: Jen-min ch'u-pan she, 1974), pp. 53-55.

36. *I-ching* 27 (April 5, 1937):7.

Bibliography of the Publications of C. Martin Wilbur

Books

The American Plant Migration, Part I: The Potato. By Berthold Laufer, prepared for publication by C. Martin Wilbur. Anthropological Series, vol. 28, no. 1, publication 418. Chicago: Field Museum of Natural History, 1938.

Slavery in China during the Former Han Dynasty, 206 B.C.–A.D. 25. Anthropological Series, vol. 34, publication 525. Chicago: Field Museum of Natural History, 1943. Reprints: New York, Russell & Russell, 1967; New York, Kraus Reprint Co., 1968.

Chinese Sources on the History of the Chinese Communist Movement: An Annotated Bibliography of Materials in the East Asiatic Library of Columbia University. East Asian Institute Studies no. 1. New York: East Asian Institute of Columbia University, 1950.

Documents on Communism, Nationalism, and Soviet Advisors in China, 1918-1927. With Julie Lien-ying How. New York: Columbia University Press, 1956. Reprint: New York, Octagon Books, 1972.

The Communist Movement in China; an Essay Written in 1924. By Ch'en Kung-po, edited with an introduction by C. Martin Wilbur. East Asian Institute Studies no. 7. New York: East Asian Institute of Columbia University, 1960. Reprint: New York, Octagon Books, 1966.

Forging the Weapons: Sun Yat-sen and the Kuomintang in Canton, 1924. Mimeographed. New York: East Asian Institute of Columbia University, 1966.

The Chinese Oral History Project. New York: The East Asian Institute of Columbia University, 1972.

Sun Yat-sen: Frustrated Patriot. New York: Columbia University Press, 1976.

Articles and Chapters

"Contribution to a Bibliography on Chinese Metallic Mirrors." *The China Journal* 20, no. 4 (April 1934):173-78.

"Japan and the Korean Farmer." *Asia* 35, no. 7 (July 1935):394-97.

"The History of the Crossbow Illustrated from Specimens in the United States National Museum." *Smithsonian Report for 1936* (publication 3438), pp. 427-38.

"Shih Jun-chang." In *Some Eminent Chinese of the Seventeenth Century: Twenty-two Biographies from a Proposed Dictionary of Ch'ing Dynasty Biography*, edited by Arthur W. Hummel, pp. 16-17. Baltimore: Waverly Press, 1936. Also in *Eminent Chinese of the Ch'ing Period*, edited by Arthur W. Hummel, vol. 2, p. 651. Washington, D.C.: U.S. Government Printing Office, 1943-44.

" 'Pieces of Eight' in China." *Field Museum News* 8, no. 4 (April 1937).

"Jades Collected by Mrs. George T. Smith Added to Exhibit at Museum." Field Museum News 8, no. 12 (December 1937).

"Chinese Exhibit Illustrates the Story of Printing." *Field Museum News* 9, no. 8 (August 1938).

"Ancient Chinese Bronze Type Reveals Some of the History of Printing." *Field Museum News* 10, no. 10 (October 1939).

"Chicago Meets Young China in Field Museum Exhibit." *Field Museum News* 11, no. 5 (May 1940).

"A Story of Fragments—How an Archaeological Object, and its History, are Both Reconstructed." *Field Museum News* 11, no. 12 (December 1940).

"Hidden Inscriptions—Discovery Leads into Ancient Politics, Tax Frauds, Even Clothes Pressing." *Field Museum News* 12, no. 1 (January 1941).

"Additional Notes on Tea." By L. Carrington Goodrich and C. Martin Wilbur. *Journal of the American Oriental Society* 62, no. 3 (1942):195-97.

"Rare Costumes of Aborigines in War-Menaced Yunnan." *Field Museum News* 14, no. 2 (February 1943).

"Slavery as Practiced in Ancient China." *Field Museum News* 14, no. 2 (February 1943).

"Carl Whiting Bishop." *The Far Eastern Quarterly* 2, no. 2 (February 1943):204-7.

"Industrial Slavery in China during the Former Han Dynasty (206 B.C.-A.D. 25)." *Journal of Economic History* 3, no. 1 (May 1943):56-69.

"Rare Collection Illustrates China's New Stone Age." *Field Museum News* 14, nos. 6, 7, and 8 (June, July, and August 1943).

"George McAfee McCune (June 16, 1908–November 5, 1948)." *The Far Eastern Quarterly* 9, no. 2 (February 1950):185-91.

"Ways to View Our Dilemma in Korea." *Barnard Bulletin* 55, no. 19 (December 11, 1950).

"The Year 1951 in China." *The American Annual 1952*, pp. 134-37.

"The Year 1952 in China." *The American Annual 1953*, pp. 128-31.

"The Year 1953 in China" and "The Year 1953 in Formosa," *The American Annual 1954*, pp. 132-35 and 259-60.

"Mao's 'Paradise' as Seen from India." *The Reporter* (May 19, 1955), pp. 14-16.

"Southeast Asia Between India and China." *Journal of International Affairs*

10, no. 1 (1956):87-99.

"Chinese Doves Flutter Over Japan." *The New York Times Magazine,* February 19, 1956, pp. 14, 32, 34, and 36.

"The Cultures of Asia in a Time of Political Change: China." In *The Cultures of Asia in a Period of Political Change: The Hofstra Forum,* pp. 1-15. Hempstead, N.Y.: Hofstra College, 1956.

"Japan and the Rise of Communist China." In *Japan between East and West,* pp. 199-239. New York: Council on Foreign Relations and Harper and Brothers, 1957.

"Political Issues between Mainland China and the United States." In *China Consultation 1958,* pp. 21-32. New York: Far Eastern Office, Division of Foreign Missions, National Council of Churches of Christ in the U.S.A., 1958.

"The Structure of Militarism in China during the 1920s." In *University Seminar on Modern East Asia: China* (January 30, 1963), mimeographed. New York: Columbia University, 1963.

"The Ashes of Defeat: Accounts of the Nanchang Revolt and Southern Expedition, August 1-October 1, 1927, by Chinese Comm·nists who Took Part." *The China Quarterly* (April-June 1964), pp. 3-54.

"Sun Yat-sen and Soviet Russia, 1922-1924." In *University Seminar on Modern East Asia: China* (March 10, 1965), mimeographed. New York: Columbia University, 1965.

"The Future of American-Chinese Relations." *Christianity and Crisis* (June 27, 1966), pp. 141-43.

"Military Separatism in China." *Chicago Today* (Spring 1967), pp. 19-24.

"Military Separatism and the Process of Reunification under the Nationalist Regime, 1922-1937." In *China in Crisis: China's Heritage and the Communist Political System,* edited by Ping-ti Ho and Tang Tsou, vol. 1, book 1, pp. 203-63. Chicago: University of Chicago Press, 1968.

"Blücher's 'Grand Plan' of 1926." Translated by Jan J. Solecki, notes by C. Martin Wilbur. *The China Quarterly* (July-September 1968), pp. 34-39.

"The Influence of the Past: How the Early Years Helped to Shape the Future of the Chinese Communist Party." *The China Quarterly* (October-December 1968), pp. 23-44. Also in *Party Leadership and Revolutionary Power in China,* edited by John Wilson Lewis, pp. 35-68. Cambridge: The University Press, 1970.

"China's Transitional Century, 1850-1950." In *China in Change: An Approach to Understanding,* edited by M. Searle Bates, pp. 33-62. New York: Friendship Press, 1969.

"Introduction to *The Constitutionalists and the Revolution of 1911 in China* by Chang Peng-yuan." *Thought and Word* 9, no. 1 (May 1971):62-63.

"The Variegated Career of Ch'en Kung-po." In *Revolutionary Leaders of Modern China,* edited by Chün-tu Hsüeh, pp. 455-70. New York and London: Oxford University Press, 1971.

"The Presidential Address: China and the Skeptical Eye." *Journal of Asian Studies* 31, no. 4 (August 1972):761-68.

"Further Reflections on Sun Yat-sen." In *University Seminar on Modern East Asia: China* (March 21, 1973), mimeographed. New York: Columbia University, 1973.

"Statement on American Policy Toward China." In *Future Importance of Taiwan and the Republic of China to U.S. Security and Economic Interests*, pp. 22-29. Hearings before the Subcommittee on Asian and Pacific Affairs of the Committee on Foreign Affairs, House of Representatives, Ninety-third Congress, First Session, July 25–August 1, 1973. Washington, D.C.: U.S. Government Printing Office, 1973.

"China, History of: XI. The Republican Period." *Encyclopedia Britannica*, 15th ed.

"Problems of Starting a Revolutionary Base: Sun Yat-sen and Canton, 1923." *Bulletin of the Institute of Modern History, Academia Sinica* 4, part 2 (December 1974):665-727.

"Speeding Recognition of the P.R.C.: A Cost too High, a Step too Soon." *Contemporary China* 1, no. 1 (October 1976):33-35.

"The Case for Not Recognizing Peking." *The Washington Post*, December 10, 1976. Reprinted in *Congressional Record* (February 1, 1977), p. E487.

"American Relations with China: An Amateur's View." *Taipei Language Institute Newsletter* (August 31, 1977), p. 4.

"Fairbank's 'Formula' Refuted by Professor." *The China Post*, September 15, 1977, p. 1.

"Sun Yat-sen and Soviet Russia—a Brief Second Look." In *Proceedings of the 30th International Congress of Orientalists*, Mexico City, August 1976, forthcoming.

"The Human Dimension and its Problems." Forthcoming as a chapter in a book on Taiwan.

"The Nationalist Revolution (From Canton to Nanking) 1923-1938." In *Cambridge History of China*, vol. 12 or 13, forthcoming.

"Sun Chung-shan Hsien-sheng yü Su O." In *Chung-hua Min-kuo Shih-liao Yen-chiu Chung-hsin Ti-liu Tz'u Hsueh-shu T'ao-lun Hui Chi-lu* (Taipei, 1977), pp. 1-30.

Reviews

Studies in Early Chinese Culture: First Series, by Herlee Glessner Creel. *American Anthropologist* 40, no. 3 (July-September 1938):512-13.

The Early Empires of Central Asia: A Study of the Scythians and the Huns and the Part They Played in World History: with Special Reference to Chinese Sources, by William Montgomery McGovern. *American Anthropologist* 42, no. 1 (January-March 1940):151-54.

Rome and China: A Study of Correlations in Historical Events, by Frederick J. Teggart. *American Historical Review* 46, no. 1 (October 1940):93-95.

Inner Asian Frontiers of China, by Owen Lattimore. *Pacific Affairs* 13, no. 4 (December 1940):498-501.

Chinese Fairy Tales and Folk Tales, collected and translated by Wolfram Eberhard. *American Journal of Folklore* 54 (1941):82-83.

Archaeological Researches in Sinkiang, Especially the Lop-nor Region, by Folke Bergman. *American Anthropologist* 44, no. 2 (April-June 1942): 311-13.

Old China Hands and the Foreign Office, by Nathan A. Pelcovits. *The Annals of the American Academy* 257 (May 1948):220-21.

The Far East: A History of the Impact of the West on Eastern Asia, by Paul Hibbert Clyde. *The Annals of the American Academy* 258 (July 1948): 136-37.

The United States and China, by John King Fairbank. *There is Another China: Essays and Articles for Chang Poling of Nankai. Political Science Quarterly* 63, no. 4 (December 1948):619-20.

The Cowrie Shell Miao of Kweichow, by Margaret M. Mickey. *American Anthropologist* 51, no. 3 (July-September 1949):478-79.

New Light on the History of the Taiping Rebellion, by Ssu-yu Teng. *Far Eastern Survey* 19, no. 10 (May 17, 1950):103-4.

History of Chinese Society: Liao (907-1125), by Karl A. Wittfogel and Fang Chia-sheng. *American Anthropologist* 52, no. 3 (July-September 1950): 399-400.

The Government and Politics of China, by Chien Tuan-sheng. *Far Eastern Survey* 20, no. 3 (February 7, 1951):32.

Mao Tse-tung, Ruler of Red China, by Robert Payne. *American Historical Review* 61, no. 3 (April 1951):662-63.

Food and Money in Ancient China: The Earliest Economic History of China to A.D. 25, translated and annotated by Nancy Lee Swan. *The Far Eastern Quarterly* 10, no. 3 (May 1951):320-22.

The Enemy Within: An Eye-witness Account of the Communist Conquest of China, by Raymond J. de Jaegher and Irene Corbally Kuhn. *New York Herald Tribune Book Review,* March 23, 1952, p. 4.

Chinese Communism and the Rise of Mao, by Benjamin I. Schwartz. *New China: Three Views,* by Otto B. Van der Sprenkel, Robert Guillain, and Michael Lindsay. *American Historical Review* 57, no. 3 (April 1952): 679-80.

Revolution in China, by Charles Patrick Fitzgerald. *The Nation* (August 23, 1952), pp. 154-55.

The American Record in the Far East, 1945-1951, by Kenneth Scott Latourette. *The Korea Story,* by John C. Caldwell in collaboration with Lesley Frost. *The Nation* (December 27, 1952), p. 610.

China, Japan and the Powers, by Meribeth E. Cameron, Thomas H. D. Mahoney, and George E. McReynolds. *The Far Eastern Quarterly* 12, no. 2 (February 1953):203-4.

Nationalism and Communism in East Asia, by W. MacMahon Ball. *The Nation* (April 4, 1953).

Nationalism and Communism in East Asia, by W. MacMahon Ball. *Political Science Quarterly* 68, no. 4 (December 1953):620-22.

Civil Service in Early Sung China, 960-1067, by E. A. Kracke, Jr. *Pacific Historical Review* 23, no. 1 (February 1954):81-82.

The China Tangle: The American Effort in China from Pearl Harbor to the Marshall Mission, by Herbert Feis. *The Annals of the American Academy* 292 (March 1954):214-15.

Shanghai, Key to Modern China, by Rhoads Murphy. *U.S. Quarterly Book Review* 10, no. 1 (March 1954):78-79.

The Great Peace: An Asian's Candid Report on Red China, by Raja Hutheesing. *China's New Creative Age,* by Hewlett Johnson. *Far Eastern Survey* 23, no. 6 (June 1954):95-96.

Moscow and the Chinese Communists, by Robert C. North. *U.S. Quarterly Book Review* 10, no. 2 (June 1954):166-67.

China in the 16th Century: The Journals of Matteo Ricci, 1583-1610, translated by Louis J. Gallagher, S.J. *United States Quarterly Book Review* 10, no. 2 (June 1954):167.

Trade and Diplomacy on the China Coast, by John King Fairbank. *United States Quarterly Book Review* 10, no. 3 (September 1954):308-9.

China's Management of the American Barbarians: A Study of Sino-American Relations, 1841-1861, by Earl Swisher. *Political Science Quarterly* 69, no. 4 (December 1954):633-34.

A Treasury of Asian Literature, by John D. Yohannan. *The Bulletin of the Marboro Book Club* 2, no. 22 (1956).

Land of the 500 Million: A Geography of China, by George B. Cressey. *American Slavic and East European Review (Slavic Review)* 15, no. 4 (December 1956):567.

Fifty Years of Chinese Philosophy, 1898-1950, by O. Briere, S.J. *Journal of the American Oriental Society* 77, no. 1 (January-March 1957):62-63.

Indian Views of Sino-Indian Relations, by Margaret W. Fisher and Joan V. Bondurant. *The Journal of Asian Studies* 16, no. 2 (February 1957):287-88.

Japanese Studies of Modern China: A Bibliographical Guide, by John King Fairbank and Masataka Banno. *Pacific Affairs* 30, no. 1 (March 1957):76-77.

The Political History of China, 1840-1928, by Li Chien-ning. *Pacific Affairs* 30, no. 2 (June 1957):178-80.

Soviet Russia in China: A Summing Up at Seventy, by Chiang Chung-cheng. *The New York Times Book Review,* June 23, 1957, pp. 1 and 25.

China: New Age and New Outlook, by Ping-chia Kuo. *Annals of the American Academy* 312 (July 1957):149-50.

The United States and China, by John King Fairbank. *The New York Times Book Review,* September 14, 1958.

The Yellow Wind: An Excursion in and around Red China with a Traveler in the Yellow Wind, by William Stevenson. *The New York Times Book Review,* November 1, 1959.

Intellectual Trends in the Ch'ing Period, by Liang Ch'i-ch'ao, translated by Immanuel C. Y. Hsü. *Pacific Historical Review* 28, no. 4 (November 1959):411-12.

The Serpent and the Tortoise: Problems of the New China, by Edgar Faure.

Decision for China: Communism or Christianity, by Paul K. T. Sih. *Far Eastern Survey* 28, no. 11 (November 1959):175.

One Chinese Moon, by J. Tuzo Wilson. *New York Times Book Review*, December 13, 1959.

A Chinese Village in Early Communist Transition, by C. K. Yang. *The Chinese Family in the Communist Revolution*, by C. K. Yang. *The New York Times Book Review*, February 7, 1960.

Red Carpet to China, by Michael Croft. *The New York Times Book Review*, March 27, 1960.

China: Its People, Its Society, Its Culture, by Chang-tu Hu and others. *New York Herald Tribune Book Review*, May 1, 1960.

The May Fourth Movement: Intellectual Revolution in Modern China, by Chow Tse-tung. *The New York Times Book Review*, May 15, 1960.

Ten Years of Storm: The True Story of the Communist Regime in China, by Chow Ching-wen. *Thought Reform of the Chinese Intellectuals*, by Theodore H. E. Chen. *The New York Times Book Review*, October 23, 1960.

China Crosses the Yalu: The Decision to Enter the Korean War, by Allen S. Whiting. *The New York Times Book Review*, November 27, 1960.

Thought Reform and the Psychology of Totalism: A Study of "Brain-washing" in China, by Robert Jay Lifton. *The New York Times Book Review*, February 5, 1961.

Sun Yat-sen and Communism, by Shao Chuan Leng and Norman D. Palmer. *The New York Times Book Review*, April 30, 1961.

A History of Japan, 1334-1615, by George Sansom. *New York Herald Tribune Book Review*, July 2, 1961.

Red China: An Asian View, by Sripati Chandra-sekhar. *The New York Times Book Review*, July 9, 1961.

The Communist Movement in China, 1921-1937: An Annotated Bibliography of Selected Materials in the Chinese Collection of the Hoover Institution on War, Revolution, and Peace, by Chun-tu Hsueh. *Pacific Historical Review* 30, no. 4 (November 1961):419-20.

Asia in the European Age, 1498-1955, by Michael Edwardes. *The New York Times Book Review*, April 7, 1963.

The Asian Century: A History of Modern Nationalism in Asia, by Jan Romein in collaboration with Jan Erik Romein. *The New York Times Book Review*, April 7, 1963.

A Man Must Choose: The Dilemma of a Chinese Patriot. New York Tribune Book Review, June 30, 1963.

The Asian Century: A History of Modern Nationalism in Asia, by Jan Romein in collaboration with Jan Erik Romein. *Asia in the European Age, 1498-1955*, by Michael Edwardes. *Political Science Quarterly* 78, no. 4 (December 1963), pp. 605-9.

Documents of the Three-Self Movement: Source Materials for the Study of the Protestant Church in Communist China, edited by Francis P. Jones. *China Notes* 2, no. 3 (April 1964).

Twentieth Century China, by O. Edmund Clubb. *The New York Times Book Review*, May 3, 1964.

The Scrutable East: A Correspondent's Report on Southeast Asia, by Robert Trumbull. *The New York Times Book Review*, June 21, 1964.

The Center of the World: Communism and the Mind of China, by Robert S. Elegant. *The New York Times Book Review*, July 19, 1964.

Studies in Frontier History: Collected Papers, 1928-1958, by Owen Lattimore. *Political Science Quarterly* 79, no. 3 (September 1964):469-71.

In Search of Wealth and Power: Yen Fu and the West, by Benjamin Schwartz. *The Journal of Asian Studies* 24, no. 1 (November 1964):150-51.

Mao and the Chinese Revolution, by Jerome Ch'en. *The New York Times Book Review*, May 23, 1965.

Scientism in Chinese Thought, 1900-1950, by D.W.Y. Kwok. *American Historical Review* 72, no. 2 (January 1967):669-70.

Le Mouvement Ouvrier Chinois de 1919 à 1927 and *Les Syndicats Chinois 1919-1927*, by Jean Chesneaux. *Journal of Asian Studies* 26, no. 2 (February 1967):293-95.

The Taiping Rebellion: History and Documents, Volume I: History, by Franz Michael in collaboration with Chung-li Chang. *Political Science Quarterly* 82, no. 3 (September 1967):491-92.

China: The People's Middle Kingdom and the U.S.A., by John King Fairbank. *American Historical Review* 75, no. 5 (June 1970):1504-5.

China in Revolution: The First Phase, 1900-1913, edited with an introduction by Mary Clabaugh Wright. *Political Science Quarterly* 86, no. 1 (March 1971):157-59.

Rebellion and its Enemies in Late Imperial China: Militarization and Social Structure, 1796-1864, by Philip A. Kuhn. *Political Science Quarterly* 87, no. 1 (March 1973):153-55.

The Taiping Rebellion: History and Documents. Volumes II and III, by Franz Michael in collaboration with Chung-li Chang. *Modern Asian Studies* 8, part 3 (July 1974):422-24.

"Proletarian Hegemony" in the Chinese Revolution and the Canton Commune of 1927, by S. Bernard Thomas. *China Quarterly*, forthcoming.

The Contributors

John DeFrancis is professor emeritus at the University of Hawaii. He is the author of *Nationalism and Language Reform in China* (Princeton, 1950) and several language texts, including *Advanced Chinese* (Yale, 1966). He is also coeditor of *Chinese Social History: Translations of Selected Studies* (Octagon, 1956).

Joshua A. Fogel is a Ph.D. candidate at Columbia University. He has written "Race and Class in Chinese Historiography," *Modern China* 3, no. 3 (1977).

James P. Harrison is professor of history at Hunter College. He is the author of *The Communists and Chinese Peasant Rebellions* (Atheneum, 1969) and *The Long March to Power* (Praeger, 1972).

Thomas L. Kennedy is professor of history at Washington State University. He has written "Chang Chih-tung and the Struggle for Strategic Industrialization," *Harvard Journal of Asiatic Studies* (1973); and *The Arms of Kiangnan* (Westview, 1978).

Olga Lang's writings include *Chinese Family and Society* (Archon, 1968) and *Pa Chin and His Writings* (Harvard, 1967).

Robert H. G. Lee is associate professor of history at the State University of New York at Stony Brook. His publications include *The Manchurian Frontier in Ch'ing History* (Harvard, 1970).

Li Yu-ning is associate professor of history at St. John's University in New York. She is the compiler and editor of *The First Emperor of China: The Politics of Historiography* (International Arts and Sciences Press, 1975) and the author of *The Introduction of Socialism to China* (East Asian Institute Occasional Papers, 1971), as well as a book-length study of Ch'ü Ch'iu-pai.

Anita M. O'Brien is presently publications manager at the East Asian Institute of Columbia University, where she received her M.A. in 1975.

Jane L. Price is lecturer in Chinese history at Columbia University. She is author of *Cadres, Commanders, and Commissars* (Westview, 1976).

William T. Rowe is a Ph.D. candidate at Columbia University. He has contributed a research note to *Ch'ing-shih wen-t'i* (December 1977).

Odoric Y. K. Wou is associate professor of history at Rutgers University, Newark, and author of *Militarism in Modern China: The Life of Wu P'ei-fu* (Dawson, 1978).

Ka-che Yip is associate professor of history at the University of Maryland—Baltimore County. He is the author of articles on Chinese education and a book-length study of Chinese students and anti-Christianism in the 1920s.

Index